T0338074

Financial Statement Analysis

Founded in 1807, John Wiley & Sons is the oldest independent publishing company in the United States. With offices in North America, Europe, Australia and Asia, Wiley is globally committed to developing and marketing print and electronic products and services for our customers' professional and personal knowledge and understanding.

The Wiley Finance series contains books written specifically for finance and investment professionals as well as sophisticated individual investors and their financial advisors. Book topics range from portfolio management to e-commerce, risk management, financial engineering, valuation and financial instrument analysis, as well as much more.

For a list of available titles, visit our Web site at www.WileyFinance.com.

Financial Statement Analysis

A Practitioner's Guide

Fifth Edition

MARTIN S. FRIDSON
FERNANDO ALVAREZ

WILEY

For general information on our other products and services or for technical support, please contact our Customer Care Department within the United States at (800) 762-2974, outside the United States at (317) 572-3993 or fax (317) 572-4002.

Wiley also publishes its books in a variety of electronic formats. Some content that appears in print may not be available in electronic formats. For more information about Wiley products, visit our web site at www.wiley.com.

Library of Congress Cataloging-in-Publication Data is Available:

ISBN 9781119457145 (Hardback)
ISBN 9781119457190 (ePDF)
ISBN 9781119457169 (ePub)

Cover Design: Wiley
Cover Image: © Billion Photos/Shutterstock

SKY10033114_022522

In memory of my father, Harry Yale Fridson, who introduced me to accounting, economics, and logic, as well as the fourth discipline essential to the creation of this book—hard work!
M. F.

For Shari, Virginia, and Armando.
F. A.

Contents

Preface to Fifth Edition

This fifth edition of *Financial Statement Analysis,* like its predecessors, seeks to equip its readers for the practical challenges of contemporary business. Once again, the intention is to acquaint readers who have already acquired basic accounting skills with the complications that arise in applying textbook-derived knowledge to the real world of extending credit and investing in securities. Just as a swiftly changing environment necessitated extensive revisions and additions in the second through fourth editions, new concerns and challenges for users of financial statements have emerged as the third decade of the twenty-first century unfolds.

A fundamental change reflected in the third edition was the shift of corporations' executive compensation plans from a focus on reported earnings toward enhancing shareholder value. Stock options became a major component of corporate leaders' pay. In theory, this new approach aligned the interests of management and shareholders, but the concept had a dark side. Chief executive officers who were under growing pressure to boost their corporations' share prices could no longer increase their bonuses by goosing reported earnings through financial reporting tricks that were transparent to the stock market. Instead, they had to devise more opaque methods that gulled investors into believing that the reported earnings gains were real.

To adapt to the new environment, corporate managers became far more aggressive in misrepresenting their performance. They moved beyond exaggeration to outright fabrication of earnings through the use of derivatives and special purpose vehicles that never showed up in financial statements and had little to do with the production and sale of goods and services. This insidious trend culminated in colossal accounting scandals involving companies such as Enron and WorldCom, which shook confidence not only in financial reporting but also in the securities markets.

Government responded to the outrage over financial frauds by enacting the Sarbanes-Oxley Act of 2002. Under its provisions, a company's chief executive officer and chief financial officer were required to attest to the integrity of the financial statements. They were thereby exposed to greater risk than formerly of prosecution and conviction for misrepresentation. Prior to enactment of this legislation, it was not unheard of for a CEO who stood to profit massively from share price appreciation to escape prosecution by implausibly disavowing knowledge of the fraud and shifting the consequences to an underling whose compensation was not tied in any way to the company's stock price.

Sarbanes-Oxley has had a profound effect. True, the fourth edition of *Financial Statement Analysis* examined several major financial reporting frauds that came to light later than 2002. Upon close examination, however, those scams turned out to have originated prior to Sarbanes-Oxley's passage, but exposed sometime later. By the 2010s, outright, large-scale financial reporting fraud was rare in the U.S. Compiling this new edition was not hampered, however, by any shortage of case studies involving accounting that deceived investors without breaking the law. In addition, flat-out financial reporting fraud continued to flourish outside the U.S.

Curiously, there have been cases since the enactment of Sarbanes-Oxley in which corporate executives have gone to prison for faking the financials, yet the CEO managed to escape prosecution. This is an outcome that Congress clearly sought to prevent. Financial writer Alison Frankel explained the snag in a July 27, 2012, Reuters article entitled, "Sarbanes-Oxley's Lost Promise: Why CEOs Haven't Been Prosecuted."

According to the legislation, a top corporate executive who knowingly signs off on a false financial report is subject to a 10-year prison term and a fine of up to $1 million. The penalties rise to 20 years and $5 million if the misconduct is willful. In practice, few executives were convicted or even charged with false certification in the first decade after passage of Sarbanes-Oxley.

Federal prosecutors attributed this to the fact that most major corporations responded to the new law by instituting multiple layers of subcertification. They required lower-level officials to affirm the financial statements' accuracy. The subcertifications insulated CEOs and CFOs from charges of false certification, making it difficult to impossible for prosecutors to prove that they signed financial reports they knew to be false.

Frankel noted that the subcertification process has forced corporations to be more vigilant at all levels about financial reporting. That likely accounted for the paucity of major accounting scandals subsequent to 2002. In short, Sarbanes-Oxley has succeeded in deterring untruthful reporting that rises to the level of a felony. As case studies presented in this fifth edition of *Financial Statement Analysis* demonstrate, however, legal subterfuges continue to expose investors and creditors to highly unpleasant surprises. Sometimes, too, corporate executives still cross the line into criminality. Therefore, users of financial statements still cannot breathe easy.

In a somewhat more favorable development, corporations' passion for granting stock options to senior managers cooled somewhat after the Financial Accounting Standards Board instituted FAS 123R, a 2006 financial accounting standard introduced by the Financial Accounting Standards Board (FASB) requiring annual expensing of equity based employee compensation amounts. The result was some shift from stock option to restricted stock units (RSUs). Unlike options, which can lose all their value if the company's stock price falls, RSUs retain part of their value if that happens. Emphasizing RSUs rather than options somewhat reduces management's incentive to raise the share price by artificial means.

To help readers avoid being misled by deceptive financial statements, we continue to prescribe a combination of solid understanding of accounting principles with a corporate finance perspective. We facilitate such integration of disciplines throughout the book, making excursions into economics and business management as well. In addition, we encourage analysts to consider the institutional context in which financial reporting occurs. Organizational pressures result in divergences from elegant theories, both in the conduct of financial statement analysis and in auditors' interpretations of accounting principles. The issuers of financial statements also exert a strong influence over the creation of the accounting principles, with powerful politicians sometimes carrying their water.

As in previous editions, we highlight success stories in the critical examination of financial statements. Wherever we can find the necessary documentation, we show not only how a corporate debacle could have been foreseen through application of basis analytical techniques but also how practicing analysts actually did detect the problem before it became widely recognized. Readers will be encouraged by these examples, we hope, to undertake genuine, goal-oriented analysis, instead of simply going through the motions of calculating standard financial ratios. Moreover, the case studies should persuade them to stick to their guns when they spot trouble, despite management's predictable litany. ("Our financial statements are consistent with generally accepted accounting principles. They have been certified by one of the world's premier auditing firms. We will not allow a band of greedy short sellers to destroy the value created by our outstanding employees.") Typically, as the vehemence of management's protests increases, conditions deteriorate further, culminating in revelations that suddenly wipe out substantial shareholder value.

As for the plan of *Financial Statement Analysis*, readers should not feel compelled to tackle its chapters in the order we have assigned to them. To aid those who want to jump in somewhere in the middle of the book, we provide cross-referencing and a glossary. Words that are defined in the glossary are shown in bold-faced type in the text. Although skipping around will be the most efficient approach for many readers, a logical flow does underlie the sequencing of the material.

In Part One, "Reading Between the Lines," we show that financial statements do not simply represent unbiased portraits of corporations' financial performance and explain why. The section explores the complex motivations of issuing firms and their managers. We also study the distortions produced by the organizational context in which the analyst operates.

Part Two, "The Basic Financial Statements," takes a hard look at the information disclosed in the balance sheet, income statement, and statement of cash flows. Under close scrutiny, terms such as *value* and *income* begin to look muddier than they appear when considered in the abstract. Even cash flow, a concept commonly thought to convey redemptive clarification, is vulnerable to stratagems designed to manipulate the perceptions of investors and creditors.

In Part Three, "A Closer Look at Profits," we zero in on the lifeblood of the capitalist system. Our scrutiny of profits highlights the manifold ways in which earnings are exaggerated or even fabricated. By this point in the book, the reader should be amply imbued with the healthy skepticism necessary for a sound, structured approach to financial statement analysis.

Application is the theme of Part Four, "Forecasts and Security Analysis." For both credit and equity evaluation, forward-looking analysis is emphasized over seductive but ultimately unsatisfying retrospection. Tips for maximizing the accuracy of forecasts are included, and real-life projections are dissected. We cast a critical eye on standard financial ratios and valuation models, however widely accepted they may be.

Financial markets continue to evolve, but certain phenomena appear again and again in new guises. In this vein, companies never lose their resourcefulness in finding new ways to skew perceptions of their performance. By studying their methods closely, analysts can potentially anticipate the variations on old themes that will materialize in years to come.

MARTIN FRIDSON
FERNANDO ALVAREZ

Acknowledgments

Mukesh Agarwal
John Bace
Mimi Barker
Mitchell Bartlett
Richard Bernstein
Richard Byrne
Richard Cagney
George Chalhoub
Tiffany Charbonier
Sanford Cohen
Chiara de Biase
Margarita Declet
Mark Dunham
Kenneth Emery
Peter Ernster
Bill Falloon
Sylvan Feldstein
David Fitton
Thomas Flynn III
Daniel Fridson
Igor Fuksman
Ryan Gelrod
Kenneth Goldberg
Susannah Gray
Evelyn Harris
David Hawkins
Emilie Herman
Alan Jones
Avi Katz
Rebecca Keim

James Kenney
Andrew Kroll
Joseph Lee
Les Levi
Ross Levy
Michael Lisk
David Lugg
Jennie Ma
Stan Manoukian
Michael Marocco
Tom Marshella
Eric Matejevich
John Mattis
Pat McConnell
Oleg Melentyev
Krishna Memani
Ann Marie Mullan
Kingman Penniman
Stacey Rivera
Richard Rolnick
Clare Schiedermayer
Gary Schieneman
Bruce Schwartz
Devin Scott
David Shapiro
Lawrence Siskind
Elaine Sisman
Charles Snow
Vladimir Stadnyk
John Thieroff

Scott Thomas
John Tinker
Kivin Varghese
Diane Vazza
Pamela Van Giessen
Sharyl Van Winkle
David Waill

Steven Waite
Douglas Watson
Burton Weinstein
Stephen Weiss
David Whitcomb
Mark Zand

Reading Between the Lines

The Adversarial Nature of Financial Reporting

Financial statement analysis is an essential skill in a variety of occupations, including investment management, corporate finance, commercial lending, and the extension of credit. For individuals engaged in such activities, or who analyze financial data in connection with their personal investment decisions, there are two distinct approaches to the task.

The first is to follow a prescribed routine, filling in boxes with standard financial ratios, calculated according to precise and inflexible definitions. It may take a little more effort or mental exertion than this to satisfy the formal requirements of many positions in the field of financial analysis. Operating in a purely mechanical manner, though, will not provide much of a professional challenge. Neither will a rote completion of all of the proper standard analytical steps ensure a useful, or even a nonharmful, result. Some individuals, however, will view such problems as only minor drawbacks.

This book is aimed at the analyst who will adopt the second and more rewarding alternative: the relentless pursuit of accurate financial profiles of the entities being analyzed. Tenacity is essential because financial statements often conceal more than they reveal. To the analyst who embraces this proactive approach, producing a standard spreadsheet on a company is a means rather than an end. Investors derive but little satisfaction from the knowledge that an untimely stock purchase recommendation was supported by the longest row of figures available in the software package. Genuinely valuable analysis begins *after* all the usual questions have been answered. Indeed, a superior analyst adds value by raising questions that are not even on the checklist.

Some readers may not immediately concede the necessity of going beyond an analytical structure that puts all companies on a uniform, objective scale. They may recoil at the notion of discarding the structure altogether when a sound assessment depends on factors other than comparisons of standard financial ratios. **Comparability**, after all, is a cornerstone of **generally accepted accounting principles (GAAP)**. It might therefore seem to follow that financial statements prepared in accordance with GAAP necessarily produce fair and useful indications of relative value.

The corporations that issue financial statements, moreover, would appear to have a natural interest in facilitating convenient, cookie-cutter analysis. These companies spend heavily to disseminate information about their financial performance. They employ investor-relations managers, they communicate with existing and potential shareholders via interim financial reports and press releases, and their senior executives participate in lengthy conference calls with securities analysts. Given that companies are so eager to make their financial results known to investors, they should also want it to be easy for analysts to monitor their progress. It follows that they can be expected to report their results in a transparent and straightforward fashion ... or so it would seem.

THE PURPOSE OF FINANCIAL REPORTING

Analysts who believe in the inherent reliability of GAAP numbers and the good faith of corporate managers misunderstand the essential nature of financial reporting. Their conceptual error connotes no lack of intelligence, however. Rather, it mirrors the standard accounting textbook's idealistic but irrelevant notion of the purpose of financial reporting. Even the renowned consultant to investment managers and author Howard Schilit, an acerbic critic of financial reporting as it is actually practiced, presents a high-minded view of the matter:

> The primary goal in financial reporting is the dissemination of financial statements that accurately measure the profitability and financial condition of a company.[1]

Missing from this formulation is an indication of *whose* primary goal is accurate measurement. Schilit's words are music to the ears of the financial statement users listed in this chapter's first paragraph, but they are not the ones doing the financial reporting. Rather, the issuers are for-profit companies, generally organized as corporations.[2]

A corporation exists for the benefit of its shareholders. Its objective is not to educate the public about its financial condition, but to maximize its shareholders' wealth. If it so happens that management can advance that objective through "dissemination of financial statements that accurately measure the profitability and financial condition of the company," then in principle, management should do so. At most, however, reporting financial results in a transparent and straightforward fashion is a means unto an end.

Management may determine that a more direct method of maximizing shareholder wealth is to reduce the corporation's **cost of capital**. Simply stated, the lower the interest rate at which a corporation can borrow or the higher the price at which it can sell stock to new investors, the greater the wealth of its shareholders. From this standpoint, the best kind of financial statement is not one that represents the corporation's condition most fully and most fairly, but rather one that produces the highest possible credit rating (see Chapter 13) and price-earnings **multiple** (see Chapter 14). If the highest ratings and multiples result from statements that measure profitability and financial condition *inaccurately,* the logic of fiduciary duty to shareholders obliges management to publish that sort, rather than the type held up as a model in accounting textbooks. The best possible outcome is a cost of capital lower than the corporation deserves on its merits. This admittedly perverse argument can be summarized in the following maxim, presented from the perspective of issuers of financial statements:

The purpose of financial reporting is to obtain cheap capital.

Attentive readers will raise two immediate objections. First, they will say, it is fraudulent to obtain capital at less than a fair rate by presenting an unrealistically bright financial picture. Second, some readers will argue that misleading the users of financial statements is not a sustainable strategy over the long run. Stock market investors who rely on overstated historical profits to project a corporation's future earnings will find that results fail to meet their expectations. Thereafter, they will adjust for the upward bias in the financial statements by projecting lower earnings than the historical results would otherwise justify. The outcome will be a stock valuation no higher than accurate reporting would have produced. Recognizing that the practice would be self-defeating, corporations will logically refrain from overstating their financial performance. By this reasoning, the users of financial statements can take the numbers at face value, because corporations that act in their self-interest will report their results honestly.

The inconvenient fact that confounds these arguments is that financial statements do *not* invariably reflect their issuers' performance faithfully. In lieu of easily understandable and accurate data, users of financial statements often find numbers that conform to GAAP yet convey a misleading impression of profits. Worse yet, companies frequently bend and sometimes break the rules for financial reporting. Not even the analyst's second line of defense, an affirmation by independent auditors that the statements have been prepared in accordance with GAAP, assures that the numbers are reliable. Reported numbers can be invalidated by subsequent revisions, typically, if not always credibly, attributed to honest mistakes.

Alternatively, issuers may emphasize supplementary, non-GAAP numbers to steer analysts toward a more favorable view of their performance. In fairness, some of the alternative metrics disseminated by issuers increase the clarity of disclosure by addressing genuine shortcomings in the financial reporting rules. The rule makers, after all, have found it challenging to keep accounting standards up to date with changes in the way corporations create wealth. Those changes are a consequence of the shift in the economy from traditional manufacturing to knowledge-based industries. At the same time, the lack of standardization in non-GAAP reporting enables issuers that are so inclined to exaggerate their financial performance.

The following case study demonstrates how an overly trusting user of financial statements can be misled.

Mattel's Accounting Games

On August 2, 2019, PricewaterhouseCoopers (PwC), Mattel's outside auditor, received a whistleblower letter suggesting that accounting errors had occurred in earlier periods and questioning whether PwC was truly independent. The toymaker disclosed the letter's receipt on August 8, 2019, and the following day its stock plunged by 15.8 percent while the Standard & Poor's 500 Index registered a minor decline of 0.7 percent. Mattel's board directed the audit committee to investigate the matter.

The investigation found that income tax expense was understated by $109 million in 2017's third quarter and overstated by the same amount in the fourth quarter, resulting in no impact for the full year. Disclosing these findings on October 29, 2019, Mattel pointed out that the errors were noncash and did not affect operating income or **EBITDA** for 2017. The company acknowledged material weaknesses in its internal control over financial reporting but said that the audit committee concluded that PwC's objectivity and impartiality were unimpaired. Mattel further announced plans to restate its 2018 Form 10-K to restate 2017's final two quarters and strengthen its internal financial reporting controls.

Details of the findings included the disturbing fact that after the errors came to light they were not disclosed to Mattel's chief executive officer and the audit committee. The internal investigation did not find that management engaged in fraud, instead blaming mishandling of the discovery of the accounting error on "a confluence of one-time events, management's reliance on the accounting advice sought and received on the error from the lead audit engagement partner of Mattel's outside auditor, and lapses in judgment by management."[3]

Mattel's audit committee determined that many of the whistleblower's allegations about PwC's independence were unfounded. In conjunction with a separate investigation by PwC, however, the audit committee concluded that the lead audit partner for Mattel violated Securities and Exchange Commission rules on auditor independence by recommending candidates for the company's senior finance positions and providing feedback on senior finance employees. PwC replaced some members of the audit team assigned to Mattel, including the lead partner, who was placed on administrative leave. (One commentator on accounting issues characterized him as the fall guy in the affair.)[4]

The bland tone of Mattel's disclosure likely reassured investors whose confidence in the company's financial reporting had been shaken by the August 8 revelations. In the following month, however, the *Wall Street Journal* presented details[5] of what happened when Mattel's tax team discovered the accounting error in early 2018, several months before the news reached the audit committee.

Brett Whitaker, who was director of tax reporting at the time, said the company's finance team discussed correcting the error and restating earnings, expecting that Mattel would have to come clean about flaws in its accounting procedures. According to Whitaker and documents that the *Wall Street Journal* reviewed, senior company finance executives and PwC decided instead to change the accounting treatment of the *Thomas & Friends* cartoon series, starring a talking locomotive. That action effectively buried the problem.

Whitaker, who stated that he was not the whistleblower, characterized the senior executives' response as a coverup and said it dumbfounded his team. He reported that one of PWC's tax partners was high-fiving people in the hallway after the decision was made to change the accounting, relieving the auditing firm of the need to admit its error. Whitaker resigned from Mattel in March 2018. Mattel, for its part, replaced its chief financial officer but said the change in accounting treatment was appropriate.

Following this blow to its credibility with investors, one might have expected a chastened Mattel to be on its best behavior with respect to financial reporting. Only a year-and-a-half after the public learned of the accounting error in the 2017 statements, however, the Securities and Exchange Commission ordered the company to stop using a non-GAAP measure it employed in the discussion and analysis section of its 2019 financial statement. "Gross sales" excluded adjustments such as trade discounts. Mattel applied it to overall revenue as well as its "power brands," namely, Barbie, Hot Wheels, Fisher Price – and Thomas the Tank Engine and his pals. Mattel agreed to switch to "gross billings," the amounts invoiced to customers.

The context of these events is instructive for users of financial statements. Mattel's share price fell by 50.2 percent between year-ends 2014 and 2017. In 2018 Mattel lost $531 million on sales of $4.5 million. The company was plagued by declining sales, particularly in the Fisher-Price and American Girl Lines. In addition, Mattel recalled all 4.7 million Rock 'n' Play Sleeper products after the U.S. Consumer Products Safety Commission reported that they were associated with more than 30 infant deaths since their 2009 introduction. (The company said it was not at fault and that the fatalities resulted from customers disregarding safety warnings and instructions.) Seasoned observers of financial reporting notice that errors frequently occur in conjunction with depressed share prices. On January 4, 2021, when the Securities and Exchange Commission ordered Mattel to stop highlighting the non-GAAP gross sales number, its share price was still 44.3 percent below its year-end 2014 level.

Mattel's story is just one of many in this book that should dispel any illusions that financial statements are always completely reliable. The outside auditor's stamp of approval is no guarantee that reported earnings accurately reflect actual results. Auditing firms, no less than corporate issuers of financial statements, are for-profit businesses with incentives to sweep their failings under the rug. Users of the statements must employ the best analytical techniques available to identify signs that the reported numbers are out of line with the company's true performance or financial condition.

THE FLAWS IN THE REASONING

As many examples that follow demonstrate, neither fear of antifraud statutes nor enlightened self-interest invariably deters corporations from cooking the books. The reasoning by which these two forces ensure honest accounting rests on hidden assumptions. None of the assumptions can stand up to an examination of the organizational context in which financial reporting occurs.

To begin with, corporations can push the numbers pretty far out of joint before they run afoul of the accounting standards, much less open themselves to prosecution for fraud. When deliberate financial reporting violations come to light, as in most other kinds of white-collar crime, the real scandal involves what is *not* forbidden. In practice, generally accepted accounting principles countenance a lot of measurement that is decidedly inaccurate, at least over the short run.

For example, corporations routinely and unabashedly smooth their earnings. That is, they create the illusion that their profits rise at a consistent rate from year to year. Corporations engage in this behavior, with the blessing of their auditors, because the appearance of smooth growth receives a higher price-earnings multiple from stock market investors than the jagged reality underlying the numbers.

Suppose that, in the last few weeks of a quarter, earnings threaten to fall short of the programmed year-over-year increase. The corporation simply borrows sales (and associated profits) from the next quarter by offering customers special discounts to place orders earlier than they had planned. *Higher*-than-trendline growth, too, is a problem for the earnings-smoother. A sudden jump in profits, followed by a return to a more ordinary rate of growth, produces volatility, which is regarded as an evil to be avoided at all costs. Management's solution is to run up expenses in the current period by scheduling training programs and plant maintenance that, while necessary, would ordinarily be undertaken in a later quarter.

These are not tactics employed exclusively by fly-by-night companies. Blue chip corporations openly acknowledge that they have little choice but to smooth their earnings, given Wall Street's allergy to surprises. In past years officials of General Electric indicated that when a division was in danger of failing to meet its annual earnings goal, it was accepted procedure to make an acquisition in the waning days of the reporting period. According to an executive in the company's financial services business, he and his colleagues hunt for acquisitions at such times, saying, "Gee, does somebody else have some income? Is there some other deal we can make?"[6] The freshly acquired unit's profits for the full quarter could be incorporated into GE's, helping to ensure the steady growth so prized by investors.

Why do auditors not forbid such gimmicks? They hardly seem consistent with the ostensible purpose of financial reporting, namely, the accurate portrayal of a corporation's earnings. The explanation is that sound principles of accounting theory represent only one ingredient in the stew from which financial reporting standards emerge.

Along with accounting professionals, the issuers and users of financial statements also have representation on the **Financial Accounting Standards Board (FASB)**, the rule-making body that operates under authority delegated by the Securities and Exchange Commission. When FASB identifies an area in need of a new standard, its professional staff typically defines the theoretical issues in a matter of a few months. Issuance of the new standard may take several years, however, as the corporate issuers of financial statements pursue their objectives on a decidedly less abstract plan.

From time to time, highly charged issues, such as executive stock options and mergers, lead to fairly testy confrontations between FASB and the corporate world. The compromises that emerge from these dustups fail to satisfy theoretical purists. On the other hand, rule making by negotiation heads off all-out assaults by the corporations' allies in Congress. If the lawmakers were ever to get sufficiently riled up, they might drastically curtail FASB's authority. Under extreme circumstances, they might even replace FASB with a new rule-making body that the corporations could more easily bend to their will.

There is another reason that enlightened self-interest does not invariably drive corporations toward candid financial reporting. The corporate executives who lead the battles against FASB have their own agenda. Just like the investors who buy their corporations' stock, managers seek to maximize their wealth. If producing bona fide economic profits advances that objective, it is rational for a chief executive officer (CEO) to try to do so. In some cases, though, the CEO can achieve greater personal gain by taking advantage of the compensation system through financial reporting gimmicks.

Suppose, for example, the CEO's year-end bonus is based on growth in earnings per share. Assume also that for financial reporting purposes, the corporation's **depreciation** schedules assume an average life of eight years for fixed assets. By arbitrarily amending that assumption to nine years (and obtaining the auditors' consent to the change), the corporation can lower its annual depreciation expense. This is strictly an accounting change; the actual cost of replacing equipment worn down through use does not decline. Neither does the corporation's tax deduction for depreciation expense rise nor, as a consequence, does cash flow[7] (see Chapter 4). Investors recognize that bona fide profits (see Chapter 5) have not increased, so the corporation's stock price does not change in response to the new accounting policy. What *does* increase is the CEO's bonus, if it is tied to the highly manipulable earnings per share figure.

This example explains why a corporation may alter its accounting practices, making it harder for investors to track its performance, even though the shareholders' enlightened self-interest favors straightforward, transparent financial reporting. The underlying problem is that corporate executives sometimes put their own interests ahead of their shareholders' welfare. They beef up their bonuses by overstating profits, while shareholders bear the cost of reductions in price–earnings ratios to reflect deterioration in the quality of **reported earnings**.[8]

The logical solution for corporations, it would seem, is to align the interests of management and shareholders. Instead of calculating executive bonuses on the basis of earnings per share, the board should reward senior management for increasing shareholders' wealth by causing the stock price to rise. Such an arrangement gives the CEO no incentive to inflate reported earnings through gimmicks that transparently produce no increase in bona fide profits and therefore no rise in the share price.

Following the logic through, financial reporting ought to have moved closer to the ideal of accurate representation of corporate performance as companies increasingly linked executive compensation to stock price appreciation in the closing decades of the twentieth century. In reality, though, no such trend was discernible. If anything, corporations became more creative and more aggressive over time in their financial reporting.

Aligning management and shareholder interests, it turns out, had a dark side. Corporate executives could no longer increase their bonuses through financial reporting tricks that were readily detectable by investors. Instead, they had to devise better-hidden gambits that fooled the market and artificially elevated the stock price. Financial statement analysts had to work harder than ever to spot corporations' subterfuges.

The Sarbanes-Oxley Act of 2002 raised hopes that analysts' lives would be made easier by enabling them to rely more heavily on the veracity of published financial statements. Enacted in the wake of a series of spectacular financial reporting scandals, the legislation required publicly traded companies' chief executive officers and chief financial officers to issue statements certifying that in all material respects their financial statements and disclosures present their companies' operations and financial condition fairly.

Spectacular financial reporting frauds did become less frequent as chief executive officers began to face the prospect of prison time if they signed off on fraudulent financial states. Fraud did not completely disappear, however. To an extent, CEOs were able to push responsibility for it down the chain of command by structuring their sign-offs on the statements as approvals of calculations by subordinates, making it difficult for prosecutors to secure convictions at the top level.

Although spectacular cases of outright fraud became less frequent after Sarbanes-Oxley went into effect, analysts needed to remain vigilant. As GAAP numbers became riskier, companies stepped up their efforts to redirect analysts' attention to non-GAAP, adjusted metrics that portrayed them in a better light. Not incidentally, many companies used the adjusted – that is, higher – earnings numbers in calculating CEOs' bonuses.

Some of the adjusted revenue and earnings figures served constructive purposes. By 2015, however, 90 percent of S&P 500 companies were reporting non-GAAP, up from about 70 percent in 2009. At that point, the Securities and Exchange Commission felt obliged to curb the trend.

The SEC cracked down on excessive use of nonstandard accounting metrics in 2016. Under the new guidelines, companies could supplement their reporting with on-GAAP numbers but had to give GAAP numbers equal or greater prominence and explain how the two different sets of figures were reconciled. The SEC crackdown had some initial impact, but financial statement issuers resumed their eager embrace of non-GAAP numbers when the COVID-19 pandemic hit.

Financial data provider Calcbench ran a calculation on the 60 companies with the greatest divergences between GAAP and non-GAAP net profits in 2020. The aggregate difference came to $132.2 billion, meaning that the companies collectively steered analysts toward adjusted earnings that were twice as great as their $130.7 billion of GAAP net income. In total, the 60 sample companies made more than 240 adjustments GAAP net income. Amortization of intangibles was the most popular device, accounting for 30 percent of all adjustments. "Companies will use whichever accounting practices make them look best and benefit their CEOs the most," commented Rosanna Landis Weaver of As You Sow, a nonprofit organization focused on corporate social responsibility.[9]

SMALL PROFITS AND BIG BATHS

Certainly, financial statement analysts do not have to fight the battle single-handedly. The Securities and Exchange Commission and the Financial Accounting Standards Board prohibit corporations from going too far in prettifying their profits to pump up their share prices. These regulators refrain from indicating exactly how far is too far, however. Inevitably, corporations hold diverse opinions on matters such as the extent to which they must divulge bad news that might harm their stock market valuations. For some, the standard of disclosure appears to be that if nobody happens to ask about a specific event, then declining to volunteer the information does not constitute a lie.

The picture is not quite that bleak in every case, but the bleakness extends pretty far. A research team led by Harvard economist Richard Zeckhauser compiled evidence that lack of perfect candor is widespread.[10] The researchers focused on instances in which a corporation reported quarterly earnings that were only slightly higher or slightly lower than its earnings in the corresponding quarter of the preceding year.

Suppose that corporate financial reporting followed the accountants' idealized objective of depicting performance accurately. By the laws of probability, corporations' quarterly reports would have included about as many cases of earnings that barely exceeded year-earlier results as cases of earnings that fell just shy of year-earlier profits. Instead, Zeckhauser and colleagues found that corporations posted small increases far more frequently than they posted small declines. The strong implication was that when companies were in danger of showing slightly negative earnings comparisons, they found enough discretionary items to squeeze out marginally improved results.

On the other hand, suppose a corporation suffers a quarterly profit decline too large to erase through discretionary items. Such circumstances create an incentive to take a big bath by maximizing the reported setback. The reasoning is that investors will not be much more disturbed by a 30 percent drop in earnings than by a 20 percent drop. Therefore, management may find it expedient to **accelerate** certain future expenses into the current quarter, thereby ensuring positive reported earnings in the following period. It may also be a convenient time to recognize long-run losses in the value of assets such as outmoded production facilities and **goodwill** created in unsuccessful acquisitions of the past. In fact, the corporation may take a larger write-off on those assets than the principle of accurate representation would dictate. Reversals of the excess write-offs offer an artificial means of stabilizing reported earnings in subsequent periods.

Zeckhauser and his associates corroborated the big bath hypothesis by showing that large earnings declines were more common than large increases. By implication, managers did not passively record the combined results of their own skill and business factors beyond their control, but intervened in the calculation of earnings by exploiting the latitude in accounting rules. The researchers' overall impression was that corporations regard financial reporting as a technique for propping up stock prices, rather than a means of disseminating objective information.[11]

If corporations' gambits escape detection by investors and lenders, the rewards can be vast. For example, an interest-cost savings of half a percentage point on $10 billion of borrowings equates to $50 million (pretax) per year. If the corporation is in a 21 percent tax bracket and its stock trades at 20 times earnings, the payoff for risk-concealing financial statements is $790 million in the cumulative value of its shares.

Among the popular methods for pursuing such opportunities for wealth enhancement, aside from the big bath technique studied by Zeckhauser, are:

- Maximizing growth expectations.
- Downplaying contingencies.

MAXIMIZING GROWTH EXPECTATIONS

Imagine a corporation that is currently reporting annual net earnings of $200 million. Assume that five years from now, when its growth has leveled off somewhat, the corporation will be valued at 20 times earnings. Further assume that the company will pay no dividends over the next five years and that investors in growth stocks currently seek returns of 25 percent (before considering capital gains taxes).

Based on these assumptions, plus one additional number, the analyst can place an aggregate value on the corporation's outstanding shares. The final required input is the expected growth rate of earnings. Suppose the corporation's earnings have been growing at a 30 percent annual rate and appear likely to continue increasing at the same rate over the next five years. At the end of that period, annual earnings will be $743 million. Applying a multiple of 20 times to that figure produces a valuation at the end of the fifth year of $14.9 billion. Investors seeking a 25 percent rate of return will pay $4.9 billion today for that future value.

These figures are likely to be pleasing to a founder or chief executive officer who owns, for the sake of illustration, 25 percent of the outstanding shares. The successful entrepreneur is worth $1.2 billion on paper, quite possibly up from zero just a few years ago. At the same time, the newly minted billionaire is a captive of the market's expectations.

Suppose investors conclude for some reason that the corporation's potential for increasing its earnings has declined from 30 to 25 percent per annum. That is still far above average for corporate America. Nevertheless, the aggregate value of the corporation's shares will decline from $4.9 billion to $4.8 billion, keeping previous assumptions intact.

Overnight, the long-struggling founder will see the value of his personal stake plummet by $25 million. Financial analysts may shed few tears for him. After all, he is still a billionaire on paper. If they were in his shoes, however, how many would accept a $25 million loss with perfect equanimity? Most would be sorely tempted, at the least, to avoid incurring a financial reverse of comparable magnitude via every means available to them under GAAP.

That all-too-human response is the one typically exhibited by owner-managers confronted with falling growth expectations. Many, perhaps most, have no intention to deceive. It is simply that the entrepreneur is by nature a self-assured optimist. A successful entrepreneur, moreover, has had this optimism vindicated. Having taken his company from nothing to $200 million of earnings against overwhelming odds, he believes he can lick whatever short-term problems have arisen. He is confident that he can get the business back onto a 30 percent growth curve, and perhaps he is right. One thing is certain: If he were not the sort who believed he could beat the odds one more time, he would never have built a company worth almost $5 billion.

Financial analysts need to assess the facts more objectively. They must recognize that the corporation's predicament is not unique, but on the contrary, quite common. Almost invariably, senior managers try to dispel the impression of decelerating growth, since that perception can be so costly to them. Simple mathematics, however, tends to make false prophets of corporations that extrapolate high growth rates indefinitely into the future. Moreover, once growth begins to level off (see Exhibit 1.1), restoring it to the historical rate requires overcoming several powerful limitations.

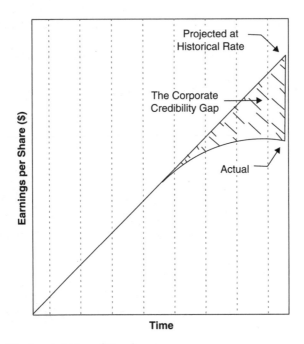

EXHIBIT 1.1 The Inevitability of Deceleration.
Note: Shifting investors' perceptions upward through the Corporate Credibility Gap between actual and management-projected growth is a potentially valuable but inherently difficult undertaking for a company. Liberal financial reporting practices can make the task somewhat easier. In this light, analysts should read financial statements with a skeptical eye.

Limits to Continued Growth

Saturation Sales of a hot new consumer product can grow at astronomical rates for a time. Eventually, however, everybody who cares to will own one (or two, or some other finite number that the consumer believes is enough). At that point, potential sales will be limited to replacement sales plus growth in population, that is, the increase in the number of potential purchasers.

Entry of Competition Rare is the company with a product or service that cannot either be copied or encroached on by a knockoff sufficiently similar to tap the same demand, yet different enough to fall outside the bounds of patent and trademark protection.

Increasing Base A corporation that sells 10 million units in Year 1 can register a 40 percent increase by selling just 4 million additional units in Year 2.

If growth continues at the same rate, however, the corporation will have to generate 59 million new unit sales to achieve a 40 percent gain in Year 10.

In absolute terms, it is arithmetically possible for volume to increase indefinitely. On the other hand, a growth rate far in excess of the **gross domestic product**'s annual increase is nearly impossible to sustain over any extended period. By definition, a product that experiences higher-than-**GDP** growth captures a larger percentage of GDP each year. As the numbers get larger, it becomes increasingly difficult to switch consumers' spending patterns to accommodate continued high growth of a particular product.

Market Share Constraints   For a time, a corporation may overcome the limits of growth in its market and the economy as a whole by expanding its sales at the expense of competitors. Even when growth is achieved by market share gains rather than by expanding the overall demand for a product, however, the firm must eventually bump up against a ceiling on further growth at a constant rate. For example, suppose a producer with a 10 percent share of market is currently growing at 25 percent a year while total demand for the product is expanding at only 5 percent annually. By Year 14, this supergrowth company will require a 115 percent market share to maintain its rate of increase. (Long before confronting this mathematical impossibility, the corporation's growth will probably be curtailed by the antitrust authorities.)

Basic economics and compound-interest tables, then, assure the analyst that all growth stories come to an end, a cruel fate that must eventually be reflected in stock prices. Financial reports, however, frequently tell a different tale. It defies common sense, yet almost has to be told given the stakes. Users of financial statements should acquaint themselves with the most frequently heard corporate versions of "Jack and the Beanstalk," in which earnings – in contradiction to a popular saw – do grow to the sky.

Real-Life Illustrations   Financial statement users who learn the above-described fables of unending earnings growth at unusually high rates will soon see that they are not merely hypothetical. The financial news frequently contains reports of companies bumping up against these limits. Here are a few examples involving well-known corporations:

Between 2010 and 2015 Under Armour's stock rose at an astounding **compound annual growth rate** of 42.5 percent. The manufacturer of sports and fitness apparel, shoes, and accessories was in the midst of a 26-quarter streak of 20 percent or greater year-over-year sales increases. Over the next year-and-a-half, however, Under Armour's shares plunged by nearly 50 percent even as the Standard & Poor's 500 stock index advanced by almost 20 percent.

The plummeting share price reflected a blow to high expectations for sales and earnings growth that investors had built into Under Armour's valuation. Even after management reported a deceleration in sales growth to 12 percent in 2016's fourth quarter, its stock remained at a lofty price-earnings **multiple** of 44 times. Among other setbacks, the company's sales were hit by a succession of bankruptcies at sporting goods retailing chains.

Concurrent with the slowdown in sales growth, Under Armour's gross margin was slipping. Management delivered the disheartening news that sustaining the high growth that investors were counting on would require heavy investment. Part of the problem was that Under Armour, which had cut its teeth in the apparel sector, was now counting on footwear to maintain the corporate-wide pace of sales gains. To compete with footwear heavyweights Adidas and Nike, Under Armour would have to spend aggressively on sponsorship and marketing.

The stock of another high-flier, Boston Beer, rose at a 26 percent compound annual rate in the 15 years through 2014. Over the next two years shareholders suffered a 41 percent decline. The S&P 500 rose by 9 percent during that span. Once again, the culprit was slowing revenue. In 2016 the brewer of Samuel Adams Lager posted its first year-over-year sales decline in 13 years, as well as a 6 percent drop in earnings per share.

"The problem for Boston Beer," wrote Avi Salzman in *Barron's*, is that craft beer appears to have reached the saturation point. Everybody and his brother now has a special brew with a cool label and a hint of cocoa."[12] In 1984, when Boston Beer was founded, the U.S. had just 97 breweries. By 2016 the number was 5,000, which included a doubling just since 2012, according to Brewers Association chief economist Bart Watson.

All that proliferation of brands may have been overwhelming beer drinkers with choices. Boston Beer's founder and chairman Jim Koch reported that some retailers were confused. Consumers were giving up on trying to choose a craft beer and just saying, "I'll have a Corona."[13] Compounding the problem, industry giants Anheuser-Busch InBev and MillersCoors were acquiring many craft brewers, making craft beer seem less special.

As with Under Armour, maintaining sales growth was expected to come at a cost that would likely put pressure on profit margins. Journalist Salzman suggested that Boston Beer's promotions budget would rise by 10 percent in the coming year.

Finally, Whole Foods Market far outpaced the S&P 500 with an 18 percent compound annual rise in its share price from 2003 to 2013. The stock index rose at just 5 percent a year during the period. Between 2013 and 2016, however, the organic food retailer's stock dropped by 47 percent versus a 21 percent gain for the S&P 500.

As with the previous examples, competition put a crimp in investors' dreams of continued high, steady sales growth. Co-founder and chief executive officer John Mackey acknowledged a similar complacency within the company, saying, "When you average 8 percent same-store sales [growth] for 35 years, it can breed a sense of 'Why do we need to change? Things are working.'"[14] Then reality stepped in.

For years, Whole Foods had a lock on the natural and organic sector, enabling it to charge high prices while spending little on promotion. Then other supermarket chains got into the game, offering similar products at lower prices. "More conventional supermarkets are copying us," Mackey lamented. "Every place we went bred the Midas touch. But it also bred envy."[15] By 2016, Kroger's natural and organic sales exceeded Whole Foods's total revenue. The warehouse-club retailer Costco Wholesale claimed honors as the top organic food retailer.

To analysts who had absorbed the lessons of countess precedents, the results should not have been surprising. Whole Foods racked up six quarters of same-store sales declines, its longest such streak since going public in 1992. Over that span, customer visits fell by as much as 14 million, according to Barclays PLC. In June 2017, with activist investors pressuring management to rebuild shareholder value, Whole Foods agreed to be acquired by online retailing giant Amazon.

Commonly Heard Rationalizations for Declining Growth

"Our Year-over-Year Comparisons Were Distorted" Recognizing the sensitivity of investors to any slowdown in growth, companies faced with earnings deceleration commonly resort to certain standard arguments to persuade investors that the true, underlying profit trend is still rising at its historical rate (see Exhibit 1.2). Freak weather conditions may be blamed for supposedly anomalous, below-trendline earnings. Alternatively, the company may allege that shipments were delayed (never canceled, merely delayed) because of temporary production problems caused, ironically, by the company's explosive growth. (What appeared to be a negative for the stock price, in other words, was actually a positive. Orders were coming in faster than the company could fill them – a high-class problem indeed.) Widely publicized macroeconomic events such as the Y2K problem[16] receive more than their fair share of blame for earnings shortfalls. However plausible these explanations may sound, analysts should remember that in many past instances, short-term supposed aberrations have turned out to be advance signals of earnings slowdowns.

"New Products Will Get Growth Back on Track" Sometimes, a corporation's claim that its obviously **mature** product lines will resume their former growth path

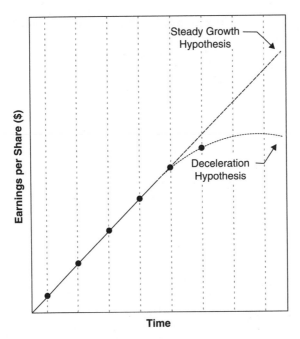

EXHIBIT 1.2 "Our Year-over-Year Comparisons Were Distorted."
Note: Is the latest earnings figure an outlier or does it signal the start of a slowdown in growth? Nobody will know for certain until more time has elapsed, but the company will probably propound the former hypothesis as forcefully as it can.

becomes untenable. In such instances, it is a good idea for management to have a new product or two to show off. Even if the products are still in development, some investors who strongly wish to believe in the corporation will remain steadfast in their faith that earnings will continue growing at the historical rate. (Such hopes probably rise as a function of owning stock on margin at a cost well above the current market.) A hardheaded analyst, though, will wait to be convinced, bearing in mind that new products have a high failure rate.

"We're Diversifying Away from Mature Markets" If a growth-minded company's entire industry has reached a point of slowdown, it may have little choice but to redeploy its earnings into faster-growing businesses. Hunger for growth, along with the quest for cyclical balance, is a prime motivation for the corporate strategy of **diversification.**

Diversification reached its zenith of popularity during the conglomerate movement of the 1960s. Up until that time, relatively little evidence had accumulated regarding the actual feasibility of achieving high earnings growth through acquisitions of companies in a wide variety of growth industries. Many corporations subsequently found that their diversification strategies worked better on paper than in practice. One problem was that they had to pay extremely high price-earnings multiples for growth companies that other conglomerates also coveted. Unless earnings growth accelerated dramatically under the new corporate ownership, the acquirer's return on investment was fated to be mediocre. This constraint was especially problematic for managers who had no particular expertise in the businesses they were acquiring. Still worse was the predicament of a corporation that paid a big premium for an also-ran in a hot industry. Regrettably, the number of industry leaders available for acquisition was by definition limited.

By the 1980s, the stock market had rendered its verdict. The price-earnings multiples of widely diversified corporations carried a conglomerate discount. One practical problem was the difficulty security analysts encountered in trying to keep tabs on companies straddling many different industries. Instead of making 2 plus 2 equal 5, as they had promised, the conglomerates' managers presided over corporate empires that traded at cheaper prices than their constituent companies would have sold for in aggregate had they been listed separately.

Despite this experience, there are periodic attempts to revive the notion of diversification as a means of maintaining high earnings growth indefinitely into the future. In one variant, management makes lofty claims about the potential for cross-selling one division's services to the customers of another. It is not clear, though, why paying premium acquisition prices to assemble the two businesses under the same corporate roof should prove more profitable than having one independent company pay a fee to use the other's mailing list. Battle-hardened analysts wonder whether such corporate strategies rely as much on the vagaries of mergers-and-acquisitions accounting (see Chapter 10) as they do on bona fide **synergy**.

All in all, users of financial statements should adopt a show-me attitude toward a story of renewed growth through diversification. It is often nothing more than a variant of the myth of above-average growth forever. Multi-industry corporations bump up against the same arithmetic that limits earnings growth for focused companies.

DOWNPLAYING CONTINGENCIES

A second way to mold disclosure to suit the issuer's interests is by downplaying extremely significant contingent liabilities. Thanks to the advent of **class-action** suits, the entire net worth of even a multibillion-dollar corporation may be at risk in litigation involving environmental hazards or product liability. Understandably, an issuer of financial statements would prefer that securities analysts focus their attention elsewhere.

At one time, analysts tended to shunt aside claims that ostensibly threatened major corporations with bankruptcy. They observed that massive lawsuits were often settled for small fractions of the original claims. Furthermore, the outcome of a lawsuit often hinged on facts that emerged only when the case finally came to trial (which by definition never happened if the suit was settled out of court). Considering also the susceptibility of juries to emotional appeals, securities analysts of bygone days found it extremely difficult to incorporate legal risks into earnings forecasts that relied primarily on **microeconomic** and **macroeconomic** variables. At most, a contingency that had the potential of wiping out a corporation's equity became a qualitative factor in determining the multiple assigned to a company's earnings.

Manville Corporation's 1982 bankruptcy marked a watershed in the way analysts have viewed legal contingencies. To their credit, specialists in the building products sector had been asking detailed questions about Manville's exposure to asbestos-related personal injury suits for a long time before the company filed. Many investors nevertheless seemed to regard the corporation's August 26, 1982, filing under **Chapter** 11 of the Bankruptcy Code as a sudden calamity. Manville's stock plunged by 35 percent on the day following its filing.

In part, the surprise element was a function of disclosure. The corporation's last quarterly report to the Securities and Exchange Commission prior to its bankruptcy had implied a total cost of settling asbestos-related claims of about $350 million. That was less than half of Manville's $830 million of shareholders' equity. On August 26, by contrast, Manville estimated the potential damages at no less than $2 billion.

For analysts of financial statements, the Manville episode demonstrated the plausibility of a scenario previously thought inconceivable. A bankruptcy at an otherwise financially sound company, brought on solely by legal claims, had become a nightmarish reality. Intensifying the shock was that the problem had lain dormant for many years. Manville's bankruptcy resulted from claims for diseases contracted decades earlier through contact with the company's products. The long-tailed nature of asbestos liabilities was underscored by a series of bankruptcy filings over succeeding years. Prominent examples, each involving a billion dollars or more of assets, included Walter Industries (1989), National Gypsum (1990), USG Corporation (1993 and again in 2001), Owens Corning (2000), and Armstrong World Industries (2000).

Massive awards to litigants do not invariably trigger corporate bankruptcies. In 2016 a federal judge approved a $20 billion settlement of civil claims against U.K.-based integrate oil giant BP arising from the largest marine oil spill in history. Also in that year, a federal judge approved a $14.7 billion settlement in litigation concerning Volkswagen's scheme to cheat on emission test of diesel cars. Neither company went bust as a result, but the events underscore the magnitude of potential losses that could blindside analysts who ordinarily focus on the potential impact of much more minor earnings surprises.

Bankruptcies connected with asbestos exposure, silicone gel breast implants, and assorted environmental hazards have heightened awareness of legal risks. Even so, analysts still miss the forest for the trees in some instances, concentrating on the minutiae of financial ratios of corporations facing similarly large contingent liabilities. They can still be lulled by companies' matter-of-fact responses to questions about the gigantic claims asserted against them.

Thinking about it from the issuer's standpoint, one can imagine several reasons that the investor-relations officer's account of a major legal contingency is likely to be rosier than the economic reality. To begin with, the corporation's managers have a clear interest in downplaying risks that threaten the value of their stock and options. Furthermore, as parties to a highly contentious lawsuit, the executives find themselves in a conflict. It would be difficult for them to testify persuasively in their company's defense while simultaneously acknowledging to investors that the plaintiffs' claims have merit and might, in fact, prevail. (Indeed, any such public admission could compromise the corporation's case. Candid disclosure may therefore not be a viable option.) Finally, it would hardly represent aberrant behavior if, on a subconscious level, management were to deny the real possibility of a company-wrecking judgment. It must be psychologically difficult for managers to acknowledge that their company could go bust for reasons seemingly outside their control. Filing for bankruptcy may prove to be the only course available to the corporation, notwithstanding an excellent record of earnings growth and a conservative balance sheet.

For all these reasons, analysts must take particular care to rely on their independent judgment when a potentially devastating contingent liability looms larger than their conscientiously calculated financial ratios. It is not a matter of sitting in judgment on management's honor and forthrightness. If corporate executives remain in denial about the magnitude of the problem, they are not deliberately misleading analysts by presenting an overly optimistic picture. Moreover, the managers may not provide a reliable assessment even if they soberly face the facts. In all likelihood, they have never worked for a company with a comparable problem. They consequently have little basis for estimating the likelihood that the worst-case scenario will be fulfilled. Analysts who have seen other corporations in similar predicaments have more perspective on the matter, as well as greater objectivity. Instead of relying entirely on the company's periodic updates on a huge class action suit, analysts should also speak to representatives of the plaintiffs' side. Their views, while by no means unbiased, will expose logical weaknesses in management's assertions that the liability claims will never stand up in court.

THE IMPORTANCE OF BEING SKEPTICAL

By now, the reader presumably understands why this chapter is titled "The Adversarial Nature of Financial Reporting." The issuer of financial statements has been portrayed in an unflattering light, invariably choosing the accounting option that will tend to prop up its stock price, rather than generously assisting the analyst in deriving an accurate picture of its financial condition. Analysts have been warned not to partake of the optimism that drives all great business enterprises, but instead to maintain an attitude of skepticism bordering on distrust. Some readers may feel they are not cut out to be financial analysts if the job consists of constant nay-saying, of posing embarrassing questions, and of being a perennial thorn in the side of companies that want to win friends among investors, customers, and suppliers.

Although pursuing relentless antagonism can indeed be an unpleasant way to go through life, the stance that this book recommends toward issuers of financial statements implies no such acrimony. Rather, analysts should view the issuers as adversaries in the same manner that they temporarily demonize their opponents in a friendly pickup basketball game. On the court, the competition can be intense, which only adds to the fun. Afterward, everyone can have a fine time going out together for pizza and beer. In short, financial analysts and investor-relations officers can view their work with the detachment of litigators who engage in every legal form of shin-kicking out of sheer desire to win the case, not because the litigants' claims necessarily have intrinsic merit.

Too often, financial writers describe the give-and-take of financial reporting and analysis in a highly moralistic tone. Typically, the author exposes a tricky presentation of the numbers and reproaches the company for greed and chicanery. Viewing the production of financial statements as an epic struggle between good and evil may suit a crusading journalist, but financial analysts need not join the ethics police to do their job well.

An alternative is to learn to understand the gamesmanship of financial reporting, perhaps even to appreciate on some level the cleverness of issuers who constantly devise new stratagems for leading investors off the track.

Outright fraud cannot be countenanced, but disclosure that shades economic realities without violating the law requires truly impressive ingenuity. By regarding the interaction between issuers and users of financial statements as a game, rather than a morality play, analysts will find it easier to view the action from the opposite side. Just as a chess master anticipates an opponent's future moves, analysts should consider which gambits they themselves would use if they were in the issuer's seat.

"Oh no!" some readers must be thinking at this point. "First the authors tell me that I must not simply plug numbers into a standardized spreadsheet. Now I have to engage in role-playing exercises to guess what tricks will be embedded in the statements before they even come out. I thought this book was supposed to make my job easier, not more complicated."

In reality, this book's goal is to make the reader a better analyst. If that goal could be achieved by providing shortcuts, the authors would not hesitate to do so. Financial reporting occurs in an institutional context that obliges conscientious analysts to go many steps beyond conventional calculation of financial ratios. Without the extra vigilance advocated in these pages, the user of financial statements will become mired in a system that provides excessively simple answers to complex questions, squelches individuals who insolently refuse to accept reported financial data at face value, and inadvisably gives issuers the benefit of the doubt.

These systematic biases are inherent in selling stocks. Within the universe of investors are many large, sophisticated financial institutions that utilize the best available techniques of analysis to select securities for their **portfolios**. Also among the buyers of stocks are individuals who, not being trained in financial statement analysis, are poorly equipped to evaluate annual and quarterly earnings reports. Both types of investors are important sources of financing for industry, and both benefit over the long term from the returns that accrue to capital in a market economy. The two groups cannot be sold stocks in the same way, however.

What generally sells best to individual investors is a story. Sometimes the story involves a new product with seemingly unlimited sales potential. Another kind of story portrays the recommended stock as a play on some current economic trend, such as declining interest rates or, at the time of the COVID-19 pandemic, a reopening of the economy. Some stories lie in the realm of rumor, particularly those that relate to possible corporate takeovers. The chief characteristics of most stories are the promise of spectacular gains, dubious logic, and a paucity of quantitative verification.

No great harm is done when an analyst's stock purchase recommendation, backed up by a thorough study of the issuer's financial statements, is translated into soft, qualitative terms for laypersons' benefit. Not infrequently, though, a story originates among stockbrokers or even in the executive offices of the issuer itself. In such an instance, the zeal with which the story is disseminated may depend more on its narrative appeal than on the solidity of the supporting analysis.

Individual investors' fondness for stories undercuts the impetus for serious financial analysis, but the environment created by institutional investors is not ideal, either. Although the best investment organizations conduct rigorous and imaginative research, many others operate in the mechanical fashion derided earlier in this chapter. They reduce financial statement analysis to the bare bones of forecasting earnings per share, from which they derive a price-earnings multiple. In effect, the less conscientious investment managers assume that as long as a stock stacks up well by this single measure, it represents an attractive investment. Much Wall Street research, regrettably, caters to these institutions' tunnel vision, sacrificing analytical comprehensiveness to the operational objective of maintaining up-to-the-minute earnings estimates on vast numbers of companies.

Investment firms, moreover, are not the only workplaces in which serious analysts of financial statements may find their style crimped. The credit departments of manufacturers and wholesalers have their own set of institutional hazards.

Consider, to begin with, the very term *credit approval process*. As the name implies, the vendor's bias is toward extending rather than refusing credit. Up to a point, this is as it should be. In Exhibit 1.3, neutral Cutoff Point A, where half of all applicants are approved and half are refused, represents an unnecessarily high credit standard. Any company employing it would turn away many potential customers who posed almost no threat of delinquency. Even Cutoff Point B, which allows more business to be written but produces no credit losses, is less than optimal. Credit managers who seek to maximize profits aim for Cutoff Point C. It represents a level of credit extension at which losses on receivables occur but are slightly more than offset by the profits derived from incremental customers.

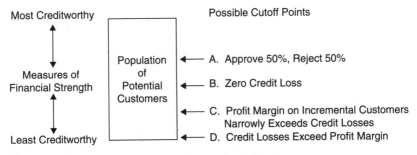

EXHIBIT 1.3   The Bias toward Favorable Credit Evaluations.

To achieve this optimal result, a credit analyst must approve a certain number of accounts that will eventually fail to pay. In effect, the analyst is required to make mistakes that could be avoided by rigorously obeying the conclusions derived from the study of applicants' financial statements. The company makes up the cost of such mistakes by avoiding mistakes of the opposite type (rejecting potential customers who will not fail to pay).

Trading off one type of error for another is thoroughly rational and consistent with sound analysis, so long as the objective is truly to maximize profits. There is always a danger, however, that the company will instead maximize sales at the expense of profits. That is, the credit manager may bias the system even further, to Cutoff Point D in Exhibit 1.3. Such a problem is bound to arise if the company's salespeople are paid on commission and their compensation is not tightly linked to the collection experience of their customers. The rational response to that sort of incentive system is to pressure credit analysts to approve applicants whose financial statements cry out for rejection.

A similar tension between the desire to book revenues and the need to make sound credit decisions exists in commercial lending. At a bank or a finance company, an analyst of financial statements may be confronted by special pleading on behalf of a loyal, long-established client that is under allegedly temporary strain. Alternatively, the lending officer may argue that a loan request ought to be approved, despite substandard financial ratios, on the grounds that the applicant is a young, struggling company with potential to grow into a major client. Requests for exceptions to established credit policies are likely to increase in both number and fervor during periods of slack demand for loans.

When considering pleas of mitigating circumstances, the credit analyst should certainly take into account pertinent qualitative factors that the financial statements fail to capture. At the same time, the analyst must bear in mind that qualitative credit considerations come in two flavors, favorable and unfavorable. It is also imperative to remember that the cold, hard statistics show that companies in the temporarily impaired and start-up categories have a higher-than-average propensity to **default** on their debt.

Every high-risk company seeking a loan can make a plausible soft case for overriding the financial ratios. In aggregate, though, a large percentage of such borrowers will fail, proving that many of their seemingly valid qualitative arguments were specious. This unsentimental truth was driven home by a massive 1989–1991 wave of defaults on high-yield bonds that had been marketed on the strength of supposedly valuable assets not reflected on the issuers' balance sheets. Bond investors had been told that the bold dreams and ambitions of management would suffice to keep the companies solvent. Another large default wave in 2001 involved early-stage telecommunications ventures for which there was scarcely any financial data from which to calculate ratios. The rationale advanced for lending to these nascent companies was the supposedly limitless demand for services made possible by miraculous new technology. Credit analysis gone awry was at the core of the Great Recession of 2008–2009. An unsustainable boom in housing prices was fueled by mortgages lending that abandoned all established standards for qualifying borrowers.

To be sure, defaults also occur among individuals and companies that satisfy established quantitative standards. When it comes to quantitative standards, though, analysts can test financial ratios against a historical record to determine their reliability as predictors of bankruptcy (see Chapter 13). No comparable testing is feasible for the highly idiosyncratic, qualitative factors that weakly capitalized companies cite when applying for loans. Analysts are therefore on more solid ground when they rely primarily on the numbers than when they try to discriminate among companies' soft arguments.

CONCLUSION

A primary objective of this chapter has been to supply an essential ingredient that is missing from many discussions of financial statement analysis. Aside from accounting rules, cash flows, and definitions of standard ratios, analysts must consider the motivations of corporate managers, as well as the dynamics of the organizations in which they work. Neglecting these factors will lead to false assumptions about the underlying intent of issuers' communications with users of financial statements.

Moreover, analysts may make incorrect inferences about the quality of their own work if they fail to understand the workings of their own organizations. If a conclusion derived from thorough financial analysis is deemed wrong, it is important to know whether that judgment reflects a flawed analysis or a higher-level decision to override analysts' recommendations. Senior managers sometimes subordinate financial statement analysis to a determination that idle funds must be put to work or that loan volume must be increased. At such times, organizations rationalize their behavior by persuading themselves that the principles of interpreting financial statements have fundamentally changed. Analysts need not go to the extreme of resigning in protest, but they will benefit if they can avoid getting caught up in the prevailing delusion.

To be sure, organizational behavior has not been entirely overlooked up until now in the literature of financial statement analysis. Typically, academic studies depict issuers as profit-maximizing firms, inclined to overstate their earnings if they can do so legally and if they believe it will boost their equity market valuation. This model lags behind the portrait of the firm now prevalent in other branches of finance.[17] Instead of a monolithic organization that consistently pursues the clear-cut objective of share price maximization, the corporation is now viewed more realistically as an aggregation of individuals with diverse motivations.

Using this more sophisticated model, an analyst can unravel an otherwise vexing riddle concerning corporate reporting. Overstating earnings would appear to be a self-defeating strategy in the long term, since it has a tendency to catch up with the perpetrator. Suppose, for example, a corporation depreciates assets over a longer period than can be justified by physical wear and tear and the rate of technological change in manufacturing methods. When the time comes to replace the existing equipment, the corporation will face two unattractive options. The first is to penalize reported earnings by writing off the remaining undepreciated balance on equipment that is obsolete and hence of little value in the resale market. Alternatively, the company can delay the necessary purchase of more up-to-date equipment, thereby losing ground competitively and reducing future earnings. Would the corporation not have been better off if it had refrained from overstating its earnings in the first place, an act that probably cost it some measure of credibility among investors?

If the analyst considers the matter from the standpoint of management, a possible solution to the riddle emerges. The day of reckoning, when the firm must pay back the reported earnings borrowed via underdepreciation, may be beyond the planning horizon of senior management. A chief executive officer who intends to retire in five years, and who will be compensated in the interim according to a formula based on reported earnings growth, may have no qualms about exaggerating current results at the expense of future years' operations. The long-term interests of the firm's owners, in other words, may not be consistent with the short-term interests of their agents, the salaried managers.

Plainly, analysts cannot be expected to read minds or to divine the true motives of management in every case. There is a benefit, however, in simply being cognizant of objectives other than the ones presupposed by introductory accounting texts. If nothing else, the awareness that management may have something up its sleeve will encourage readers to trust their instincts when some aspect of a company's disclosure simply does not ring true. In a given instance, management may judge that its best chance of minimizing analysts' criticism of an obviously disastrous corporate decision lies in stubbornly defending the decision and refusing to change course. Even though the chief executive officer may be able to pull it off with a straight face, however, the blunder remains a blunder. Analysts who remember that managers may be pursuing their own agendas will be ahead of the game. They will be properly skeptical that management is genuinely making tough choices designed to yield long-run benefits to shareholders, but which individuals outside the corporation cannot envision.

Armed with the attitude that the burden of proof lies with those making the disclosures, the analyst is now prepared to tackle the basic financial statements. Methods for uncovering the information they conceal, as well as that which they reveal, constitute the heart of the next three chapters. From that elementary level right on up to making investment decisions with the techniques presented in the final two chapters, it will pay to maintain an adversarial stance at all times.

The Basic Financial Statements

CHAPTER 2

The Balance Sheet

The balance sheet is a remarkable invention, yet it has two fundamental shortcomings. First, while it is in theory quite useful to have a summary of the values of all the assets owned by an enterprise, these values frequently prove elusive in practice. Second, many kinds of things have value and could be construed, at least by the layperson, as assets. Not all of them can be assigned a specific value and recorded on a balance sheet, however. For example, proprietors of service businesses are fond of saying, "Our assets go down the elevator every night." Everybody acknowledges the value of a company's human capital – the skills and creativity of its employees – but no one has devised a means of valuing it precisely enough to reflect it on the balance sheet. Accountants do not go to the opposite extreme of banishing all intangible assets from the balance sheet, but the dividing line between the permitted and the prohibited is inevitably an arbitrary one.[1]

During the late 1990s, doctrinal disputes over accounting for assets intensified as intellectual capital came to represent growing proportions of many major corporations' perceived value. A study conducted on behalf of Big Five accounting firm Arthur Andersen showed that between 1978 and 1999, **book value** fell from 95 percent to 71 percent of the stock market value of public companies in the United States.[2] Increasingly, investors were willing to pay for things other than the traditional assets that generally accepted accounting principles (GAAP) had grown up around, including buildings, machinery, inventories, receivables, and a limited range of capitalized expenditures.

The link between book values and market-estimated values continued to loosen in the twenty-first century. In early 2021, the book values per share reported by Bloomberg for the fabled FAANG stocks ranged from 3 percent to 15 percent of the companies' **market capitalizations.** These five stocks – Facebook, Amazon, Apple, Netflix, and Alphabet (formerly known as Google) – accounted for about 15 percent of the Standard & Poor's 500

Index's total value at the time and frequently dominated large moves in the index's level.

Prominent accounting theorists argued that financial reporting practices rooted in an era more dominated by heavy manufacturing grossly understated the value created by research and development outlays, which GAAP was resistant to capitalizing. They observed further that traditional accounting generally permitted assets to rise in value only if they were sold. "Transactions are no longer the basis for much of the value created and destroyed in today's economy, and therefore traditional accounting systems are at a loss to capture much of what goes on," argued Baruch Lev of New York University. As examples, he cited the rise in value resulting from a drug passing a key clinical test and from a computer software program being successfully beta-tested. "There's no accounting event because no money changes hands," Lev noted.[3]

THE VALUE PROBLEM

The problems of value that accountants wrestle with have also historically plagued philosophers, economists, tax assessors, and the judiciary. Moral philosophers over the centuries grappled with the notion of a fair price for merchants to charge. Early economists attempted to derive a product's intrinsic value by calculating the units of labor embodied in it. Several distinct approaches have evolved for assessing real property. These include **capitalization** of rentals, inferring a value based on sales of comparable properties, and estimating the value a property would have if put to its highest and best use. Similar theories are involved when the courts seek to value the assets of bankrupt companies, although vigorous negotiations among the different classes of creditors play an essential role in the final determination.

With commendable clarity of vision, the accounting profession long ago cut through the thicket of competing theories by establishing **historical cost** as the basis for valuing nonfinancial assets. The cost of acquiring or constructing an asset has the great advantage of being an objective and verifiable figure. As a benchmark for value, it is, therefore, compatible with accountants' traditional principle of conservatism.

Whatever its strengths, however, the historical cost system also has disadvantages that are apparent even to the beginning student of accounting. As already noted, basing valuation on transactions means that no asset can be reflected on the balance sheet unless it has been involved in a transaction. The most familiar difficulty that results from this convention involves goodwill. Company A has value above and beyond its tangible assets, in the form of well-regarded brand names and close relationships with merchants built up over many years. None of this intangible value appears on Company A's balance sheet, however, for it has never figured in a transaction. When Company B acquires Company A at a premium to book value, though, the intangibles are suddenly recognized. To the benefit of users of financial statements, Company A's assets become more fully reflected. On the negative side, Company A's balance sheet now says it is more valuable than Company C, which has equivalent tangible and intangible assets but has never been acquired.

The difficulties a person may encounter in the quest for true value are numerous. Consider, for example, a piece of specialized machinery, acquired for $50,000. On the day the equipment is put into service, even before any controversies surrounding depreciation rates arise, value is already a matter of opinion. The company that made the purchase would presumably not have paid $50,000 if it perceived the machine to be worth a lesser amount. A secured lender, however, is likely to take a more conservative view. For one thing, the lender will find it difficult in the future to monitor the value of the collateral through comparables, since only a few similar machines (perhaps none, if the piece is customized) are produced each year. Furthermore, if the lender is ultimately forced to foreclose, there may be no ready purchaser of the machinery for $50,000, since its specialized nature makes it useful to only a small number of manufacturers. All of the potential purchasers, moreover, may be located hundreds of miles away, so that the machinery's value in a liquidation would be further reduced by the costs of transporting and reinstalling it.

The problems encountered in evaluating one-of-a-kind industrial equipment might appear to be eliminated when dealing with actively traded commodities such as crude oil reserves. Even this type of asset, however, resists precise, easily agreed-on valuation. Since oil companies frequently buy and sell reserves in the ground, current transaction prices are readily available. These transactions, however, are based on estimates of eventual production from unique geologic formations, for there are no means of directly measuring oil reserves. Even when petroleum engineers employ the most advanced technology, their estimates rely heavily on judgment and inference. It is not unheard of, moreover, for a well to begin to produce at the rate predicted by the best scientific methods, only to peter out a short time later, ultimately yielding just a fraction of its estimated reserves. With this degree of uncertainty, recording the true value of oil reserves is not a realistic objective for accountants. Users of financial statements can, at best, hope for informed guesses, and there is considerable room for honest people (not to mention rogues with vested interests) to disagree.

If anything, this particular valuation issue is becoming even more problematic as the global economy moves toward greater reliance on environmentally friendlier energy sources. Already, a largescale shift from coal to natural gas, a cleaner fuel, has produced huge write-downs of asset values. For example, the reported asset value of all of Peabody Energy's U.S. thermal coal mining assets dropped by 52 percent in the first half of 2020.[4]

Thinking more broadly than just about the energy sector, a wide range of companies are vulnerable to disruption in today's economy. Scale economies achieved through massive purchases of assets provide no sure protection against inroads by new competitors armed with innovative technologies or business models. Salvage values may be minimal on assets dedicated to obsolete modes of operation. Accordingly, analysts must closely monitor the returns that companies are earning on their assets to ascertain whether the accounting-based values are durable.

COMPARABILITY PROBLEMS IN THE VALUATION OF FINANCIAL ASSETS

The numerous difficulties of evaluating physical assets make historical cost an appealing, if imperfect, solution by virtue of its objectivity. Some financial assets are unaffected by those difficulties, however. They trade daily and actively in well-organized markets such as the New York Stock Exchange. It is feasible to value such assets on the basis of market quotations at the end of the financial reporting period, rather than according to historical cost, and achieve both objectivity and accuracy.

Analysts must keep in mind, however, that the values assigned to huge amounts of financial assets on many companies' balance sheets are *not* verifiable on the basis of continuously quoted prices determined in deep, liquid markets. Under **Fair Value Accounting**, an asset of this sort is valued at the amount at which it currently could be bought or sold in a transaction between willing parties, not including a liquidation sale. If no active market for the asset exists, a company can determine its balance sheet value on the basis of quoted prices for similar assets that do trade actively. In this case, the company must make assumptions about how the market would adjust for the fact that the actively traded and non-actively traded assets are not identical. If no comparables exist, a company can use its own assumptions about the assumptions market participants would use to offer or bid for the asset it is valuing. Users of financial statements can reasonably expect that some companies' assumptions about assumptions will be on the liberal side, potentially inflating the value of non-actively traded assets. Abuse of this discretion was one element of the Enron fraud (see Chapter 11).

Thanks to market innovations of recent decades, a large category of subjectively valued financial assets consists of non-exchange-traded **derivatives**. (The collective term for these assets reflects that their valuations derive from the values of other assets, such as commodities or indexes of securities.) In a financial market crisis, the price at which such instruments can be bought or sold is subject to violent swings. Companies understandably would prefer that the investors who determine their stock prices not see or consider such losses in value, which the companies invariably (but not always correctly) characterize as temporary. For a financial institution, an even bigger worry is that its regulator will declare the institution insolvent, based on a market-induced and genuinely temporary decline in the balance sheet value of its derivatives.

Seeing these disadvantages to themselves, issuers of financial statements have resisted the imposition of full-blown fair value accounting. Under the compromise embodied in the 1993 Statement of Financial Accounting Standards (**SFAS**) 115, financial instruments are valued according to their intended use by the company issuing the financial statements. If the company intends to hold a debt security to maturity, it records the value at amortized cost less impairment, if any. (The amortization is the write-down of a premium over face value or write-up of discount from face value, over the remaining period to maturity. Impairment is a loss of value arising from a clear indication that the obligor will be unable to satisfy the terms of the obligation.) If the company intends to sell a debt or equity security in the near term, hoping to make a trading profit, it records the instrument at fair value and includes unrealized gains and losses in earnings. A third option is for the company to classify a debt or equity security as neither held-to-maturity or a trading security, but instead in the noncommittal category of available for sale. In that case, the instrument is recorded at fair value, but unrealized gains and losses are excluded from earnings and instead reported in other comprehensive income, a separate component of shareholders' equity. SFAS 157, issued in 2006, sought to clarify further the fair value definition.

The essential point is that an asset may be valued on one company's balance sheet at a substantially different value than an identical asset is valued on another company's balance sheet, all based on the different companies' representations of their intentions.

It is even possible for an asset to be carried at two different values on a single balance sheet. For instance, when equity values plummeted in 2008, managers of leveraged buyout partnerships varied in the severity with which they wrote down their holdings. Many deals were shared by multiple private equity firms. A university endowment fund or pension plan sponsor might be a limited partner in a privately owned company held by two or more private equity funds that placed different values on the company. Underlying the value for those funds on the institution's balance sheet would be nonequivalent valuations of identical shares.

Inconsistent valuations can also undermine the integrity of an enterprise's balance sheet without involvement of outside parties such as private equity firms. An inquest into the September 2008 bankruptcy of Lehman Brothers found that each trading desk within the investment bank had its own methodology for pricing assets. Methodologies differed even within a single asset class, and the Product Control Group, which was supposed to enforce standardization in valuation, was understaffed for the task. Incidentally, some of the methodologies employed at Lehman Brothers were dubious, to say the least. For example, the investment bank based its second-quarter 2008 prices for one group of assets on a Morgan Stanley research note published in the first quarter of that year.[5]

INSTANTANEOUS WIPEOUT OF VALUE

Because the value of many assets is so subjective, balance sheets are prone to sudden, arbitrary revisions. To cite one example, in 2018 General Electric wrote off $17 billion in value of the power equipment businesses purchased in 2015 from France's Alstom. The reduction in value exceeded the total amount GE paid for the businesses, which was $10 billion. This apparent anomaly arose from the **goodwill** recorded in the acquisition.

When GE sorted out accounting for the acquisition a year after it was completed, the company placed a value of $21 billion on the power businesses' gross assets and valued its liabilities at $23 billion. After removing some minority interests, GE concluded that the acquired operations had a net worth of –$7 billion. The $17 billion difference between that figure and the $10 billion purchase price constituted the goodwill that GE wrote down on the acquired Alstom businesses, just three years after the deal closed. The company wrote down $6 billion of other assets at the same time.

In 2016 GE justified paying $10 billion for businesses with –$7 billion of book value on the basis of expected synergy (possibly the most dangerous word in finance), including incremental revenue from cross-selling opportunities. The following year, GE chief executive officer John Flannery remarked that if GE could go back in a time machine, it would pay far less than it shelled out for the Alstom assets. Unfortunately, time machines were not part of GE's product line and Flannery was ousted as in conjunction with the total $23 billion write-off.

Jonathan Ford of the *Financial Times* suggested there was more than bad timing or bad luck behind the swift evaporation of the asset value attributed to the Alstom assets.[6] Writing in 2018, Ford noted that the total amount of goodwill on the balance sheets of S&P 500 companies ballooned from $1.8 trillion to $2.9 trillion. He attributed this dramatic rise to a protracted merger boom, combined with the economy's shift from manufacturing to services. Many leading companies, he pointed out, now have little in the way of tangible assets, meaning that larger portions of acquisition prices than formerly would be chalked up to goodwill.

Up until 2000 in the U.S. and 2005 in Europe, acquirers that paid more than the purchased assets' tangible value had to amortize the resulting goodwill year-by-year. That reduced the reported profits generated by the acquired business. With that requirement now removed, said the *Financial Times* columnist, corporate CEOs could "buy earnings" and thereby increase their growth-based bonuses and report respectable profits even on mediocre businesses acquired at excessive prices.

The game is up only when the accountants determine that the asset in question has become impaired. Ford asserted that the test for a write-down-triggering impairment, namely, deterioration in expected future cash flows, can easily be gamed. The day of reckoning cannot be deferred indefinitely, but in the meantime unwary investors will have an inflated notion of the acquirer's asset value.

Ideally, analysts will not wait for the accountants to make it official that acquired assets have deteriorated in value. Instead, they will adjust a company's balance sheet to reflect telltale signs of overstatement. By paying attention to these early warning signals, they can potentially avoid being caught off guard by asset revaluations.

By way of illustration, on January 18, 2013, Caterpillar Inc. said it was taking a noncash goodwill impairment charge of approximately $580 million. The impaired assets came with the June 2012 acquisition of Mining Machinery Limited (ERA), including its wholly owned subsidiary. Zhengzhou Siwei Mechanical & Electrical Manufacturing Co., Ltd., commonly referred to as "Siwei."

Caterpillar attributed the discrepancy between the value attributed to the assets at the time of the acquisition and the written-down value less than a year later to "deliberate, multi-year, coordinated accounting misconduct" by Siwei senior managers.[7] Duncan Mavin of the *Wall Street Journal* pointed out, however, that due diligence prior to the acquisition "must have raised red flags."[8] In Mavin's view, ERA appeared to be headed for a working capital crisis, based on a 37 percent jump in accounts receivable from 2010 to 2011, far exceeding the 10 percent increase in sales over the same period. Inventories not yet shifted to customers meanwhile rose by 234 percent.

When China's economy slowed, ERA's directors lent the company cash to keep lid on its high borrowing costs. In March 2012 the company warned that rising raw material costs and swelling bad debt allowance would cause it to miss a profit target. The hope was that being acquired by Caterpillar, a much bigger company, would bring efficiencies and cheaper financing. Those benefits, however, would not solve the basic problem that ERA had to offer customers credit and favorable terms in order to compete with state-owned rivals.

The ERA write-down did not cause Caterpillar's stock to plummet. Neither did it prompt downgrades by the bond-rating agencies (see Chapter 13). In many other instances, shareholders and bondholders have not been so fortunate. Analysts can help investors avoid unpleasant surprises by paying attention to the sort of early warning signals detailed by Mavin.

If this seems a daunting task, the reader may take encouragement from the success of the bond-rating agencies in sifting through the financial reporting folderol to get to the economic substance. The bursting of Tech Bubble of the 1990s in 2001 produced numerous multibillion-dollar goodwill write-offs. They did not, as one might have expected, set off a massive wave of rating downgrades. As in many previous instances of companies writing down assets, Moody's and Standard & Poor's did not equate changes in accounting values with reduced protection for lenders. To be sure, if a company wrote off a billion dollars' worth of goodwill, its ratio of assets to liabilities declined. Its ratio of *tangible* assets to liabilities did not change, however. The rating agencies monitored both ratios but had customarily attached greater significance to the version that ignored intangible assets such as goodwill.

HOW GOOD IS GOODWILL?

By maintaining a skeptical attitude to the value of intangible assets throughout the **New Economy** excitement of the late nineties, Moody's and Standard & Poor's were bucking the trend. The more stylish view was that balance sheets constructed according to GAAP seriously understated the value of corporations in dynamic industries such as computer software and e-commerce. Their earning power, so the story went, derived from inspired ideas and improved methods of doing business, not from the bricks and mortar for which conventional accounting was designed. To adapt to the economy's changing profile, proclaimed the heralds of the new paradigm, the accounting rule makers had to allow all sorts of items traditionally expensed to be capitalized onto the asset side of the balance sheet. Against that backdrop, analysts who questioned the value represented by goodwill, an item long deemed legitimate under GAAP, look conservative indeed.

In reality, the stock market euphoria that preceded some mind-boggling write-offs illustrated in classic fashion the reasons for rating agency skepticism toward goodwill. Through stock-for-stock acquisitions, the sharp rise in equity prices during the late 1990s was transformed into increased balance sheet values, despite the usual assumption that fluctuations in a company's stock price do not alter its stated net worth. It was an awesome form of financial alchemy.

The link between rising stock prices and escalating goodwill is illustrated by the fictitious example in Exhibit 2.1. In Scenario I, the shares of Associated Amalgamator Corporation ("Amalgamator") and United Consolidator Inc. ("Consolidator") are both trading at multiples of 1.0 times book value per share. Shareholders' equity is $200 million at Amalgamators and $60 million at Consolidator, equivalent to the companies' respective market

EXHIBIT 2.1   Pro Forma Balance Sheets, December 31, 2021 ($000,000 omitted)

	Associated Amalgamator Corporation	United Consolidator Inc.	Purchase Price	Combined Companies Pro Forma
Scenario I				
Tangible assets	$1,000	$400		$1,400
Intangible assets	0	0		20
Total assets	1,000	400		1,420
Liabilities	800	340		1,140
Shareholders' equity (SE)	200	60	80	280
Total liabilities and SE	$1,000	$400		$1,420
Tangible assets/total liabilities	1.25	1.18		1.23
Total assets/total liabilities	1.25	1.18		1.25
Market capitalization	200	60		280
Scenario II				
Tangible assets	$1,000	$400		$1,400
Intangible assets	0	0		60
Total assets	1,000	400		1,460
Liabilities	800	340		1,140
Shareholders' equity (SE)	200	60	120	320
Total liabilities and SE	$1,000	$400		$1,460
Total assets/total liabilities	1.25	1.18		1.28
Tangible assets/total liabilities	1.25	1.18		1.23
Market capitalization	300	90		480*

*Ignores possible impact of earnings per share dilution.

capitalizations. Amalgamator uses stock held in its treasury to acquire Consolidator for $80 million. The purchase price represents a premium of 33 1/3 percent above the prevailing market price.

Let us now examine a key indicator of credit quality. Prior to the acquisition, Amalgamator's ratio of total assets to total liabilities (see Chapter 13) is 1.25 times, while the comparable figure for Consolidator is 1.18 times. The stock-for-stock acquisition introduces no new hard assets (e.g., cash, inventories, or factories). Neither does the transaction eliminate any existing liabilities. Logically, then, Consolidator's 1.18 times ratio should drag down Amalgamator's 1.25 times ratio, resulting in a figure somewhere in between for the combined companies.

In fact, though, the total-assets-to-total-liabilities ratio after the deal is 1.25 times. By paying a premium to Consolidator's tangible asset value, Amalgamator creates $20 million of goodwill. This intangible asset represents just 1.4 percent of the combined companies' total assets, but that suffices to enable Amalgamator to acquire a company with a weaker debt-quality ratio without showing any deterioration on that measure.

If this outcome seems perverse, consider Scenario II. As the scene opens, an explosive stock market rally has driven up both companies' shares to 150 percent of book value. The ratio of total assets to total liabilities, however, remains at 1.25 times for Amalgamator and 1.18 times for Consolidator. Conservative bond buyers take comfort from the fact that the assets remain on the books at historical cost less depreciation, unaffected by euphoria on the stock exchange that may dissipate at any time without notice.

As in Scenario I, Amalgamator pays a premium of 33 1/3 percent above the prevailing market price to acquire Consolidator. The premium is calculated on a higher market capitalization, however. Consequently, the purchase price rises from $80 million to $120 million. Instead of creating $20 million of goodwill, the acquisition gives rise to a $60 million intangible asset.

When the conservative bond investors calculate the combined companies' ratio of total assets to total liabilities, they make a startling discovery. Somehow, putting together a company boasting a 1.25 times ratio with another sporting a 1.18 times ratio has produced an entity with a ratio of 1.28 times. Moreover, a minute of experimentation with the numbers will show that the ratio would be higher still if Amalgamator had bought Consolidator at a higher price. Seemingly, the simplest way for a company to improve its credit quality is to make stock-for-stock acquisitions at grossly excessive prices.

Naturally, this absurd conclusion embodies a fallacy. In reality, the receivables, inventories, and machinery available to be sold to satisfy creditors' claims are no greater in Scenario II than in Scenario I. Given that the total-assets-to-total-liabilities ratio is lower at Consolidator than at

Amalgamator, the combined companies' ratio logically must be lower than at Amalgamator. Common sense further states that Amalgamator cannot truly have better credit quality if it overpays for Consolidator than if it acquires the company at a fair price.

As it happens, there is a simple way out of the logical conundrum. Let us exclude goodwill in calculating the ratio of assets to liabilities. As shown in the exhibit, Amalgamator's ratio of *tangible* assets to total liabilities following its acquisition of Consolidator is 1.23 times in both Scenario I and Scenario II. This is the outcome that best reflects economic reality. To ensure that they reach this commonsense conclusion, credit analysts must follow the rating agencies' practice of calculating balance sheet ratios both with and without goodwill and other intangible assets, giving greater emphasis to the latter version.

Calculating ratios on a tangibles-only basis is not equivalent to saying that the intangibles have no value. Amalgamator is likely to recoup all or most of the $60 million accounted for as goodwill if it turns around and sells Consolidator tomorrow. Such a transaction is hardly likely, however. A sale several years hence, after stock prices have fallen from today's lofty levels, is a more plausible scenario. Under such conditions, the full $60 million probably will not be recoverable.

Even leaving aside the possibility of a plunge in stock prices, it makes eminent sense to eliminate or sharply downplay the value of goodwill in a balance-sheet-based analysis of credit quality. Unlike inventories or accounts receivable, goodwill is not an asset that can be readily sold or **factored** to raise cash. Neither can a company enter into a **sale-leaseback** of its goodwill, as it can with its plant and equipment. In short, goodwill is not a separable asset that management can either convert into cash or use to raise cash to extricate itself from a financial tight spot. Therefore, the relevance of goodwill to an analysis of asset protection is questionable.

On the whole, the rating agencies appear to have shown sound judgment during the 1990s by resisting the New Economy's siren song. While enthusiasm mounted for all sorts of intangible assets, they continued to gear their analysis to tangible-assets-only versions of key balance sheet ratios. By and large, therefore, companies did not alter the way they were perceived by Moody's and Standard & Poor's when they suddenly took an ax to their intangible assets.

More generally, asset write-offs do not usually cause ratings to fall. Occasionally, to be sure, the announcement of a write-off coincides with the disclosure of a previously unrevealed impairment of value, ordinarily arising from operating problems. That sort of development may trigger a downgrade. In addition, a write-off sometimes coincides with a decision to close down certain operations. The associated severance costs (payments to terminated employees) may represent a substantial cash outlay that does weaken the company's financial position. Finally, a write-off can put a company in violation of a debt covenant (see Chapter 12). Nervous lenders may exploit the **technical default** by canceling the company's credit lines, precipitating a **liquidity** crisis. In and of itself, however, adjusting the balance sheet to economic reality does not represent a reduction in credit protection measures.

LOSING VALUE THE OLD-FASHIONED WAY

Goodwill write-offs by high-tech, asset-light companies make splashy headlines in the financial news, but they by no means represent the only way in which balance sheet assets suddenly and sharply decline in value. In the "Old Economy," where countless manufacturers earn slender margins on low-tech industrial goods, companies are vulnerable to long-run erosion in profitability. Common pitfalls include fierce price competition and a failure, because of near-term pressures to conserve cash, to invest adequately in modernization of plants and equipment. As the rate of return on their fixed assets declines, producers of industrial commodities such as paper, chemicals, and steel must eventually face up to the permanent impairment of their reported asset values.

It is not feasible, in the case of a chronically low rate-of-return company, to predict precisely the magnitude of a future reduction in accounting values. Indeed, there is no guarantee that a company will fully come to grips with its overstated net worth, especially on the first round. To estimate the expected order of magnitude of future write-offs, however, an analyst can adjust the shareholders' value shown on the balance sheet to the rate of return typically being earned by comparable corporations.

To illustrate, suppose Company Z's average net income over the past five years has been $24 million. With most of the company's modest earnings being paid out in dividends, shareholders' equity has been stagnant at around $300 million. Assume further that during the same period, the average return of companies in the Standard & Poor's 400 index of industrial corporations has been 14 percent.

Does the figure $300 million accurately represent Company Z's equity value? If so, the implication is that investors are willing to own the company's shares and accept a return of only 8 percent ($24 million divided by $300 million), even though a 14 percent return is available on other stocks. There is no obvious reason that investors would voluntarily make such a sacrifice, however. Therefore, Company Z's book value is almost certainly overstated.

A reasonable estimate of the low-profit company's true equity value would be the amount that produces a return on equity equivalent to the going rate:

$$\frac{\text{Company Z average earnings stream}}{X} = \frac{\text{Average return on equity}}{\text{for U.S. corporations}}$$

$$\frac{\$24 \text{ million}}{X} = 14\%$$

$$X = \$171 \text{ million}$$

Although useful as a general guideline, this method of adjusting the shareholders' equity of underperforming companies neglects a number of important subtleties. For one thing, Company Z may be considered riskier than the average company. In that case, shareholders would demand a return higher than 14 percent to hold its shares. Furthermore, cash flow may be a better indicator of the company's economic performance than net income. This would imply that the adjustment ought to be made to the ratio of cash flow to market capitalization, rather than return on equity. Furthermore, investors' rate-of-return requirements reflect expected future earnings, rather than past results. Depending on the outlook for its business, it might be reasonable to assume that Company Z will either realize higher profits in the next five years than in the past five or see its profits plunge further. By the same token, securities analysts may expect the peer group of stocks that represent alternative investments to produce a return higher or lower than 14 percent in coming years. The further the analyst travels in search of true value, it seems, the murkier the notion becomes.

TRUE EQUITY IS ELUSIVE

What financial analysts are actually seeking, but are unable to find in the financial statements, is equity as economists conceive of it. In scholarly studies, the term *equity* generally refers not to accounting book value, but to the present value of future cash flows accruing to the firm's owners. Consider a firm that is deriving huge earnings from a trademark that has no accounting value because it was developed **internally** rather than acquired. The present value of the profits derived from the trademark would be included in the economist's definition of equity but not in the accountant's, potentially creating a gap of billions of dollars between the two.

The contrast between the economist's and the accountant's notions of equity is dramatized by the phenomenon of negative equity. In the economist's terms, equity of less than zero is synonymous with bankruptcy. The reasoning is that when a company's liabilities exceed the **present value** of all future income, it is not rational for the owners to continue paying off the liabilities. They will stop making payments currently due to lenders and trade creditors, which will in turn prompt the holders of the liabilities to try to recover their claims by forcing the company into bankruptcy. Suppose, on the other hand, that the present value of a highly successful company's future income exceeds the value of its liabilities by a substantial margin. If the company runs into a patch of bad luck, recording net losses for several years running and writing off selected operations, the book value of its assets may fall below the value of its liabilities. In accounting terms, the result is negative shareholders' equity. The economic value of the assets, however, may still exceed the stated value of the liabilities. Under such circumstances, the company has no reason to consider either suspending payments to creditors or filing for bankruptcy.

The Western Union Company's September 2006 spin-off from First Data Corporation demonstrated that negative equity in an accounting sense is not synonymous with insolvency. In connection with the spin-off, the provider of money transfer services distributed approximately $3.5 billion to First Data in the form of cash and debt securities. Net of other events during the period, shareholders' equity fell to –$314.8 million on December 31, 2006, from $2.8 billion one year earlier. By producing solid earnings over the next three years, Western Union boosted shareholders' equity to $353.5 million by December 31, 2009. Anyone who mistook the year-end 2006 negative figure as an indication of Western Union's economic value would have deemed its stock grossly overvalued at $18.85 a share. Through the end of 2009, however, Western Union shares performed far better than the stock market as a whole. The Standard & Poor's 500 Index fell by 21.4 percent versus a decline of only 15.9 percent for Western Union.

BOOK VALUE MAY OVERSTATE REALITY

Just as book value can understate equity in an economic sense, it can overstate it too. Consider Celadon Group, which at the time of the events described here was the twelfth largest U.S. trucker focusing on truckload shipments. As detailed in an April 5, 2017, report by Prescience Point Research Group[9], securities analysts generally valued Celadon's shares at one times tangible book value (TBV), which is calculated by subtracting goodwill from companywide book value (total assets minus total liabilities). As reported by Celadon, TBV equated to $10.80 per share at the time of Prescience Point's report, implying that its shares were significantly undervalued at $6.25. The research firm maintained, however, that Celadon's true TBV was $0.42 per share.

Taking into account as well other signs of financial misreporting, Prescience Point valued Celadon's shares at zero. That price target was not reached in the near term, but less than a month after publication of the report the stock closed at $1.55, down by 75 percent. In the interim, the company announced that Chief Operating Officer Eric Meek had resigned after its auditor, BKD, LLP, determined that investors should not rely on the fiscal 2016 financial statements. By the end of 2019 Celadon had filed for bankruptcy and its shares, long since delisted by the New York Stock Exchange, were quoted at less than $0.02. In addition, the former president of a former Celadon subsidiary had pleaded guilty to a fraud by which Celadon avoided disclosing substantial losses and misrepresented its financial condition. Two of his superiors were under indictment.

Among the factors that pointed to a vast overstatement of tangible book value was an exhibit in a Securities and Exchange Commission 10-Q filing. It concerned a 50/50 off-balance sheet joint venture (JV) that Celadon formed with Element Fleet Management. The transaction's background was that under terms of its sales of tractors (which pull the semi-trailers in tractor-trailer units) to Element, Celadon agreed to cover up to 10 percent of Element's losses on its purchases. (These losses arose if the prices Element obtained in the used tractor market were less than the tractors' depreciated cost.) In addition, Celadon agreed to cover, on an interim basis, any shortfall on lease payments from Element's operators. Element was obligated to repay these "lease shortfall advances" at some point.

These arrangements became very costly for Celadon when used tractor prices and lease utilization rates began to plummet in late 2015. Cash flow turned negative as Celadon shelled out $74 million to cover Element's losses on its purchased tractors and $31.9 million for lease shortfalls. Under the new JV arrangement Cedalon would no longer have to make up shortfalls at Element.

Element contributed $100 million of equity to the JV, consisting of $667.5 million of equipment and $567.6 million of debt. Celadon likewise contributed $100 million of equity – $36.4 million in cash and $63.6 million of equipment. Based on those reported values, Celadon valued its 50 percent stake in the $200 million joint venture at $100 million.

Prescience Point questioned that valuation. To begin with, Celadon represented that just before the JV was formed it recovered $31.8 million of previous lease shortfall advances from Element. According to the JV subscription agreement included as an exhibit in Celadon's 10-Q filing, however, Element made a $31.8 million "Daylight Loan" to the JV, which in turn advanced the money to Celadon. That was the source of the cash that

Celadon contributed to the JV, which immediately used it to repay the Daylight Loan. Prescience Point concluded that the transactions constituted a sham loan designed to create the false appearance of recovery by Celadon of its earlier lease shortfall advances. With $31.8 million of Celadon's supposed $100 million equity contribution going to repay the Daylight Loan made a short while earlier, Celadon's actual equity contribution was just $68.2 million, said Prescience.

As for the other partner's ostensible $100 million equity contribution, Prescience Point argued that the equipment valued at $567.6 million by Element was under-depreciated by $171.5 million. In the 1.7 years in which Element had owned equipment purchased from Celadon, it had recorded $80.9 million in depreciation on $740.0 million of equipment. That equated to 6.4 percent annual depreciation, implying that Element was assuming a 15-year average useful life, which Prescience Point deemed not even remotely consistent with tractors' actual useful lives. Celadon was assuming a useful life of only four years and a 40 percent salvage value, resulting in a much higher 15 percent annual depreciation rate. Two peer companies were applying 15 percent and 17 percent rates. The $171.5 million by which Prescience Point estimated that Element's contributed equipment was overvalued exceeded the sum of Element's stated $100 million equity contribution and the $68.2 million valid portion of Celadon's nominal $100 million equity contribution. (The nominal amount was reduced by the $31.8 million that was quickly shuffled in and out). That left the joint venture with no actual equity value. Fifty percent of nothing is nothing, leading to the conclusion that the $100 million joint venture stake on Celadon's balance sheet was overstated by $100 million.

Celadon further inflated its TBV by increasing the useful lives of both its tractors and its trailers. Separate from that balance sheet effect, Prescience Point spied another red flag in the company's firing of the top-tier audit firm KPMG in 2013, a year after KPMG required Celadon to restate its financials. KPMG's replacement was a regional auditor, BKD LLP. Between fiscal 2014 and fiscal 2016 Celadon's annual audit fees increased by 179.6 percent. Prescience Point noted that in two of the largest financial frauds in history, Enron (see Chapter 11) and Satyam, outsized audit fees compromised the auditors' ability or willingness to carry out their duties adequately.

Predictably, Celadon's management brushed off Prescience Point's criticisms, alleging that the research firm was short its stock. One securities analyst sprang to the company's defense, urging investors to buy Celadon's stock on the dip. That proved an ill-timed recommendation in light of the one-day 55 percent drop that followed on May 2. Users of financial statements should expect – and regard with skepticism – reflexive and sometimes outraged denials by management when financial reporting irregularities come to light.

PROS AND CONS OF A MARKET-BASED EQUITY FIGURE

Relying on market capitalization is the practical means by which financial analysts commonly estimate the economists' more theoretically rigorous definition of equity as the present value of expected future cash flows. Monumental difficulties confront anyone who instead attempts to arrive at the figure through conventional financial reporting systems. The problem is that traditional accounting favors items that can be objectively measured. Unfortunately, future earnings and cash flows are unobservable. Moreover, calculating present value requires selecting a **discount rate** representing the company's **cost of capital.** Determining the cost of capital is a notoriously controversial subject in the financial field, complicated by thorny tax considerations and risk adjustments. The figures needed to calculate economists' equity are not, in short, the kind of numbers accountants like to deal with. Their ideal value is a price on an invoice that can be independently verified by a canceled check.

Market capitalization has additional advantages beyond its comparative ease of calculation. For one thing, it represents the consensus of large numbers of analysts and investors who constantly monitor companies' future earnings prospects as the basis for their evaluations. In addition, an up-to-the-minute market capitalization can be calculated on any day that the stock exchange is open. This represents a considerable advantage over the shareholders' equity shown on the balance sheet, which is updated only once every three months. Market capitalization adjusts instantaneously to news such as a surprise product launch by a competitor, an explosion that halts production at a key plant, or a sudden hike in interest rates by the Federal Reserve. In contrast, these events may never be reflected in book value in a discrete, identifiable manner. Ardent advocates of market capitalization cannot conceive of any more accurate estimate of true equity value.

Against these advantages, however, the analyst must weigh several drawbacks to relying on market capitalization to estimate a company's actual equity value. For one thing, while the objectivity of a price quotation established in a competitive market is indeed a benefit, it is obtainable only for corporations with publicly traded stocks. For privately owned companies, the proponents of market capitalization typically generate a proxy for true equity through reference to industry-peer public companies. For example, to calculate the equity of a privately owned paper producer, an analyst might multiply the publicly traded peer group's average price-earnings ratio (see Chapter 14) by the private company's earnings. Often, the peer-group multiple is based on **EBITDA** (see Chapter 8) rather than net income. This method can expand the peer group to include companies no longer publicly traded but recently acquired in leveraged buyouts. A limitation of the peer-group approach is that it fails to capture company-specific factors and therefore does not reap one major benefit of using market capitalization as a gauge of actual equity value.

Even if analysts restrict their reliance on market capitalization to publicly traded companies, they will still encounter pitfalls. Consider, for example, that on Monday, February 5, 2018, the **Dow Jones Industrial Average** plunged by 1,175 points, or 4.6 percent. The price of Dow component Boeing dropped by 5.7 percent, representing a $20 billion loss in market value. No major negative news was reported about the aerospace company that day and stock analysts had recently raised their earnings-per-share estimates on the company. Just ten days later, with the stock market gauge on the rebound, Boeing's shares had more than fully recovered their Friday, February 2, 2018, value.

Notwithstanding the theoretical arguments for regarding market capitalization as a company's true equity value, short-run changes of the magnitude experienced by Boeing on February 5, 2018, raise a caution. In a literal interpretation, even a huge, sudden swing in market capitalization indicates a change in a company's earnings prospects. In extreme cases, though, a temporary shift in the aggregate value of a company's shares can appear to reveal more about the dynamics of the stock market. An inference along those lines is supported by extensive academic research conducted under the rubric of behavioral finance. In contrast to more traditional financial economists, the behavioralists doubt that investors invariably process information accurately and act on it according to rules of rationality, as defined by economists. Empirical studies by adherents of behavioral finance show that instead of faithfully tracking companies' intrinsic values, market prices frequently overreact to news events. Even though investors supposedly evaluate stocks on the basis of expected future dividends (see Chapter 14), the behavioralists find that the stock market is far more volatile than the variability of dividends can explain.[10]

To be sure, these conclusions remain controversial. Traditionalists have challenged the empirical studies that underlie them, producing a vigorous debate. Nevertheless, the findings of behavioral finance lend moral support to analysts who find it hard to believe that the one-day erasure of billions of market capitalization must automatically be a truer representation of the company's change in equity value than a figure derived from financial statement data.

Market capitalization, then, is a useful tool but not one to be heeded blindly. In the end, true equity remains an elusive number. Instead of striving for theoretical purity on the matter, analysts should adopt a flexible attitude, using the measure of equity value most useful to a particular application.

For example, stated balance sheet figures, derived mainly from historical cost, are the ones that matter in estimating the risk that a company will violate a loan covenant requiring maintenance of a minimum ratio of debt to net worth (see Chapter 12). The historical cost figures are less relevant to a liquidation analysis aimed at gauging creditors' asset protection. That is, if a company were sold to pay off its debts, the price it would fetch would probably reflect the market's current valuation of its assets more nearly than the historical cost of those assets.

Neither measure, however, could be expected to equate precisely to the proceeds that would actually be realized in a sale of the company. Between the time that a sale was decided on and executed, its market capitalization might change significantly, purely as a function of the stock market's dynamics. By the same token, the current balance sheet values of certain assets could be overstated, through tardy recognition of impairments in value, or understated, reflecting the prohibition on writing up an asset that has not changed hands.

THE COMMON FORM BALANCE SHEET

Deterioration in a company's financial position may catch investors by surprise because it occurs gradually and is reported suddenly. It is also possible for an increase in financial risk to sneak up on analysts even though it is reported as it occurs. Many companies alter the mix of their assets, or their methods of financing them, in a gradual fashion. To spot these subtle yet frequently significant changes, it is helpful to prepare a common form balance sheet.

Also known as the percentage balance sheet, the common form balance sheet converts each asset into a percentage of total assets and each liability or component of equity into a percentage of total liabilities and shareholders' equity. Exhibit 2.2 applies this technique to the 2019 balance sheet of WEC Energy, a generator and distributor of natural gas.

The analyst can view a company's common form balance sheets over several quarters to check, for example, whether inventory is increasing significantly as a percentage of total assets. An increase of that sort might signal **involuntary inventory buildup** resulting from an unforeseen slowdown in sales. Similarly, a rise in accounts receivable as a percentage of assets may point to increasing reliance on the extension of credit to generate sales

EXHIBIT 2.2   WEC Energy Group Inc. Balance Sheet in Millions

	Dec. 31, 2019	Percent Total
Assets		
Current assets		
Cash and cash equivalents	$ 37.5	0.11%
Accounts receivable and unbilled revenues, net of reserves of $140.0	1,176.5	3.37%
Materials, supplies, and inventories	549.8	1.57%
Prepayments	261.8	0.75%
Other	68	0.19%
Current assets	2,093.6	5.99%
Long-term assets		
Property, plant, and equipment, net of accumulated depreciation and amortization of $8,878.7	23,620.1	67.58%
Regulatory assets	3,506.7	10.03%
Equity investment in transmission affiliates	1,720.8	4.92%
Goodwill	3,052.8	8.73%
Other	957.8	2.74%
Long-term assets	32,858.2	94.01%
Total assets	$34,951.8	100.00%
Liabilities and shareholders' equity		
Current liabilities		
Short-term debt	830.8	2.38%
Current portion of long-term debt	693.2	1.98%
Accounts payable	908.1	2.60%
Accrued payroll and benefits	199.8	0.57%
Other	550.8	1.58%
Current liabilities	3,182.7	9.11%
Long-term liabilities		
Long-term debt	11,211	32.08%
Deferred income taxes	3,769.3	10.78%
Deferred revenue, net	497.1	1.42%
Regulatory liabilities	3,992.8	11.42%
Environmental remediation liabilities	589.2	1.69%
Pension and OPEB obligations	326.2	0.93%
Other	1,128.9	3.23%
Long-term liabilities	21,514.5	61.55%
Commitments and contingencies (Note 23)		
Common shareholders' equity		
Common stock – $0.01 par value; 325,000,000 shares authorized	3.2	0.01%
Additional paid in capital	4,186.6	11.98%

EXHIBIT 2.2 (*Continued*)

	Dec. 31, 2019	Percent Total
Retained earnings	5,927.7	16.96%
Accumulated other comprehensive loss	(4.1)	−0.01%
Common shareholders' equity	10,113.4	28.94%
Preferred stock of subsidiary	30.4	0.09%
Noncontrolling interests	110.8	0.32%
Total liabilities and shareholders' equity	**$34,951.8**	100.00%

Source: Company 10K and author calculations.

or a problem in collecting on credit previously extended. Over a longer period, a rise in the percentage of assets represented by a manufacturing company's property, plant, and equipment can signal that a company's business is becoming more capital-intensive. By implication, fixed costs are probably rising as a percentage of revenues, making the company's earnings more volatile.

CONCLUSION

By closely examining the underlying values reflected in the balance sheet, this chapter emphasizes the need for a critical, rather than a passive, approach to financial statement analysis. The concepts and case studies underscore the chapter's dominant theme, the elusiveness of true value. Mere tinkering with the conventions of historical cost cannot bring accounting values into line with equity as economists define it and, more to the point, as financial analysts would ideally like it to be. Market capitalization probably represents a superior approach in many instances. Under certain circumstances, however, serious questions can be raised about the validity of a company's stock price as a standard of value. In the final analysis, users of financial statements cannot retreat behind the numbers derived by any one method. They must instead exercise judgment to draw sound conclusions.

CHAPTER 3

The Income Statement

The goal of analyzing an income statement is essentially to determine whether the story it tells is good, bad, or indifferent. To accomplish this objective, the analyst draws a few initial conclusions, then puts the income statement into context by comparing it with income statements of earlier periods, as well as statements of other companies. These steps are described in the section of this chapter titled "Making the Numbers Talk."

Simple techniques of analysis can extract a great deal of information from an income statement, but the quality of the information is no less a concern than the quantity. A conscientious analyst must determine how accurately the statement reflects the issuer's revenues, expenses, and earnings. This deeper level of scrutiny requires an awareness of imperfections in the accounting system that can distort economic reality.

The section titled "How Real Are the Numbers?" documents the indefatigability of issuers in devising novel gambits for exploiting these vulnerabilities. Analysts must be equally resourceful. In particular, students of financial statements must keep up with innovations in transforming rising stock values into revenues of dubious quality. Abuses in reporting supplementary, non-**GAAP** numbers frequently facilitate such chicanery.

MAKING THE NUMBERS TALK

By observing an income statement in its raw form, the reader can make several useful, albeit limited, observations. Jack in the Box's income statement for 2019 (Exhibit 3.1) shows, for example, that the company was profitable rather than unprofitable. The statement also provides some sense of the firm's cost structure. Cost of goods sold (COGS) was the largest component of total costs, at about nine times selling, general, and administrative expenses (SG&A). Depreciation and amortization, essentially a fixed expense in the short run, was a minor factor.

EXHIBIT 3.1 Jack in the Box Inc. Income Statements in $ Thousands

For Fiscal Year 2019 12 months	Jack in the Box Inc. (NASDAQ GS: JACK)
Sales/Revenue	950,107
Cost of goods sold (COGS) including D&A	660,438
COGS excluding D&A	605,257
Depreciation	55,081
Amortization of intangibles	100
Gross income	**289,669**
Gross profit margin	30%
SG&A expense	76,357
Research & development	–
Other SG&A	76,357
Unusual expense	21,456
Non-operating income/expense	(18,202)
Non-operating interest income	1,060
Interest expense	**58,942**
Pretax income	**115,772**
Pretax margin	0
Income tax – current domestic	19,925
Income tax – current foreign	–
Income tax – deferred domestic	4,100
Consolidated net income	91,747
Minority interest expense	–
Net income	**91,747**
Extraordinaries & discontinued operations	2,690
Discontinued operations	2,775
Net income after extraordinaries	94,437
Net income available to common	**94,522**
Basic shares outstanding	25,823
EBITDA	**268,493**
EBITDA margin	28%
Market capitalization	1,900,000
Market cap/EBITDA	**7.1**

Source: Barron's, Bloomberg, and author calculations.

Based on these observations, we can infer that Jack in the Box's profitability is highly sensitive to changes in the prices of materials and labor that are included in COGS. Companies generally have limited control over those costs. Management has more discretion with SG&A, but changes in that category have a proportionally smaller impact on profits.

The relative importance of the various cost components is largely a function of Jack in the Box's business, which consists of operating and franchising quick-service restaurants that offer burgers, breakfast sandwiches, and other items. Depreciation is a larger component of the income statements of heavy manufacturing companies that require huge production facilities (e.g., steel mills, automobile plants).

Jack in the Box's income statement is void in a category that is a significant cost item for many other companies – research and development (R&D). For pharmaceutical producers and companies that create and market electronics and computer software, R&D is generally a significant cost element.

Even within an industry, the breakdown of expenses can vary from company to company as a function of differing business models and financial policies. This is illustrated by Exhibit 3.2, which compares the income statements of Jack in the Box and two other restaurant chains, Shake Shack and Yum! Brands. To facilitate the comparison, the exhibit converts the components of the companies' income statements to percentages of revenues. Note that percentage breakdowns are also helpful for comparing a single company's performance with its results in previous years and for comparing two different companies on the basis of their effectiveness in controlling costs.

Despite being in the same general line of business, the three companies' business profiles differ in significant ways. Like Jack in the Box, Shake Shack emphasizes burgers in its menu, but the format of its restaurants is fast casual rather than fast food. Yum! Brands differs from the other two by operating under multiple fast food brands, namely KFC, Pizza Hut, and Taco Bell. Another important difference among the three companies is the percentage of restaurants that they franchise rather than operate directly. For Shake Shack it is 3 percent, for Jack in the Box 65 percent, and for Yum! Brands 98 percent.

The divergent levels of franchising contribute to the three restaurant companies' dissimilar cost structures. For chains that franchise high percentages of their restaurants, franchise fees constitute a large portion of revenues and items such as ingredients and labor represent comparatively small portions of their costs. Accordingly, COGS (excluding depreciation and amortization) ranges from a low of 46.76 percent at mostly franchising Yum! Brands to a high of 75.12 percent at Shake Shack, which relies the least on franchising among the three companies. The larger components of COGS at Shake Shack and Jack in the Box make their profit margins more sensitive than Yum! Brands's to increases in food and labor costs.

Differences in cost sensitivities among companies in the same industry can occur at a more micro level as well. For example, as the U.S. economy emerged from the COVID-19 pandemic in 2021, CEO Dave Boennighausen

EXHIBIT 3.2 Shake Shack Inc., Jack in the Box Inc., and Yum! Brands Inc. Income Statements in $ Thousands

Income Statement in $ Thousands For fiscal year 2019 12 months	Shake Shack Inc. (NYSE: SHAK)		Jack in the Box Inc. (NASDAQ GS: JACK)		Yum! Brands Inc. (NYSE: YUM)	
Sales/Revenue	594,519	100.00%	950,107	100.00%	5,597,000	100.00%
Cost of goods sold (COGS) including D&A	487,311	81.97%	660,438	69.51%	2,783,000	49.72%
COGS excluding D&A	446,607	75.12%	605,257	63.70%	2,617,000	46.76%
Depreciation	40,392	6.79%	55,081	5.80%	114,000	2.04%
Amortization of intangibles	312	0.05%	100	0.01%	52,000	0.93%
Gross income	107,208	18.03%	289,669	30.49%	2,814,000	50.28%
Gross profit margin		18.03%		30.49%		50.28%
SG&A expense	65,337	10.99%	76,357	8.04%	917,000	16.38%
Research & development	0		0		0	
Other SG&A	65,337	10.99%	76,357	8.04%	917,000	16.38%
Unusual expense	-194	-0.03%	21,456	2.26%	87,000	1.55%
Non-operating income/expense	(14,117)	-2.37%	(18,202)	-1.92%	58,000	1.04%
Non-operating interest income	0		1,060	0.11%	10,000	0.18%
Interest expense	434	0.07%	58,942	6.20%	501,000	8.95%
Pretax income	27,514	4.63%	115,772	12.19%	1,373,000	24.53%
Pretax margin		4.63%		12.19%		25%
Income tax – current domestic	7,267	1.22%	19,925	2.10%	145,000	2.59%
Income tax – current foreign	2,183	0.37%	0		166,000	2.97%
Income tax – deferred domestic	(6,064)	-1.02%	4,100	0.43%	-19,000	-0.34%
Consolidated net income	24,128	4.06%	91,747	9.66%	1,294,000	23.12%
Minority interest expense	4,301	0.72%	0		0	
Net income	19,827	3.33%	91,747	9.66%	1,294,000	23.12%

Extraordinaries & discontinued operations	0		2,690	0.28%	0	
Discontinued operations	0		2,775	0.29%	0	
Net income after extraordinaries	19,827	3.33%	94,437	9.94%	1,294,000	23.12%
Net income available to common	19,827	3.33%	94,522	9.95%	1,294,000	23.12%
Basic shares outstanding	31,381	5.28%	25,823	2.72%	306,000	5.47%
EBITDA 1	82,575	13.89%	268,493	28.26%	2,059,000	36.79%
EBITDA margin	13.89%		28.26%	0		
Market capitalization	2,700,000		1,900,000		35,200,000	
Market cap/EBITDA	32.70		7.08		17.10	

Source: Barron's and author calculations.

maintained that Noodles & Co. would be less affected by potential rises in meat prices than some other restaurant chains. Wisconsin Mac & Cheese was among the favorites on its menu and recent additions focused on noodle items based on zucchini (Zoodles) and cauliflower (Caulifloodles).[1]

Continuing with the data displayed in Exhibit 3.2, a comparatively small COGS cost component means that other costs, particularly SG&A, represent a larger portion of total costs and expenses. Yum! Brands, with the lowest COGS percentage, has the highest SG&A percentage, 16.38 percent, twice the level of Jack in the Box, at 8.04 percent. As noted, SG&A expenses may be more controllable than COGS during business downturns, conferring an advantage on companies with a higher concentration of the cost side of their business in SG&A.

Shake Shack stands out in the category of interest expense, which accounts for just 0.07 percent of its sales. That compares with 6.20 percent for Jack in the Box and 8.95 percent for Yum! Brands. With their greater reliance on debt financing, the latter two companies' profitability is more sensitive than Shake Shack's to fluctuations in interest rates.

Another factor that may give rise to differences in cost structures within an industry is the availability of **economies of scale**, as discussed later. Greater size does not invariably confer an advantage in profitability. In this particular comparison, however, pretax margin is highest on the company with the largest revenue (Yum! Brands) and lowest on the one with the smallest revenue (Shake Shack).

Costs as percentages of sales also vary among competitors within an industry for reasons other than differences in business models. Some companies operate more efficiently than others, generating more revenue from each dollar of expenditures. Where a company stands in its life cycle can also make a difference. A long-established restaurant chain can reach the point of saturating its market. A younger chain's profitability may be helped by not having to choose more marginal locations in order to maintain the pace of new store openings.

The variation in cost structures and profit margins that Jack in the Box, Shake Shack, and Yum! Brands exhibit within the restaurant business is paralleled in other industries. For example, some pharmaceutical manufacturers also produce and market medical devices, nonprescription health products, toiletries, and beauty aids. A more widely diversified manufacturer can be expected to have a higher percentage of product costs, as well as a lower percentage of research and development expenses, than industry peers that focus exclusively on prescription drugs. Analysts must take care not to mistake a difference that is actually a function of business strategy as evidence of inferior or superior management skills.

Segment reporting data in the notes to financial statements can provide a measure of insight into the underlying differentiators of profit margins among companies that tend to be grouped together. Unfortunately, companies have considerable discretion in defining their segments, resulting in a lack of standardization that often makes comparisons difficult. In such cases, an analyst must dig deeper for an understanding of the competitors' cost structures by obtaining as much information as their **investor relations officers** will divulge and drawing on industry sources.

HOW REAL ARE THE NUMBERS?

Many individuals are attracted to business careers not only by monetary rewards but also by the opportunity, lacking in many other professions, to be measured against an objective standard. The personal desire to improve the bottom line, that is, a company's net profit, challenges a businessperson in much the same way that an athlete is motivated by the quantifiable goal of breaking a world record. The income statement is the stopwatch against which a company runs; net profit is the corporation's record of wins and losses for the season.

The analogy between business and athletics extends to the fact, which is apparent to any close observer, that superior skills and teamwork alone do not win championships. A baseball manager can intimidate the umpire by heatedly protesting a call on the base paths, hoping thereby to have the next close ruling go in his team's favor. A corporation has the power to fire its auditor and may use that power to influence accounting decisions that are matters of judgment rather than clear-cut reporting standards. A baseball team's front office can shorten the right-field fence in its home stadium to favor a lineup stocked with left-handed power hitters; a corporation's management can select the accounting method that shows its results in the most favorable light. Collectively, the team owners can urge the rules committee to move the pitching mound further back from the plate if they believe that a predictable increase in base hits and runs will boost attendance. Similarly, a group of corporations can try to block the introduction of new accounting standards that might reduce their reported earnings.

Attempts to alter the yardstick become most vigorous when the measure of achievement becomes more important to participants than the accuracy of the measure itself. Regrettably, this is often the case when corporations seek to motivate managers by linking their compensation to the attainment of specific financial goals. Executives whose bonuses rise in tandem with earnings per share have a strong incentive not only to generate bona fide earnings but also to use every lawful means of inflating the figures through accounting sleight of hand.

It would take many more pages than are allotted to this chapter to detail all the ways that companies can manipulate the accounting rules to inflate their earnings. Instead, the following examples should convey to the reader the thought process involved in this rule bending. Equipped with an understanding of how the rule benders think, users of financial statements will be able to detect other ruses they are sure to encounter.

Not All Sales Are Final

"Take care of the top line and the bottom line will take care of itself." So goes a business bromide that was popularized by Apple co-founder Steve Jobs. It underscores the importance of revenues (the top line) to net income (the bottom line). The point is that if a company wants to cure an earnings problem, it should concentrate on bringing in more sales.

Generally, this is sound advice, as long as the requisite sales are brought in by the sales force. A company can ultimately worsen its operating troubles if the financial staff makes up the shortfall in revenues through accounting gimmicks. Some revenue-inflating tricks are achievable within GAAP boundaries, while others clearly fall outside the law. They all produce similar ill effects, however. Enhancements to reported sales boost reported earnings without increasing cash flow commensurately.

Often, a company's earnings and cash flow diverge to an extent that becomes unsustainable. The eventual result is an abrupt adjustment to the financial statements of previous periods. In the process, earnings and cash flow come back into alignment, but management's credibility plummets. Even when no such shock occurs, the practice of pumping up revenues through discretionary accounting decisions represents a hazard for analysts. At a minimum, it reduces the comparability of a company's financial statements from one period to the next.

Additional Reasons to Be Skeptical about Revenues

Unfortunately for analysts, companies do not always spell out in the notes to financial statements the means by which they have artificially inflated their revenues. A company might lower the credit standards it applies to prospective customers without simultaneously raising the percentage of reserves it establishes for losses on receivables. The result would be a rise in both revenues and earnings in the current period, with the corresponding increase in credit losses not becoming apparent until a later period. Alternatively, a manufacturer may institute short-term discounts that encourage its dealers or wholesalers to place orders earlier than they otherwise would. In this case, sales and earnings will be higher in the current quarter than they would be in the absence of the incentives, but the difference will represent merely a shifting of revenues from a later to an earlier period. Analysts will face disappointment if they extrapolate from the inflated quarterly data to project future revenues.

Although the current-period income statement may offer no clues that these gambits have been used, several techniques can help the analyst detect artificial expansion of revenues. On a retrospective basis, a surge in credit losses or an unexpected shortfall in revenues may indicate that revenues were inflated in an earlier period with the techniques described in the preceding paragraph. (Hindsight of this kind is not without value; an analyst who finds a historical pattern of hyperbolized sales at a company will be appropriately skeptical about future income statements of that company looking surprisingly strong.) On a current basis, analysts should take notice if a company posts a substantially greater sales increase than its competitors. If discussions with the company and other industry sources fail to elicit a satisfactory explanation (such as the introduction of a successful new product), artificial methods may be the root of the matter. Industry sources can also provide direct testimony about tactics being used to shift revenues from future periods to the present.

Unusual Items

To most individuals who examine a company's income statement, the document is less important for what it tells about the past than for what it implies about future years.[2] Last year's earnings, for example, have no direct impact on a company's stock price, which represents a discounting of a future stream of earnings (see Chapter 14). An equity investor is therefore interested in a company's prior-year income statement primarily as a basis for forecasting future earnings. Similarly, a company's creditors do not have to wait for the income statement to be published to know whether they were paid the interest that came due in the past year. Their motivation for studying the document is to form an opinion about the likelihood of payment in the current year and in years to come.

In addition to recognizing that readers of its income statement will view the document primarily as an indicator of the future, a company knows that creating more favorable expectations about the future can raise its stock price and lower its borrowing cost. It is therefore in the company's interest to persuade readers that a major setback to last year's earnings will not adversely affect future earnings. One way of achieving this is to suggest that any large loss suffered by the company was somehow outside the normal course of business, anomalous, and, by implication, unlikely to recur.

Prior to 2015, the **FASB**'s rules distinguished between "unusual" and "extraordinary" items.[3] The latter were reported on an after-tax basis below the net income line, creating an especially strong impression that they were one-off events that ought not influence analysts' projections of future earnings. FASB's 2015 rule change eliminated the concept of extraordinary items on the grounds that issuers were unduly burdened by the cost and complexity of satisfying the standards for using the designation.

Numerous financial statement items continue to be presented as "unusual" or "nonrecurring," obliging analysts to make judgments about the likelihood of similar events affecting future earnings. These labels have no official standing under GAAP and are applied at the discretion of management. That is to say, adverse events that could very well be repeated are made to seem aberrant by people who stand to benefit from unwary analysts producing unrealistically high earnings forecasts and thereby propelling the company to a higher valuation than it truly deserves.

FASB's pre-2015 rules prohibited certain items from being classified as extraordinary:

- Write-offs of receivables and inventories.
- Gains or losses on foreign currency translation (even when they result from major devaluations or revaluations).
- Gains or losses on disposal of a segment of a business or the sale or abandonment of property, plant, or equipment.

Because these items did not meet FASB's standard for being characterized as especially far outside the normal course of business, analysts should be particularly wary of treating them as unique events, to be ignored when thinking about possible disruptions to future earnings. Allegedly nonrecurring items have a nasty habit of recurring.

Over time, restructuring has become a catchall for charges that companies wish analysts to consider outside the normal course of business but that do not qualify for below-the-line treatment. The term has a positive connotation, implying that the corporation has cast off its money-losing operations and positioned itself for significantly improved profitability. If abused, the segregation of restructuring charges can create too rosy a picture of past performance. It can entrap the unwary analyst by downplaying the significance of failed business initiatives, which have a bearing on management's judgment. Additionally, the losses associated with a restructuring may be blamed on the company's previous chief executive officer, provided they are booked early in the successor CEO's tenure. Within a year's time, the new kingpin may be able to take credit for a turnaround, based on an improvement in earnings relative to a large loss that can be conveniently attributed to the predecessor regime.

Even more insidiously, companies sometimes write off larger sums than warranted by their actual economic losses on a failed business. Corporate managers commonly perceive that the damage to their stock price will be no greater if they take (for sake of argument) a $1.5 billion write-off than if they write off $1.0 billion. The benefit of exaggerating the damage is that in subsequent years, the overcharges can be reversed in small amounts that do not generate any requirement for specific disclosure. Management can use these gains to supplement and smooth the corporation's bona fide operating earnings.

The most dangerous trap that users of financial statements must avoid, however, is inferring that the term *restructuring* connotes finality. Some corporations have a bad habit of remaking themselves year after year. For such companies, the analyst's baseline for forecasting future profitability should be earnings after, rather than before, restructuring charges.

Procter & Gamble (P&G) is a case in point. As of April 2001, the consumer goods company had booked restructuring charges in seven consecutive quarters, aggregating to $1.3 billion. Moreover, management indicated that it planned to continue taking these ostensibly nonrecurring charges until mid-2004, ultimately charging off approximately $4 billion.

Defending its reporting, P&G said that Securities and Exchange Commission (SEC) accounting rules precluded it from taking one huge charge at the outset of the restructuring program launched in June 1999. Instead, the company was required to record the charges in the periods in which it actually incurred them. Granting the point, the SEC did not compel Procter & Gamble to segregate the costs of closing factories and laying off workers from its other operating expenses. Indeed, the arguments were stronger for treating the charge-offs as normal costs of operating in P&G's highly competitive consumer goods business, where countless products fail or become obsolete over time.

Abstract issues of accounting theory, however, had little impact on brokerage house securities analysts' treatment of P&G's earnings record. All 14 analysts who followed the company and submitted earnings per share forecasts to Thomson Financial/First Call excluded the restructuring charges from their calculations, and P&G management was bound to like Wall Street's interpretation of the numbers. Including all of the ostensibly unusual gains and losses, operating income declined in all four quarters of 2000. Leaving out all the items deemed aberrant by management, net income rose in all quarters but the first. The latter interpretation surely gave investors a more optimistic view of P&G's prospects than the sourpuss GAAP numbers.[4]

Naturally, companies encourage analysts to *include* special items in their earnings calculations when they happen to be gains, rather than losses. They evidently reason that turnabout is fair play, and judging by the results, many securities analysts apparently agree. The 14 Wall Street analysts mentioned earlier unanimously chose to include in their "core net earnings" figures the gains that Procter & Gamble classified as nonrecurring or extraordinary, even as they excluded the extraordinary and nonrecurring losses.

A Shortcut to Higher Sales

At the same time that corporate managers have been supplementing their traditional tactics with new adjustments to earnings, they have also concentrated in recent years on applying their ingenuity to revenues. This focus is understandable in the context of huge stock market valuations for many young tech companies that have yet to achieve positive GAAP earnings. One metric applied to such companies is the price-to-sales ratio, as opposed to the more conventional price-to-earnings ratio. Even for more conventional companies, reporting rapid sales growth can foster investor confidence that impressive profit growth will follow in due course.

Amassing sales is a vital business task, but not easily achieved. Competitors are forever striving to snatch away revenues by introducing superior products or devising means of lowering prices to customers. From the standpoint of maximizing value to consumers and promoting economic efficiency, management's optimal response to this challenge is to upgrade its own products and generate cost savings that it can pass along to customers. Stepping up expenditures on advertising or expanding the sales force can also lead to increased revenues. Along with effective execution of product design or marketing plans, however, another option exists. Management can boost sales through techniques that qualify as corporate finance rather than sales or marketing.

Raising the rate of revenue increases through mergers and acquisitions is the most common example. A corporation can easily accelerate its sales growth by buying other companies and adding their sales to its own. Creating genuine value for shareholders through acquisitions is more difficult, although unwary investors sometimes fail to recognize the distinction.

In the fictitious example in Exhibit 3.3, Big Time Corporation's sales increase by 5 percent between Year 1 and Year 2. Small Change, a smaller, privately owned company in the same industry, also achieves 5 percent year-over-year sales growth. Suppose that at the end of Year 1, Big Time acquires Small Change with shares of its own stock. The Big Time

EXHIBIT 3.3 Small Sales Growth Acceleration without Profitability Improvement: Big Time Corporation and Small Change Inc. ($000,000 omitted)

| | Non-acquisition scenario | | | | Acquisition scenario | |
| | Big Time Corporation | | Small Change Inc. | | Big Time Corporation | |
	Year 1	Year 2	Year 1	Year 2	Year 1	Year 2
Sales	$5,000.00	$5,250.00	$238.10	$250.00	$5,000.00	$5,500.10
Costs and expenses						
Cost of goods sold	$3,500.10	$3,672.60	$162.40	$173.00	$3,500.10	$3,345.60
Selling, general, and administrative expense	$1,250.00	$1,315.00	$61.90	$62.50	$1,250.00	$1,377.50
Interest expense	$60.0	$63.0	$4.8	$5.0	$60.0	$68.0
Total costs and expenses	$4,810.1	$5,050.6	$229.1	$240.5	$4,810.1	$5,291.1
Income before income taxes	$189.9	$199.4	$9.0	$9.5	$189.9	$208.9
Income taxes	$39.9	$41.9	$1.9	$2.0	$39.9	$43.9
Net income	$150.00	$157.50	$7.10	$7.50	$150.00	$165.00
Year-over-year sales increase	~	5%	~	5%	~	5%
Net income as a percentage of sales	3%	3%	3%	3%	3%	3%
Shares outstanding (million)	75	75			75	78.6
Earnings per share	$2.00	$2.10			$2.00	$2.10
Price-earnings multiple (times)	14	14			14	14
Price per share	$28.00	$29.40			$28.00	$29.40

income statements under this assumption ("Acquisition Scenario") show a 10 percent sales increase between Year 1 and Year 2. (Note that Year 1 is shown as originally reported, with Small Change still an independent company, while in Year 2, the results of the acquired company, Small Change, are consolidated into the parent's financial reporting. Analysts might also examine a pro forma income statement showing the levels of sales, expenses, and earnings that Big Time would have achieved in Year 1, if the acquisition had occurred at the beginning of that year.)

On the face of it, a company growing at 10 percent a year is sexier than one growing at only 5 percent a year. Observe, however, that Big Time's profitability, measured by net income as a percentage of sales, does not improve as a result of the acquisition. Combining two companies with equivalent profit margins of 3 percent produces a larger company that also earns 3 percent on sales. Shareholders do not gain anything in the process, as the supplementary figures in Exhibit 3.3 demonstrate.

If Big Time decides not to acquire Small Change, its number of shares outstanding remains at 75.0 million. The earnings increase from $150.0 million in Year 1 to $157.5 million in Year 2 raises earnings per share from $2.00 to $2.10. With the price-earnings multiple constant at 14 times, equivalent to the average of the company's industry peers, Big Time's stock price rises from $28.00 to $29.40 a share.

In the Acquisition Scenario, on the other hand, Big Time pays its industry-average earnings multiple of 14 times for Small Change, for a total acquisition price of $7.1 million × 14 = $99.4 million. At Big Time's Year 1 share price of $28.00, the purchase therefore requires the issuance of $99.4 million ÷ $28.00 = 3.6 million shares. With the addition of Small Change's net income, Big Time earns $165.0 million in Year 2. Dividing that figure by the increased number of shares outstanding (78.6 million) produces earnings per share of $2.10. At a price-earnings multiple of 14 times, Big Time is worth $29.40 a share, precisely the price calculated in the Non-acquisition Scenario. The mere increase in annual sales growth from 5 percent to 10 percent has not benefited shareholders, whose shares increase in value by 5 percent whether Big Time acquires Small Change or not.

Analysts should note that this analysis is sensitive to the assumptions underlying the scenarios. Suppose, for instance, that instead of issuing stock, Big Time finances the acquisition of Small Change with borrowed money. Let us suppose that Big Time must pay interest at a rate of 4 percent on the $99.4 million of new borrowings. Interest expense in Year 2 of the Acquisition Scenario is now $72.0 million, rather than $68.0 million. Pretax income therefore falls from $208.9 million to $204.9 million, reducing net income from $165.0 million to $161.9 million at the company's effective tax rate of 21 percent. Only 75.0 million shares are outstanding at the conclusion of the transaction, however, rather than the 78.6 million observed in the acquisition-for-stock case. As a result, Big Time's earnings per share rise to $161.9 million ÷ 75.0 million = $2.16.

Assuming the market continues to assign a multiple of 14 times to Big Time's earnings, the stock is now worth $30.24, a 3 percent increase over the Non-acquisition Scenario. In practice, though, the investors may reduce Big Time's price-earnings multiple slightly to reflect the heightened risk represented by its decreased interest coverage. (Following the formulas laid out in Chapter 13, income before interest and taxes declines from $276.9 million ÷ $68.0 million = 4.1 times in the stock-acquisition case to $276.9 million ÷ $72.0 million = 3.8 times in the debt-financed-acquisition case.) If the price-earnings multiple falls only from 14 to 13.61 times as a result of this decline in debt protection, Big Time's stock price in this variant again comes to $29.40, equivalent to the Year 2 price in the Non-acquisition Scenario. As in the case of Big Time paying with stock for the acquisition of Small Change, shareholders do not benefit if Big Time instead borrows the requisite funds, assuming investors are sensitive to the impact of the company's increased debt load on its credit quality.

Internal versus External Growth

More important than the fine-tuning of the calculations is the principle that a company cannot truly increase shareholders' wealth by accelerating its revenue growth without also improving profitability. This does not dissuade companies from attempting to mesmerize analysts with high rates of sales growth generated by grafting other companies' sales onto their own through acquisitions. Analysts may fall for the trick by failing to distinguish between **internal growth** and **external growth.**

Internal growth consists of sales increases generated from a company's existing operations, while the latter represents incremental sales brought in through acquisitions. An internal (or organic) growth rate greater than the average recorded for the industry implies that the company is gaining market share from its competitors. As a precaution, the analyst must probe further to determine whether management has merely increased unit sales by accepting lower gross margins. If that is not the case, however, the company may in fact be improving its competitive position and, ultimately, increasing its value. On the other hand, if Company A generates external growth by acquiring Company B and neither Company A nor its new subsidiary increases its profitability, then the intrinsic value of the merged companies is no greater than the sum of the two companies' values.

External growth can increase shareholders' wealth, however, if the mergers and acquisitions lead to improvements in profitability. This effect is commonly referred to as *synergy*. It is a term much abused by companies that promise to achieve operating efficiencies, without offering many specific examples, through acquisitions that appear to offer few such opportunities. Nevertheless, even analysts who have grown cynical after years of seeing purported synergies remain unrealized will acknowledge the existence of several bona fide means of raising a company's profit margins through external growth.

For one thing, a company may be able to reduce its cost per unit by increasing the size of its purchases. Suppliers commonly offer volume discounts to their large customers, which they can service more efficiently than customers who order in small quantities. If the cost of materials, fuel, and transportation required to produce each widget goes down while the selling price of widgets remains unchanged in a stable competitive environment, the company's gross margin increases.

Another way to increase profitability through external growth involves **economies of scope.** In a simple illustration, a manufacturer of potato chips has a sales force calling on retail stores. Much of the associated expense represents the time and transportation costs incurred as the salespeople travel from store to store, as well as the salespeople's health insurance and other benefits. Now suppose that the potato chip manufacturer acquires a pretzel manufacturer. For the sake of explication, assume that the pretzel company formerly relied on food brokers rather than an in-house sales force. The acquiring company terminates the contracts with the brokers and adds pretzels to its potato chip sales force's product line. Revenues and gross profits per sales call rise with the addition of the pretzel line. The number of sales calls per salesperson remains essentially constant, because taking orders for the additional product consumes little time. Accordingly, time and transportation costs per sales call do not rise materially, while the cost of health insurance and other benefits does not rise at all. Adding it all up, the profitability of selling both potato chips and pretzels through the same distribution channel is greater than the profitability of selling one snack food only.

Analysts should be forewarned that claims of potential economies of scope often prove, in retrospect, to be exaggerated. Over a period of several decades, for example, banks, brokerage houses, and insurance companies have frequently proclaimed the advent of the financial supermarket, in which a single distribution channel will efficiently deliver all classes of financial services to consumers. A fair amount of integration between these businesses has certainly occurred, but cultural barriers between the businesses have turned out to be more formidable than corporate planners have foreseen. Considerable training is required to teach salespeople how to shift gears between the fast-paced business of dealing in stocks and the more painstaking process of selling insurance policies. In general, the less closely related the combining businesses are, the less certain it is that the hoped-for economies of scope will be realized. When disparate companies combine in pursuit of novel synergies, analysts should treat with extreme caution the margin increases shown in pro forma income statements produced by management.

Capturing Economies of Scale

Finally, and perhaps most famously, mergers can genuinely increase profitability and shareholder wealth through economies of scale. As illustrated in Exhibit 3.4, Central Widget is currently utilizing only 83.3 percent of its productive capacity. At the present production level, the company's **fixed costs** amount to $300 million ÷ 250 million units = $1.20 per unit, or 12 percent of each sales dollar. These irreducible costs represent a major constraint on the company's net profit margin, just 2.0 percent, and in turn its return on equity (see Chapter 13), which is an unexciting 11.1 percent.

Central Widget spies an opportunity in the form of its smaller competitor, Excelsior Widget. Because the two companies operate in the same geographic region, it would be feasible to consolidate production in Central Widget's underutilized factories. Management proposes a merger premised on achieving economies of scale.

Excelsior's cost structure is similar to Central's, except that its general and administrative expense is higher as percentage of sales (6.7 percent versus 3.0 percent). The problem is that certain costs (such as the upkeep on a headquarters building and salaries of senior executives) are nearly as great for Excelsior as for Central, but Excelsior has a smaller base of sales over which to spread them. As a result, Excelsior is running at a loss at current operating levels. Its board of directors therefore accepts the acquisition offer. Central pays $23.40 worth of its own stock (0.72 shares) for each share of Excelsior, a 30 percent premium to Excelsior's prevailing market price.

Unlike the acquisition of Small Change by Big Time depicted in Exhibit 3.3, this transaction not only increases the acquiring company's sales but also improves its profitability. Following the acquisition, on a pro forma basis, Central Widget's fixed cost per unit is $299.0 million ÷ 280 million = $1.07, down from $1.15. The net margin is up from 2.0 percent to 2.6 percent, while earnings per share have jumped from $2.50 to $3.33, pro forma. If the market continues to assign a multiple of 13 times to Central's earnings, the stock should theoretically trade at $56.03, up from $44.98 before the transaction. Realistically, that increase probably overstates the actual rise that Central Widget shareholders can expect. Aside from severance costs not shown in the pro forma income statement, investors may reduce the price-earnings multiple to reflect the myriad uncertainties faced in any merger, such as potential loss of key personnel

EXHIBIT 3.4 Economies of Scale

Selected Production and Financial Statement Data

	Central Widget	Excelsior Widget	Central Widget (Pro Forma)
Units of capacity (millions)	300	36	300
Unit sales (millions)	250	30	280
Capacity utilization	83.3%	83.3%	93.3%
Price per unit	$ 10.00	$ 10.00	$ 10.00
Variable costs per unit			
Labor	$ 4.75	$ 4.75	$ 4.75
Materials	$ 3.00	$ 3.00	$ 3.00
Variable sales costs	$ 0.75	$ 0.75	$ 0.75
Total	$ 8.50	$ 8.50	$ 8.50
Total fixed costs ($million)			
Depreciation	$ 200.00	$ 24.00	$ 200.00*
Interest expense	$ 12.50	$ 1.50	$ 14.00
General and administrative	$ 75.00	$ 20.00	$ 85.00**
Total	$ 287.50	$ 45.50	$ 299.00
($000,000 omitted)			
Sales	$2,500.00	$300.00	$2,800.00
Variable costs	$2,125.00	$255.00	$2,380.00
Fixed costs	$ 287.50	$ 45.50	$ 299.00
Income before income taxes	$ 87.50	($0.50)	$ 121.00
Income tax	$ 18.38	($0.11)	$ 25.41
Net income	$ 69.13	($0.39)	$ 95.59
Net income as a percentage of sales.	2.8%	–0.1%	3.4%
Shares outstanding (million)	20	3	22.2***
Earnings per share	$ 3.46	($0.13)	$ 4.31
Price-earnings multiple (times)	13	N.M.	13
Price per share	$ 44.98	$ 18.00	$ 56.03

*Assumes closure of Excelsior Widget factory.
**Assumes elimination of 50% of Excelsior Widget's general and administrative expense through closure of company headquarters.
***Assumes acquisition price of $23.40 per Excelsior Widget share.

and the predictable traumas of melding distinct corporate cultures. After all the dust has settled, however, Central Widget's shareholders will assuredly benefit from the economies of scale achieved through the acquisition of Excelsior Widget.

Scale economies become available for a variety of reasons. Technological advances can make a sizable portion of existing capacity redundant. For example, the advent of computerization increased the productivity of financial services workers engaged in clearing transactions. **Consolidation** in the banking and brokerage industries was hastened by cost savings achievable through handling two companies' combined volume of transactions with fewer back office workers than the companies previously employed in aggregate. In retailing, mergers have sometimes produced savings by enabling distribution centers to serve larger numbers of stores.

Economies of scale also arise through consolidation of a mom-and-pop business, that is, an industry characterized by many small companies operating within limited market areas. For example, waste hauling has evolved from a highly localized business to an industry with companies operating on a national scale. Among the associated efficiencies is the ability to reduce garbage trucks' idle time by employing them in several adjacent municipalities. "Rollup" consolidations of this sort have also merged large numbers of medical practices.

Behind the Numbers: Fixed versus Variable Costs

As synergies go, projections of economies of scale in combinations of companies within the same business tend to be more plausible than economies of scope purportedly available to companies in tangentially connected businesses. The existence of chronically underutilized capacity is apparent to operations analysts within corporations and to outside management consultants. Word inevitably spreads from there until the possibility of achieving sizable efficiencies through consolidation becomes common knowledge among investors. Companies' published financial statements typically provide too little detail to directly quantify the potential for realizing economies of scale.

Companies do not generally break out their fixed and **variable costs** in the manner shown in Exhibit 3.4. Instead, they include a combination of variable and fixed costs in cost of goods sold. Somewhat helpfully, the essentially fixed costs of depreciation and interest appear as separate lines. On the whole, however, a company's published income statement provides only limited insight into its **operating leverage,** or the rate at which net income escalates once sales volume rises above the **breakeven rate.** This is unfortunate, because a breakout of fixed and variable costs would be immensely helpful in quantifying the economies of scale potentially achievable through a merger. More generally, such information would greatly facilitate the task of forecasting a company's earnings as a function of projected sales volume.

Exhibit 3.5 uses data from the Central Widget example to plot the relationship between sales volume and pretax income (income before income taxes). The company breaks even at a sales volume of 200 million units, the

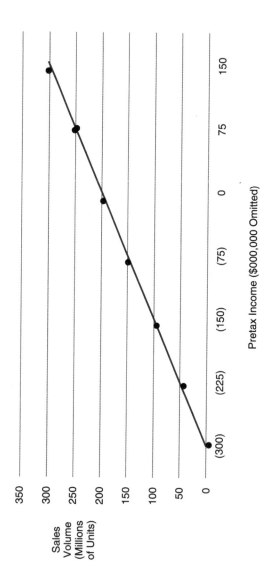

Pretax Income ($000,000 Omitted)

Units *	= Contribution per Unit	= Contribution	- Fixed Costs	= Pretax Income
0	$1.50	$0	$300	($300)
50	1.50	$75	300	($225)
100	1.50	$150	300	($150)
150	1.50	$225	300	($75)
200	**1.50**	**$300**	**300**	**$0**
250	1.50	$375	300	$75
300	1.50	$450	300	$150

(Units in millions. Contribution, fixed costs, and pretax income in millions of dollars.)

*Price per unit	- Variable cost per Unit	= Contribution per Unit
$10.00	$8.50	$1.50

EXHIBIT 3.5 Operating Leverage – Central Widget.

level at which the $1.50 per unit **contribution** (margin of revenue over variable cost) exactly offsets the $300 million of fixed costs. Once fixed costs are covered, the contribution on each incremental unit sold flows directly to the pretax income line. At full capacity, 300 million units, Central Widget earns $150 million before taxes. (Note that analysts can alternatively remove interest expense from the calculation and base a breakeven analysis on operating income.)

In theory, an analyst can back out the fixed and variable components of a company's costs from reported sales and income data. The object is to produce a graph along the lines of the one shown in Exhibit 3.5, while also estimating the contribution per unit. At that point, the analyst can create a table like that shown in the exhibit and establish the sensitivity of profits to the portion of capacity being utilized.

Exhibit 3.6 presents the fictitious case of West Coast Whatsit. The top graph plots the company's reported unit sales volume versus pretax income for each of the past 12 years. (West Coast is debt-free and has no other nonoperating income or expenses, so the company's operating income is equivalent to its pretax income.) Observe that the plotted points are concentrated in the upper right-hand corner of the graph, reflecting that annual sales volume never declined to less than 380 million units (63 percent of capacity) during the period. At that low ebb, pretax income dropped below zero.

The next step is to fit a diagonal line through the points, as shown in the upper graph. (Statistical tools available online make it easy to fit a regression line to data.) According to the line derived from the empirical observations, the company's breakeven sales volume is 400 million units, that is, the point on the diagonal line that corresponds to zero on the horizontal scale (pretax income). Although West Coast Whatsit has not utilized 100 percent of its capacity in any of the past 10 years, the graph indicates that at that level (600 million on the vertical scale), pretax income would amount to $400 million.

To complete the analysis, the analyst must also plot the reported unit sales volume versus dollar sales for the past 10 years, as shown in the lower graph. The remaining task is to back into the data required to fill in the table at the bottom of Exhibit 3.6. At the outset, the analyst knows only the figures shown in boldface, which can be derived directly from the two graphs. For example, the fitted line shows that at full capacity (600 million units), sales would total $3.0 billion.

According to the known data, the increase in pretax income between the breakeven volume (400 million units) and a volume of 500 million units is $200 million. That dollar figure must represent the contribution on 100 million units. Dividing $200 million by 100 million yields the contribution per unit of $2.00, enabling the analyst to fill in that whole column. Dividing

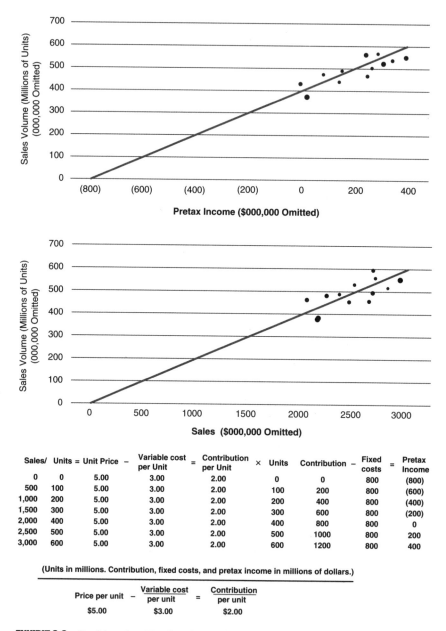

Sales/	Units	= Unit Price	−	Variable cost per Unit	=	Contribution per Unit	× Units	Contribution	−	Fixed costs	=	Pretax Income
0	0	5.00		3.00		2.00	0	0		800		(800)
500	100	5.00		3.00		2.00	100	200		800		(600)
1,000	200	5.00		3.00		2.00	200	400		800		(400)
1,500	300	5.00		3.00		2.00	300	600		800		(200)
2,000	400	5.00		3.00		2.00	400	800		800		0
2,500	500	5.00		3.00		2.00	500	1000		800		200
3,000	600	5.00		3.00		2.00	600	1200		800		400

(Units in millions. Contribution, fixed costs, and pretax income in millions of dollars.)

Price per unit	−	Variable cost per unit	=	Contribution per unit
$5.00		$3.00		$2.00

EXHIBIT 3.6   Backing Out Fixed and Variable Cost – Coast Whatsit.

any figure in the sales column by its corresponding number of units (e.g., $2.5 billion and 500 million) provides the unit price of $5.00, which goes on every line in that column. Variable cost per unit, by subtraction, is $3.00.

At the breakeven level (pretax income = $0), the contribution totals 400 million units times $2.00 = $800 million. The analyst can put that number on every line in the entire "Fixed Costs" column. All that remains is to fill in the "Contribution" column by multiplying each remaining line's number of units by the $2.00 contribution per unit figure.

Regrettably, the elegant procedure just described tends to be highly hypothetical, even though it is useful to go through the thought process. To begin with, companies engaged in a wide range of products do not disclose the explicit unit volume figures that the analysis requires. Relating their sales volumes to prices and costs is more complicated than in the case of a producer of a basic metal or a single type of paper. The management discussion and analysis section of a multiproduct company's financial report may disclose period-to-period *changes* in unit volume, but not absolute figures, by way of explaining fluctuations in revenues. A rise or drop in revenue, however, may also reflect changes in the sales price per unit, which may in turn be sensitive to industrywide variance in capacity utilization. In addition, revenue may vary with product mix. When a recession causes consumers to turn cautious about spending on major appliances, for example, they may trade down to lower-priced models that provide smaller contributions to the manufacturers. Finally, multiproduct companies' product lines typically change significantly over periods as long as the 12 years assumed in Exhibit 3.6.

For all these reasons, analysts generally cannot back out fixed and variable costs in practice. When projecting a company's income statement for the coming year, they instead work their way down to the operating income line by making assumptions about cost of goods sold (COGS) and selling, general, and administrative expenses (SG&A) as percentages of sales (see Chapter 12). They try in some sense to take into account the impact of fixed and variable costs, but they cannot be certain that their forecasts are internally consistent.

In Exhibit 3.6, total pretax costs are equivalent to the sum of COGS and SG&A. (Remember that West Coast Whatsit has no interest expense or other nonoperating items.) An analyst who projects that the two together will represent 92 percent of sales is making a forecast consistent with sales volume of 500 million units, or 83 percent of capacity. At that unit volume, variable costs total 500 million × $3.00 = $1.5 billion, which when added to fixed costs of $800 million, produces total costs of $2.3 billion, or 92 percent of sales measuring $2.5 billion. The assumption of a total pretax cost 92 percent ratio would be too pessimistic if the analyst actually expected West

Coast to operate in line with the whatsit industry as a whole at 90 percent of capacity. That would imply unit sales of 540 million, resulting in variable costs of $1.62 billion and total costs of $2.42 billion. The ratio of operating expenses to sales of $2.7 billion (540 million units @ $5.00) would be only 90 percent. Observe that not only operating income but also the operating margin rises as sales volume increases.

Estimating COGS and SG&A as percentages of sales is an imperfect, albeit necessary, substitute for an analysis of fixed and variable costs. Conscientious analysts must strive to mitigate the distortions introduced by the shortcut method. They should avoid the trap of uncritically adopting the projected COGS and SG&A percentages kindly provided by companies' investor relations departments. Analysts who do so risk sacrificing their independent judgment. After all, the preceding paragraph demonstrates that a forecast of the operating margin must reflect an implicit assumption about sales volume. Accordingly, a company's **guidance** regarding COGS and SG&A percentages necessarily incorporates management's assumption about the coming year's sales volume. At the risk of stating the obvious, management's embedded sales projection will often be more optimistic than the analyst's independently generated forecast.

Readers should not infer from the absence of disclosure about fixed and variable costs that the information is unimportant to understanding companies' financial performance. On the contrary, a company's fixed-variable mix can be a dominant factor in analyzing both its credit quality and its equity value (see Chapters 13 and 14, respectively). A company with relatively large fixed costs has a high breakeven level. Even a modest economic downturn will reduce its capacity utilization below the rate required to keep the company profitable. A cost structure of this sort poses a substantial risk of earnings falling below the level needed to cover the company's interest expense. On the other hand, if the same company has low variable costs, its earnings will rise dramatically following a recession. Each incremental unit of sales will contribute prodigiously to operating income. Two real-life examples demonstrate the analytical company's cost structure, even though it may not be feasible to document the mix precisely from the financial statements.

As an amusement park operator, Cedar Fair exemplifies the high-fixed-cost company. Attendance (and therefore revenue) shows wide seasonal variations, but the company's costs are concentrated in categories that do not vary with attendance. Examples include occupancy, depreciation on rides, insurance, and wages of employees who must be on site whether the parks are full or nearly empty.

A time series of the company's cost of sales as a percentage of sales (see Exhibit 3.7) shows wide quarterly fluctuations, largely reflecting

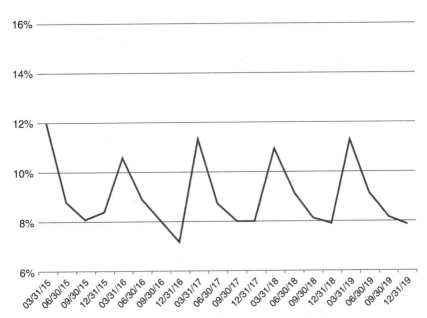

EXHIBIT 3.7 Cedar Fair Cost of Goods Sold as a Percentage of Sales.
Source: Stock Investor Pro and author calculations.

extreme seasonality in the company's business. In 2019, for example, the warm-weather second and third calendar quarters accounted for 78 percent of the year's sales. Profit margins are highest during the third quarter, essentially the summer months. Cedar Fair generally reports losses in the first quarter.

Archer Daniels Midland (see Exhibit 3.8) represents the opposite extreme of cost structures. Seasonality is not a material factor for the food processor and commodities trader, as demand for its products is steady. In the five-year period depicted in Exhibit 3.8, ADM's cost of goods sold as a percentage of sales never strayed outside the range of 92 percent to 95 percent. The ratio remained inside those bounds even during the pandemic-wracked, recession year of 2020.

Notwithstanding the generally stable pattern of margins depicted in Exhibit 3.8, Archer Daniels Midland experienced a sharp earnings drop-off in 2016. Net income as a percentage of sales fell from 2.73 percent to 2.05 percent and basic earnings per share from continuing operations fell by 27 percent. Contributing factors included compressed grain handling margins in the first half of the year, low market volatility that limited forward merchandising opportunities, weak barge demand and lower freight rates in

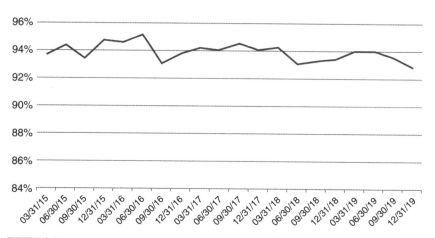

EXHIBIT 3.8 Archer Daniels Midland Cost of Goods Sold as a Percentage of Sales.
Source: Stock Investor Pro and author calculations.

the Transportation segment, reduced global soy crush margins, and smaller soybean and corn crops than in 2015.

Those results demonstrate that even in a business with built-in safe-guards against wide period-to-period swings, events beyond management's control may periodically cut down the bottom line. Even so, credit analysts generally perceive greater risk in the pattern exemplified by Cedar Fair. For highly seasonal companies, classically represented by toy manufacturers and general merchandisers, a lackluster winter holiday sales season can drive operating income below the level required to cover interest expense.

Playing with Price-Earnings Multiples Vigilance, as exemplified by the need to watch for earnings discontinuities, has been a recurring theme throughout this exploration of the ins and outs of income statements. Other pitfalls to watch out for include unrealizable synergies and company-furnished projections of cost ratios that incorporate management's assumptions regarding sales volume. Before moving on, vigilant analysts should familiarize themselves with a device that companies have developed to get around the general proposition that mergers do not increase value unless they increase profitability.

Turning back to the fictitious acquisition case presented in Exhibit 3.3, let us change one assumption (see Exhibit 3.9). As a comparatively small company within its industry, Small Change probably will not command as high a price-earnings multiple as its larger industry peers. Therefore, we shall assume that Big Time is able to acquire the company for only 12 times earnings, rather than 14 times, as assumed in Exhibit 3.3.

EXHIBIT 3.9 Exploiting a Difference in Price-Earnings Multiples: Big Time Corp. and Small Change Inc. ($000,000 omitted)

| | Non-acquisition scenario | | | | Acquisition scenario | |
| | Big Time Corp | | Small Change Inc. | | Big Time Corp | |
	Year 1	Year 2	Year 1	Year 2	Year 1	Year 2
Sales	$ 5,000.0	$ 5,250.0	$ 238.1	$ 250.0	$ 5,000.0	$ 5,500.0
Cost and expenses						
Cost of goods sold	$3,500.10	$3,672.60	$162.40	$173.00	$3,500.10	$3,845.60
Selling, general, and administrative expenses	1250.0	1315.0	61.9	62.5	1250.0	1377.5
Interest expense	$ 60.0	$ 63.0	$ 4.8	$ 5.0	$ 60.0	$ 68.0
Total costs and expenses	$ 4,810.1	$ 5,050.6	$ 229.1	$ 240.5	$ 4,810.1	$ 5,291.1
Income before income taxes	$ 189.9	$ 199.4	$ 9.0	$ 9.5	$ 189.9	$ 208.9
Income taxes	$ 39.9	$ 41.9	$ 1.9	$ 2.0	$ 39.9	$ 43.9
Net income	$ 150.0	$ 157.5	$ 7.1	$ 7.5	$ 150.0	$ 165.0
Year-over-year sales increase		5%		5%		10%
Net income as a percentage of sales	3%	3%	3%	3%	3%	3%
Shares outstanding (million)	75.0	75.0			75.0	78.0
Earnings per share	$ 2.00	$ 2.10			$ 2.00	$ 2.12
Price-earnings multiple (times)	14	14			14	14
Price per share	$ 28.00	$ 29.40			$ 28.00	$ 29.68

Our revised assumption does not alter the income statements in either year under either the Acquisition Scenario or the Non-acquisition Scenario. The acquisition price, however, falls from $99.4 million to $7.1 million × 12 = $85.2 million. Big Time issues only $85.2 million ÷ $28.00 = 3.0 million shares to pay for the acquisition, rather than 3.6 million under the previous assumption. Consequently, Big Time has 78.0 million shares outstanding at the end of Year 2 under the Acquisition Scenario, instead of 78.6 million. Earnings per share come to $165.0 million ÷ 78.0 million = $2.12. At a price-earnings multiple of 14 times, Big Time's stock is valued at $29.68 a share following the Small Change acquisition, slightly higher than the $29.40 figure shown in the Non-acquisition Scenario. Big Time could vault its share price to a considerably loftier level by making a series of acquisitions on a similar basis.

In contrast to the outcome depicted in Exhibit 3.3, Big Time increases the value of its stock through the acquisition of Small Change. The company achieves this effect without realizing operating efficiencies through the combination. Following the transaction, Big Time's ratio of net income to sales is 3 percent, unchanged from its preacquisition level.

The rational explanation of this apparent alchemy lies in Big Time's ability to exchange its stock for shares of privately owned Small Change on highly favorable terms. By acquiring the smaller company at a price of 12 times earnings with stock valued at a multiple of 14 times, Big Time spreads Small Change's earnings across fewer shares than would be the case if the market valued the two companies at the same multiple. The effect, achieved purely through financial engineering, is a parody of the economies of scale realized in mergers premised instead on improvements in operations.

In fairness to the many real-world companies that have exploited disparities in price-earnings multiples over the years, Big Time's share-price-enhancing acquisition rests squarely within the bounds of fair play. Companies legitimately take advantage of favorable currency exchange rates when deciding whether to purchase materials and equipment domestically or overseas. If the dollar is high relative to the euro, companies based in the United States can source goods more economically in Europe than at home. In principle, it is no less appropriate or beneficial to shareholders to buy earnings with a highly valued acquisition currency, that is, its own stock.

Furthermore, as shareholders of a private company, Small Change's owners do not have to be coerced to sell out to Big Time. The disparity in price-earnings multiples is justified by the private company's owners' opportunity to exchange an illiquid investment for public stock, for which a deep and active trading market exists. If anything, the difference between Big Time's multiple of 14 times and Small Change's 12 times understates the valuation gap between the public and private shares. Lacking a secondary market that would reward higher reported income with a higher share price, private owner-managers commonly extract compensation through perquisites that their companies can lawfully account for as business expenses. The result is lower net income than comparably successful public companies would report, but with the value of the perks delivered on a pretax basis. Instead of buying cars with dividends distributed from after-tax income, the owner-managers can drive fancier, more expensive company-provided cars purchased with pretax dollars. After adjusting Small Change's reported income for expenses that would not be incurred at a public company such as Big Time, the $85.2 million acquisition price might represent a multiple of only 10 or 11 times, rather than 12 times.

In short, there is nothing inherently unsavory about paying for low-multiple companies with high-multiple stock. Why, then, does the technique warrant special focus in a chapter covering the broad subject of income statements? The answer is that like many other legitimate financial practices, exploiting disparities in price-earnings multiples is prone to abuse. Capitalizing on disparities in price-earnings multiples can lead to trouble in several ways.

To begin with, suppose a high-multiple company acquires a low-multiple company during a period of exceptionally wide dispersion in valuations. In a shift from normal conditions to a two-tiered market, the respective multiples might go, for the sake of example, from 15 and 12 to 25 and 10. Selling stockholders of the low-multiple company would probably consider it a fair exchange to accept payment in shares of the high-multiple company at the prevailing market price. Their feelings would probably change dramatically, however, if the two-tiered market abruptly ended with the purchaser's stock receding from 25 times earnings to a more ordinary 15 times. Sellers who retained the acquiring company's shares would discover that their value received had suddenly fallen by 40 percent. (It is reasonable to assume that many shareholders would have held on to the shares, because doing so would ordinarily delay the incurrence of capital gains taxes on the sale. Unlike cash-for-stock transactions, stock-for-stock acquisitions generally qualify as tax-free exchanges.)

Readers might accuse the selling shareholders of being crybabies. After all, they knew when they accepted the acquiring company's shares as payment that they would be exposed to stock market fluctuations, much as they were prior to the deal. The difference, however, is that if they had held on to their low-multiple stock, their loss would not have been 40 percent, but only 17 percent; that is, from 12 times to 10 times earnings. (A complete comparison must also take into account any premium over the previously prevailing stock price received by the selling shareholders.)

Financial statement analysis would not have warned the selling shareholders of the impending marketwide drop in price-earnings (P/E) multiples. Careful scrutiny of the acquiring company's income statement might very well have determined, however, that its shares were susceptible to a sharp decline. Over the years, many voracious acquirers have temporarily achieved stratospheric multiples on their acquisition currency through financial reporting gimmicks that hard-nosed analysts were able to detect before the share prices fell back to earth.

In some instances, the basis for an exaggerated P/E multiple is rapid earnings per share (EPS) growth achieved through financial engineering rather than bona fide synergies. Starting with a modest multiple on its stock, a company can make a few small acquisitions of low-multiple companies to get the earnings acceleration started. Each transaction may be too small to be deemed material in itself. That would eliminate any obligation on the company's part to divulge details that would make it easy for analysts to quantify the impact of the company's exploitation of disparities in P/E multiples. As quarter-to-quarter percentage increases in EPS escalate, the company's equity begins to be perceived as a high-growth glamour stock. Obliging investors award the stock a higher multiple, which increases the company's ability to buy earnings on favorable terms. Management may succeed in pumping up the P/E multiple even further by asserting that it can achieve economies of scope through acquiring enterprises outside, yet in some previously unrecognized way, complementary to the company's core business.

The conglomerate craze of the 1960s relied heavily on these techniques, and with variations, they have been reused in more recent times. Massive declines in the share prices of the insatiable acquirers' stock prices have frequently resulted. Contributing to the downslides have been the practical problems of integrating the operations of diverse companies. Deals that work on paper have often foundered on incompatible information systems, disparate distribution channels, clashes of personality among senior executives, and contrasting corporate cultures. In addition, the process of boosting earnings per share through acquisition of lower-multiple companies may prove unsustainable. For example, if competition heats up among corporations seeking to grow through acquisition, the P/E gap between acquirers and target companies may narrow. That could get in the way of the continuous stream of acquisitions needed to maintain EPS growth in the absence of profit improvements. Inevitably, too, the voracious acquirer will suffer a normal cyclical decline in the earnings of its existing operations. The company's price-earnings multiple may then decline relative to the multiples of its potential targets, interrupting the necessary flow of acquisitions.

It is no small task to dissect the income statement of a corporation that makes frequent acquisitions and discloses as few details as possible. Nevertheless, an energetic analyst can go a long way toward segregating ongoing operations from purchased earnings growth. Acquisitions of public companies leave an information trail in the form of regulatory filings. Conscientious searching of the media, including the industry-specialized periodicals and local newspapers, may yield useful tidbits on acquisitions of private companies. Such investigations will frequently turn up the phrase "terms of the acquisition were not disclosed," but reliable sources may provide informed speculation about the prices paid. Finally, the acquirers may furnish general information regarding the range of earnings multiples paid in recent deals. If an analysis of the available data indicates that management is expanding its empire without creating additional value through genuine economies of scale or scope, the prudent action is to sell before the bottom falls out.

CONCLUSION

At several points in this chapter, analysis of the income statement has posed questions that could be answered only by looking outside the statement. Mere study of reported financial figures never leads to a fully informed judgment about the issuer. Financial statements cannot capture certain nonquantitative factors that may be essential to an evaluation. These include industry conditions, corporate culture, and management's ability to anticipate change and respond effectively.

CHAPTER 4

The Statement of Cash Flows

The present version of the financial statement that traces the flow of funds in and out of the firm, the statement of cash flows, became mandatory, under Statement of Financial Accounting Standards (SFAS) 95, for issuers with fiscal years ending after July 15, 1988. Exhibit 4.1, the 2019 cash flow statement of Motorola Solutions, illustrates the statement's division into cash flows from operating activities, investing activities, and financing activities. The predecessor of the statement of cash flows, the statement of changes in financial position, was first required under Accounting Principles Board (APB) opinion 19, in 1971.

Prior to 1971, going as far back as the introduction of **double-entry bookkeeping** in Italy during the fifteenth century, financial analysts had muddled through with only the balance sheet and the income statement. Anyone with a sense of history will surely conclude that the introduction of the cash flow statement must have been premised by expectations of great new analytical insights. Such an inference is in fact well founded. The advantages of a cash flow statement correspond to the shortcomings of the income statement and, more specifically, the concept of profit. Over time, profit has proven so malleable a quantity, so easily enlarged or reduced to suit management's needs, as to make it useless, in many instances, as the basis of a fair comparison among companies.

An example of the erroneous comparisons that can arise involves the contrasting objectives that public and private companies have in preparing their income statements.

For financial-reporting (as opposed to tax-accounting) purposes, a publicly owned company generally seeks to maximize its reported net income, which investors use as a basis for valuing its shares. Therefore, its incentive in any situation where the accounting rules permit discretion is to minimize expenses. The firm will capitalize whatever expenditures it can and depreciate its fixed assets over as long a period as possible. All that restrains the public company in this respect (other than conscience) is the wish to avoid

EXHIBIT 4.1 Motorola Solutions, Inc. Cash Flow Statement

Consolidated Statements of Cash Flows – USD ($) in Millions	12 Months Ended
	Dec. 31, 2019
Operating	
Net earnings (loss) attributable to Motorola Solutions, Inc.	$ 868
Earnings attributable to noncontrolling interests	3
Net earnings (loss)	871
Adjustments to reconcile net earnings (loss) to net cash provided by operating activities:	
Depreciation and amortization	394
Non-cash other charges	35
Pension settlement losses	359
(Gain) losses from the extinguishment of long term debt	50
Share-based compensation expense	118
Gains on sales of investments and businesses, net	(5)
Changes in assets and liabilities, net of effects of acquisitions, dispositions, and foreign currency translation adjustments:	
Accounts receivable	(79)
Inventories	(74)
Other current assets and contract assets	49
Accounts payable, accrued liabilities, and contract liabilities	198
Other assets and liabilities	(5)
Deferred income taxes	(84)
Net cash provided by operating activities	1,823
Investing	
Acquisitions and investments, net	(709)
Proceeds from sales of investments	16
Capital expenditures	(248)
Proceeds from sales of property, plant and equipment	7
Net cash used for investing activities	(934)
Financing	
Repayment of debt	(2,039)
Net proceeds from issuance of debt	1,804
Issuances of common stock	114
Purchases of common stock	(315)
Settlement of conversion premium on 2.00% senior convertible notes	(326)
Payment of dividends	(379)
Payment of dividends to noncontrolling interest	(3)
Deferred acquisition costs	0
Net cash provided by (used for) financing activities	(1,144)
Effect of exchange rate changes on cash and cash equivalents	(1)

EXHIBIT 4.1 (*Continued*)

Consolidated Statements of Cash Flows – USD ($) in Millions	12 Months Ended
Net increase (decrease) in cash and cash equivalents	$(256)
Cash and cash equivalents, beginning of period	1,257
Cash and cash equivalents, end of period	1,001
Cash paid during the period for:	
Interest, net	221
Income and withholding taxes, net of refunds	138
Convertible debt	
Adjustments to reconcile net earnings (loss) to net cash provided by operating activities:	
(Gain) losses from the extinguishment of long-term debt	(4)
Long-term debt, excluding convertible debt	
Adjustments to reconcile net earnings (loss) to net cash provided by operating activities:	
(Gain) losses from the extinguishment of long-term debt	50

Source: Company 10K and author calculations.

being perceived as employing liberal accounting practices, which may lead to a lower market valuation of its reported earnings. Using depreciation schedules much longer than those of other companies in the same industry could give rise to such a perception.

In contrast, a privately held company has no public shareholders to impress. Unlike a public company, which shows one set of statements to the public and another to the Internal Revenue Service, a private company typically prepares one set of statements, with the tax authorities foremost in its thinking. Its incentive is not to maximize, but to minimize the income it reports, thereby minimizing its tax bill as well. If an analyst examines its income statement and tries to compare it with those of public companies in the same industry, the result will be an undeservedly poor showing by the private company.

THE CASH FLOW STATEMENT AND THE LEVERAGED BUYOUT

Net income becomes even less relevant when one analyzes the statements of a company that has been acquired in a **leveraged buyout (LBO)** (Exhibit 4.2)[1]. In a classic LBO, a group of investors acquires a business

EXHIBIT 4.2 Leveraged Buyout Forecast – Base Case ($000,000 omitted)

Capitalization

December 31, 2019

Senior debt	900	45%
Subordinated debt	500	25%
Total debt	1,400	70%
Common equity	600	30%
Total capital	$2,000	100%

Projected income statement

	2019 Actual	2020	2021	2022	2023	2024
Sales	1,429	$1,543	$1,667	$1,800	$1,944	$2,100
Cost of sales	800	864	933	1,008	1,089	1,176
Depreciation	100	108	117	126	136	147
Selling, general, and administrative expense	286	309	333	360	389	420
Operating income	243	262	283	306	331	357
Interest expense	30	71	63	55	46	35
Income before income taxes	213	192	220	251	285	322
Provision (credit) for income taxes	45	40	46	53	60	68
Net income	$ 168	$ 152	$ 174	$ 198	$ 225	$ 254
EBITDA	$ 343	$ 370	$ 400	$ 432	$ 467	$ 504
Valuation	1989	2148	2320	2506	2706	2923
Initial investment as % of value	30%	28%	26%	24%	22%	21%

Projected cash flow

	2020	2021	2022	2023	2024
Net income	$ 152	$ 174	$ 198	$ 225	$ 254
Depreciation	108	117	126	136	147
Cash from operations	$ 259	$ 290	$ 324	$ 361	$ 401
Less: property and equipment additions	100	108	117	126	136
Cash available for debt reduction	$ 160	$ 182	$ 208	$ 235	$ 265

Projected capitalization

	Actual 2019	2020	2021	2022	2023	2024
Senior debt	$ 900	$ 740	$ 558	$ 350	$ 115	($150)
Subordinated debt	500	500	500	500	500	500
Total debt	1,400	1,240	1,058	850	615	350
Common equity	600	$ 752	$ 925	$1,124	$1,349	$1,603
Total capital	$2,000	$1,992	$1,983	$1,974	$1,964	$1,953

by putting up a comparatively small amount of equity and borrowing the balance (70 percent in this example) of the purchase price. As a result of this highly leveraged capital structure, interest expense is so large that the formerly quite profitable company reports a reduced net income in its first year as an LBO (2020). Hardly an attractive investment, on the face of it, and one might also question the wisdom of lenders who provide funds to an enterprise that is assured of becoming less profitable.

A closer study, however, shows that the equity investors are no fools. In 2020, the company's sales are expected to bring in $1,543 million in cash. Cash outlays include cost of sales ($864 million); selling, general, and administrative expense ($309 million); and interest expense ($71 million), for a total of $1,244 million. Adding in depreciation of $108 million produces total expenses of $1,352 million, which when subtracted from sales results in a $191 million pretax profit. The amount attributable to depreciation, however, does not represent an outlay of cash in the current year. Rather, it is a bookkeeping entry intended to represent the gradual reduction in value, through use, of physical assets. Therefore, the funds generated by the leveraged buyout firm equal sales less the cash expenses only. (Note that the assumed tax rate in this projection is 21 percent.)

Viewed in terms of cash inflows and outflows, rather than earnings, the leveraged buyout begins to look like a sound venture. In 2024, net income has increased by only 8 percent since 2020, despite a 26 percent advance in sales, but the company is generating cash and has reduced its borrowings. (Note that in this illustration, the equity investors take no dividends but instead dedicate any surplus cash generated to debt reduction.)

The story improves further in subsequent years. As sales grow at an 8 percent annual rate, the projected income statement shows a steady increase in operating income. In addition, the paydown of debt causes interest expense to decline, so net income increases over time. With depreciation rising as well, funds from operations in this example keep ahead of the growing capital expenditure requirements.

If the projections prove accurate, the equity investors will, by the end of 2024, own a company with $2.1 billion in sales and $357 million of operating income, up from $1.4 billion and $243 million, respectively, in 2019. They will have captured that growth without having injected any additional cash beyond their original $600 million investment.

Suppose the investors then decide to monetize the increase in firm value represented by the growth in earnings. Assuming they can sell the company for the same multiple of EBITDA (earnings before interest, taxes, depreciation, and amortization)[2] that they paid for it, they will realize net proceeds of $1,740 million, derived as follows ($000,000 omitted):

1. Calculate the multiple of EBITDA paid in 2019.

$$= \frac{\text{Purchase price (Equity + Borrowed funds)}}{\text{Net income + Income taxes + Interest expense} + \text{Depreciation and Amortization}}$$

$$= \frac{\$2{,}000}{\$133 + \$65 + \$45 + \$100}$$

$$= 5.8$$

2. Multiply this factor by 2024 EBITDA to determine sale price in that year.

$$(5.8) \times (\$254 + \$68 + \$35 + \$147) = \$2{,}932$$

3. From this figure, subtract remaining debt to determine pretax proceeds.

$$\$2{,}932 - \$350 = \$2{,}573$$

4. Subtract 20 percent capital gains tax on the gain over original equity investment to determine net proceeds.

$2,573	Pretax proceeds
−600	Original equity investment
$1,973	Capital gain
× 0.20	Capital gains tax rate
$395	Tax on capital gain
$2,573	Pretax proceeds
−395	Tax on capital gain
$2,178	Net proceeds

The increase in the equity holders' investment from $600 million to $2,178 million over five years represents a compounded annual return of 29 percent after tax. Interestingly, the annual return on equity (based on reported net income and the beginning-of-year book value of equity) is significantly lower. It declines from 20 percent in 2020 to 16 percent in 2024, as equity grows faster than income. Analysts evaluating the investment merits of the LBO proposal would miss the point if they focused on earnings rather than cash flow.

The same emphasis on cash flow, rather than reported earnings, is equally important in analyzing the downside in a leveraged buyout.

As one might expect, the equity investors do not reap such spectacular gains without taking substantial risk. There is a danger that everything will not go according to plan and that they will lose their entire investment. Specifically, there is a risk that sales and operating earnings will fall short of expectations, perhaps as a result of a recession or because the investors' expectations were unrealistically high at the outset. With a less debt-heavy capital structure, a shortfall in operating earnings might not be worrisome. In a leveraged buyout, however, the high interest expense can quickly turn disappointing operating income into a sizable net loss (Exhibit 4.3). The loss may be so large that even after depreciation is added back, the company's funds generated from operations may decline to zero or to a negative figure. (Note that the shortfall shown here resulted from a 10 percent drop in sales from 2019 and deviations of just 10 percent each in the projections for cost of sales, and selling, general, and administrative expense, shown in Exhibit 4.2.)

Now the future does not look so rosy for the equity investors. If they cannot reduce operating expenses sufficiently to halt the cash drain, they will lack the cash required for the heavy interest expenses they have incurred, much less the scheduled principal payments. Most of the choices available,

EXHIBIT 4.3   Leveraged Buyout Forecast – Pessimistic Case ($000,000 omitted)

Projected Income Statement	2020
Sales	$1,286
Cost of sales	849
Depreciation	108
Selling, general, and administrative expense	386
Operating income	(57)
Interest expense	71
Income before income taxes	(128)
Provision (credit) for income taxes	(27)
Net income	$ (101)
Net income	$ (101)
Plus: depreciation	$ 108
Equals: cash generated	$ 7
Compare to Exhibit 4.2 results: Cash from operations	$ 260

if they cannot cut costs sufficiently, are unappealing. One option is for the investors to inject more equity into the company. This will cause any profits they ultimately realize to represent a smaller percentage return on the equity invested, besides possibly straining the investors' finances. Alternatively, the existing equity holders can sell equity to a new group of investors. The disadvantage of this strategy is that anyone putting in new capital at a time when the venture is perceived to be in trouble is likely to exact terms that will severely dilute the original investors' interest and, possibly, control. Comparably harsh terms may be expected from lenders who are willing (if any are) to let the company try to borrow its way out of its problems. A distressed exchange offer, in which bondholders accept reduced interest or a postponement of principal repayment, may be more attractive for the equity holders but is likely to meet stiff resistance.

If all these options prove unpalatable or infeasible, the leveraged company will default on its debt. At that point, the lenders may force the firm into bankruptcy, which could result in a total loss for the equity investors. Alternatively, the lenders may agree to reduce the interest rates on their loans and postpone mandatory principal repayments, but they will ordinarily agree to such concessions only in exchange for a larger say in the company's management. In short, once cash flow turns negative, the potential outcomes generally look bleak to the equity investors.

The key point here is that the cash flow statement, rather than the income statement, provides the best information about a highly leveraged firm's financial health. Given the overriding importance of generating (and retaining) cash to retire debt, and because the equity investors do not seek dividends, there is no advantage in showing an accounting profit, the main consequence of which is incurrence of taxes, resulting in turn in reduced cash flow. Neither are there public shareholders clamoring for increases in earnings per share. The cash flow statement is the most useful tool for analyzing highly leveraged companies because it reflects the true motivation of the firm's owners — to generate cash, rather than to maximize reported income.

ANALYTICAL APPLICATIONS

Although privately held and highly leveraged companies illustrate most vividly the advantages of the cash flow statement, the statement also has considerable utility in analyzing publicly owned and more conventionally capitalized firms. One important application lies in determining where a company is in its life cycle, that is, whether it is taking off, growing rapidly, maturing, or declining. Different types of risk characterize these various stages of the life cycle. Therefore, knowing which stage a company is in can focus the analyst's efforts on the key analytical factors. A second use of the cash flow statement is to assess a company's **financial flexibility**. This term refers to a company's capacity, in the event of a business downturn, to continue making expenditures that, over the long term, minimize its cost of capital and enhance its competitive position. Finally, the cash flow statement is the key statement to examine when analyzing a troubled company. When a company is verging on bankruptcy, its balance sheet may overstate its asset value, as a result of write-offs having lagged the deterioration in profitability of the company's operations. On the other hand, the balance sheet may fail to reflect the full value of certain assets recorded at historical cost, which the company might sell to raise cash. The income statement is not especially relevant in the context of pending bankruptcy. For the moment, the company's key objective is not to maintain an impeccable earnings record, but to survive. The cash flow statement provides the most useful information for answering the critical question: Will the company succeed in keeping its creditors at bay?

Cash Flows and the Company Life Cycle

Business enterprises typically go through phases of development that are in many respects analogous to a human being's stages of life. Just as children are susceptible to illnesses different from those that afflict the elderly, the risks of investing in young companies are different from the risks inherent in mature companies. Accordingly, it is helpful to understand which portion of the life cycle a company is in and which financial pitfalls it is therefore most likely to face.

Revenues build gradually in the introductory phase, when the company is just organizing itself and launching its products. From a small base, revenues accelerate rapidly during the growth phase, as the company's products penetrate the market and production reaches a profitable scale. In the maturity phase, sales opportunities are limited to the replacement of products previously sold, plus new sales derived from growth in the population. Price competition often intensifies at this stage, as companies seek sales growth through increased market share (a larger piece of a pie that is growing at a lesser rate). The decline stage does not automatically follow maturity, but over long periods, some industries do get swept away by technological change. Sharply falling sales and earnings, ultimately resulting in corporate bankruptcies, characterize industries in severe decline.

Exhibit 4.4 depicts the business life cycle in terms of operating activities and financing activities, which are usually sources of cash flow, and investing activities, which is ordinarily a use of cash flow. Observe that the financing

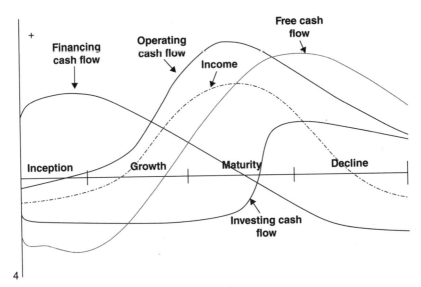

EXHIBIT 4.4 Relevance of Cash Flows and Income over a Company's Life Cycle.
Source: Anonymous Scholar

curve peaks in the earlier (introductory-growth) portion of the life cycle, while the operating and investing curves peak in the later (maturity-decline) portion. A crossover occurs in the maturity phase as cash flows from operating and investing begin to exceed cash flows from financing.

Introductory stage companies subsist primarily on financing as they build their operations toward the point at which they will begin to generate cash. Growth companies can be highly profitable, but they require extensive external capital to keep **funding** their expansion. Mature companies may achieve less impressive profit margins, but as their need to invest levels off, they become self-funding and, ultimately, net generators of cash. This is indicated in the graph by the financing curve falling into negative territory. Companies that throw off cash can be good leveraged buyout candidates. Alternatively, they may seek to bolster profits through industry consolidation (i.e., mergers and acquisitions that reduce the number of competitors) to achieve economies of scale. Declining companies reach a point at which deteriorating cash flows from operating and investing activities cause them to become net cash users. They cannot fill the gap with external financing (as shown by the financing curve moving into the negative zone), because they represent poor credit risks and offer unattractive returns to equity investors.

Intellia Therapeutics (NTLA) illustrates the cash flow pattern of a company in the introductory phase of its life cycle (Exhibit 4.5). This biotech

EXHIBIT 4.5 Intellia Therapeutics (NTLA) Consolidated Statements of Cash Flows – USD ($) in Thousands

	12 Months Ended					
	Dec. 31, 2015	Dec. 31, 2016	Dec. 31, 2017	Dec. 31, 2018	Dec. 31, 2019
Sales/revenue	16,479	26,117	30,434	43,103	57,994
Cash flows from operating activities:					
Net loss	(12,397)	(31,634)	(67,543)	(85,343)	(99,533)
Adjustments to reconcile net loss to net cash provided by (used in) operating activities:					
Acquired in-process research and development					
Depreciation and amortization	328	1104	2,994	4,464	5,587
Loss on disposal of property and equipment	9	13	166	75	1
Equity-based compensation	1308	6715	15,322	17,046	15,091
Benefit from intraperiod tax allocation	(1,012)				
Accretion of investment discounts	–	–		(676)	(3,725)
Changes in operating assets and liabilities:					
Accounts receivable		(5,454)	(4,017)	2,924	2,927
Prepaid expenses and other current assets	(525)	(979)	(1,893)	310	(1,763)
Operating right-of-use assets	–	–			5,728
Other assets	(76)	(6,435)	902	1,022	153
Accounts payable	335	1,784	(488)	232	1,880
Accrued expenses	805	3,050	2,394	2,780	2,310
Deferred revenue	9,312	67,975	(12,988)	(3,936)	(27,122)
Operating lease liabilities	–	–			(4,774)
Other long-term liabilities	150	(30)	(125)	(155)	

(Note: The 2015 column also includes: Acquired in-process research and development 6055; Depreciation and amortization 3; Equity-based compensation 308; Net loss (9,539); Prepaid expenses and other current assets (285); Accounts payable 163; Accrued expenses 1,056; Other long-term liabilities 173)

Net cash provided by (used in) operating activities	(2,322)	(1,763)	36,109	(65,276)	(61,257)	(103,240)

	Col1	Col2	Col3	Col4	Col5	Col6
Net cash provided by (used in) operating activities	(2,322)	(1,763)	36,109	(65,276)	(61,257)	(103,240)
Cash flows from investing activities:						
Purchases of property and equipment	(275)	(2,554)	(6,165)	(10,091)	(6,358)	(6,794)
Proceeds from sale of property and equipment	—	—	—	—	131	—
Acquisition of in-process research and development	(300)	—	—	—	(254,555)	(297,030)
Purchases of marketable securities	—	—	—	—	—	329,000
Maturities of marketable securities	—	—	—	—	—	25,176
Net cash provided by (used in) investing activities	(575)	(2,554)	(6,165)	(10,091)	(260,782)	25,176
Cash flows from financing activities:						
Proceeds from sale of Class A-1 and A-2 preferred units and Series B preferred	12,651	74,661	—	—	—	—
Payments to acquire in-process research and development	—	(1,100)	(600)	—	—	—
Payment of preferred unit and preferred stock issuance costs	(258)	(2,671)	(100)	—	—	—
Proceeds from sale of common units	349					—
Proceeds from common stock offerings, net of offering costs			170,507	141,000	28,547	72,256
Proceeds from options exercised			2	1,156	10,652	3,086
Issuance of shares through employee stock purchase plan			259	825	1,018	1,092
Payment of common stock offering costs		(602)	(2,764)	—	—	—

(Continued)

EXHIBIT 4.5 (*Continued*)

	12 Months Ended				
	Dec. 31, 2015	Dec. 31, 2016	Dec. 31, 2017	Dec. 31, 2018	Dec. 31, 2019
Net cash provided by financing activities	12,742	167,304	142,981	40,217	76,434
Net increase in cash and cash equivalents	65,971	197,248	67,614	(281,822)	(1,630)
Cash and cash equivalents, beginning of period	9,845	75,816	273,064	340,678	58,856
Cash and cash equivalents, end of period	75,816	273,064	340,678	58,856	57,226
Supplemental disclosures of cash flow information:					
Purchases of property and equipment unpaid at period end	36	219	3,090	805	1,071
Acquisition of in-process research and development unpaid at period end	1,700		—	—	800
Noncash portion of acquired in-process research and development	4,055		—	—	—
Financing costs incurred but unpaid at period end	970				
Conversion of convertible preferred stock to common stock		88,557	—	—	—
Right-of-use assets acquired under operating leases	—	—	—	—	2,554

Source: Company 10K and author calculations.

company, founded in 2014, engages in research and clinical development of gene editing therapies for patients with genetically based diseases. The company was privately owned during the initial period shown in the exhibit, going public only in May 2016.

Intellia recorded negative net income throughout the period shown. Book losses are not unusual for companies at the introductory stage. In the case of capital-intensive manufacturing companies, it may take several years for sales to reach a level sufficient to cover the substantial fixed costs that are essential to operations.

During the period shown in Exhibit 4.5, Intellia was at a relatively early stage of developing therapies from its CRISPR gene editing technology. As late as 2019, the company's research and development expense was 2.5 times its revenue. The profits and cash flow from operations sought by shareholders were still to come, keeping Intellia dependent on raising outside funds.

After its initial public offering the company continued to raise cash from common stock offerings in 2017, 2018, and 2019. In those years, the company had modest expenditures for property and equipment. Much of the cash raised by the stock offerings was used in the purchase and sale of marketable securities, likely in anticipation of negative operating cash flow.

Carvana (Exhibit 4.6) is an example of a rapidly growing company that has emerged from its introductory phase. It was founded in 2012 as an e-commerce platform that buys and sells used cars. The company went public in 2015 and over the five years depicted in the cash flow statements grew its sales at a 134 percent annual rate. Clearly, this is a business in which year-to-year sales increases derive from rising popularity of its service, rather than mere population growth, as is the case with a mature company.

As Carvana's sales grew, so did its reported losses, leading to increasingly negative cash flow from operating activities. (In an illustration of the weakening link between GAAP income and equity valuations discussed in Chapter 5, investors awarded Carvana a **market capitalization** of $14 billion as of the end of fiscal 2019.) Investing activities, primarily purchases of property and equipment, rendered cash flow even more negative before taking into account financing activities. In 2015–2017 Carvana financed its growing operations mainly with a floor plan facility, which consists of short-term loans provided to a big-ticket retailer by a traditional bank, specialty lender, or finance arms of a manufacturer and then repaid as the inventoried items are sold. As the scale of operations grew, the company relied mostly on revolving credit, long-term debt, and equity offerings.

Cash flow statements of mature companies look like Kimberly-Clark's (Exhibit 4.7). Founded in 1872, the company manufactures consumer products made from natural or synthetic fibers, with brands such as Depend,

EXHIBIT 4.6 Carvana Co (CVNA) Consolidated Statements of Cash Flows – USD ($) in Thousands

	12 Months Ended					
	Dec. 31, 2015	Dec. 31, 2016	Dec. 31, 2017	Dec. 31, 2018	Dec. 31, 2019	Dec. 31, 2020
Sales and operating revenues:	124,972	341,989	796,915	1,955,467	3,939,896	5,586,565
Cash flows from operating activities:						
Net loss	$ (36,780)	$ (93,112)	$ (164,316)	$ (254,745)	$ (364,639)	$ (462,222)
Adjustments to reconcile net loss to net cash used in operating activities:						
Depreciation and amortization expense	2,800	4,658	11,568	23,539	41,265	73,791
Loss on disposal of property and equipment	0	0	958	575	1,714	6,130
Provision for bad debt and valuation allowance	299	1,348	1,375	1,917	11,922	20,962
Gain on loan sales, including $0, $269, and $0 from related parties, respectively	0	(7,446)	(21,697)	(51,729)	(137,301)	(217,643)
Equity-based compensation expense	490	555	5,611	24,095	33,063	25,088
Amortization and write-off of debt issuance costs and bond premium	0	0	1,646	2,305	5,541	7,959
Loss on early extinguishment of debt	0	0	0	0	0	33,683
Originations of finance receivables	(80,070)	(224,169)	(529,153)	(1,259,539)	(2,625,351)	(3,579,156)
Proceeds from sale of finance receivables	0	269,262	527,265	1,633,519	2,643,912	3,634,520
Purchase of finance receivables	0	0	0	(387,445)	(161,781)	0
Proceeds from sale of finance receivables to related party	79,362	13,015	0	0	0	0
Purchase of finance receivables from related party	0	(74,589)	0	0	0	0

Principal payments received on finance receivables held for sale	0	0	0	0	85,017	50,235
Unrealized (gain) loss on beneficial interest in securitization	0	0	0	0	964	(3,823)

Changes in assets and liabilities:

Accounts receivable	(2,711)	(3,492)	(8,715)	(19,212)	(9,741)	(42,995)
Vehicle inventory	(41,667)	(117,468)	(40,839)	(183,068)	(344,861)	(263,321)
Other current assets	(789)	(7,157)	(6,605)	0	0	0
Other assets	0	0	(1,019)	(12,249)	(32,619)	(25,415)
Accounts payable and accrued liabilities	4,122	17,922	16,986	68,550	97,912	94,179
Accounts payable to related party	21,436	(19,552)	(82)	0	0	0
Operating lease right-of-use assets	0	0	0	(46,928)	(32,044)	0
Operating lease liabilities	0	0	0	45,195	38,057	0
Other liabilities	0	0	7,093	(853)	(418)	(397)
Net cash used in operating activities	(53,508)	(240,225)	(199,924)	(414,340)	(757,134)	(608,412)

Cash flows from investing activities:

Purchases of property and equipment	(13,950)	(39,539)	(78,490)	(143,668)	(230,538)	(359,801)
Change in restricted cash	(2,115)	(8,151)	(4,177)	0	0	0
Principal payments received on beneficial interests in securitizations	0	0	0	0	2,799	13,875
Business acquisitions, net of cash acquired	0	0	0	(6,670)	0	0

(*Continued*)

EXHIBIT 4.6 (*Continued*)

	12 Months Ended					
	Dec. 31, 2015	Dec. 31, 2016	Dec. 31, 2017	Dec. 31, 2018	Dec. 31, 2019	Dec. 31, 2020
Net cash used in investing activities	(16,065)	(47,690)	(82,667)	(150,338)	(227,739)	(345,926)
Cash flows from financing activities:						
Proceeds from floor plan facility	125,080	410,562	949,144	0	0	0
Payments on floor plan facility	(88,397)	(287,551)	(865,665)	0	0	0
Proceeds from Verde Credit Facility	0	0	35,000	0	0	0
Payments on Verde Credit Facility	0	0	(35,000)	0	0	0
Proceeds from short-term revolving facilities	0	0	0	1,848,051	4,485,917	4,429,185
Payments on short-term revolving facilities	0	0	0	(1,899,880)	(4,219,415)	(4,958,205)
Proceeds from issuance of long-term debt, including $25,000 in 2018 from related parties	0	0	32,698	399,063	481,772	1,335,779
Payments on long-term debt	0	(284)	(2,259)	(35,522)	(15,683)	(653,589)
Payments of debt issuance costs, including $1,000, $0, and $0 to related parties, respectively	(150)	(728)	(2,055)	(11,390)	(11,445)	(29,394)
Proceeds from note payable to related party	50,000	0	0	0	0	0
Payment of note payable to related party	(11,752)	0	0	0	0	0
Net proceeds from issuance of Class A common stock	0	0	0	172,287	297,611	1,058,940
Net proceeds from initial public offering	0	(398)	206,198	0	0	0
Net proceeds from issuance of Class A convertible preferred stock	0	0	98,682	(12)	0	0

Proceeds from exercise of stock options	0	0	48	795	1,696	5,419
Tax withholdings related to restricted stock awards	0	0	(704)	(2,509)	(5,830)	(23,145)
Class C redeemable preferred units issuance costs	(400)					0
Class C redeemable preferred units	65,000	162,446				
Proceeds from issuance of Class C redeemable preferred units						
Class C redeemable preferred units issuance costs	$ (470)	$ (82)				
Purchases of property and equipment, including $21,657 and $6,282 in 2020 and 2019, respectively, from related parties	0	0	0	0	(6,282)	(21,657)
Proceeds from issuance of long-term debt, including $25,000 in 2018 from related parties	0	0	0	25,000	0	0
Class A convertible preferred stock	0	0	0	0	0	0
Dividends paid on Class A convertible preferred stock	0	0	0	$ (4,619)	$ 0	$ 0
Dividends paid	(33,533)	0	0	0	0	0
Net cash provided by financing activities	105,778	283,965	416,087	466,264	1,014,623	1,164,990
Net increase (decrease) in cash and cash equivalents	36,205	(3,950)	133,496	(98,414)	29,750	210,652
Cash and cash equivalents at beginning of period	6,929	43,134	39,184	187,123	88,709	118,459
Cash, cash equivalents, and restricted cash at end of period	43,134	39,184	172,680	88,709	118,459	329,111

Source: Company 10K and author calculations.

EXHIBIT 4.7   Kimberly-Clark Corp. (KMB) Consolidated Statements Of Cash Flows – USD ($) in Millions

	12 Months Ended					
	Dec. 31, 2014	Dec. 31, 2015	Dec. 31, 2016	Dec. 31, 2017	Dec. 31, 2018	Dec. 31, 2019
Net sales	$19,724	$18,591	$18,202	$18,348	$18,486	$18,450
Operating activities						
Net income	$ 1,595	$ 1,066	$ 2,219	$ 2,319	$ 1,445	$ 2,197
Depreciation and amortization	**862**	**746**	**705**	**724**	**882**	**917**
Asset impairments	0	0	0	0	74	0
Stock-based compensation	52	75	77	76	41	96
Deferred income taxes	63	(255)	(15)	(69)	2	29
Net (gains) losses on asset dispositions	0	0	0	21	52	(193)
Equity companies' earnings (in excess of) less than dividends paid	28	(10)	(4)	26	18	(6)
Decrease (increase) in operating working capital	(176)	(445)	334	(148)	389	(288)
Pension and other postretirement benefit expense	(102)	930	(50)	2	(25)	13
Adjustments related to Venezuelan operations	462	153	(11)	0	0	0
Other	61	46	(23)	(22)	92	(29)
Cash provided by operations	**2,845**	**2,306**	**3,232**	**2,929**	**2,970**	**2,736**
Investing activities						
Capital spending	(1,039)	(1,056)	(771)	(785)	(877)	(1,209)
Proceeds from sales of investments	127	0	28	3	51	242
Investments in time deposits	(151)	(146)	(221)	(214)	(353)	(568)
Maturities of time deposits	239	164	188	183	272	542
Other	54	(12)	44	(38)	5	(49)
Cash used for investing	(770)	(1,050)	(732)	(851)	(902)	(1,042)
Financing activities						
Cash dividends paid	(1,256)	(1,272)	(1,311)	(1,359)	(1,386)	(1,408)

Change in short-term debt	721	303	(908)	360	(34)	303
Debt proceeds	1,257	1,100	1,293	937	507	706
Debt repayments	(123)	(553)	(598)	(1,481)	(407)	(707)
Redemption of redeemable preferred securities of subsidiary	(500)	0	0	0	0	0
Proceeds from exercise of stock options	127	140	107	121	62	228
Acquisitions of common stock for the treasury	**(1,939)**	**(861)**	**(739)**	**(911)**	**(800)**	**(800)**
Cash transferred to Halyard Health, Inc. related to spin-off	(120)	0	0	0	0	0
Shares purchased from noncontrolling interest	0	(151)	0	0	0	0
Other	(60)	(4)	(29)	(88)	(57)	(114)
Cash used for financing	**(1,893)**	**(1,298)**	**(2,185)**	**(2,421)**	**(2,115)**	**(1,792)**
Effect of exchange rate changes on cash and cash equivalents	(447)	(128)	(11)	36	(30)	1
Increase (decrease) in cash and cash equivalents	(265)	(170)	304	(307)	(77)	(97)
Cash and cash equivalents – beginning of year	1,054	789	619	923	616	539
Cash and cash equivalents – end of year	$ 789	$ 619	$ 923	$ 616	$ 539	$ 442

Source: Company 10K and author calculations.

Huggies, Kleenex, Kotex, and Scott. Its business can rely on steady, but not rapidly growing demand.

Without major needs to expand production, Kimberly-Clark funded 84 percent of its capital expenditures from depreciation and amortization in the six years shown in the exhibit. Rather than needing to reinvest the bulk of its earnings at this stage of the life cycle, the company paid out 74 percent of its net income in dividends during the period. Borrowings essentially provided cash to return additional capital to shareholders through stock repurchases.

Not all companies that find their businesses maturing settle into the sort of pattern portrayed in Exhibit 4.7. Some instead elect to reinvest the greater part of their positive cash flow by launching or acquiring businesses with higher growth potential than their original core operations. The older operations become cash cows to be milked for funding the newer activities.

BlackBerry (Exhibit 4.8) displays cash flow characteristics of a company in the decline phase of its life cycle. Founded in 1984 as Research in Motion (RIM), this Canadian company enjoyed huge success as the early leader in smartphones. Even after Apple introduced its first iPhone in 2007, RIM racked up sizable market share gains. Its 2008 BlackBerry Storm model received poor reviews, however. BlackBerry's U.S. user base peaked in 2012. The iPhone and Google's Android system overtook BlackBerry's and by 2016 fewer than one percent of U.S. smartphone users were running the BlackBerry system. Layoffs, losses, and executive turnover accompanied the company's competitive setbacks.

BlackBerry's revenues stagnated in the four years covered by Exhibit 4.8. Losses in fiscal years 2020 and 2021 put the company in the red for the full period. Net cash provided by operating activities dropped off sharply after fiscal 2018. BlackBerry's business does not require substantial capital spending ("Acquisition of property, plant and equipment"). Nevertheless, the company's cash balance declined at a rate of $212 million a year in fiscal years 2019–2021.

Note that business setbacks do not always evolve into downward spiraling cash flows. As detailed in Exhibit 4.9a, in 2015 Microsoft suffered a largest-ever quarterly loss. A year earlier the company had acquired Nokia's handset unit in an attempt to turn around its own money-losing smartphone business. The deal did little to gain ground with mobile phone users, however, and Microsoft wrote off most of the purchase cost of the acquisition. In addition to that non-cash charge, the company incurred large restructuring costs associated with terminating 7,800 employees and other integration efforts.

Net cash from operations declined in fiscal 2015. As shown in Exhibit 4.9b, however, that performance measure rebounded strongly in fiscal 2016 and grew strongly in each of the subsequent three years. This

EXHIBIT 4.8 BlackBerry (BB) Consolidated Statements of Cash Flows – USD ($) in Millions

	12 Months Ended				
	Feb. 28, 2018	Feb. 28, 2019	Feb. 29, 2020	Feb. 28, 2021
Revenue	$ 932	$ 904	$1,040	$ 893
Cash flows from operating activities				
Net income (loss)	$ 405	$ 93	$ (152)	$(1,104)
Adjustments to reconcile net income (loss) to net cash provided by operating activities:				
Amortization	177	149	212	198
Deferred income taxes	(7)	(25)	0	(3)
Stock-based compensation	49	67	63	44
Impairment of goodwill	0	0	22	594
Impairment of long-lived assets held-for-use	11	0	10	43
Non-cash consideration received from contracts with customers	0	(46)	(8)	0
Debentures fair value adjustment	191	(117)	(66)	372
Other long-term assets	18	0	37	0
Other long-term liabilities	5	(12)	2	(3)
Operating leases	0	0	(9)	(4)
Other	3	6	10	1
Net changes in working capital items				
Accounts receivable, net	49	(9)	18	29
Other receivables	(44)	52	5	(11)
Income taxes receivable	2	17	3	(4)
Other assets	39	(1)	2	55
Accounts payable	(82)	(15)	(17)	(11)

(*Continued*)

EXHIBIT 4.8 (*Continued*)

	12 Months Ended			
	Feb. 28, 2018	Feb. 28, 2019	Feb. 29, 2020	Feb. 28, 2021
Accrued liabilities	(36)	(21)	(15)	(20)
Income taxes payable	4	(2)	1	(15)
Deferred revenue	(44)	(36)	(18)	(79)
Net cash provided by operating activities	704	100	26	82
Cash flows from investing activities				
Acquisition of long-term investments	(27)	(2)	(1)	(5)
Proceeds on sale or maturity of long-term investments	77	2	19	0
Acquisition of property, plant and equipment	(15)	(17)	(12)	(8)
Proceeds on sale of property, plant and equipment	3	1	0	0
Acquisition of intangible assets	(30)	(32)	(32)	(36)
Business acquisitions, net of cash acquired	0	(1,402)		
Change in consideration for business acquisition			1	0
Acquisition of restricted short-term investments	0	0	0	(24)
Acquisition of short-term investments	(3,499)	(2,895)	(1,180)	(1,039)
Proceeds on sale or maturity of short-term investments	2,861	3,970	1,017	1,047
Net cash used in investing activities	(630)	(375)	(188)	(65)
Cash flows from financing activities				
Issuance of common shares	8	5	9	19
Common shares repurchased	(18)	0	0	0
Finance lease, principal payments	0	0	2	0
Repurchase of 3.75% debentures				(1)
Issuance of 1.75% debentures				(610)
				365

Net cash provided by (used in) financing activities	(10)	5	7	(227)
Effect of foreign exchange gain (loss) on cash and cash equivalents	6	(3)	(1)	2
Cash, cash equivalents, restricted cash and restricted cash equivalents, period increase (decrease), including exchange rate effect	70	(273)	(156)	(208)
Cash, cash equivalents, restricted cash and restricted cash equivalents, beginning of period	785	855	582	426
Cash, cash equivalents, restricted cash and restricted cash equivalents, end of period	$ 855	$ 582	$ 426	$ 218

111

EXHIBIT 4.9a Microsoft Consolidated Statement of Cash Flows in Millions (USD $), unless otherwise specified

	12 Months Ended				
	Jun. 30, 2011	Jun. 30, 2012	Jun. 30, 2013	Jun. 30, 2014	Jun. 30, 2015
Product				72,948	75,956
Service and other				13,885	17,624
Revenue	69,943	73,723	77,849	86,833	93,580
Operations					
Net income	23,150	16,978[1]	21,863[2]	22,074	12,193[3]
Adjustments to reconcile net income to net cash from operations:					
Goodwill impairment	0	6,193	0	0	7,498
Depreciation, amortization, and other	2,766	2,967	3,755	5,212	5,957
Stock-based compensation expense	2,166	2,244	2,406	2,446	2,574
Net recognized losses (gains) on investments and derivatives	–362	–200	80	(109)	(443)
Excess tax benefits from stock-based compensation	–17	–93	–209		
Deferred income taxes	2	954	–19	(331)	224
Deferral of unearned revenue	31,227	36,104	44,253	44,325	45,072
Recognition of unearned revenue	(28,935)	(33,347)	(41,921)	(41,739)	(44,920)
Changes in operating assets and liabilities:					
Accounts receivable	(1,451)	(1,156)	(1,807)	(1,120)	1,456
Inventories	(561)	184	(802)	(161)	(272)
Other current assets	(1,259)	493	(129)	(29)	62
Other long-term assets	62	(248)	(478)	(628)	346
Accounts payable	58	(31)	537	473	(1,054)
Other current liabilities	(1,146)	410	146	1,075	(624)
Unearned revenue					

Income taxes	0	0	0	0	0
Other current liabilities	1,599	1,014	1,158	174	1,294
Other long-term liabilities					
Net cash from operations	**29,668**	**32,502**	**28,833**	**31,626**	**26,994**
Financing					
Short-term debt repayments, maturities of 90 days or less, net	4,481	500	0	0	(186)
Proceeds from issuance of debt	1C,680	10,350	4,883	0	6,960
Repayments of debt	(1,500)	(3,888)	(1,346)	0	(814)
Common stock issued	634	607	931	1,913	2,422
Common stock repurchased	**(14,443)**	**(7,316)**	**(5,360)**	**(5,029)**	**(11,555)**
Common stock cash dividends paid	(9,882)	(8,879)	(7,455)	(6,385)	(5,180)
Excess tax benefits from stock-based compensation	362	(39)	209	93	17
Other			(10)	0	(40)
Net cash used in financing	**(9,668)**	**(8,665)**	**(8,148)**	**(9,408)**	**(8,376)**
Investing					
Additions to property and equipment	(5,944)	(5,485)	(4,257)	(2,305)	(2,355)
Acquisition of companies, net of cash acquired, and purchases of intangible and other	(3,723)	(5,937)	(1,584)	(10,112)	(71)
Purchases of investments	(98,729)	(72,690)	(75,396)	(57,250)	(35,993)
Maturities of investments	15,013	5,272	5,130	15,575	6,897
Sales of investments	70,848	60,094	52,464	29,700	15,880
Securities lending payable	(466)	(87)	(168)	(394)	1,026

(Continued)

EXHIBIT 4.9a (*Continued*)

	12 Months Ended				
	Jun. 30, 2011	Jun. 30, 2012	Jun. 30, 2013	Jun. 30, 2014	Jun. 30, 2015
Net cash used in investing	(14,616)	(24,786)	(23,811)	(18,833)	(23,001)
Effect of exchange rates on cash and cash equivalents	103	(104)	(8)	(139)	(73)
Net change in cash and cash equivalents	4,105	(2,672)	(3,134)	4,865	(3,074)
Cash and cash equivalents, beginning of period	5,505	9,610	6,938	3,804	8,669
Cash and cash equivalents, end of period	9,610	6,938	3,804	8,669	5,595

[1]Includes a goodwill impairment charge related to our OSD business segment, which decreased net income by $6.2 billion and diluted earnings per share by $0.73.

[2]Includes a charge related to a fine imposed by the European Commission in March 2013, which decreased net income by $733 million (€561 million) and diluted earnings per share by $0.09. Also includes a charge for Surface RT inventory adjustments recorded in the fourth quarter of fiscal year 2013, which decreased net income by $596 million and diluted earnings per share by $0.07.

[3]Includes $7.5 billion of goodwill and asset impairment charges related to our phone business, and $2.5 billion of integration and restructuring expenses, Integration Plan and Phone Hardware Restructuring Plan, primarily associated with our Phone Hardware, which together decreased net income and diluted EPS by $9.5 billion and $1.15, respectively.

Source: Company 10K and author calculations.

EXHIBIT 4.9b Microsoft Consolidated Statement of Cash Flows in Millions (USD $), unless otherwise specified

	12 Months ended			
	Jun. 30, 2016	Jun. 30, 2017	Jun. 30, 2018	Jun. 30, 2019
Product	61,502			
Service and other	23,818			
Revenue	85,320[a]	96,571	110,360	125,843
Operations				
Net income	16,798[4]	$ 25,489	$ 16,571	$ 39,240
Adjustments to reconcile net income to net cash from operations:				
Goodwill impairment	630			
Depreciation, amortization, and other	6,622	8,778	10,261	11,682
Stock-based compensation expense	2,668	3,266	3,940	4,652
Net recognized losses (gains) on investments and derivatives	(223)	(2,073)	(2,212)	(792)
Excess tax benefits from stock-based compensation		0		
Deferred income taxes	332	(829)	(5,143)	(6,463)
Deferral of unearned revenue	57,072			
Recognition of unearned revenue	(48,498)			
Changes in operating assets and liabilities:				
Accounts receivable	(530)	(1,216)	(3,862)	(2,812)
Inventories	600	50	(465)	597
Other current assets	(1,167)	1,028	(952)	(1,718)
Other long-term assets	(41)	(917)	(285)	(1,834)
Accounts payable	88	81	1,148	232
Other current liabilities	(260)			
Unearned revenue		3,820	5,922	4,462

(*Continued*)

EXHIBIT 4.9b (*Continued*)

	12 Months ended			
	Jun. 30, 2016	Jun. 30, 2017	Jun. 30, 2018	Jun. 30, 2019
Income taxes	0	1,792	18,183	2,929
Other current liabilities		356	798	1,419
Other long-term liabilities	(766)	(118)	(20)	591
Net cash from operations	33,325	39,507	43,884	52,185
Financing				
Short-term debt repayments, maturities of 90 days or less, net	7,195	(4,963)	(7,324)	0
Proceeds from issuance of debt	13,884	44,344	7,183	0
Repayments of debt	(2,796)	(7,922)	(10,060)	(4,000)
Common stock issued	668	772	1,002	1,142
Common stock repurchased	(15,969)	(11,788)	(10,721)	(19,543)
Common stock cash dividends paid	(11,006)	(11,845)	(12,699)	(13,811)
Excess tax benefits from stock-based compensation				
Other	(369)	(190)	(971)	(675)
Net cash used in financing	(8,393)	8,408	(33,590)	(36,887)
Investing				
Additions to property and equipment	(8,343)	(8,129)	(11,632)	(13,925)
Acquisition of companies, net of cash acquired, and purchases of intangible and other	(1,393)	(25,944)	(888)	(2,388)
Purchases of investments	(129,758)	(176,905)	(137,380)	(57,697)
Maturities of investments	22,054	28,044	26,360	20,043
Sales of investments	93,287	136,350	117,577	38,194
Securities lending payable	203	(197)	(98)	0

Net cash used in investing	(23,950)	(46,781)	(6,061)	(15,773)
Effect of exchange rates on cash and cash equivalents	(67)	19	50	(115)
Net change in cash and cash equivalents	915	1,153	4,283	(590)
Cash and cash equivalents, beginning of period	5,595	6,510	7,663	11,946
Cash and cash equivalents, end of period	6,510	$ 7,663	$ 11,946	$ 11,356

(a)Reflects the impact of the net revenue deferral from Windows 10 of $1.3 billion, $1.7 billion, $1.6 billion, and $2.0 billion, for the first, second, third, and fourth quarter of fiscal year 2016, respectively, and $6.6 billion for fiscal year 2016.

(4)Includes $630 million of asset impairment charges related to our phone business, and $480 million of restructuring charges associated with our 2016 restructuring plans, which together decreased net income and diluted EPS by $895 million and $0.11, respectively.

Source: Company 10K and author calculations.

experience highlights an important point about financial forecasting: It is essential to analyze a company's business prospects, rather than simply extrapolate recent results and account for the business cycle.

The Concept of Financial Flexibility

Besides reflecting a company's stage of development, and therefore the categories of risk it is most likely to face, the cash flow statement provides essential information about a firm's financial flexibility. By studying the statement, an analyst can make informed judgments on such questions as:

- How safe (likely to continue being paid) is the company's dividend?
- Could the company fund its needs internally if external sources of capital suddenly become scarce or prohibitively expensive?
- Would the company be able to continue meeting its obligations if its business turned down sharply?

Exhibit 4.10 provides a condensed format that can help answer these questions. At the top is basic cash flow, defined as net income (excluding noncash components), depreciation, and deferred income taxes. This format helps the analyst quantify the company's capacity for **discretionary** outlays.

In difficult times, when a company must cut back on various expenditures to conserve cash, management faces many difficult choices. A key

EXHIBIT 4.10   Walmart Inc.

Analysis of Financial Flexibility Fiscal Period ending Jan-31-2019 ($000 omitted)	
Basic cash flow[1]	$ 27,458.0
Changes in adjusted working capital[2]	295.0
Operating cash flow	27,753.0
Capital expenditures	(10,344.0)
Discretionary cash flow	17,409.0
Total dividends paid	(6,102.0)
Other investing activities	0
Cash flow before financing	$ 11,307.0

[1]Includes net income, depreciation, and amortization, deferred income taxes, and other.
[2]Excludes cash and notes payable.
Source: Barron's and author calculations.

objective is to avoid damage to the company's long-term health. Financial flexibility is critical to meeting this objective.

Walmart, the world's largest retailer, exhibited exceptional financial flexibility in the fiscal year ending January 31, 2019. Cash generated by operations, at a robust $27.8 billion, easily covered the company's ambitious $10.3 billion capital spending program. Internally generated funds also covered the company's $6.1 billion of dividends, which, as discussed below, represent an expenditure made at the board's discretion.

Even after those uses, Walmart generated $11.3 billion of cash that was available for $7.4 billion of stock repurchases. Walmart had the flexibility to make that highly discretionary outlay because it was self-sufficient with respect to its non-discretionary expenditures. The company needed external funding, in the form of debt, mainly because it chose to make $14.7 billion of acquisitions.

Walmart's ability to self-finance its **organic growth** constitutes a huge competitive advantage. At times, new financing becomes painfully expensive, as a function of high interest rates or depressed stock prices. During the credit crunches that occasionally befall the business world, external financing is unavailable at any price.

Underlying Walmart's lack of dependence on external funds is a highly profitable discount store business. If this engine were to slow down for a time, as a result of an economic contraction or increased competitive pressures, the company would have two choices. It could reduce its rate of store additions and profit-enhancing investments in technology, or it could become more dependent on external financing. The former approach could further impair profitability, while the latter option would earmark a greater portion of Walmart's EBITDA for interest and dividends, meaning less would be available for investments to maintain or enhance competitiveness. Loss of financial flexibility, in short, leads to further loss of financial flexibility.

If a corporation's financial strain becomes acute, the board of directors may take the comparatively extreme step of cutting or eliminating the dividend. (About the only measures more extreme than elimination of the dividend are severe retrenchment, entailing a sell-off of core assets to generate cash, and cessation of interest payments, or default.) Reducing the dividend is a step that corporations try very hard to avoid, for fear of losing favor with investors and consequently suffering an increase in cost of capital. Boards sometimes go so far as to borrow to maintain a dividend at its existing rate. This tactic cannot continue over an extended period, lest interest costs rise while internal cash generation stagnates, ultimately leading to insolvency.

Notwithstanding the lengths to which corporations sometimes go to preserve dividends, reducing the dividend must be viewed as a potential means of maintaining financial flexibility in a period of depressed earnings. After all, the term *discretionary*, applied to the cash flow that remains available after operating expenses and capital expenditures, emphasizes that dividends are not contractual payments, but disbursed at the board's discretion. When preservation of the dividend jeopardizes a company's financial well-being, shareholders may actually urge the board to cut the **payout** as a means of enhancing the stock value over the longer term.

To gauge the safety of the dividend, analysts can calculate the margin by which discretionary cash flow covers it. In Walmart's case, the ratio is a comfortable $16.971 billion ÷ $6.102 billion = 2.78×. In fact, if Walmart had earned zero profit for the year, its discretionary cash flow still would have more than sufficed to make the intended dividend payment.

Walmart's degree of financial flexibility is exceptional. A significant drop in the net income of many other companies would reduce their discretionary cash flow below the level of planned dividend payments. These companies typically have an additional cushion, however, in the form of potential cutbacks in their capital budgets. A retailer could not only reduce the pace of store additions but also defer planned refurbishment of existing stores. The latter measure, though, could cut into future competitiveness. Retailers find that their sales drop off if their stores start to look tired. Similarly, an industrial company can lose its competitive edge if it drops back to maintenance-level capital spending for any extended period. This is the amount required just to keep existing plant and equipment in good working order, with no expenditures for adding to capacity or modernizing facilities to enhance productivity. Incidentally, analysts should seek independent confirmation of the figure that management cites as the maintenance level, possibly from an engineer familiar with the business. Companies may exaggerate the extent to which they can reduce capital spending to conserve cash in the event of a downturn.

One final factor in assessing financial flexibility is the change in adjusted working capital. Unlike conventional working capital (current assets minus current liabilities), this figure excludes notes payable, as well as cash and short-term investments. A company's inventories and receivables generally expand as its sales grow over time. If it has a strong balance sheet it can fund much of that cash need by increasing its trade payables (credit extended by vendors). External financing may be required, however, if accumulation of unsold goods causes inventories to rise disproportionately to sales. Similarly, if customers begin paying more slowly than formerly, receivables can widen the gap between working capital requirements and trade credit availability.

The resulting deterioration in credit quality measures (see Chapter 13), in turn, may cause vendors to reduce the amount of credit they are willing to provide. Once again, loss of financial flexibility can feed on itself. Exhibit 4.10 shows that Walmart was well insulated against such problems in the fiscal year ending January 31, 2019. The company generated $295 million of cash by increasing accounts payable and other short-term liabilities by more than the amount by which accounts receivable and inventories grew to support sales growth.

IN DEFENSE OF SLACK

Conditions are tough enough when credit is scarce, either because of general conditions in the financial markets or as a result of deterioration in a company's debt quality measures. Sometimes the situation is much worse, as a company finds itself actually prohibited from borrowing. Bank credit agreements typically impose restrictive covenants, which may include limitations on total indebtedness (see "Projecting Financial Flexibility" in Chapter 12). Beyond a certain point, a firm bound by such covenants cannot continue borrowing to meet its obligations.

A typical consequence of violating debt covenants or striving to head off bankruptcy is that management reduces discretionary expenditures to avoid losing control. Many items that a company can cut without disrupting operations in the short run are essential to its long-term health. Advertising and research are obvious targets for cutbacks. Their benefits are visible only in future periods, while their costs are apparent in the current period. Over many years, a company that habitually scrimps on such expenditures can impair its competitiveness, thereby transforming a short-term problem into a long-term one.

Avoiding this pattern of decline is the primary benefit of financial flexibility. If during good times a company can generate positive cash flow before financing, it will not have to chop capital expenditures and other outlays that represent investments in its future. Nor, in all likelihood, will a company that maintains some **slack** be forced to eliminate its dividend under duress. The company will consequently avoid tarnishing its image in the capital markets and raising the cost of future financings.

Despite the blessings that financial flexibility confers, however, maintaining a funds cushion is not universally regarded as a wise corporate policy. The opposing view is based on a definition of *free cash flow* as "cash flow in excess of that required to fund all of a firm's projects that have positive **net present values** when **discounted** at the relevant cost of capital."[3] According to this argument, management should dividend all excess cash flow to shareholders. The only alternative is to invest it in low-return projects (or possibly even lower-return marketable securities), thereby preventing shareholders from earning fair returns on a portion of their capital. Left to their own devices, argue the proponents of this view, managers will trap cash in low-return investments because their compensation tends to be positively related to the growth of assets under their control. Therefore, management should be encouraged to remit all excess cash to shareholders. If encouragement fails to do the trick, the threat of **hostile takeover** should be employed, say those who minimize the value of financial flexibility.

The argument against retaining excess cash flow certainly sounds logical. It is supported, moreover, by numerous studies[4] indicating the tendency of companies to continue investing even after they have exhausted their good opportunities. Growing as it does out of economic theory, though, the argument must be applied judiciously in practice. Overinvestment has unquestionably led, in many industries, to prolonged periods of excess capacity, producing in turn chronically poor profitability. In retrospect, the firms involved would have served their shareholders better if they had increased their dividend payouts or repurchased stock, instead of constructing new plants. That judgment, however, benefits from hindsight. Managers may have overinvested because they believed forecasts of economic growth that ultimately proved too optimistic. Had demand grown at the expected rate, a firm that had declined to expand capacity might have been unable to maintain its market share. In the long run, failing to keep up with the scale economies achieved by more expansion-minded competitors could have harmed shareholders more than a few years of excess capacity. The financial analyst's job includes making judgments about a firm's reinvestment policies – without the benefit of hindsight – and does not consist of passively accepting the prevailing wisdom that low returns in the near term prove that an industry has no future opportunities worth exploiting.

A subtler point not easily captured by theorists is that financial flexibility can translate directly into operating flexibility. Keeping cash trapped in marketable securities can enable a firm to gain an edge over lean-and-mean competitors when tight credit conditions make it difficult to finance working capital needs. Another less obvious risk of eschewing financial flexibility is the danger of permanently losing experienced skilled workers through temporary layoffs occasioned by recessions. Productivity suffers during the subsequent recovery as a consequence of laid-off skilled employees finding permanent jobs elsewhere. It may therefore be economical to continue to run plants, thereby deliberately building up inventory, to keep valued workers on the payroll. This strategy is difficult to implement without some capability of adjusting to a sudden increase in working capital financing requirements.

CONCLUSION

Over the past five decades, the statement of cash flows has become a valuable complement to the other statements. It is invaluable in many situations where the balance sheet and income statement provide only limited insight. For example, the income statement is a dubious measure of the success of a highly leveraged company that is being managed to minimize, rather than maximize, reported profits. Similarly, it is largely irrelevant whether the balance sheet of a company with an already substantially depleted net worth shows 10 percent lower equity in the current quarter than in the previous one. The primary concern of the investor or creditor at such times is whether the company can buy enough time to solve its operating problems by continuing to meet its near-term obligations.

The cash flow statement does more than enrich the analysis of companies encountering risks and opportunities that the income statement and balance sheet are not designed to portray. It also helps to identify the life cycle categories into which companies fit. At all stages of development, financial flexibility is essential to meeting the types of challenges that typically arise. The cash flow statement is the best tool for measuring flexibility, which, contrary to a widely held view, is not merely a security blanket for squeamish investors. In the hands of aggressive but prudent management, a cash flow cushion can enable a company to sustain essential long-term investment spending when competitors are forced to cut back.

A Closer Look at Profits

What Is Profit?

Profits hold an exalted place in the business world and in economic theory. The necessity of producing profits imposes order and discipline on business organizations. It fosters cost-reducing innovations, which in turn promote the efficient use of scarce resources. The profit motive also encourages savings and risk taking, two indispensable elements of economic development. Finally, profitability is a yardstick by which businesspeople can measure their achievements and justify their claims to compensation.

In view of all these essential economic functions, one might suppose that users of financial statements would have long since devised a universally agreed-upon definition of profit. This is the case, however, only at the following, extremely rudimentary level:

$$\text{Profit} = \text{Revenue} - \text{Costs}$$

Defining profit in such a manner merely stirs up questions, however: What is revenue? Which costs count? Or, more precisely, which costs count now, and which count later? Because these questions can be answered in many different ways, countless definitions of profit are in common use. For analysts of financial statements, the most important distinction to understand is between bona fide profits and accounting profits.

BONA FIDE PROFITS VERSUS ACCOUNTING PROFITS

In defining **bona fide profits,** the simple formula, revenue minus costs, represents a useful starting point. When calculating this kind of profit, the analyst must take care to consider only genuine revenues and to deduct all relevant costs. A nonexhaustive list of costs includes labor, materials, occupancy, services purchased, depreciation of equipment, and taxes. No matter how

meticulously the analyst carries out these computations, however, no calculation of profit can be satisfactory unless it passes a litmus test:

> *After a company earns a bona fide profit, its owners are wealthier
> than they were beforehand.*

To underscore the point, there can be no bona fide profit without an
increase in wealth. Bona fide profits are the only kind of profits that truly
matter in financial analysis.

As for accounting profits, generally accepted accounting principles
(GAAP) define voluminous rules for calculating them with extraordinary
precision. For financial analysts, however, the practical definition of an
accounting profit is simple:

> *An accounting profit is whatever the accounting rules say it is.*

If, during a stated interval, a business adds nothing to its owners'
wealth, but the accounting rules state that it has earned a profit, that is good
enough. An accounting profit that reflects no genuine increase in wealth is
certainly sufficient for many stock market investors. They cheerfully assign
a price-earnings multiple to any number that a reputable accounting firm
waves its magic wand over and declares to be a profit.

What Is Revenue?

Suppose, for example, that an entrepreneur launches a restaurant-franchising
business. The fictitious Salsa Meister International does not operate any
Salsa Meister restaurants. It merely sells franchises to other entrepreneurs
and collects franchise fees.

The franchised restaurants, sad to say, consistently lose money. That fact
has no bearing on Salsa Meister International's accounting profit, however.
The restaurants' operations are not part of Salsa Meister International, their
revenues are not its revenues, and their costs are not its costs. Salsa Meister International's income consists entirely of franchise fees, which it earns
by rendering the franchisees such services as developing menus, providing
accounting systems, training restaurant employees, and creating advertising
campaigns.

An astute analyst will ask how money-losing franchisees come up with
cash to pay fees. The diagram in Exhibit 5.1 answers this riddle. Salsa Meister International sells stock to the public and then lends the proceeds to
the franchisees. The franchisees send the cash right back to Salsa Meister
International under the rubric of fees. Salsa Meister International gratefully

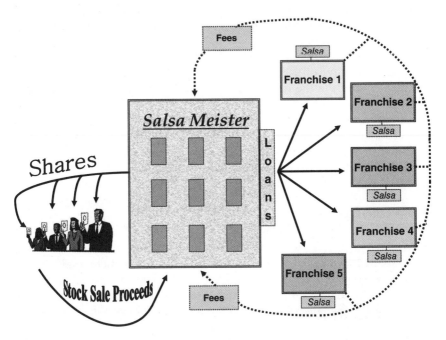

EXHIBIT 5.1 Turning Stock Market Proceeds into Revenue.

accepts the fees, which exceed the modest costs of running a corporate head-quarters, and renames them revenue.

According to GAAP, Salsa Meister International has earned a profit. Investors apply a price-earnings multiple to the accounting profit. On the strength of that valuation, the company goes forward with its next public stock offering. Once again, the proceeds finance the payment of fees by franchisees, whose numbers have meanwhile increased in connection with the Salsa Meister chain's expansion into new regions. Accounting profits rise, and the cycle of relabeling stock market proceeds, first as fees and finally as earnings, starts all over again.

The astute analyst is troubled, however. Cutting through the form of the transactions to the substance, it is clear that Salsa Meister International's wealth has not increased. Cash has simply traveled from the shareholders to the company, to the franchisees, and then back to the company, undergoing a few name changes along the way.

Merely circulating funds, it is clear, does not increase wealth. If Jack hands Jill a dollar, which she promptly hands right back to him, neither party is better off after the so-called transaction than before it. By definition, neither Jack nor Jill has earned a bona fide profit. Salsa Meister International has not earned a bona fide profit either, regardless of what GAAP may say about accounting profits.

Sooner or later, investors will come to this realization. When that happens, the company will lose its ability to manufacture accounting profits by raising new funds in the stock market. Salsa Meister's stock price will then fall to its intrinsic value—zero. Investors will suffer heavy losses, which they could have avoided by asking whether the company's reported profits truly reflected increases in wealth. Moreover, the investors will continue making similar mistakes unless they begin to understand that bona fide profits sometimes differ radically from accounting profits.

WHICH COSTS COUNT?

The willingness to take accounting profits at something other than face value is an essential element of genuinely useful financial statement analysis. It is likewise imperative that analysts exercise care in deciding what to substitute for a GAAP definition of profit. Once they leave the GAAP world of agreed-upon rules, analysts enter a free market of ideas, where numerous parties hawk competing versions of earnings.

Corporations have vastly increased their promulgation of non-GAAP numbers in this century. By 2017, the independent research provider Audit Analytics found that fully 97 percent of S&P 500 companies included some self-produced measures in their earnings releases, up from a little over half two decades earlier. Between 1996 and 2016 the average number of non-GAAP items in those statements rose from just over two to more than seven.[1]

Analysts need to be discriminating in their use of these alternative presentations of reality, but the same can be said of GAAP numbers. Economist Andrew Smithers found that in the ten-year periods ending 1957 to 2002, the reported earnings of the companies constituting the S&P 500 were about as volatile as the top-down corporate earnings drawn from U.S. national accounts. In subsequent years, Smithers found, the companies' reported earnings were five times more volatile than the after-tax profits reported in the national accounts.[2]

Smithers deemed it highly unlikely that the national accounts data had become unreliable. The other explanation for his findings was that accounting reforms of the 1990s rendered GAAP earnings much more volatile than formerly. Shifting numerous items from **historical cost** accounting to **fair value** accounting was meant to promote more efficient allocation of capital. The unintended effect was to make reported earnings more procyclical, as asset prices incorporated estimates of future profits as well as currently realized earnings. This was one reason reported earnings became less closely correlated with movements in stock prices. Analysts who deployed their skills within investment organizations had little choice but to pay greater attention to companies' non-GAAP figures, notwithstanding the underlying calculations' lack of standardization.

Many of the deviations from GAAP hang on the question of which costs to eliminate from the calculations. While some of the popular income statement variants offer insight into knotty problems of financial statement analysis, others have the opposite effect of obscuring the facts. Many issuers of financial statements attempt to exploit dissatisfaction with GAAP by encouraging analysts to adopt earnings measures that make their own profits appear higher than either their accounting profits or their bona fide profits.

In 2020, some companies broke new ground by adding back costs imposed by the COVID-19 pandemic. German manufacturer Schenck Process turned a 16 percent year-over-year earnings decline in that year's first quarter into an increase of nearly 20 percent by steering analysts toward its EBITDAC, i.e., earnings before interest, tax, depreciation, amortization, and coronavirus.[3]

Not surprisingly, corporations' stepped-up use of non-GAAP has attracted regulators' attention. The Securities and Exchange Commission's Regulation G does not prohibit companies from presenting non-standard numbers in their earnings releases. In those releases, however, companies are required to explain why they are providing a non-GAAP metric and quantitatively reconcile it with the most directly comparable GAAP metric. Companies must also present the comparable GAAP metric at least as prominently as the non-GAAP one.

The archetype for many alternative earnings measures is a version that adds back depreciation. As far back as 1930, one investment expert urged investors to ignore accounting-based earnings in the following words:

> *Textbooks will advise the investor to look for earnings figures which give effect to depreciation charges. But depreciation, after all, is a purely accounting item, and can be adjusted, within limits, to show such net earnings as are desired. Therefore it would seem preferable for the investor to obtain, if possible, earnings before depreciation, and to make his own estimate of depreciation in arriving at approximate net earnings.*[4]

Observe that the author does not dispute the relevance of depreciation to the calculation of earnings. Rather, he objects that it is too malleable.[5] The issuer of the statements can raise or lower its reported earnings simply by using its latitude to assume shorter or longer average lives for its depreciable assets.

It is fair to assume, in the case of financial statements that companies present to potential investors, that "such net earnings as are desired" are higher than the company's bona fide profits. Therefore, the necessary adjustment is to *increase* depreciation and thereby *reduce* earnings. The author agrees with today's boosters of alternative earnings measures that proper analysis requires adjustments to reported income, but he is very far from urging analysts to ignore depreciation altogether.

Promoters of many companies with negligible reported earnings, on the other hand, are not bashful about urging investors to disregard depreciation. This audacious assault on the very foundations of **accrual accounting** draws its inspiration from the world of privately owned real estate, where the logic of managing a public company is turned upside down. Instead of exploiting every bit of latitude in the accounting rules to maximize reported earnings, private owners of real estate strive to minimize reported income and, by extension, income taxes. Accordingly, when a private investor acquires a building (a depreciable), the investor typically attributes a large portion and the land that it sits on (which is not depreciable), they typically attribute as large a portion of the purchase price as possible to the building. That treatment maximizes the depreciation expense and minimizes the owner's taxes.

Let us suppose that annual rental revenue on the building offsets the landlord's out-of-pocket expenses, such as maintenance, repairs, property taxes, and interest on the property's mortgage. The owner, in other words, is breaking even, before taking into account the noncash expense of depreciation. Including depreciation, the property shows an annual loss, which reduces the owner's income tax bill. Let us also assume that after a few years, the owner sells the land and building. After paying of the mortgage balance, the owner walks away with more cash than originally invested, thanks to the tendency of real estate values to rise over time.

Recapping, the real estate investor has sold the property for more than was paid. Their gain has not been reduced along the way by net cash outlays on operations. The investor's gain has not been reduced along the way by net cash outlays on operations. On the contrary. . . the rise in the investor's wealth. The key point is that the investor is wealthier now than prior to purchasing the building. According to our definition, the investor has realized a bona fide profit, despite reporting losses every single year. Adding to the paradox is the investor's success in selling the property for a gain. Economic theory states that an investment has value only because it produces profits. By extension, the value can increase only if the profits increase. In this instance, however, the property's value rose despite an uninterrupted flow of red ink.

Naturally, these curious events have a rational explanation. The rate at which the tax code allows owners to write off property overstates actual wear and tear. Over the typically very long life of a building, it may get depreciated several times over for tax purposes. The disparity between economic depreciation and tax-based depreciation may be viewed as a subsidy for socially productive investment. Alternatively, it can be seen as a testament to the real estate operators' influence over the legislators who write the tax code.

Either way, a conventional income statement provides a cockeyed view of the profitability of buying and selling buildings. A closer approximation of reality ignores the depreciation expense altogether and focuses on **cash-on cash-profit**. In the simplest terms, the owners lay out a sum at the beginning of the investment and take out a bigger sum at the end, while also generating cash – through tax savings – during the period in which they own the building.

How Far Can the Concept Be Stretched?

To a limited extent, a profitability analysis that ignores depreciation is applicable outside the world of real estate. In the broadcasting business, companies typically record depreciation and amortization expense that far exceeds physical wear and tear on assets. For example, when a company buys a radio or television station, the price reflects a comparatively small component of plant and equipment. The larger portion of the station's value derives from its exclusive right to utilize part of the broadcasting spectrum, a scarce resource that tends to become more valuable over time. Much as in the real estate illustration, the broadcaster may show perennial losses after depreciation, yet realize a handsome profit when it finally sells the station. Instead of analyzing broadcasters on the basis of conventional net income, it is appropriate for analysts to focus on **broadcast cash flow**, usually defined as:

operating income + depreciation and amortization + corporate overhead

(A more meticulous calculation of broadcast cash flow deducts cash outlays for acquisition of new programming while adding back the amortization of the cost of previously acquired programming; both items can be found on the statement of cash flows.)

Clearly, the deliberate neglect of depreciation is an analytical option that should be used with discretion. In many industries, fixed assets consist mainly of machines or vehicles that really do diminish in value through use. The major risk of analytical error does not arise from the possibility that reported depreciation expense will substantially exceed economic depreciation, but the reverse.

Through a false analogy with real estate and broadcasting, any marginally unprofitable company in a capital-intensive business can declare itself to be in the black. The trick is simply to proclaim that analysts should no longer consider depreciation. Supposed earnings generated in such fashion qualify as neither accounting profits nor bona fide profits, however.

CONCLUSION

Despite the critical importance of measuring profit, businesspeople cannot produce a definition that is satisfactory in every situation. Even the simple formula of revenue minus costs founders on the malleability of accounting-based revenues and costs. As Chapters 6 and 7 demonstrate, these basic measures of corporate performance are far too subject to manipulation and distortion to be taken at face value. Also, our brief discussions of real estate and leveraged buyouts show that net earnings can be calculated in perfect accordance with GAAP yet bear little relation to an investor's rate of return.

In light of such observations, financial analysts must walk a fine line. On the one hand, they must not lose touch with economic reality by hewing to accounting orthodoxy. On the other hand, they must not accept the version of reality that seekers of cheap capital would like to foist on them. Analysts should be skeptical of claims that a business's alleged costs are mere accounting conventions and that anyone who believes otherwise is a fuddy-duddy.

CHAPTER 6

Revenue Recognition

Experience teaches that it can be dangerous to accept reported revenues at face value, even if they have been audited. Many corporations employ highly aggressive recognition practices that comply with GAAP yet distort the underlying economic reality. Sometimes, executives hell-bent on making their numbers will cross the line into fraudulent revenue recognition. Often, outward signs of exceptional success indicate in reality a high probability of downward revisions of previously reported revenues. Under intense pressure to maintain their stock prices, companies characterized by extremely rapid sales growth seem particularly prone to taking liberties.

MAKING IT UP AT GOWEX

Gowex had a lot to celebrate in March 2014. Since its initial public offering four years earlier, the Spanish provider of wi-fi hotspots and support services for mobile phone carriers had seen its stock rise by 2,700 percent. On March 20 the company announced its preliminary consolidated sales figures for 2013, which it described as "more than outstanding."[1] At €182.8 million, sales were up by 60 percent over 2012 and exceeded the company's own forecasts by 7.53 percent.

Lavish outside recognition had accompanied Gowex's financial success. In 2011 the company won the Internet Day prize for Best Company. Two years later the first European Small & Mid-Cap Awards honored Gowex as the Best New Listed Company. In 2014 the Spanish government added its Start-Ex award to the company's plaudits. On March 28 Gowex's stock reached an all-time high of €26.00, up from just €4.32 one year earlier. On June 25, 2014, founder and Chief Executive Officer Jenaro Garcia predicted that Gowex would soon be providing wi-fi service to 20 percent of the earth's population.

The following week, in an astounding reversal of fortune, Gowex's shares plunged by 60 percent in just two days, closing at €7.92 on July 2.

(The stock had already fallen by 23 percent from its March 28 peak.) Gowex stock was suspended from trading on July 3.

On July 5 CEO Garcia resigned after admitting that he had falsified Gowex's financial statements by overstating revenues for at least the last four years. A few days later he acknowledged that the fakery dated back to at least 2005. The company announced that it would file for insolvency. On July 16 Santander Private Banking Gestion reported that it had placed a value of zero on the Gowex shares in three investment funds that it managed.

Clues to the fraudulent accounting responsible for Gowex's downfall were detectable by astute financial analysts. In fact, it was a report[2] alleging a tenfold overstatement of revenues, published on July 1, 2014, by Gotham City Research LLC, that precipitated the stock price collapse. The short-selling firm's analysis concluded that Gowex's actual revenues were no more than 10 percent of what the company reported.

In a classic response, Garcia initially denied the research report's accusations, calling it "categorically false"[3] and "defamatory."[4] He threatened legal action against Gotham City. The company's auditor made jokes about the comic book character Batman, who lives in the fictitious Gotham City.

Before long, however, Garcia conceded that the charges were true. Court testimony by Chief Financial Officer Francisco Martinez Marugan detailed Garcia's orders to employees to falsify financial data and engage in double billing. Garcia admitted that Gowex had created fictitious customers, in one instance by paying his maid €300 to sign papers creating a bogus company.

Gowex's share price began its slide before Gotham City's bombshell landed, even as Garcia conducted a cross-European roadshow with institutional investors. Analysts worried that the shares had gotten overvalued and also expressed concerns about the company's transparency. Two analysts said they had never managed to meet with or speak to the company's investor relations manager – CEO Garcia's wife, Florencia Mate Garabito.

In eight months of intensive research, digging into publicly available information and speaking to Gowex executives and the company's competitors, Gotham City uncovered additional reasons for skepticism. For example, Gowex said it was receiving €7.5 million for a contract with New York City, but then told Gotham that the payment was €2 million. The New York Economic Development Corp. said the true figure was just $245,000, equivalent to roughly €179,000 on July 1, 2014.

Gotham City found another discrepancy in statements made at various times about Gowex's revenue. In 2003 Garcia stated that the company cleared a large profit on turnover (revenue) of €42.0 million in 2002. According to Gowex's IPO offering circular in 2010, however, revenues totaled only €2.7 million in 2003.

Further doubts about the integrity of Gowex's financial reporting arose from the fact that its audit fee totaled only 0.04 percent to 0.06 percent of revenues during 2011–2013. Gotham showed that over the same period, five comparable companies' fees collectively averaged 0.77 percent to 0.94 percent of revenues. Gowex's audit fee, by Gotham City's reckoning, implied a business 5 to 10 percent its supposed size.

Gowex's auditor constituted another red flag. As Gotham pointed out, it is very rare for a company with $1 billion to $2 billion of market value to select an obscure auditor. Gowex's appeared to be the only public company client of M&A Auditores, S.L., a name largely unknown even within Spain. M&A's office was a small room in an apartment complex. The auditor's business card did not contain a business email address, so he wrote his personal Gmail address on the back of the card he provided to Gotham's research staff.

Gotham's 93-page research report concluded that Gowex's revenues were 90 percent less than reported and that its true stock value was zero. Its investigations found that 90 percent of the company's Telecom revenue originated from undisclosed, related parties. Gowex Telecom's website had not been updated in years, suggesting to Gotham that it was no longer in business.

Troublingly, too, Gowex did not publicly disclose such basic metrics as its hotspot count or segment details of its wireless revenue. When pressed by Gotham, Garcia said Gowex's hotspots numbered in the 100,000s. Another analyst said Garcia quoted him a figure of 200,000. Examination of Gowex's hotspot map produced a count of only 5,530.

Just one example of Gotham's methodology involved Gowex's listing of Telefonica among its largest customers. Gotham confirmed that there was a contract between the two companies but established that no payments were going from Telefonica to Gowex. Gowex was making payments to Telefonica for purposes that Gotham could not determine.

Gotham's deep dive into the underlying facts clearly established that Gowex's reported numbers were not credible. On a completely different track, Messod Daniel Beneish of the Kelley School of Business at Indiana University analyzed the company's reported numbers with a model he devised to ferret out evidence of earnings manipulation. Shortly before the revelations of fraudulent reporting devastated the company's market value, Beneish's model indicated a 71.3 percent probability that Gowex was manipulating its financials. That meant, by Beneish's reckoning, that Gowex was 103.3 times as likely to be a fraud than the average firm in the market.

Beneish's model is described in a 1999 *Financial Analysts Journal* article.[5] The model's explanatory variables and the reasoning behind them are shown below. "High" levels for variables 3, 4, and 7 are in comparison to averages of industry peer companies.

1. *Days' sales in receivables index.* Definition: Current year's ratio of days' sales in receivables divided by previous year's. If days' sales in receivables increases sharply, it may indicate that the company is booking fictitious sales on which cash is not being collected.

2. *Gross margin index.* Definition: Previous year's gross margin divided by current year's gross margin. If this ratio exceeds 1x, gross margin has deteriorated. That is a sign that a company's prospects are worsening, potentially tempting management to manipulate its earnings.

3. *Asset quality index.* Definition: Current year's ratio of noncurrent assets other than property, plant, and equipment (PP&E) to total assets, divided by previous year's ratio. The future benefits of non-PP&E assets are potentially less certain than those of PP&E assets. A rise in the asset quality index is a hint that the company may be increasingly deferring, rather than expensing, costs, which would imply an overstatement of current earnings.

4. *Sales growth index.* Definition: Ratio of current year's sales to previous year's sales. High sales growth does not automatically imply manipulation. High-growth companies, however, often experience intense pressure to achieve earnings targets. Knowing that the first indication of a slowdown will deal a severe blow to its stock price, such a company has a greater incentive to manipulate earnings than one for which investors expect only sales growth in line with nominal (inflation-included) Gross Domestic Product.

5. *Sales, general, and administrative expenses index.* Definition: Current year's ratio of sales, general, and administrative expenses to sales, divided by previous year's ratio. A high level of this index suggests poor prospects for the company, hence a strong incentive for manipulation.

6. *Leverage index.* Definition: Current year's ratio of total debt to total assets, divided by previous year's ratio. If this index is greater than one, indicating rising leverage, the company may have an incentive to manipulate its earnings in order to avoid triggering a default on its debt covenants.

7. *Total accruals to total assets.* Definition: Change in working capital accounts other than cash less depreciation, divided by total assets. If this ratio is high, it may indicate that management is making discretionary accounting choices to alter earnings.

As detailed in his *Financial Analysts Journal* article, Beneish adjusted the inputs through quantitative techniques designed to eliminate distortion that may arise from a ratio employed in a year-over-year comparison having a small denominator.

Beneish has made his model available free of charge at https://apps .kelley.iu.edu/Beneish/MScore/mscore/MScoreInput. Whether or not the above-listed variables are fed into Beneish's model, calculating them can help to identify potential manipulators. Beneish drew on previous empirical research in choosing which ratios and indexes to incorporate. The key for variables 3, 4, and 7 is to use them to compare a company to its industry peers. Beneish identified peers via two-digit Standard Industry Classification codes, which are used by various U.S. government agencies.

Any one of the variables may emit a seemingly worrisome signal that turns out to have an innocent explanation. Multiple indications of trouble, however, suggest that there is indeed fire where the smoke has been spotted. The company's revenues may even turn out to be as phony as Gowex's were.

GLOBO'S FORESEEN FALL FROM GRACE

Globo, an Athens-based producer of mobile-device software, suffered a seemingly sudden reversal of fortune in 2015. From its 2014 year-end price of £40.00 the company's stock soared to £62.25 on June 10. Nine days later, Standard & Poor's assigned the proposed $180 million senior secured note offering by Globo's U.S. subsidiary a BB– rating, a comparatively high grade within the speculative category. The rapidly expanding company planned to use the proceeds of the debt sale primarily to fund acquisitions. On August 18, the International Data Corporation's 2014 report on Worldwide Enterprise Mobility Management noted that Globo's latest year-over-year 116.9 percent revenue increase measured more than four times the industry growth rate. A little more than two months later, however, the company requested a suspension of trading in its shares. By then the stock price was less than half the June 10 peak, at £28.25. On October 26, Standard & Poor's downgraded the company from BB– to CCC and withdrew its rating on Globo's still uncompleted bond offering.

The event that triggered Globo's swift fall from grace was the October 22, 2015, publication of a research report, authored by hedge fund firm Quintessential Capital Management, labeling the company a fraud. Predictably, Globo initially denied all of the report's allegations. On October 24, however, Founder and Chief Executive Officer Costis Papadimitrakopoulos submitted his resignation at an emergency meeting of the board of directors and confirmed the falsification of financial data and misrepresentation of the company's financial position. The board accepted the CEO's resignation, as well as that of Chief Financial Officer Dimitris Gryparis.

To observers not previously familiar with Globo, its demise appeared to be an overnight event. Long before October 2015, however, there were numerous clues that something was amiss. To begin, with, in 2014's first quarter Globo fired its auditor. In a letter to shareholders dated March 6, 2014, CEO Papadimitrakopoulos stated that the board had decided to replace BDO with Grant Thornton because BDO's proposed cost of its audit was not competitive. In a statement under Section 519 of the U.K.'s Companies Act of 2006, however, BDO said that it was asked to resign because of an inability to agree on the scope of the audit. BDO specified that under Globo's terms it would not have sufficient involvement in the work of component auditors, without which it could not obtain sufficient information on which to base its opinion.

Even prior to the appearance of that classic red flag, however, Ennismore Fund Management detected several trouble signs in Globo's financial statements. To begin with, Globo's 2013 Interim Results announcement reported that €10 million of it €30 million total revenues for the period came from its GO!Enterprise product, an app by which a company's employees can obtain remote access to work servers from their own personal mobile devices. (This product category goes by the acronym BYOD, for "bring your own device.") Of the €10 million of GO!Enterprise revenues, said Globo, 57 percent came from license sales. Globo declined Ennismore's request to name any GO!Enterprise customers. The London-based investment management firm attempted to contact most of the corporate customers named in Globo results and presentations. None of them confirmed that they were GO!Enterprise BYOD product licensees and some stated that they were not, although some apparently used other Globo products or services.

Globo reported in its 2012 final results that GO!Enterprise had a total of 250,000 active licensees through two license schemes. Revenue growth reported for the first half of 2013 implied a significant increase in active licensees during that period. The company's investor relations department confirmed to Ennismore that end users accessed the GO!Enterprise software via download from Apple's AppStore or Android Market, with two-thirds of users utilizing Google's Android operating system.

According to Ennismore, the company mentioned no other download method in its September 2012 discussions. Yet as of August 29, 2013, the GO!Enterprise app had been downloaded from Google Play, the largest app store by far for Android users, only 1,000 to 5,000 times. By Ennismore's calculation, that amounted to less than 5 percent of the end users implied by the product's reported revenue. By contrast, Good Technology's comparable BYOD product had been downloaded 500,000 to 1,000,000 times on Google Play, supporting the notion that downloading from app stores is the industry-standard distribution method.

Ennismore also noted that Globo had not generated positive free cash flow in any year since 2004, the first year for which financial statements were available. The firm's report further stated that "from the growth in receivables, it appears that little revenue has been collected over the past year." Precisely pinning down the increase in trade receivables was not feasible because the figure reported by Globo did not adjust for the disposal of 51 percent of the company's Greek subsidiary near the end of 2012. Ennismore calculated, however, that if the subsidiary's year-end 2012 trade receivables approximated those of June 30, 2012, then trade receivables for continuing operations rose by about 150 percent in 2012, an amount roughly equivalent to all of the year's reported GO!Enterprise revenue.

Internally, Ennismore conducted further analysis that compared Globo with mobile products industry peers on a variety of financial ratios. The companies displayed in Exhibit 6.1 include both the industry leader, Good Technology Corporation, and the field's one other listed company, Mobile-Iron, Inc. The other three shown in the table are large companies with mobile security among their product offerings.

In each category, Globo Plc was an outlier in 2014. For example, the first column of numbers shows that its operating margin was 32 percent, even though Good Technology and MobileIron were at deeply negative levels.

EXHIBIT 6.1   Mobile Products Company Peer Comparison – 2014

Company	Operating Profit as % of Revenues	Trade Receivables Days Sales Outstanding	Accrued Income as % of Revenues	Unearned Income as % of Revenues	Funding from Working Capital as % of Revenues
Citrix Systems	14 (4)	58 (5)	63 (6)	49 (4)	−67 (3)
Globo Plc	32 (1)	164 (1)	263 (1)	4 (6)	56 (1)
Good Technology Corporation	−36 (5)	90 (2)	109 (2)	201 (1)	−70 (4)
Mobilelron, Inc.	−67 (6)	83 (3)	83 (4)	43 (5)	−67 (3)
Symantec Corporation	21 (2)	42 (6)	72 (5)	54 (3)	−85 (6)
VMware, Inc.	19 (3)	70 (4)	99 (3)	76 (2)	−83 (5)

Source: Ennismore Fund Management.

Strong margins in a business in which direct competitors were losing money justified skepticism about the validity of the profits Globo was reporting.

Further evidence that Globo's sales were inflated appeared in the form of its 164 days sales outstanding (DSO) of trade receivables. That was almost double the level reported by industry leader Good Technology. Bloated receivables balances are a classic red flag, indicating that sales are not turning into cash receipts – possibly because they are fictitious. Furthermore, software companies do not ordinarily generate large receivables. They typically sell their products through licenses, with cash paid in advance, or by subscription.

Globo's way-outside-the-mainstream accrued income as a percentage of revenues raised similar concerns. This item refers to revenue that the company has already recognized but for which customers have not yet been billed. Even more troubling, Globo showed only a negligible 4 percent of unearned income as a percentage of revenue. That contrasted radically with Good Technology's 201 percent and MobileIron's 43 percent. Unearned income is generally a large item for software companies, which have an obligation to provide services for which they have already been paid.

As a result of its high DSO and low unearned income, Globo required substantial outside funding of its working capital. Its peers, on the other hand, *generated* sizable funds from working capital, as indicated in the table by negative working capital funding as a percentage of revenue.

To seasoned analysts, Globo's sharp divergences from industry norms on all of these ratios raised questions about the validity of its balance sheet. Globo drew down roughly €25 million of a revolving credit facility in the first half of 2015, even though it reported that it ended 2014 with €82 million in cash and €40 million in net (of debt) cash. Ennismore noted that revolvers are there to be drawn when needed. Why would the company incur significant interest costs when it supposedly had as much cash as it required sitting in the bank? That troubling question helps to explain why the 2015 Quintessential Capital Management report that precipitated the company's collapse was titled, "Our Final Opinion: It's a Greek Parmalat." (See Chapter 11. A major red flag prior to that company's bankruptcy was its heavy borrowing despite claiming to have a huge cash balance.)

Based on its findings, Ennismore sold Globo's shares short, as disclosed in its January 22, 2014, report. Short-selling, to be sure, is not part of every investor's repertoire. Applying the techniques detailed in Ennismore's report can, however, benefit long-only market players. They may avoid future collapses of stocks that skyrocketed with the help of misleading or even fraudulent financial reporting.

CHANNEL-STUFFING IN THE DRUG BUSINESS

On April 3, 2002, Bristol-Myers Squibb shares plummeted by as much as 14 percent in after-hours trading after the company said first-quarter earnings from operations would be $0.44 to $0.47 a share. Analysts surveyed by Thomson Financial/First Call had been expecting $0.56. For the full year, said the pharmaceutical producer, earnings would drop by at least 25 percent from 2001's $2.41 a share.

In the wake of the negative surprise, Chief Executive Officer Peter Dolan assumed direct responsibility for the worldwide medicines business. The previous head of the unit left the company. Two weeks later, the company announced that its chief financial officer would step down as well.

The explanation for the sudden drop in projected earnings was that in 2001 Bristol-Myers gave wholesalers discounts to induce them to buy its products at a much faster rate than necessary to fill prescriptions at pharmacies. That boosted revenues for certain drugs in 2001, as sales to wholesalers ran above end demand by consumers. In 2002, however, instead of reordering, wholesalers worked down their bloated inventories to supply their pharmacy customers. Bristol-Myers's sales to wholesalers consequently slackened. Dolan told analysts and investors that the company was cutting back shipments and that 2002 profits would depend on how quickly the wholesalers' inventory levels could be reduced.

Channel-stuffing is a security analysts' term for the financial reporting gimmick that Bristol-Myers employed to accelerate future revenues to the current period. Drug wholesalers were happy to hold more inventory than they needed, as long as the discounts they received were large enough to cover the related **carrying costs**. Expiration dates for the drugs they took into inventory were typically about two years in the future, so there was little risk that the products would lose their value while sitting in the wholesalers' warehouses. Furthermore, wholesalers that bought extra drugs at the current price stood to gain from subsequent increases in the retail price by the manufacturer. The price hikes would allow them to take higher markups on inventory purchased at the old price.

Why, though, would Bristol-Myers bother to stuff its wholesale distribution channels, especially considering that the discounts represented sales dollars forgone and never to be recovered? Wholesalers could absorb only so much redundant inventory. Sooner or later, the scheme would have to end, making it apparent that the company had overstated earnings by borrowing sales from future periods.

That is exactly what happened to Bristol-Myers. On March 10, 2003, the company restated its financial statements for 1999 through 2001 to correct "errors and inappropriate accounting." The company chopped earnings from continuing operations by about $900 million, partially offset by an upward revision for 2002. Earlier, the company had told investors that its planned restatement would merely shift reported revenues from earlier periods to 2002 and 2003. As it turned out, however, the company deleted $2.5 billion from the earlier years and booked only $1.9 billion in the later years, explaining that the disappearance of $0.6 billion was "primarily due to changes in accruals from sales returns, rebates,"[6] and accounting changes. Bristol-Myers stock, which had reached a peak of $70.37 at the end of 2000, closed at $22.51. Even after this damage to investors, Bristol-Myers was not done with its revisions. On March 16, 2004, the company restated its 1999 through 2002 earnings and its 2003 earnings upward.

Background of a Doomed Scheme

The stock's precipitous decline during 2001 and 2002 helped to explain why Bristol-Myers manipulated its earnings in a manner that was sure to prove unsustainable. Along with other pharmaceutical producers, Bristol-Myers was feeling profit pressures due to difficulties in developing new drugs to replace sales of products on which patent protection was expiring. The company had not generated a single major drug from billions of research dollars since the 1989 merger of Bristol-Myers and Squibb. Management's biggest hope, the hypertension drug Vanlev, failed to obtain Food and Drug Administration approval in 2000 after adverse side effects were discovered. In 2001, the company suffered embarrassment when it agreed to pay $2 billion for cancer drug Erbitux, a discovery of biotechnology company ImClone Systems that later failed to obtain Food and Drug Administration approval.

In 1996, then-CEO Charles Heimbold Jr. promised investors 12 percent annual earnings growth through 2000. That target proved elusive as industry competition escalated and a low-priced generic alternative threatened sales of a top-selling Bristol-Myers cancer drug. Following a late 1999 meeting, Heimbold replaced Donald Haydon Jr., the head of the medicines group. According to past and present company executives interviewed by the *Wall Street Journal*,[7] Haydon was known for speaking candidly about Bristol-Myers's declining sales prospects. Consequently, his reassignment was taken as a message that executives must meet their sales quotas at all costs. At that point, the medicines group began offering wholesalers discounts to induce them to order at higher levels than expected pharmacy prescriptions justified.

In addition, according to the interviewed executives, Bristol-Myers started to pump up the bottom line by taking into earnings portions of restructuring reserves created in earlier periods. This was contrary to Securities and Exchange Commission (SEC) accounting policy, reiterated in a 1999 bulletin, requiring that such reserves be used exclusively for specified purposes and prohibiting them from being taken into earnings in small amounts over time. Also suspect was Bristol-Myers's repeated practice of establishing restructuring reserves that exactly equaled gains on asset sales. In addition, the executives said, the company frequently added a penny or two to earnings per share (EPS) through gains on sales of small product lines, without reporting the divestments or highlighting them as one-time events. The SEC frowned on withholding information about such transactions on claims of immateriality and stated that even if one small transaction could be legitimately ignored, failing to disclose a number of them could be materially misleading. Finally, some of the interviewed executives contended that in mid-2001, Bristol-Myers overstated the portion of its $7.8 billion acquisition of DuPont's drug business that was attributable to in-process research and development and therefore qualified for immediate write-off under GAAP. The SEC had long claimed that companies were overvaluing in-process R&D to minimize the amount of goodwill that might cause a subsequent write-down. Executives interviewed by the *Wall Street Journal* contended that the company overstated the in-process R&D write-off to create the possibility of reversing portions of it in the future, as yet one more way to tweak reported earnings.

Company officials strenuously denied that its accounting policies were geared toward managing earnings or, by extension, maximizing the compensation of senior executives whose compensation was linked to the company's stock price. Bristol-Myers's March 10, 2003, write-down, however, came in the context of accelerating SEC and Federal Bureau of Investigation inquiries into senior management's role in the improper accounting.

In August 2004, Bristol-Myers agreed to pay $150 million to settle SEC charges of accounting fraud. This was followed in June 2005 by a $300 million settlement of Justice Department charges that also arose from inventory manipulation. The company further agreed that CEO Dolan would surrender the title of chairman and pledged to endow a chair in business ethics at Seton Hall University Law School. Christopher J. Christie, the U.S. attorney in Newark who was subsequently elected governor of New Jersey, said the scheme reflected a corporate culture that emphasized higher sales at all costs. "These people had knowledge which they should have disclosed to the investing public, which they did not," Christie commented. "It's not a channel-stuffing case. It's a failure-to-disclose case."[8]

Detecting Excessive Inventory

Not everyone was caught entirely off guard by Bristol-Myers's revelation of clogged-up distribution channels. Several days before the company's April 3, 2002, announcement, Merrill Lynch analyst Steven Tighe wrote that the inventory in the wholesale distribution chain for the company's top 10 core retail brands could total $500 million to $800 million.[9] That would approximate 2.42 times average weekly sales, an abnormally high level. Tighe estimated that the resulting sales deceleration would penalize Bristol-Myers earnings per share by $0.02 to $0.03 in 2002's first quarter.

The analyst derived his estimate of wholesale inventories for Bristol Myers's 10 major drugs, representing 50 percent of pharmaceutical revenues, from price and prescription statistics of IMS Health, a vendor of health care data. For example, IMS reported that pharmacy-level sales of Pravachol, a cholesterol-reducing drug, grew by 8 percent in 2001 and the retail price increased by 6 percent. Bristol-Myers reported a 21 percent sales gain for the year, implying a gap of 7 percent versus the sell-through at pharmacies.[10] The largest such sales disparity, amounting to $1.7 billion, involved Glucophage, an oral antidiabetic. According to IMS, prescriptions declined by 8 percent, offsetting an 8 percent retail price increase, yet Bristol-Myers recorded an 18 percent sales gain. Tighe reckoned that Glucophage wholesale inventories equaled a staggering 78 percent of his estimated 2002 sales for the brand.

It turned out that the inventory bloat and resulting earnings impact were even greater than Tighe's analysis suggested. Still, the detection of channel-stuffing was an alarm bell for the impending stock price decline. More impressively still, UBS Warburg analyst C. J. Sylvester warned of excess inventory on the order of $550 million in September 2001, half a year before the company dropped its bombshell.

Unfortunately for most users of financial statements, annual subscriptions to the data required for this sort of analysis, provided by companies such as IMS and NDCHealth, run into tens of thousands of dollars. The Bristol-Myers Squibb case study nevertheless illustrates the value of testing a company's reported earnings against independently provided information. Publicly available statistics for sales in certain industries, such as automobiles and casinos, can provide a helpful check.

A SECOND TAKE ON EARNINGS

What I like to do is get in the car and drive around and do drive-by shootings. You can haul someone out of their car and beat on them and steal their money and their car. It's kind of amusing that you have that ability.[11]

These are not the words of a career criminal, but of one of the many devotees of *Grand Theft Auto 3*, a video game produced by Take-Two Interactive Software. Another way that players score in the hugely popular game is to have sex with a prostitute, then murder her and steal her money. Other popular strategies consist of shooting random pedestrians and bludgeoning them with a baseball bat. Such features have earned *Grand Theft Auto 3* the distinction of being banned in Australia.

Less brutal, but nonimaginary, misdeeds won Take-Two a place in the annals of financial misrepresentation. The story began to unfold after the company's share price more than doubled in less than six months. Even at that, some experts considered the stock undervalued relative to industry peers such as Electronic Arts and Activision, giving rise to speculation that Take-Two might be an attractive candidate for acquisition by Microsoft.

Near-term dreams of continued upward momentum in the stock were shattered on December 14, 2001. Take-Two plunged by $4.72 to $10.33, a 31 percent drop, on rumors that the company might have to restate its earnings. The rumors proved on the mark. Take-Two announced on December 17 that it would restate its earnings for the first three quarters of the fiscal year ending October 31, 2001. According to management, the adjustment arose because the company recorded revenue on some games it sold to "certain independent third-party distributors," but which were later returned to or repurchased by Take-Two. The company estimated that earnings per share for fiscal 2000 would be restated from $0.88 to $0.75–$0.77.

Surprisingly to some observers, Take-Two's stock rose by $3.23 to $13.56, a 31 percent gain, on December 17. To short seller Marc Cohodes of Rocker Partners, the company's announcement was evidence that it was relying on accounting gimmickry. As he characterized it, Take-Two had been selling products to itself and including those sales in its revenues.[12] President Paul Eibeler, however, complained that the restatements were overshadowing Take-Two's "underlying strength"[13] and that the company's prospects for fiscal 2002 were strong. Some Wall Street analysts shared that view. Wedbush Morgan Securities's Miguel Iribarren reiterated his buy recommendation with a one-year price target of $25. Commerce Capital Markets' Richard Zimmerman confirmed his strong buy with a target of $20.

For the next few months, the financial reporting news got worse. On January 22, 2002, Take-Two announced that it would postpone the release of its fourth quarter and fiscal year-end results. The Nasdaq stock market promptly halted trading in Take-Two's shares. On February 12, the company restated its fiscal year 2001 earnings per share from $0.88 to $0.23, while also slightly reducing its reported per-share loss for the first nine months of fiscal 2002 from ($0.11) to ($0.09). In addition, Take-Two disclosed that the SEC had launched an investigation of its accounting. The following day, another classic red flag appeared, as the company's chief financial officer, Albert Pastino, resigned.

Despite these adverse developments, when trading in Take-Two shares resumed on February 15, some analysts remained upbeat. Morgan Keegan's Bob DeLean commented, "On the negative side, management has no credibility and you have historically aggressive accounting. But going forward, they are having success with a couple of big hits and the balance sheet is going to look a lot better."[14] He rated the stock outperform, with a six-month target of $30–$35. Rocker Partners' Cohodes remained the skeptic, arguing, "The numbers have been made up, that we know for sure. Everything else is speculation."[15]

In this instance, contrary to the lesson taught by many other cases of financial misreporting, it paid to accept the discredited management's assurances that the company's business prospects looked bright. Analyst Iribarren's target of $20 by December 2002 was achieved in April of that year, with the Standard & Poor's 500 Index nearly unchanged over the period. The lower end of DeLean's six-month target of $30–$35 by August 2002 was likewise reached, albeit tardily, in November 2002, notwithstanding a 15 percent drop in the S&P.

All this good news for shareholders came despite the fact that the revenue recognition misreporting ultimately turned out to be more extensive than the company disclosed in 2002. On January 31, 2004, Take-Two announced it would restate earnings back as far as fiscal 1999. The latest discrepancies involved the recording of reserves for price concessions.

On June 9, 2005, Take-Two agreed to a penalty of $7.5 million to settle SEC charges of accounting fraud. Former Chairman Ryan Brant consented to a penalty of $500,000 and disgorgement and prejudgment interest of $3.1 million, representing bonuses based on the originally reported earnings. Former Chief Operating Officer Larry Muller and former Chief Financial Officer James David Jr. also agreed to penalties and disgorgement of bonuses.

None of the parties admitted or denied the allegations in the SEC's complaint, but those allegations were as disturbing, in their own way, as descriptions of mayhem in *Grand Theft Auto 3*. The commission charged that Take-Two systematically booked revenue from approximately 180 separate so-called parking arrangements. At or around the end of fiscal years or quarters, the commission contended, the company shipped hundreds of thousands of video games to distributors who were under no obligation to pay for them, fraudulently booked the shipments as if they were sales, then accepted returns of the products in later periods. In many instances, the SEC claimed, management created fraudulent invoices to disguise the returns as "purchases of assorted product."[16] Furthermore, according to the complaint, Take-Two improperly recognized revenues on games that were still being manufactured and therefore could not be shipped. Finally, the SEC charged, the company accounted improperly for the acquisition of two video game publishers and failed to establish proper reserves for reductions in the retail prices of its games. Reminiscent of the treatment of innocent bystanders in the company's most notorious game, GAAP received the equivalent of a beating with a baseball bat at the hands of Take-Two's management.

MAKING THE NUMBERS AT M/A-COM

On February 2, 2015, M/A-Com Technology Solutions Holdings reported sales of $114.9 million, meeting (just barely) Wall Street analysts' expectations of around $114 million. Investors noticed, however, that the semiconductor producer cleared the hurdle only with the help of a well-timed accounting change. Instead of holding firm in acknowledgement that expectations had been met, M/A-Com's share price dropped by 0.6 percent on a day when the Russell 3000 Technology Index rose by 0.9 percent.

The accounting change, disclosed in conjunction with M/A-Com's earnings release, involved sales to distributors, which represented nearly 25 percent of total sales in the previous year. Formerly, the company recognized revenue when the distributors sold M/A-Com's products to end users. Under the newly instituted procedure, M/A-Com recognized revenue upon selling to distributors and established a reserve against future returns.[17]

Analyst Sam McBride of independent research firm New Constructs pointed out that the newly adopted "sell-in" method raised the possibility that **channel-stuffing** was occurring. That is, under pressure to meet quarterly sales targets, M/A-Com might have overloaded its distributors with more inventory than they could possibly sell. The company would make its numbers for the quarter, but might subsequently experience large returns, resulting in a reversal of previously booked revenue. Earnings could take a further hit from distributors requiring larger pricing adjustments or refunds than M/A-Com had reserved for, giving investors an unpleasant surprise.

Worryingly, M/A-Com's *days sales outstanding* (DSO) increased to 65 days in the fiscal second quarter ending April 3, 2015, from 57 days one year earlier. This kind of rise, coinciding with a shift to "sell-in," could be a sign of channel-stuffing, which is otherwise difficult to detect. Companies are not required to disclose the amount of their products sitting in distributor inventories.

Journalist Vito Racanelli detailed this financial reporting concern in *Barron's* in June 2015. He also questioned M/A-Com's calculation of non-GAAP earnings per share, which the company asserted was a better reflection of its operations than the GAAP figures. Racanelli noted that the non-GAAP results excluded various expenses that seemed recurring for a tech company relying partly on acquisitions for its growth. Specifically, he cited share-based compensation, some cash compensation, merger and acquisition costs, and earn-out costs. The *Barron's* columnist also drew attention to the ongoing dilution of existing shareholders, pointing out that shares outstanding had more than quadrupled over the proceeding four years. Racanelli concluded, "The shares could be vulnerable to a selloff if revenue disappoints."[18]

Those words proved prophetic. In the third quarter of 2017 M/A-Com's revenue, gross margin, and adjusted earnings per share came in somewhat shy of consensus estimates. More disturbingly, the company issued EPS **guidance** for the fourth quarter of $0.45–$0.50, well below the bottom range of analysts' $0.68-$0.79 estimates. As for revenue, the company's guidance was 19 percent below consensus forecasts. M/A-Com's stock plunged by 20 percent at the opening on August 2, 2017, while the Russell 3000 Technology Index was down by less than 0.2 percent.

By the end of the day, M/A-Com shares had fallen by 25 percent. The company blamed weakness in China for its disappointing results. According to Cowen analyst Paul Silverstein, recent channel checks indicated that M/A-Com's inventory buildup in China exceeded previous market expectations. This finding did not necessarily prove that M/A-Com had been stuffing the channels, but it was consistent with that explanation.

Reviewing these events a few years later, analyst McBride (then no longer at New Constructs) cast some doubt on M/A-Com's explanation of its third-quarter disappointment. He cited a press release by Oclaro, a key M/A-Com customer, concerning its own third-quarter 2017 results. The manufacturer of optical components said that softness in its Chinese revenues was in line with expectations. This implies that the slowdown in demand that M/A-Com blamed for its surprisingly low fourth-quarter guidance should have been baked into its revenue outlook well before the beginning of August.

McBride identified one other possible indication that M/A-Com's numbers leading up to the third-quarter 2017 bombshell were not completely reliable. In seven of the eight previous quarters, he said, the company beat the analysts' EPS consensus (as reported by Seeking Alpha) by $0.01 to $0.02. That sort of pattern can indicate aggressive efforts to make reported earnings hit a desired level, regardless of the underlying reality.

Whatever connection there was or was not between the questions raised in 2015 about M/A-Com's financial reporting and the August 2017 negative surprise, the company's stock did not quickly rebound. On April 10, 2019, the share price was 70 percent below its July 31, 2017, level. Between those same two dates, the Russell 3000 Technology Index rose by 34 percent.

On April 11, 2019, M/A-Com dropped by 11 percent versus a 0.2 percent gain for the tech index. That day the company announced the resignation of its chief financial officer. M/A-Com's management deemed it necessary to specify that the CFO's sudden departure was unrelated to any matters involving its financial statements or accounting practices.

Many factors other than the quality of a company's financial reporting influence its share price. M/A-Com's stock might have declined as much as it did between 2017 and 2019 even if the company had been lauded for its accounting practices instead of having its revenue recognition practices questioned by skeptical analysts. Even so, investors' experience with numerous companies over many years teaches that it is worth paying attention to issues like those raised by McBride and Racanelli in 2015.

ASTRAY ON LAYAWAY

On August 9, 2000, Wal-Mart Stores (as Walmart Inc. was then known) reported a 28 percent year-over-year increase in net income for its fiscal second quarter ending July 31. At $0.36, earnings per share (diluted) were up by 29 percent. Sales rose by a healthy 20 percent, climbing 5 percent at Wal-Mart units open for more than one year.

In light of these results, which one analyst characterized as "a very good quarter," the discount chain's share price might have been expected to rise. At the very least, investors would have expected the stock to hold steady, given that the EPS increase was in line with Wall Street analysts' consensus forecast, as reported by First Call/Thomson Financial. As it turned out, however, Wal-Mart's shares fell by $4.375 to $53.125. That represented an 8 percent decline on a day on which the Dow Jones Industrial Average changed only modestly (down 0.6 percent).

Both the *Wall Street Journal*[19] and the *Bloomberg* newswire[20] linked the paradoxical drop in Wal-Mart's stock to an accounting change that was expected to reduce the following (third) quarter's earnings. The retailer's management advised analysts to lower their earnings per share estimates for the August-to-October period by 1.5 to 2 cents, to reflect a shift in the company's method of accounting for layaway sales. In such transactions, customers reserve goods with down payments, then make additional payments over a specified period, receiving their merchandise when they have paid in full. Prior to the change in accounting practice, which Financial Accounting Standard (FAS) 101 made mandatory, Wal-Mart booked layaway sales as soon as it placed the merchandise on layaway. Under the new and more conservative method, the company began to recognize the sales only when customers completed the required payments and took possession of the goods.

According to one analyst, Wal-Mart's 8 percent stock price decline represented "somewhat of an overreaction." In reality, the price drop was an overreaction in its entirety. Changing the accounting method altered neither the amount of cash ultimately received by the retailer nor the timing of its receipt. The planned change in Wal-Mart's revenue recognition process therefore entailed no loss in time value of money. Lest anyone mistakenly continue to attribute economic significance to the timing of the revenue recognition, Wal-Mart explained that the small reduction in reported earnings in the third fiscal quarter would be made up in the fourth. On top of everything else, management had already announced the accounting change prior to its August 9 conference call.

An institutional portfolio manager spoke truly when he called the market's reaction to the supposed news "more confusion than anything else." If taken at face value, the press reports indicate that investors bid the shares down on so-called news that was both dated and irrelevant. Alternatively, investors may have had other reasons for driving down the shares. For one thing, store traffic declined in the three months ended July 31 from the preceding quarter's level. Additionally, German operations posted a larger loss than management had forecast. If these events were the true causes of Wal-Mart's slide, then the *Wall Street Journal* and the *Bloomberg* newswire erred in attributing the sell-off to an accounting change with no real economic impact. Either way, confusion reigned; the only question is whether it was the investors or the journalists who were confused.

RECOGNIZING MEMBERSHIP FEES

Bally Total Fitness provided another case in which questions about revenue recognition contributed to an unfavorable stock market reaction to seemingly upbeat earnings news. On July 30, 1998, the health club chain reported diluted earnings per share of $0.08, up from a year-earlier loss of $0.59. According to the *Wall Street Journal*,[21] the improved profits were "unexpectedly encouraging." They suggested that the success of the company's newer, more upscale clubs was bolstering overall performance. In the month following the earnings report, however, Bally's shares declined by 44 percent. The Dow Jones Industrial Average fell by a less severe 16 percent over the same period. In the wake of Bally's report, moreover, short sales (representing bets that the price would fall) accounted for 15 percent of all outstanding shares. During the first quarter of 1998, the company's **short interest ratio** fluctuated in a range of 3 percent to 5 percent.

Investors were unwilling to accept Bally's earnings increase at face value because of the company's growing reliance on memberships that it financed, as opposed to selling for cash. Bally's financed customers' initial membership fees, which ranged from $600 to $1,400, for up to 36 months, charging annual interest rates of 16 percent to 18 percent.[22] (Ongoing dues represented just 27.9 percent of net revenues, with approximately 90 percent of members paying an average of only about $7 a month in 1998.) On the whole, the company's reported profit margins benefited from the increase in financed memberships as a percentage of total revenues. The reported earnings, however, rested on assumptions regarding the percentage of customers who would ultimately fail to make all of the scheduled installments.

Even under the best of circumstances, a considerable portion of any health club's new members let their memberships lapse, despite paying an initial fee. As New York University accounting professor Paul Brown notes, "People have little to lose from walking away from a health-club membership. It's not a health-care plan we're talking about, or even a car, which they might need for transportation."[23]

To be sure, Bally set aside reserves for uncollectible amounts, consistent with good accounting practice. The size of the reserves, however, required judgment about the credit quality of the new members. Because financed memberships were not entirely new to Bally, management had some experience on which to base its assumptions. In addition, the company had succeeded in increasing the use of an electronic funds transfer payment option in recent years. Collection rates were higher for members whose credit cards or bank accounts were automatically charged for fees than for those billed through monthly statements. There were risks, though, in stepping up reliance on customers who needed to borrow in order to join. As in any sales situation, aggressive pursuit of new business could result in acceptance of more marginally qualified customers. On average, the newer members might prove to be less financially capable or less committed to physical fitness than the previous purchasers of financed memberships. If more members failed on their payments than management assumed, Bally would prove in hindsight to have been too aggressive in recognizing revenue and would have to rescind previously reported income.

By taking the second-quarter 1998 earnings with a grain of salt, users of financial statements were not necessarily casting aspersions on Bally's management. Rather, they were understandably applying caution in evaluating a company in a service industry historically identified with questionable revenue recognition practices. Some analysts sprang to Bally's defense following the *Wall Street Journal*'s critical article by highlighting the company's adoption of a conservative practice at the Securities and Exchange Commission staff's behest in July 1997. Previously, Bally had fully recognized initial membership fees at the time that the memberships were sold. A health club operator could abuse this approach by using high-pressure tactics to book financed memberships for individuals who were highly unlikely to keep up their payments. Outsiders relying on the financial statements would perceive a growth in revenues that must, in time, prove unsustainable. Under the new accounting treatment, Bally spread the revenues from the initial fees over the expected membership lives – 36 months for sales made for cash on the barrelhead and 22 months for financed sales.

The SEC's urging of Bally to spread out its recognition of membership fees was part of a broader effort extending beyond the health club industry. There was no change in the accounting principle, namely, the matching concept. In the case of a health club, members' upfront fees represent payments for services received over the term of their membership. Club operators should therefore recognize the revenue over the period in which they render the service. During the late 1990s, the underlying theory underwent no change, but the SEC intensified its focus on membership fees after determining that some companies were interpreting the rules too liberally. Among the industries that came under increased scrutiny were the membership club retailers. In this type of operation, consumers pay upfront fees for the privilege of shopping at stores that sell discounted merchandise.

On October 19, 1998, BJ's Wholesale Club switched from immediate recognition of its annual membership fee (typically $35 for two family members) to incremental recognition of the fee over the full membership term, generally 12 months. In conjunction with the change in accounting policy, BJ's restated its net income for the fiscal first half ending August 1 to $10.4 million. That was down 64 percent from the previously reported $28.6 million. The restatement reflected a one-time charge for the accounting change's cumulative effect on preceding years, as well as a $1.1 million after-tax charge arising from a change to more conservative accounting for new-store preopening expenses.

Just a month and a half before these events, BJ's had issued a press release asserting that its practice of immediately recognizing annual membership fees was consistent with GAAP.[24] Management had also argued that no deferral was required, on the grounds that BJ's offered its members the right to cancel and receive refunds for only 90 days after enrollment. A mere 0.5 percent of members actually requested refunds. In contrast to the situation at Bally Total Fitness, moreover, membership fees represented a minor portion of BJ's revenues, 98 percent of which derived from merchandise sales.

Under GAAP, however, the general requirement was to spread membership fees over the full membership period. If a company offered refunds, it could not book *any* of the revenue until the refund period expired, unless there was a sufficiently long history to enable management to estimate future experience with reasonable confidence. At most, BJ's refund record might have entitled the company to begin booking the fees on the date that members enrolled. Spreading the revenue recognition over the membership period would have been mandatory in any case.[25]

In December 1999, the SEC staff clarified the point by issuing "Staff Accounting Bulletin No. 101 – Revenue Recognition in Financial Statements" (SAB 101). The staff stated its preference that companies not book membership fees until refund privileges expired. MemberWorks, a provider of membership programs offering services and discounts in a wide range of fields including health care, personal finance, and travel, altered its accounting in response to SAB 101, effective July 1, 2000. A one-time noncash charge of $25.7 million resulted, reflecting the deferral of previously recognized membership fees.[26]

A POTPOURRI OF LIBERAL REVENUE RECOGNITION TECHNIQUES

By intensifying its enforcement of established revenue recognition rules in SAB 101, the SEC put a stop to techniques that the staff considered overly aggressive. Professional Detailing, a recruiter and manager of sales staff for pharmaceutical companies, had to stop including in revenues the reimbursements that it received from clients for placing help-wanted ads. Within a month, the company's share price fell by 31 percent. Physician & Hospital Systems & Services, a unit of National Data Corporation, abandoned its long-standing policy of booking revenues for its back-office services not merely before it completed the work, but before it mailed out bills. National Data ended the practice and took a $13.8 million one-time charge to correct the previous pumping up of revenues. First American Financial took a cumulative $55.6 million charge when it embraced the matching principle by beginning to book revenues for loan services over the loan's duration, rather than immediately.[27]

Percentage-of-Completion Method

Under certain circumstances, a company engaged in long-term contract work can book revenue before billing its customer. This result arises from GAAP's solution to a mismatch commonly observed at construction firms. A variety of service companies, defense contractors, and capital goods manufacturers come up against the same accounting issue.

Typically, the company agrees to bill its customers in several installments over the life of the contract. The billing may lag behind the company's incurring of expenses to fulfill its obligations. Without some means of correcting this mismatch, reported profit will be inappropriately high in the contract's early stages and inappropriately low in the late stages.

The percentage-of-completion method is how GAAP addresses the problem. It permits the company to recognize revenue in proportion to the amount of work completed, rather than in line with its billing. The percentage-of-completion method can rectify the mismatch but may also entail considerable subjectivity. This is particularly so when the company specializes in finding creative solutions to particular companies' unique problems, a sort of work that cannot be readily measured by engineering standards. Management can speed up revenue recognition on such contracts by making assumptions that are liberal yet difficult for the auditors to reject on objective grounds. As is generally the case with artificial acceleration, taking liberties with the percentage of completion borrows future revenues, making a surprise shortfall inevitable at some point.

Crossing the Line

In the foregoing cases, the regulators merely complained that the companies' existing revenue recognition policies painted too rosy a picture, but in other instances, management has been accused of misrepresentation. For example, in 1996, the SEC claimed that computer manufacturer Sequoia Systems and four former executives engaged in a "fraudulent scheme" aimed at inflating the company's revenue and income. According to the complaint filed in U.S. District Court in Washington, the ex-chairman and three other officials booked letters of intent as revenue, backdated some purchase orders, and granted customers special terms that Sequoia never disclosed. Furthermore, charged the SEC, the executives profited from the scheme by selling stock before a true picture of the company's financial condition emerged. The company and its former officials settled the SEC's civil charges without admitting or denying guilt.[28]

FATTENING EARNINGS WITH EMPTY CALORIES

Doughnut maker Krispy Kreme went public at $21 a share in April 2000. Its stock soared by 76 percent to $37 on the first day of trading. That put its price-earnings ratio at 78 times, more than triple the multiple on the Standard & Poor's Food Index of around 23 times.

Notwithstanding the undeniably addictive quality of its doughnuts, some analysts thought Krispy Kreme's shares had risen too high. Investors were encouraged, however, by a growth rate far in excess of the typical food company. **Same-store sales** had jumped by 14 percent in fiscal 2000 (ended January 30). The number of stores had vaulted 20 percent to 144–58 company-owned and 86 franchised – since the end of fiscal 1998. Whenever a new store was slated to launch, eager customers lined up in droves to satisfy their cravings the instant the doors opened. Propelled by consumers' sugar high, Krispy Kreme shares continued to surge, reaching $108.50 in November 2000.

The mania could not last forever. In 2003, the pace of new store openings slackened, throwing into question Krispy Kreme's valuation as a super growth stock. At this point, according to a Securities and Exchange Commission complaint released in 2009, Krispy Kreme revised its senior executive compensation plan.[29] Henceforth, officers would receive no bonuses unless the company reported earnings in each quarter that exceeded its earnings per share **guidance** by at least $0.01.

To continue to clear the bar that it set for itself, the SEC said, management began to manipulate certain expense accruals to produce EPS at least one penny above the guidance. Ultimately, Krispy Kreme strung together 13 consecutive quarters in which it exceeded that threshold. In addition, said the SEC, Krispy Kreme improperly recorded questionable transactions involving company purchases of franchised stores.

The Long Slide Begins

On May 7, 2004, the company issued a first-ever profit warning, telling investors that its earnings would be 10 percent lower than it previously expected. Krispy Kreme blamed its faltering profits on the new popularity of low-carbohydrate diets, but some analysts suspected that the real problem was overexpansion. They noted that there was no sign of carb consciousness hurting business at rival Dunkin' Donuts. Krispy Kreme shares, which had split twice in 2001, suffered a one-day, 29 percent decline on the news. Later that month, the *Wall Street Journal* detailed questionable aspects of the franchise repurchases, based on information by a person familiar with the transactions.[30]

In 2003, according to the account, Krispy Kreme began a negotiation to buy back its struggling seven-store Michigan franchise. Dough-Re-Mi reportedly owed Krispy Kreme several million dollars for franchise fees, equipment, and ingredients and was delinquent on its payments. The *Journal* reported that the parties reached a preliminary agreement in which Krispy Kreme asked its franchisee to absorb the cost of closing down two underperforming stores and to repay past-due interest. Then, according to the *Journal*'s informant, Krispy Kreme agreed to increase the purchase price by the amount of these additional costs.

Why would Krispy Kreme try to recover the store-closing costs and over-due interest, only to pay it right back? The motivation might have been to increase reported earnings. If the transaction was structured as the *Journal* stated, the extra money paid out to Dough-Re-Mi became part of an intangible asset, reacquired franchise rights, which would not amortize. That is, no scheduled, bit-by-bit write-down would reduce future earnings. On the other hand, when the very same dollars came back to Krispy Kreme, they would be recorded as interest income. In essence, according to the *Wall Street Journal*'s story, Krispy Kreme manufactured earnings by taking money out of one pocket and putting it into another.

The money given to Dough-Re-Mi to cover the closing costs also became an intangible asset, again assuming the *Journal*'s account was accurate. Had Krispy Kreme instead repurchased the franchises and then closed the stores, it would have incurred an expense. The catch is that an asset is supposed to be something that creates future economic value. Terminated stores would not seem to satisfy that definition.

Krispy Kreme's defense of its accounting was a classic of the genre. To begin with, said the company, the auditor approved its handling of the items. This was not a strong justification, judging by the many borderline actions that corporations' auditors approve every year. Second, argued Krispy Kreme, Dough-Re-Mi's interest payment was unrelated to the acquisition. By a remarkable coincidence, however, it occurred on the very same day, and it was deducted from Krispy Kreme's final remittance to the franchise seller.

There was yet another strange aspect to the deal. Originally, Krispy Kreme said it would pay the equivalent of $24.5 million for the Michigan franchise. Later on, the price jumped by 26 percent to $32.1 million. The company's chief financial officer claimed that the disparity arose from an initially incomplete assessment of the costs of the transaction. Krispy Kreme, he said, should have included in the price the potential added costs of a promissory note that Dough-Re-Mi's top executive and major shareholder took in exchange for agreeing to defer his portion of the purchase price while he stayed on as a Krispy Kreme employee. Krispy Kreme, however, dismissed the executive soon after the transaction closed, triggering a payment $5 million greater than the amount originally attributed to the promissory note. This extra money, too, became part of the nonamortizing, intangible asset known as reacquired franchise rights. The shortness of the interval between the transaction and the increased payment raised the question whether at least a portion of the disbursement was in substance a severance payment to the executive. If it had been booked that way, Krispy Kreme would have realized an immediate expense. Krispy Kreme's dubious rebuttal was that the payment was not severance because it went to Dough-Re-Mi, rather than directly to the executive.

Further undercutting Krispy Kreme's credibility were details of a second franchise repurchase, in northern California. The 10-K filed in May 2002 reported that as of January 2001 CEO Scott Livengood held a 3 percent share of the franchise. In reality, his stake amounted to 6 percent, but in August 2001 he ceded 3 percent to his wife as part of a separation agreement. The couple divorced in June 2002. A Krispy Kreme spokeswoman blamed the 10-K discrepancy on a proofreading error, but the company had a potential motive for wanting to state as low a figure as possible. Allowing executives to hold nontrivial stakes in franchises was unusual. Some other franchised food companies prohibited the practice, viewing it as a conflict of interest.

On July 29, 2004, Krispy Kreme disclosed that the SEC had opened an informal inquiry into its accounting practices. The company's stock plunged by 16 percent on the news. One focus of the investigation was franchise repurchases. Camelback Research Alliance noted that Krispy Kreme's practice of not amortizing the reacquired rights was nonstandard in the franchising industry. The company parried that it believed the franchise rights had indefinite lives and therefore should not be written off over time.

Camelback co-founder Donn W. Vickrey also suggested that Krispy Kreme had paid inflated prices in some franchise repurchases.[31] He noted that in 2003 the company paid $67.5 million for franchises in Dallas and Shreveport owned by two former directors. The assets included five stores and one commissary, a production facility that served off-premises customers. At the same time, Krispy Kreme was declining to buy back a southern California franchise that was for sale for a reported $80 million and held 22 stores. Vickrey questioned whether the California stores could truly be so much less valuable. The questions about valuation of the franchise repurchases raised the specter of questionable transactions with related parties. Taking into account all of Krispy Kreme's accounting practices, Camelback gave the company an F for earnings quality, a designation the research firm customarily awarded only to companies with three characteristics:

1. Flat or declining fundamentals, providing a motivation to prettify the financials.
2. Visible evidence of unusual or improper accounting or transactions.
3. Evidence of weak corporate governance.

The Heat Goes Up

Vickrey's criticisms proved astute. Krispy Kreme's chief operating officer resigned less than a month later, a top-level executive change that analyst Skip Carpenter of Thomas Weisel Partners viewed as a sign of more problems to come.[32] A major earnings disappointment followed later the same month. The company declined to provide earnings guidance, which is usually a reason to worry. David Rocker of Rocker Partners further noted that most, if not all, of the cash on Krispy Kreme's balance sheet appeared to have come from a sale-and-leaseback transaction, rather than from operations.[33] On September 12, 2004, auditor PricewaterhouseCoopers refused to complete its review of the latest quarter's financial statements until an outside law firm hired by the board completed certain procedures that the auditor requested.

On October 8, 2004, the SEC upgraded its inquiry to a formal investigation of Krispy Kreme's financial reporting practices. Less than a week later, two former directors were slapped with a lawsuit alleging that they pumped up the price Krispy Kreme agreed to pay for the Dallas-Shreveport franchise, which they owned, by obtaining an outside bid that they never seriously considered. On November 22, 2004, Krispy Kreme stock fell 16 percent to $9.64 as the company announced its first-ever loss as a public company. That was down from an August 2003 peak, adjusted for splits, of $49.74. Among other depressing statistics, same-store sales declined by more than 6 percent, and it cost the company $3 million to deal with the SEC probe and pending litigation. Departing from customary practice for earnings calls, management declined to answer any questions and withdrew its previous projection of 15 percent sales growth in 2005.

Krispy Kreme could no longer pin its troubles on the low-carbohydrate diet fad, which appeared to be fading. A Legg Mason analyst charged the company with carelessness in selecting new store locations and failure to train new franchisees properly. In addition, the company had saturated the market by selling its goodies in supermarkets and convenience stores. Instead of a long line of customers camped out in sleeping bags, the manager of a new Krispy Kreme store in San Antonio found only his employees waiting for him when he arrived to open up. The city already had three other Krispy Kreme outlets, and its doughnuts were being sold in Albertsons and H-E-B supermarkets. There were also possible signs of strain among franchisees. A Midwestern franchisee exercised an option to sell 11 percent of its shares back to the company, and Krispy Kreme disclosed a $2 million charge for doubtful accounts from two franchisees.

On December 16, 2004, Krispy Kreme conceded that some of the payment to Dough-Re-Mi's former owner should have been treated as compensation expense. Lawyers hired by the board, however, found no intentionally improper conduct in the incident. Management also acknowledged errors in its accounting for the acquisition of a California franchise. Krispy Kreme stock rose by 8.7 percent on the news, as analysts rejoiced that the disclosures were not worse. PricewaterhouseCoopers, however, continued to refuse to complete its review of results for two prior quarters, pending completion of the ongoing investigation by a special committee of the board and the outside law firm.

It quickly became clear that the company was not yet out of the woods. On January 4, 2005, Krispy Kreme said it would reduce its previous year's reported profit and that it would be in default on its $150 million bank credit line due to its failure to file financial statements and probably also as a result of its earnings decline. Without the ability to draw further on its bank line, said Krispy Kreme, it would be unable to honor its guarantees of franchisees' debts, of which $16.7 million was in default. In February, the company said that it needed additional credit by the end of March to remain in business. By this time, more than a dozen shareholder lawsuits had piled up, including one alleging that Krispy Kreme had tried to meet investors' expectations for earnings growth by ordering some employees to ship more doughnuts than wholesale customers had ordered.

In response to its deteriorating situation, Krispy Kreme replaced chief executive Scott Livengood with a turnaround specialist. On February 24, 2005, the U.S. attorney's office for the Southern District of New York launched an investigation on top of the SEC's ongoing probe. Several new elements entered the disclosures of financial reporting problems on April 9, 2005, when Krispy Kreme increased the size of the corrections to its fiscal 2004 results from the $3.8 million to $4.9 million range to a range of $5.2 million to $6.2 million. The previously undisclosed problems involved derivatives transactions, errors in accounting for leases and improvements related to leases, and reversal of income related to equipment sold to a franchisee before Krispy Kreme bought that operation. Management said further restatements probably would be needed on the last item, as the basis for recognizing the revenue would be changed to the installation date of the equipment, rather than the shipping or delivery date.

The Resolution

After 10 months, the board special committee submitted a report of its investigation. The carefully worded document indicated that although all employees and franchisees who were interviewed denied deliberately distorting Krispy Kreme's earnings or being ordered to do so, "the number, nature, and timing of the accounting errors strongly suggest that they resulted from an intent to manage earnings."[34] The report criticized "round-trip transactions" in which money flowed out to franchise sellers, then flowed back in and was booked as revenue, enabling management to achieve its bogey of $0.01 above guidance.

The denouement came in 2009, when former CEO Livengood and former CFOs John Tate and Randy Casstevens settled SEC charges that they were instrumental in inflating Krispy Kreme's earnings in an alleged scheme to increase their compensation. They did not admit or deny the allegations but agreed to surrender money the SEC said they earned illegally, pay civil penalties, and be permanently enjoined from committing future violations. The SEC complaint also alleged that Krispy Kreme management conducted misleading conference calls with securities analysts, helping to keep the stock price higher than it would have been without the alleged financial manipulation, which the SEC said the executives knew about but failed to disclose. Livengood, Tate, and Casstevens collectively sold approximately 324,000 shares of stock in August 2003, close to the price peak.

Learning Lessons from Doughnuts

Krispy Kreme was not a case of massively fictitious earnings. Rather, the SEC complaint depicted a process of nickel-and-diming, through a wide range of financial statement items, to beat earnings guidance by $0.01 in every single quarter. Security analysts found no clear-cut evidence within the reported numbers that stated profits were inaccurate. Still, users of financial statements can draw some lessons for future reference.

To begin with, an exceptionally long record of beating guidance or posting year-over-year gains in quarterly earnings is a reason to suspect earnings management. Businesses tend to grow unevenly over time, reflecting such factors as the business cycle, waxing and waning of competitive pressures, and fluctuations in input costs. A second lesson of the Krispy Kreme case is that related-party transactions and deceptive financial reporting often go hand in hand. Finally, when management offers an excuse for deteriorating earnings that does not stand up to scrutiny, as Krispy Kreme did by citing the low-carb craze, it may be using financial reporting tricks to try to conceal the true causes.

TARDY DISCLOSURE AT HALLIBURTON

In 2002, the *New York Times* reported on a 1998 change in accounting policies by the Halliburton Corporation that enabled the industrial construction company to book more than $100 million of disputed costs as revenue.[35] Halliburton did not disclose the change in its treatment of cost overruns until more than a year later. Apparently in response to the *Times* article, the Securities and Exchange Commission initiated an investigation that eventually led to charges of filing materially misleading financial reports.

The Halliburton affair probably attracted disproportionate attention for an accounting controversy of less than gargantuan proportions because of the identity of the chief executive officer on whose watch it occurred.

By the time Halliburton's tardy disclosure became public knowledge, CEO Dick Cheney had moved on to become vice president of the United States. Inconveniently for the White House, a shareholder lawsuit alleging a massive scheme to defraud investors was filed against Cheney and other Halliburton executives on the day after President George W. Bush called for a crackdown on accounting abuses. Bush advocated tougher prison sentences for corporate officials engaging in fraud and a strengthening of the SEC's ability to uncover financial reporting scams.

Additional embarrassment for the administration arose from Cheney's close ties to Arthur Andersen, which incurred massive criticism for its auditing of Enron and ultimately went out of business. In a 2000 memo to his colleagues, Arthur Andersen's Terry Hatchett boasted that his relationship with Cheney was so tight that he remained lead partner on the Halliburton account even after leaving the Dallas office to head Asian operations. Additionally, Cheney appeared in a marketing video hailing Arthur Andersen's capabilities.

The Accounting Issues

The accounting issues involved cost overruns incurred in construction projects. Depending on the terms of the contract and the nature of the overrun, Halliburton could potentially recover the associated cost from a customer. Prior to 1998, the company recognized income from recovery of overrun costs in the quarter in which it resolved the claim. Beginning in the second quarter of 1998, however, Halliburton departed from its traditional practice and began recognizing revenues by offsetting its losses on certain projects with estimated probable recoveries on claims that it had not yet resolved.

Both the old and the new accounting treatment were acceptable under GAAP. The new treatment, however, boosted reported pretax income by $200 million between the second quarter of 1998 and the third quarter of 1999. In the fourth quarter of 1998, the change in accounting policy raised reported pretax profits by 46 percent. The numbers that investors saw during this period were not comparable to those reported for earlier periods, meaning they did not obtain an accurate picture of Halliburton's profit trend. Not until March 2000 did the company reveal, in its 1999 Form 10-K filing, that it had changed its accounting policy.

In 2001, Halliburton adopted an even more aggressive approach to recognizing revenue. For some projects, Halliburton began reporting sales months before billing customers for the work. Previously, the policy was to book revenues only if the company expected to bill clients within one month. In addition, the company began keeping some disputed bills on the books for over a year instead of writing them off and reporting losses. The previous policy was to refrain from a write-off only if it believed it would collect most of the claim within one year. As a result of this change, disputed claims doubled from $113 million in 2000 to $234 million in 2001.

Chief Financial Officer Doug Foshee said he could not imagine that Cheney had specifically approved the 1998 change in accounting policy. He characterized it as a routine business decision prompted by a shift in the company's business mix. Up until the late 1990s, Halliburton worked mostly under cost-plus contracts, in which it was guaranteed a profit over whatever costs it incurred. By 1998, most contracts were on a fixed-price basis. Under this arrangement, the company had to complete the work for a predetermined fee or else negotiate repayment for cost overruns and for costs arising from changes in specifications of the work.

Those changed circumstances may well have affected Halliburton's accounting policies, but the adoption of a more liberal revenue recognition policy occurred in the context of pressure on the company's stock price due to its 1998 merger with Dresser Industries. Dresser faced potentially large legal liabilities from asbestos-related litigation. Furthermore, conditions were difficult in Halliburton's energy services business. Corporate-wide sales and profits fell in the fourth quarter of 1998 from the year-earlier period.

Halliburton's financial statements provided further hints that in response to these pressures the company took liberties to present its results in a favorable light. When Cheney became CEO in October 1995, the company had about $0.95 of receivables for each dollar of quarterly revenues. At the end of his tenure, in July 2000, the figure stood at $1.20. This increase did not appear to reflect a general change in industry conditions. Over that same span, the average ratio of receivables to sales at five major competitors declined from $0.92 to $0.86. On the face of it, Halliburton became more aggressive about booking revenues before getting paid, a classic technique for pumping up reported earnings.[36]

The Resolution

On August 3, 2004, the SEC announced that Halliburton and its former controller, Robert C. Muchmore Jr., had agreed to settle charges of filing materially misleading financial statements by paying penalties of $7.5 million and $50,000, respectively. The administrator of the commission's Fort Worth office, Harold F. Degenhardt, commented, "The SEC's action today emphasizes the importance of complete transparency in a company's financial disclosures. Important information bearing on a company's results should be clearly and timely disclosed, even if those results are calculated in accordance with Generally Accepted Accounting Principles (GAAP)."[37]

The company and Muchmore neither admitted to nor denied the SEC charges. Vice President Cheney's attorney noted that the SEC had investigated the matter very thoroughly and had found no responsibility for nondisclosure on the part of either the board or the CEO. He declined to answer a question about whether Cheney knew of the effect of the accounting change on Halliburton's profits.

Lessons from Halliburton

An auditor's seal of approval does not guarantee that a company's financial reporting is reliable. Arthur Andersen went along with Halliburton's decision not to disclose an important change in accounting policies in the year in which it was made. Immateriality is a common rationale for such a decision, yet in the fourth quarter of 1998, the change in accounting for cost overruns produced nearly a 50 percent overstatement of pretax earnings. By the by, Halliburton fired Arthur Andersen in April 2002, the month before the *New York Times* raised questions about the company's accounting practices.

Neither should users of financial statements be complacent just because a prestigious individual has ultimate responsibility for the integrity of the numbers. Halliburton CEO Dick Cheney was a former congressman, White House chief of staff, and secretary of defense. By some accounts, he was a hands-off manager who would not have concerned himself with the accounting decision that eventually resulted in a settlement with the Securities and Exchange Commission. On the other hand, he evidently felt familiar enough with accounting matters to praise Arthur Andersen's work in a marketing video. In any case, if earnings look suspiciously strong during a rough patch for the company's industry, users of financial statements should never automatically rule out the possibility that manipulative accounting explains the disparity.

MANAGING EARNINGS WITH RAINY DAY RESERVES

Overstating near-term reported earnings by recognizing sales prematurely is the revenue-related abuse that creates the greatest notoriety. Analysts must also watch out for the opposite sort of finagling, however. Sometimes, management *delays* revenue recognition to *understate* short-run profits. The motive for this paradoxical behavior is a desire to report the sort of smooth year-to-year earnings growth that equity investors reward with high price-earnings multiples (see Chapter 14).

Steady earnings growth rarely occurs naturally. A company can produce it artificially, however, by creating a rainy day reserve. When net profit happens to be running above expectations, management stows part of it in a rainy day reserve. Later on, when the income is needed to boost results to targeted levels, management pulls the earnings out of storage. Smoothing the bottom line is not uncommon, but companies are touchy about the subject.

Chemical producer W. R. Grace reacted with indignation when it was accused of managing its earnings through improper reserves. On December 22, 1998, the Securities and Exchange Commission charged the company and six of its former executives with falsely reporting earnings over the preceding five years by improperly shifting revenue. Grace followed the standard script, declaring that it would "vigorously contest"[38] the charges, stating its belief that its financial reporting was proper and pointing out that its outside auditors had raised no objections to the accounting. An attorney for former Grace Chief Executive Officer J. P. Bolduc, who was among the accused executives, said that his client would fight the charges and expected to be vindicated. The SEC, complained the lawyer, was trying to punish Bolduc for carrying out his duties exactly as he should have.

The SEC specifically alleged that Grace had declined to report $10 million to $20 million of revenue that its kidney dialysis services subsidiary, National Medical Care (NMC), received in the early 1990s as the result of a change in Medicare reimbursement rules. According to the commission's enforcement division, the Grace executives reckoned that with earnings already meeting Wall Street analysts' forecasts, the windfall would not help the company's stock price. Such an inference would have been consistent with investors' customary downplaying of profits and losses that they perceive to be generated by one-time events (see Chapter 3). In fact, it was possible that the unexpected revenue would actually hurt the stock price down the road by causing NMC's profits to increase by 30 percent, an above-target and unsustainable level.

To solve the perceived problem of excessively high profits at NMC, Grace's management allegedly placed the extra revenue in another account, which it later drew on to increase the health care group's reported revenues between 1993 and 1995. As an example, claimed the SEC, senior managers of Grace asked NMC's managers to report an extra $1.5 million of income in the fourth quarter of 1994, when corporate earnings needed a boost.

Brian J. Smith, who was Grace's chief financial officer until July 1995, testified in a deposition that because the kidney dialysis unit could not maintain its pace of earnings increases, "We believed that it was prudent to reduce the growth rates."[39] His attorney denied, however, that the goal was to please Wall Street analysts by keeping reported earnings smooth, as former Grace and NMC employees asserted. Smith had bona fide liabilities in mind, claimed the attorney.

A senior partner at Grace's auditing firm, Price Waterhouse, did not agree that the additions to reserves were appropriate. Eugene Gaughan testified that in 1991, he pointed out that the accounting rules clearly stated that profits could be set aside only for foreseeable and quantifiable liabilities; GAAP did not give companies discretion to create rainy day funds.

In its year-end audit, Price Waterhouse proposed reversing the reserves, but management refused. According to the auditing firm's records, the Grace executives said that they wanted a "cushion for *unforeseen* future events"[40] (italics added). Eventually, Price Waterhouse allowed the additions to reserves to stand. The auditors' decision reflected a finding that the amount placed in the reserve was not material from Grace's corporate-wide standpoint, although it would be if NMC were a stand-alone company. (At the time, auditors generally judged an item material if it affected earnings by 5 percent or 10 percent. The Securities and Exchange Commission later established the criterion that an event was material if it would affect an investor's decision.)

According to Gaughan, Price Waterhouse objected again around the end of 1992, after seeing a memo that described Grace's use of reserves to influence reported growth in profits, while gearing NMC executives' incentive compensation to "actual results." Another Price Waterhouse partner, Thomas Scanlon, said that he told Grace CEO Bolduc that stockpiling reserves was wrong and would have to stop. By that time, the contents of the rainy day reserve had grown to about $55 million.

It appears, in short, that Grace's 1998 statement that its auditors had raised no objections to its accounting for the Medicare reimbursement windfall was true only in the technical sense that Price Waterhouse issued clean financials, based on materiality considerations. As a spokeswoman for the auditing firm pointed out, such an opinion does not imply agreement with everything in the statements. As late as April 1999, however, Grace was still insisting that Price Waterhouse had approved its accounting "without reservation."[41]

On June 30, 1999, Grace settled the case without admitting or denying the SEC's charges. The company agreed to cease and desist from further securities law violations and also to set up a $1 million education fund to promote awareness of and education about financial statements and generally accepted accounting principles. Adhering again to the standard script, the corporation explained that it settled the case "because we think it is in the best interests of our employees and shareholders to put this matter behind us and move forward."[42]

The Grace affair serves as a reminder that almost invariably, an allegation of irregularities in corporate financial reporting is followed by a vehement, formulaic denial. No matter how offended the company purports to be about having its integrity questioned, analysts should take the protests of innocence with a grain of salt. The record does not suggest that the companies that bray loudest in defending their accounting practices are sure to be vindicated in the end.

FUDGING THE NUMBERS: A SYSTEMATIC PROBLEM

As the preceding examples demonstrate, manipulation of reported revenue is distressingly common. Readers may nevertheless wonder whether this discussion presents too bleak a picture of human nature. Are not most people basically honest, after all? To a novice analyst who has never been blindsided by revisions of previously reported sales figures that proved misleading or fraudulent, it may seem paranoid to view every company's income statement with suspicion.

Harvard Business School Professor Emeritus Michael C. Jensen observes, however, that misrepresenting revenues is the inevitable consequence of using budget targets in employee compensation formulas.[43] "Tell a manager that he will get a bonus when targets are realized and two things will happen," writes Jensen. "First, managers will attempt to set easy targets, and, second, once these are set, they will do their best to see that they are met even if it damages the company." He cites real-life examples of managers who "did their best" through such stratagems as:

- Shipping fruit baskets that weighed exactly the same amount as their product and booking them as sales.
- Announcing a price increase, effective January 2, to induce customers to order before year-end and thereby help managers achieve their sales targets. The price hike put the company out of line with the competition.
- Shipping unfinished heavy equipment from a plant in England (resulting in revenue recognition in the desired quarter) to the Netherlands. At considerable cost and inconvenience, the manufacturer then completed the assembly in a warehouse located near its customer.

Compounding the problem of managers who play games with their revenues is the willingness of some corporate customers to play along. "All too often, companies wouldn't be able to accomplish the frauds without the assistance of their customers," observes Helane L. Morrison, a district administrator for the Securities and Exchange Commission.[44] For example, one-third of wireless communications provider Hybrid Networks' revenue in the fourth quarter of 1997 consisted of a sale made on the final day of the reporting period to a distributor, Ikon Office Solutions. Ikon agreed to purchase $1.5 million worth of modems from Hybrid, despite knowing that it had no customers for the equipment. Hybrid closed the sale by providing a side letter essentially permitting Ikon to return the modems without paying for them. Ikon exercised that option in 1998, yet Ronald Davies, the Ikon executive who handled the purchase, sent an e-mail to Hybrid denying any knowledge of the side letter. Unfortunately, Hybrid later gave a copy of the side letter to its auditors. The SEC then sued Hybrid, which was forced to restate its revenues to eliminate the nonfinal sale of modems to Ikon. Furthermore, Davies received a cease-and-desist order to refrain from further violations of the securities laws. In certain other enforcement actions alleging improper recognition of sales as well, the SEC has charged executives of corporate customers with collusion.

How widespread are revenue recognition gambits that enrich managers but impair bona fide profits? According to Ikon executive Davies, "It's very common for a manufacturer to call you up and say, 'I need to hit my quarterly number, would you mind giving me a purchase order for $100,000?"[45] In the litigation surrounding W. R. Grace's alleged delay of revenue recognition to smooth earnings, the chief financial officer's attorney defended his client's action by arguing, "Any CFO anywhere has managed earnings in a way the SEC is now jumping up and down and calling fraud."[46] Michael Jensen chimes in, "Almost every company uses a budget system that rewards employees for lying and punishes them for telling the truth." He proposes reforming the system by severing the link between budget targets and compensation. Realistically, however, radical reforms are not likely to occur any time soon.

Analysts therefore need to scrutinize carefully the revenues of every company they examine. Even in the case of the bluest of the blue chips, watching for rising levels of accounts receivable or inventory, relative to sales, should be standard operating procedure. Regardless of management's programmed reassurances, conspicuous surges in unbilled receivables and deferred income are telltale danger signals. It is imperative that analysts raise a red flag when a membership-based company's registrations deviate from their customary relationship with reported sales. "Budget-gaming is rife," says Jensen, and "in most corporate cultures, much of this is expected, even praised." Let the analyst beware.

Restatements of revenues and earnings arise in a wide range of circumstances. Many well-publicized cases involve young companies in comparatively new industries. Until the potential abuses have been demonstrated, management may be able to take greater liberties than the auditors will countenance at a later point. On the other hand, major, long-established corporations are sometimes overzealous in booking sales. Mature companies may pump up revenues out of a desire to meet high expectations created by earlier rapid growth.

After the fact, companies variously attribute excesses in reporting to misjudgment, bookkeeping errors, deliberate misrepresentation by rogue managers, or some combination of the three. Seasoned analysts, having been burned on many occasions by revenue revisions, tend to doubt that overstatements are ever innocent mistakes. To gain some of the veterans' perspective, if not necessarily their jaundiced view of human nature, it is worthwhile to review a few case histories of misstated revenues.

In November 2002, Enterasys Networks restated its revenue downward by 11 percent for a 19-month period in 2000 and 2001, blaming accounting mistakes. The network equipment maker's net loss for the period rose by the same amount. (A change in the fiscal year accounted for the unusual 19-month interval.) The purported mistakes that contributed to the elimination of $153 million of sales included revenues booked in the wrong periods, inflated valuations of stock received as payment for products, and expected payments that were booked as revenues but failed to materialize during the 19-month interval. Enterasys was the major surviving subsidiary of Cabletron Systems, cofounded by Craig Benson, who had just been elected governor of New Hampshire when the revisions were announced. The *Wall Street Journal* received no response to its call to a spokesman for the transition team of governor-elect Benson, who had served on the Enterasys audit committee since June 2000.

Cincinnati Milacron credited an anonymous tip for its uncovering of a $2.3 million overstatement of sales in the first half of 1993. The "isolated" incident, said the company, involved a failure by the Sano plastic machinery unit to observe the "sales cutoff" rule. Contrary to Cincinnati Milacron's policy, Sano had counted in sales units that had not been shipped. The obligatory firing centered on a senior manager, while others escaped with reprimands.[47]

First Financial Management blamed accounting errors, rather than policy violations, for its restatement of revenues for the first nine months of 1991. (Some of the employees at fault were fired, all the same.) The problem arose in the Basis Information Technologies subsidiary, a unit that First Financial had formed by consolidating 19 separate companies. Basis Information Technologies reportedly lost track of certain accruals of revenue, which should have been reduced as contracts expired. While uncovering the mess, First Financial also found that certain acquisition-related expenses had been amortized improperly.[48]

In a June 2003 interview with *Fortune,* Lucent Technologies' outside counsel commented on the company's booking of $125 million of revenue in a deal that the Securities and Exchange Commission had questioned. Paul Saunders of Cravath, Swaine & Moore characterized the telecommunications equipment manufacturer's handling of the transaction with Winstar as a "failure of communication," rather than as accounting fraud. Asked if the failure was intentional, Saunders replied, "I don't know. I don't think so."[49] One month later, Lucent was forced to publish a retraction in which it acknowledged that Saunders's comments were inaccurate and that it had falsified documents. On May 17, 2004, Lucent and three former executives agreed to settle, without admitting or denying the allegations, SEC charges that the company fraudulently and improperly recognized about $1.148 billion of revenue and $470 million in pretax earnings during fiscal 2000. The SEC complaint asserted that nine current and former Lucent executives improperly granted or failed to disclose side agreements and other incentives to induce customers to buy the company's products, all in order to meet internal sales targets and obtain sales-based bonuses. Furthermore, the SEC charged, the executives violated internal accounting controls and misled corporate finance and accounting personnel about the existence of extracontractual commitments. This case did not result in a restatement of financial results, but the SEC fined Lucent $25 million for not cooperating with its investigation.

CONCLUSION

Motivational speakers assure their audiences that if they visualize success, success will follow. Some of the corporate executives who live by the self-help creed take this advice a bit too literally. Seeing conditional sales and dubious memberships, they visualize GAAP revenues, believing that reality will follow. They transfer their own mirage to the financial statements, pumping up their companies' perceived market value and credit quality. When the revenues derived from wishful thinking fail to materialize, the managers may resort to fraud to maintain the illusion. The positive mental attitude that overstates revenues in the early stage is no less damaging, however, than the fraud responsible at a later point. When evidence of overly aggressive revenue recognition appears, analysts must act swiftly and decisively, lest they become infected by the managers' dangerous optimism.

CHAPTER 7

Expense Recognition

A s Chapter 6 illustrated, companies can grossly distort their earnings through aggressive revenue recognition. Analysts who arm themselves with appropriate skepticism about financial statements are bound to wonder whether companies also pump up the bottom line by taking liberties in booking expenses. The answer is resoundingly affirmative. Corporate managers are just as creative in minimizing and slowing down the recognition of expenses as they are in maximizing and speeding up the recognition of revenues.

DIAMOND FOODS'S MOVABLE EXPENSES

On February 8, 2012, Diamond Foods announced that it would restate its earnings for the previous two years. The snack food producer also found material weaknesses in its financial reporting controls. Chief executive officer Michael J. Mendes and chief financial officer Steven M. Neill were placed on administrative leave and fired the following day.

Diamond's shares fell as much as 44 percent in after-hours trading. Jefferies stock analyst Thilo Wrede wrote in a research bulletin that the company would probably violate its debt covenants as a result of the coming reduction of reported earnings. In addition, Standard & Poor's reduced its outlook for the company's credit rating from Stable to Slightly Negative.

The company's planned earnings restatement involved payments to walnut growers of $20 million in August 2010 and $60 million in September 2011 that were booked in the wrong periods. Shareholders who were suing the company alleged that the payments were used to shift costs one fiscal year forward. That gambit likely would have overstated earlier profits, goosing reported earnings and, by extension, Diamond's share price.

An inflated share value would have advantaged the company in its pending acquisition of the Pringles potato chip business. With that planned deal, originally valued at $2.35 billion, Diamond was poised to become the second largest snack company behind Pepsico, the parent of Frito-Lay. The potato chip maker's owner, Procter & Gamble, was to be paid mostly in Diamond Foods stock.

In the wake of Diamond's announcement, a P&G spokesperson indicated that Pringles had attracted "considerable interest" from other possible buyers. The consumer goods giant, he said, would keep its options open. A week later, P&G pulled the plug on its deal with Diamond, selling Pringles instead to Kellogg, which thereby snatched the number-two spot in snack foods.

Early Signs of Trouble

Five months before the restatement announcement that torpedoed Diamond's share price, the *Wall Street Journal*'s John Jannarone warned that "investors should take a closer look at its historical business: walnuts."[1] Jannarone's article followed by two days an Off Wall Street Consulting report by Mark Roberts that raised questions about Diamond's accounting. Roberts estimated that if Diamond had booked its costs properly, fiscal 2011 earnings per share would have been as little as $1.14 a share rather than the $2.16 that the company reported. Had the company reported the lower figure, the stock with which it planned to pay for Pringles probably would have represented much less valuable acquisition currency.

The story began with Diamond Foods's 1912 origin as a walnut growers' cooperative. Michael J. Mendes, the CEO who was fired following the restatement announcement, persuaded the cooperative's members to take the operation public in 2005. He soon began creating a snack food empire through acquisitions. *Barron's* contributor Jannarone noted that friction had developed with growers over multi-year contracts that allowed Diamond to set walnut prices unilaterally.

When walnut prices surged for the 2010 crop, Diamond paid growers considerably less than most buyers, according to the *Wall Street Journal*'s sources. On September 2, 2011, however, Diamond made a "momentum payment" to growers. A similar "continuity" payment had been made in August 2010 and growers said they could not tell whether the payments were for the years in which they were paid or for the preceding years.

Had the September 2011 payment been made by July 31, 2011, the end of Diamond's fiscal year, it would have taken a big bite out of fiscal 2011 earnings. Jannarone estimated just how big a hit that might be by conservatively assuming that Diamond bought 20 percent of the 2010 California walnut crop. (The company had disclosed that in 2005 it bought about 40 percent of the California production.) The Department of Agriculture reported the size of the 2010 crop as one billion pounds. At an average of $0.25 a pound, as growers reported to Jannarone, the momentum payment would have totaled $50 million, more than half of Diamond's $93 million in operating income. That estimate proved close to the approximately $60 million that the company later admitted was recorded in the wrong period.

Even including the 2011 momentum payment, it appeared that walnut growers had received a bit less than $1.00 a pound from Diamond. The Department of Agriculture reported an average price of $1.06 a pound for the 2010 California crop, with some varieties fetching far more. Growers had the ability to obtain better prices, once their contracts with Diamond expired, by selling into burgeoning export markets in China and Turkey. That would spell trouble for Diamond, which derived nearly 30 percent of its sales from walnuts. Its stock priced had risen 31 percent since the tentative deal to buy Pringles from P&G was announced, so shareholders faced substantial downside if Diamond's nut business began to crack.

Indeed, Diamond's share price fell by as much as 8.5 percent during the September 27, 2011, trading session that coincided with the *Barron's* revelations. (The S&P 500 Index rose by 1.0 percent that day.) On November 1, 2011, Diamond and Procter & Gamble agreed to delay the Pringles closing while Diamond's audit committee probed the company's accounting for walnut-crop payments. Four days later Bill Alpert presciently wrote in *Barron's Online*, "After Diamond's walnut accounting gets scrutiny, the stock could get crushed again."[2] In short, the stock plunge that was triggered by the restatement announcement three months later was by no means a bolt from the blue.

When Diamond officially restated its earnings on November 15, 2012, its shares closed at $15.36, down 21 percent on the day. Equity analyst Ashkay Jagdale of KeyBanc Capital Markets said the size of the restatements was in line with expectations. Diamond, however, also reported a $53.4 million loss for the first three quarters of 2012, partly due to a weakening of its walnut business. Back when the company was still a Wall Street darling based on its plan to acquire Pringles, its stock closed at $92.47 on September 20, 2011.

Notably, Diamond Foods's earnings manipulation commenced after the passage of the Sarbanes-Oxley Act that is appropriately credited with substantially reducing the incidence of financial reporting fraud in the United States. Diamond did not even go public until three years after Sarbox became the law of the land in 2002. The company's shifting of expenses, at a time when it was desperate to shore up its share price and keep a transformative acquisition on track, showed that analysts could not afford to let their guard down just because CEOs now faced greater risk of going to prison for falsifying financial statements.

The Aftermath

Nine months after Diamond's restatement announcement, the company filed restated consolidated financial statements for fiscal 2010 and 2011 and interim periods ending January 2010 to July 2011. The revised statements reduced pretax income by $17 million in fiscal 2010 and by $39.5 million in fiscal 2011. Two company directors stepped down from the board at that time.

In 2013 Diamond Foods reached a settlement with investors who acquired its stock between October 10, 2010, and February 8, 2012. The company paid $11 million in cash and issued 4.45 million common shares to resolve all outstanding claims, while denying all claims of wrongdoing or liability. Insurance funded a substantial portion of the cash payment.

The following year Diamond Foods paid $5 million to settle Securities and Exchange Commission charges that it concocted an accounting scheme to falsify its costs. The alleged motive was to increase its earnings and thereby meet equity analysts' estimates. Diamond neither admitted nor denied the charges. Its former chief financial officer Steven M. Neill likewise settled in 2015 without admitting or denying the charge against him. He paid $125,000 and forfeited his claim for approximately $1 million in stock options awarded partly during the time that the alleged fraud occurred.

Deposed chief executive officer Michael J. Mendes followed a similar route, paying $125,000 and returning more than $4 million in bonuses and other benefits. That was on top of missing out on his scheduled November 2011 headline spot at an investor bash at New York's Metropolitan Opera House that featured Sting and James Taylor. Mendes landed on his feet, however, eventually becoming CEO of Just Desserts, producer of such delicacies as Chocolate Dipped Vegan Vanilla Bundt Cake. He made a clean break from his earlier affiliation; Just Desserts proudly stated that its artisan baking processes were nut-free.

NORTEL'S DEFERRED PROFIT PLAN

Nortel Networks illustrated the distorting power of accruals, one of the most abused features of financial reporting. Founded in 1882 as the Bell Telephone Company of Canada's department for manufacturing telephones and telephone equipment, the unit was spun off as the Northern Electric and Manufacturing Company Limited in 1895. It went through various ownership and name changes, eventually becoming known as Nortel Networks to signify the company's quest to dominate the global market for public and private telecommunications networks.

Nortel grew into North America's largest telecommunications equipment manufacturer and rode the late-1990s boom in fiber optics equipment.

From the mid-1990s until mid-2000, its market capitalization soared more than tenfold, and the company shelled out $30 billion for acquisitions. Nortel's showy advertisements featured celebrities such as Elton John.

The Tech Wreck brought those heady days to an end in 2000. It became apparent that like many of its high-tech peers, the showpiece of Canadian industry had paid exorbitant prices for ill-considered acquisitions, extended credit to customers on unsound terms, and made overly optimistic earnings forecasts. Between September 2000 and August 2002, Nortel's market capitalization sank by 99 percent, devastating Canadian pension plans that were heavily invested in its shares.

First Indications of Accounting Discrepancies

New CEO Frank Dunn moved aggressively to stabilize the company, slashing the workforce from 95,000 to 35,000 and exiting several major businesses. The turnaround ran into a snag on October 23, 2003, however. Nortel announced that it had made accounting "mistakes" that required a reduction of previously stated losses totaling $740 million for 2000, 2001, 2002, and the first half of 2003. A review found that the company's balance sheet overstated liabilities by $900 million for the period in question, with the associated losses partly offset by $160 million in corresponding tax benefits. In addition, the company's second look at its books revealed that $92 million in revenues from the three-and-a-half-year span should have been deferred to later periods.

Dunn, who had been chief financial officer in 2000 and much of 2001, explained that the errors were made during a volatile period for the high-tech industry. "I want to assure Nortel Networks stakeholders that we are committed to working to identify the causes of the mistakes," said Dunn, "and to implement the appropriate measures to ensure that the problems will not recur in the future."[3] Shareholders were not entirely reassured, as Nortel's shares fell by 6 percent in after-hours trading. On the whole, though, investors concluded that because the planned restatements were modest and would reduce previous losses, the news was not all that bad.

Three months later, Nortel and its CEO appeared to have regained any lost ground with investors as the company announced its first annual profit in six years. "Great execution," exulted one Wall Street analyst. "The numbers look really good."[4]

Unfortunately, the numbers proved not to be as good as they looked. On March 10, 2004, Nortel disclosed that an investigation by its audit committee was likely to necessitate another revision of past earnings. As a result, the company had to wave a classic red flag with respect to the credibility of its financial statements by delaying the filing of its 2003 financial reports. The following week, Nortel placed Chief Financial Officer Douglas C. Beatty and

Controller Michael J. Gollogly on indefinite paid leaves of absence. Based on the unusual procedure of putting the executives on leave, rather than firing them, accounting experts suspected the company's problems were acute and might involve a disagreement with auditor Deloitte & Touche.

Some brokerage house analysts, however, continued to express confidence in the company's outlook. "In my opinion Nortel has made mistakes in the past, but I'd like to believe that they learned their lesson,"[5] commented one analyst who maintained his buy recommendation. An analyst at an independent equities research firm acknowledged there was an issue of trust in management but expressed hope that the accounting changes would be minor and have little impact on Nortel's share price. "When you're adjusting prior year numbers, who cares, I'm buying the stock today,"[6] the analyst said.

That remark would prove misguided by a long shot. More skeptical observers were apt to wonder whether the latest accounting inaccuracies were truly inadvertent errors. In 2003, Nortel had introduced a special bonus scheme. Senior executives' bonuses were tied to profits, and according to Toronto's *Globe and Mail,* 16 executives had collected a total of $43.6 million under the plan. Dunn and Beatty had reportedly received $2.15 million and $831,000, respectively.[7]

From Bad to Worse

Nortel was the most heavily traded stock on the New York Stock Exchange on March 5, 2004, falling by 3.7 percent, as the U.S. Securities and Exchange Commission (SEC) announced that it had upgraded its inquiry into the company's accounting to a formal investigation. John Gavin, president of the regulatory research firm SEC Insight Inc., commented that the SEC's upgrading of its probe, which empowered the commission to issue subpoenas, might indicate that Nortel was "not cooperating as much as they say they are."[8] The Ontario Securities Commission was also looking into Nortel's financial reporting, and an inquiry by the Royal Canadian Mounted Police later evolved into a criminal investigation.

Analysts who had downplayed the significance of the accounting revelations were dealt a blow on April 28, 2004. Nortel dropped a bombshell in the form of a 50 percent cut in its previously announced 2003 earnings of $732 million. The company said some of those profits would be shifted to earlier years, for which it reported losses. Nortel also delayed the reporting of its results for the first quarter of 2003, further damaging its credibility.

In addition to dashing hopes that the new round of accounting statements would be minor, Nortel rattled the market by firing CEO Dunn, CFO Beatty, and controller Gollogly. They were terminated for cause, but under

Canadian law that phrase included incompetence, so the dismissal did not necessarily imply any criminal acts. Nortel also placed the finance chiefs of its four operating divisions on paid leave. The company's stock price dropped by 28 percent, and Standard & Poor's downgraded its corporate credit rating from B to B–.

Some observers suggested that the senior executives were scapegoats for the board's failure to police the company's accounting practices. Dunn continued to receive high marks for his response to the 2001 business downturn. Furthermore, industry experts considered the company well positioned from a technological standpoint.

Notwithstanding these purported operational strengths, the credibility of Nortel's financial reporting continued to deteriorate. On June 2, 2004, the company indicated that the 50 percent cut in its 2003 earnings would not necessarily be the last revision. The possibility of further restatements arose as Nortel turned its attention to its reporting for the second half of 2003.

Management's credibility continued to shrink as the company kept pushing back its target date for producing definitive earnings restatements. Nortel had 650 employees devoted to the task, augmented by a host of outside auditors and consultants. By August 2004, their efforts had produced only "estimated limited preliminary unaudited" numbers.[9]

Three months later, the company still had not reported any results for 2004, and it once again delayed the release of its financials. On August 11, 2004, a new chapter opened. Nortel's investigation, which previously had focused on accruals and provisions, had turned to revenue recognition. The company said that $250 million of the $2.5 billion in 2000 revenue that had been slated for shifting to later years would be eliminated altogether. Incorrect recognition of that amount resulted from a combination of non-transfer of legal title to customers, failure to meet criteria for recognizing revenue prior to shipment, collectability questions, and other incorrect steps. Duncan Stewart, a fund manager with Terra Capital in Toronto, said Nortel's senior managers were "looking like clowns"[10] for failing to meet self-imposed deadlines for filing financial statements and for announcing major new financial reporting problems after many months of investigating.

On January 10, 2005, Nortel finally filed its 2003 financial statements. Reflecting the heavy criticism of the board's oversight of the company's accounting, five directors said they would not seek re-election, although they were not charged with any wrongdoing. In a highly unusual step, 12 senior executives agreed to return $8.6 million in bonuses they received based on erroneous accounting.

Nortel settled SEC civil charges of accounting fraud for $35 million, but rumors of poor financial condition persisted. The company was unable to obtain governmental financial assistance, and the recession of the late 2000s struck a further blow. On January 19, 2009, Nortel filed for bankruptcy in the United States, Canada, and the United Kingdom. The company initially hoped to reorganize and emerge from bankruptcy, but in June 2009 announced that it would instead liquidate all of its assets.

Lessons from Nortel

Nortel followed a time-honored (albeit not honorable) strategy of taking a big bath in its money-losing period of 2001–2002. Overstating losses created cookie-jar reserves that could be taken into profits later years. The big bath strategy is premised on the belief that magnifying an annual loss will not hurt the stock price as much as magnifying an annual profit will help it in a subsequent year.

Perhaps even more important in Nortel's case was the impact on bonuses that were paid as a function of returning to profitability. This was the arrangement for most Nortel employees even before the new plan for senior executives was adopted in 2003. In this sort of scheme, current bonuses are not reduced from zero if a reported loss is pumped up through unjustified accruals, but future bonuses are increased if those accruals are taken into profits later on, in a profitable year.

Based on past examples of big baths and cookie jar reserves, investors' muted reaction to the October 2003 announcement of a restatement, on the grounds that it lowered previously reported losses, was naive. Nortel's experience shows that if a company uses accruals to understate profits, it will have no compunction about overstating profits through aggressive revenue recognition. Instead of blowing over, the 2003 announcement proved to be the beginning of a situation that kept getting worse and worse.

The accruals that Nortel abused arose from contractual liabilities. For example, suppose the company missed a deadline on a $5 million contract and reasonably estimated the failure would cost it $500,000 through a customer refund. The amount of the expected refund would be booked as an expense, reducing current-year profits, and would be recorded as a liability until it was paid. If the customer subsequently agreed to accept a refund of only $300,000, the remaining $200,000 would be recognized as a profit in the period in which the refund was paid. The investigation by Nortel's board found that in 2003 management raided the cookie jar, taking reserves off its balance sheet without legitimate triggers for doing so. Furthermore, management overstated the reserves to create a bigger cookie jar into which it could dip.

Abuse of accruals was deeply embedded in Nortel's culture. Executives used the term *hardness* to describe the state of having ample reserves in place to draw on later as a means of managing earnings. The *Wall Street Journal* got access to an internal company document showing quarterly earnings targets. During the first half of 2003, the profit line kept rising as another number labeled *balance sheet* also kept changing, suggesting that management was generating the earnings increases by drawing on reserves.[11]

For internal purposes that included calculation of bonuses, Nortel used a figure it called "pro forma income." Its initial, publicly reported net income for the first quarter of 2003 was $54 million. The internal figure, on the other hand, included approximately $361 million in reserves, of which roughly $160 million was inappropriately reversed, according to the board's investigation. In the second quarter, Nortel publicly reported a $14 million loss, but the pro forma profit was $34 million, triggering bonuses of 10 to 25 percent of annual salary for most employees and two to four times salary for top managers, once four quarters of cumulative profits were recorded. Ultimately, the scheme unraveled when the board ordered management to clean up the company's balance after years of accumulated reserve accounting that gave rise to confusion.

An important takeaway from the Nortel case is that seemingly small items can prove highly significant. Investors paid little attention to a few hundred million dollars of reserve-related losses in the context of a total of $34 billion of losses recorded from 2000 to 2004. Those additions to reserves, however, added to accrued liabilities that grew to $5 billion by the summer of 2002, giving management a vast opportunity to manipulate earnings to enhance its bonuses.

GRASPING FOR EARNINGS AT GENERAL MOTORS

Rebates are another frequently abused element of expense recognition. General Motors's fiddling with this device shows the important role of corporate culture in the integrity of financial reporting. The corporate culture problem more familiar to many users of financial statements is the casual attitude toward the niceties of generally accepted accounting principles (GAAP) that characterizes many young, fast-growing companies with soaring stock prices. Sticking with blue chips, however, is no guarantee that the books are immaculate. A long-established company with a strong balance sheet and a lengthy record of stable earnings may have a corporate culture that includes going by the book on accounting matters, but that culture may change if profitability starts to erode.

General Motors (GM) illustrated this pathology as its fortunes deteriorated in the early 2000s.[12] During its long reign as the world's largest automaker, GM displayed all the insignia of a blue chip. When it was first rated by Moody's and Standard & Poor's in 1953, the company achieved the top ranking of AAA. Far from cutting corners in its financial reporting, GM in its heyday exceeded the requirements, providing investors audited financial statements before it became mandatory under the Securities Act of 1933.

Over time, however, GM lost its commanding position in the auto industry. This was partly because foreign manufacturers captured market share by catering to changes in consumer preferences to which U.S. producers GM, Ford, and Chrysler were slow to respond. By 1981, GM's AAA ratings were gone, and its attitude toward financial reporting began to shift. The company liberalized some of its policies in 1982 and soon became a regular proponent of looser accounting standards at hearings of the Financial Accounting Standards Board.

By 2005, GM's bond ratings had slid all the way to the speculative grade category, at BB. In the same year, disturbing signs began to surface that an aggressive approach to financial reporting had become embedded in GM's corporate culture. On October 26, 2005, the company disclosed that the Securities and Exchange Commission was investigating various aspects of its accounting. The probe, replete with subpoenas, addressed accounting for retirement benefits; certain transactions with Delphi, a bankrupt supplier that was formerly a division of GM; and the treatment of recovery of recall costs from suppliers.

On November 9, 2005, GM announced that it would have to restate its financial results for 2001 and possibly for subsequent years. The company said it had "erroneously" booked credits from suppliers, resulting in an overstatement of 2001 income by $300 million to $400 million.[13] That represented a hefty chunk of the $601 million in net income that the automaker originally showed in its 2001 annual report. The figure was down from $4.45 billion in 2000, underscoring the intense earnings pressure that GM was feeling.

At issue in GM's restatement was the recording of rebates and other credits from suppliers. The accounting rules stated that if the rebates involved not only current business but were upfront inducements to place large orders over several years, they should be taken into earnings over time, rather than booked immediately. In March 2005, Chief Financial Officer John Devine had stated that GM's "very clear" policy was to take no rebates from suppliers. In conjunction with the announcement of a coming restatement, however, spokeswoman Toni Simonetti backtracked on that claim. "I will say that some years ago we did say that we would generally discontinue this practice and generally we have," she explained. "I'm not sure if it's been stopped completely across the board."[14]

Judging by the range of accounting practices that the SEC was looking into, it appeared that the inappropriate handling of rebates was not an isolated incident, but symptomatic of widespread aggressiveness in GM's reporting. Coincident with its November 9, 2005, restatement announcement, the company disclosed that it had evaluated the effectiveness of its controls and procedures for determining whether assets should be deemed impaired and written off. Chairman Rick Wagoner said that he and CFO Devine had concluded that the company's controls were not effective at the SEC-defined "reasonable assurance level." As a result, GM had failed to reduce the value of its investment in Fuji Heavy Industries, the producer of Subaru cars, in a timely manner.

Yet another blow to the credibility of GM's financial reporting arrived on March 16, 2006. The company said that some cash flows from its mortgage subsidiary that should have been classified among its investing activities were instead booked as operating activities. This revelation puzzled accounting experts because the applicable rules were unambiguous. Extending a loan or receiving repayment fell into investing activities; interest payments were included in operating cash flow. It was difficult to see how an error could arise.

Similarly troubling was GM's revelation that in 2000 it booked a $27 million gain on the sale of precious metals in its inventory, even though it had agreed to repurchase the metals the following year. The repurchase agreement made the transaction a financing, rather than a sale, so the company should have recorded no income. Running afoul of such a fundamental accounting principle did not sound like an honest mistake. Rather, it had the scent of a transaction concocted for no economic purpose but rather to generate reported earnings at a company desperate to appear profitable.

It further developed that GM's aggressive accounting had not ended in 2000–2001. The company told investors that it had understated its loss in 2005's first quarter by $149 million. Management said it had prematurely increased the value of vehicles it was leasing to car-rental companies, assuming they would be worth more after those companies were through with them.

In the wake of the latest accounting-related disclosures, GM delayed the filing of its 10-K annual report to the SEC, a classic warning sign of financial distress. Another such indication had already come in December 2005 with an abrupt senior management change. Chief Financial Officer John Devine was replaced by Frederick "Fritz" Henderson, who later succeeded Wagoner as chief executive officer.

These telltale events did not turn out to be false warnings. On June 1, 2009, General Motors filed for bankruptcy. By then, the company's stock price had plummeted to $0.75 from its year-end 2005 level of $19.42. Even as late as 2005–2006, many investors found it hard to imagine a bankruptcy filing by a company once regarded as the bluest of blue chips. To close watchers of financial reporting, however, that outcome was by no means inconceivable. The mounting evidence of aggressive accounting strongly suggested that GM's corporate culture was deteriorating as its ability to generate bona fide profits waned.

TIME-SHIFTING AT FREDDIE MAC

Ordinarily, a company's stock price rises when its reported earnings unexpectedly increase. The opposite occurred, however, after Freddie Mac announced on January 22, 2003, that it would revise upward its earnings for previous years. Between January 21 and January 23, the mortgage finance company's shares fell nearly 5 percent while the S&P 500 Index was essentially unchanged.

The explanation of this seemingly strange response was the concern that the announcement raised among investors about the reliability of the financial statements of the government-sponsored enterprise (GSE) officially known as the Federal Home Loan Mortgage Corporation. Even before the news, investors were apprehensive about the complexity of Freddie Mac's accounting. Anxiety increased when the company's auditor, PricewaterhouseCoopers (PwC), raised questions about the way the company treated past accounting for certain hedging transactions. After Arthur Andersen surrendered its licenses to audit public companies following its conviction on criminal charges relating to its handling of Enron's audit (see Chapter 11), PwC had taken over as Freddie Mac's auditor. When PwC reviewed the 2002 results, it questioned company accounting decisions that Arthur Andersen had approved, raising the possibility that further problems would emerge.

Freddie Mac steadfastly denied that its handling of derivatives was aimed at smoothing its earnings. That is, the company contended that it did not deliberately hold down its reported profits during good times, making it easier to later post the steady earnings increases that security analysts craved. On June 25, 2003, however, Freddie Mac admitted that in some instances it manipulated its earnings to match Wall Street earnings forecasts. Management nevertheless claimed that most of the understatement of net income for 2000 through 2002, which it estimated at $1.5 billion to $4.5 billion, was accidental. (The figure rose to nearly $5 billion by the time a review of the company's financial reporting was completed in November 2003.)

Even if it was true that intentional misrepresentations were the lesser part of the earnings understatement, the company's questionable practices had a huge impact that even conscientious analysts could not detect from the outside. Freddie Mac time-shifted $420 million of pro forma profits (the measure the company was then urging investors to focus on) through linked swaps. In these transactions, the company bet on a rise in interest rates at the same time that it bet on a decline in interest rates. The net economic benefit was nil, and there was minimal business justification for the swaps, other than altering the timing of profits. Freddie Mac structured the swaps such that it made its payments in one month and received payment for the offsetting trade in the following month. That reduced net income in one year and raised it in the next.

Freddie Mac's non-economically driven financial engineering also displayed a characteristic frequently observed in accounting manipulation, namely snowballing misrepresentation. The company initiated its use of linked swaps in 2001 because falling interest rates were creating an earnings blizzard. If interest rates had leveled off, bringing profits down to a more normal growth rate, Freddie Mac could have begun working down the earnings reserve it had created. Instead, rates continued to fall. To keep the game going and avoid reporting an unwanted earnings spike, management had to undertake bigger and bigger linked-rate swaps. The final swap shifted more income than the first eight combined.[15]

Freddie Mac's manipulation did not end there. Another ploy to hide earnings consisted of ceasing to use market prices for certain derivatives. Outside investigators labeled this action "results-oriented, reverse engineered, and opportunistic."[16] Incredibly, it turned out that after all of management's maneuvers were stripped away, the net effect was that the company *overstated* its 2001 earnings by almost $1 billion.

Encouragingly, from the standpoint of dissuading future abusers of GAAP, Freddie Mac's misdeeds brought retribution. The board fired the company's president and obtained the resignations of its chief executive officer and chief financial officer. The CEO was succeeded by the former chief investment officer, but he, too, eventually lost his job after his role in the linked-rate swaps came to light. In addition, the company paid a $125 million fine in a settlement with the Office of Federal Enterprise Oversight. The regulator's report traced the origins of Freddie Mac's inappropriate practices back to the mid-1990s.

Furthermore, the revelations about Freddie Mac's accounting practices lent fuel to politicians' intent on reining in Freddie Mac and its fellow GSE, Fannie Mae. The two companies later became central figures in the financial crisis of 2008 and were placed under government conservatorship. Financial reporting issues were not the immediate cause of their fall from grace, but they were symptomatic of unhealthy corporate cultures that led to unsound financial practices.

CONCLUSION

Just as companies have myriad ways of exaggerating revenues, they follow a variety of approaches in downplaying expenses. Corporate managers make liberal assumptions about costs that may be capitalized, pile up unjustified accruals, dilute expenses with one-time gains, relocate them in time, and jump the gun in booking rebates from suppliers. These gambits are often exceedingly difficult to detect in companies' public financial statements, but seemingly minor yet unprecedented or unconventional entries can foreshadow major restatements. To pick up such clues, analysts must be disciplined enough to disbelieve the innocent explanations that companies routinely provide for abnormalities that point to trouble down the road.

CHAPTER 8

The Applications and Limitations of EBITDA

As noted in Chapter 3, corporations have attempted to break free of the focus on after-tax earnings that historically dominated their valuation and continues to be the key focus of Wall Street research. The impetus for trying to redirect investors' focus to operating income or other variants has been the minimal net profits recorded by many **New Economy** companies. Conventionally calculated price-earnings (P/E) multiples of such companies, most inconveniently, make their stocks look expensive. Old Economy companies generally have larger denominators (the E in P/E), so their multiples look extremely reasonable by comparison.

Long before the dot-com companies of the 1990s began seeking alternatives to net income, users of financial statements had discovered certain limitations in net income as a valuation tool. They observed that two companies in the same industry could report similar income yet have substantially different **total enterprise values**. Similarly, credit analysts realized that in a given year, two companies could generate similar levels of income to cover similar levels of interest expense yet represent highly dissimilar risks of defaulting on their debt in the future.

The earnings per share figure was not, despite equity investors' obsession with it, a standard by which every company's value and risk could be fairly compared. Had analysts thought deeply about the problem, they might have hypothesized that *no* single measure could capture financial performance comprehensively enough to fulfill such a role. Instead, they set off on a quest for the correct single measure of corporate profitability, believing in its existence as firmly as the conquistadors who set off in search of El Dorado.

EBIT, EBITDA, AND TOTAL ENTERPRISE VALUE

When equity analysts recommend a company's stock, they typically highlight its prospects for earnings growth. They may also apply various valuation metrics to argue that the stock is cheap relative to others they consider comparable. Sometimes, analysts also allude to upside related to the company's attractiveness as an acquisition target. An acquirer generally has to pay a significant premium to the prevailing share price to consummate the deal. The fictitious example in Exhibit 8.1 helps to bring out the shortcomings of after-tax earnings in estimating a company's "takeout value" in the acquisition scenario.

Suppose a suitor has a choice between acquiring thingamabob manufacturer Deep Hock Corporation and its direct competitor Breathing Room Inc. Assuming the going rate for acquisitions in the thingamabob industry is 25 times net income, Breathing Room is far more valuable, at 25 × $24.0 million = $600 million, versus 25 × $19.8 million = $495 million for Deep Hock. On the face of it, the higher valuation on Breathing Room is surprising, given its much lower rate of return on equity (net income ÷ shareholders' equity), i.e., 12.0 percent versus 18.0 percent on Deep Hock.

That paradox is explained by the contrast between Breathing Room's debt-free balance sheet and Deep Hock's comparatively aggressive financial leverage:

EXHIBIT 8.1 Comparative Financial Data ($000,00 omitted) Year Ended December 31, 2020

	Deep Hock Corporation	Breathing Room Inc.
Total debt	$90.0	$0.0
Shareholders' equity	110.0	200.0
Sales	250.0	250.0
Cost of sales	200.0	200.0
Depreciation and amortization	12.5	12.5
Selling, general, and administrative expense	<u>7.1</u>	<u>7.1</u>
Operating income	30.4	30.4
Interest expense	<u>5.4</u>	<u>0.0</u>
Income before income taxes	25.0	30.4
Provision for income taxes	<u>5.2</u>	<u>6.4</u>
Net income	<u>$19.8</u>	<u>$24.0</u>
Return on equity	18.0%	12.0%

$$\text{Debt-to-Total Capital} = \frac{\text{Total Debt}}{\text{Total Debt} + \text{Shareholders' Equity}}$$

$$= \frac{\$90.0}{\$90.0 + \$110.0}$$

$$= 45\%$$

The difference in valuation created by nonequivalent debt ratios does not truly affect an acquired company's post-acquisition value to the acquirer. For example, if the acquirer operates Breathing Room as a separately financed subsidiary, it can boost the return on its equity investment in the subsidiary by adding debt to Breathing Room's capital structure. On the other hand, if the acquirer's own balance sheet is debt-free, it may retire Deep Hock's debt. (Note that the need to pay off Deep Hock's debt will affect the amount of cash the acquirer will pay for the shares.)

A further complication in the calculations is that all things being equal, a leveraged company's price-earnings ratio will be lower than an unleveraged company's. That is because leverage increases earnings volatility and investors prefer steady earnings to volatile earnings. In our example, Deep Hock would have been trading at the same price-earnings multiple pre-acquisition as Breathing Room only if it surpassed Breathing Room in other multiple-enhancing characteristics.

For all these reasons, it would not in fact make sense for a would-be acquirer to apply a single multiple of earnings across the board to all potential acquirees within a given industry. To remove from the picture the incumbent managements' financial strategies, which will cease to be relevant following the acquisition, the acquirer can apply a multiple of earnings before interest and taxes, or EBIT. In our example, applying an EBIT multiple of 20 times would produce the same acquisition price for both Deep Hock and Breathing Room:

	Deep Hock	Breathing Room
Net income	$19.8	$24.0
+ Taxes	5.2	6.4
+ Interest	5.4	0.0
EBIT	$30.4	$30.4
× 20 =	$608	$608

During the 1980s, the potential acquirers that equity analysts contemplated in their Buy recommendations increasingly became **leveraged buyout** (LBO) firms. At the start of that decade, **Tobin's Q** was unusually low, with the result that many companies' private market values far exceeded their **market capitalizations.** LBO firms' typical strategy was to pay for a company with a sliver of equity and a lot of borrowed money, then apply cash generated by the business toward retiring debt. These acquirers sought to bring debt down to modest levels within about five years, then realize a profit by taking the company public again or selling it to a "strategic" buyer, that is, a larger company seeking to expand its footprint in the industry.

In that context, it made sense for the acquirers of choice, the LBO firms, to evaluate a potential acquiree not only without respect to its existing capital structure, but also without respect to some major non-cash charges, depreciation of tangible assets and amortization of intangible assets. Naturally, to maintain the company's effectiveness over the long run, those assets had to be replaced. That is, depreciation and amortization had to be offset by equivalent expenditures – or even by somewhat greater expenditures to take growth and technological advances into account. Over a five-year timeframe, however, a company might direct cashflow primarily to debt paydown without impairing its long-run competitiveness.

As LBO firms delivered handsome profits to their limited partners on several high-profile deals, their "war chests" (funds available for investment) expanded greatly. All but the very largest public companies became plausible targets for LBOs, initiated either in the form of a hostile takeover or with the involvement of incumbent management. Equity investors increasingly evaluated companies as LBO firms did, on the basis of earnings before interest, taxes, depreciation, and amortization (EBITDA). A market capitalization of $600 million for either of the two companies shown in Exhibit 8.1 would equate to an EBITDA multiple of 14 times.

	Deep Hock	Breathing Room
Net income	$19.8	$24.0
+ Taxes	5.2	6.4
+ Interest	5.4	0.0
+ Depreciation and amortization	12.5	12.5
= EBITDA	$42.9	$42.9
$600 ÷ EBITDA =	14.0 ×	14.0 ×

Another advantage of calculating total enterprise value as a multiple of EBITDA had to do with countering financial reporting trickery. If a target company uses liberal depreciation accounting to inflate its earnings, adding back depreciation puts it on an equal footing with a company that employs a more conservative approach.

Exhibit 8.2 shows how Conniving Corp.'s management has planned to report the company's annual earnings before learning, in the weeks between year-end and the scheduled date for filing its financial statements, that the private equity firm Middlebelt Partners is interested in proposing an LBO deal. Conniving's C-suite executives naturally want to maximize the value of their stock options. Chief Financial Officer Evan Chewley hatches a creative solution.

Currently, Conniving's stock is trading at 20 times earnings of $163 million, producing a $3.260 billion market capitalization. Based on terms of recent LBOs, management can expect the company to fetch a 30 percent premium, or a multiple of 26 times and a market capitalization of $4.238 billion. CFO Chewley points out that Conniving can boost its 2020 net income by the simple expedient of revising from eight to ten years the

EXHIBIT 8.2 Conniving Corp. ($000,000 omitted) December 31, 2020

	Conservative	Liberal	Change
Sales	$1,913	$1,913	
Cost of goods sold	1,334	1,334	
Depreciation	120	96	−24
Selling, general, and administrative expense	182	182	
Operating income	277	301	+24
Interest expense	71	71	
Net income before income taxes	206	230	
Provision for income taxes	43	48	
Net income	$163	$182	+19
Property, plant and equipment (2019)	$960		
Average life for depreciation (years)	8	10	+2
EBIT (2020)	$277	$301	+24
EBITDA (2020)	397	397	0

Takeover valuation sensitivity to depreciation accounting

Takeover value	Conservative	Liberal	Increase
@ 26 times earnings (30% premium)	$4.238	$4.732	$494
@ 15 times EBIT	4.155	4.515	360
@ 11 times EBITDA	4.367	4.367	0

average depreciable lives of its fixed assets, or property, plant, and equipment. With that switch to a more liberal practice, depreciation expense will fall by $24 million. Of that amount, $19 million will drop to the bottom line. At the expected LBO multiple of 26 times, Middlebelt will pay $494 million more for Conniving than under the old accounting.

Some readers may wonder whether an abrupt shift from an eight- to a ten-year depreciation schedule is a realistic plan for Conniving. In 2016, the luxury brand company Prada announced, not in connection with any M&A plans, that it would end its policy of capping the depreciation periods on its store leases at ten years. Some of its leases ran as long as 18 years, although the average was about eight years. This liberalization was expected to increase full-year 2016 earnings by around 50 million euros, or about $56 million at the then-prevailing exchange rate, with no impact on cash flow. Based on this real-world example, fictional CFO Chewley's scheme is definitely feasible.

Luckily for their investors, Middlebelt's negotiators know the ins and outs of financial reporting. They realize that lengthening the lives of depreciable assets generates no incremental cash. (Conniving already employs a more accelerated depreciation schedule in its tax reporting.) Middlebelt will not shell out an extra $494 million for a change in accounting practices.

Basing the acquisition price on EBIT rather than net income would go some way toward maintaining Conniving's comparability with companies that adhere to its industry's customary accounting standards. At a multiple of 15 times, the valuation gap created by the switch to ten-year average lives declines from $494 million to $360 million. Middlebelt can eliminate the gap altogether, though, by insisting on using a multiple of EBITDA to determine the acquisition price. EBITDA is $397 million, regardless whether Conniving uses the more conservative or the more liberal depreciation schedule. Either way, an EBITDA multiple of 11 times produces a $4.367 billion acquisition price. EBITDA's popularity as a valuation tool derives in part from this attribute of leveling the playing field in comparisons of companies' valuations.

Useful though EBITDA is in foiling this particular ploy that involves depreciation accounting, analysts involved in acquisitions should not jump to the conclusion that the starting point of every negotiation is a number that buyers and sellers can safely accept at face value. Whether they are trying to attract a higher price from an acquirer or engineer a higher valuation in the stock market, corporate managers frequently try to shift attention to "adjusted EBITDA" rather than the GAAP version.

Some adjustments make sense, as when a clearly unusual, non-recurring event happens to depress operating income in the 12 months preceding commencement of an acquisition negotiation. Also, abused though the term often is, bona fide synergies do emerge from many merger-and-acquisition transactions. If an entire layer of the acquiree's management will be eliminated through consolidation with the acquirer, it is reasonable to modify the historical EBITDA figure for that predictable saving. Less defensible are some attempts to substitute a **run rate** for a short period – in extreme cases, as little as one month – for actual results over the latest 12 months. That sort of adjusted EBITDA can be upwardly skewed by seasonal factors or special events such as new-product launches.

THE ROLE OF EBITDA IN CREDIT ANALYSIS

In the decades since LBOs first began to influence equity analysis, EBITDA has also become a fixture in credit analysis. As in valuing businesses to assess stock prices, EBITDA can discriminate among companies that look similar when judged in terms of EBIT. Consider the fictitious examples of Rock Solid Corporation and Hollowman, Inc. (Exhibit 8.3).

Measured by conventional fixed charge coverage (see Chapter 13), the two companies look equally risky, with ratios of 3.62× and 3.58×, respectively:

Fixed charge coverage:

$$\text{Net Income} + \text{Income Taxes} + \text{Interest Expense}$$

EXHIBIT 8.3 Comparative Financial Data ($000,000 omitted) Year Ended December 31, 2020

	Rock Solid Corporation	Hollowman, Inc.
Total debt	$950.0	$875.0
Shareholders' equity	750.0	675.0
Total capital	1700.0	1550.0
Sales	2000.0	1750.0
Cost of goods sold	1600.0	1400.0
Depreciation and amortization	75.0	30.0
Selling, general, and administrative expense	115.0	130.0
Operating income	210.0	190.0
Interest expense	58.0	53.0
Income before income taxes	152.0	137.0
Provision for income taxes	32.0	29.0
Net income	120.0	108.0

Interest expense:

$$\text{Rock Solid Corp.} : \frac{\$120.0 + 32.0 + 58.0}{\$58} = 3.62\times$$

$$\text{Hollowman, Inc.} : \frac{\$108.0 + 29.0 + 53.0}{\$53} = 3.58\times$$

For convenience of exposition, we refer to this standard credit measure as the EBIT-based coverage ratio. Note that for some companies, the sum of net income, income taxes, and interest expense is not equivalent to EBIT, reflecting the presence of such factors as extraordinary items and minority interest below the pretax income line.

As it happens, Hollowman and Rock Solid are almost perfectly matched on **financial leverage**, another standard measure of credit risk. (For a discussion of calculating the total-debt-to-total-capital ratio in more complex cases, see Chapter 13.)

Total-debt-to-total-capital ratio:

$$\frac{\text{Total Debt}}{\text{Total Debt} + \text{Equity}}$$

$$\text{Rock Solid Corp.:} \frac{\$950.00}{\$950.0 + 750.0} = 55.9\%$$

$$\text{Holloman, Inc.:} \frac{\$875.0}{\$875.0 + 675.0} = 56.5\%$$

By these criteria, lending to Hollowman, Inc. is as safe a proposition as lending to Rock Solid Corp. Bringing EBITDA into the analysis, however, reveals that Rock Solid is better able to keep up its interest payments in the event of a business downturn.

In the current year, Rock Solid's gross profit – $2,000 million sales less $1,600 million cost of goods sold – is $400 million. Suppose that through a combination of reduced revenue and margin deterioration, the figure drops by 55 percent to $1,800 million – $1,620 million = $180 million, while other operating expenses remain constant (Exhibit 8.4). Net income now comes to –$53.7 million. Adding to that a $14.3 million tax credit and $58 million of interest expense produces EBIT of –$10.0 million.

Is Rock Solid truly unable to pay the $58 million interest on its debt? No, because the $75.0 million of depreciation and amortization charged against income is an accounting entry, rather than a current-year outlay of cash. Adding back these noncash charges shows that the company keeps its head above water, covering its interest by a margin of 1.29 times:

EBITDA coverage of interest:

$$\frac{\text{Net Income} + \text{Income Taxes} + \text{Interest Expense} + \text{Depreciation and Amortization}}{\text{Interest Expense}}$$

$$\frac{(53.7) + (14.3) + 68.0 + 75.0}{58.0} = 1.29\times$$

By contrast, if Hollowman's gross profit falls by 55 percent to $1,575.0 million − $1,480.5 million = $94.5 million, as also shown in Exhibit 8.4, its interest coverage not only drops below 1.0 times but turns negative, even on an EBITDA basis:

$$\frac{(\$93.5) + (25.0) + 53.0 + 30.0}{53.0} = -0.67\times$$

Rock Solid can sustain a larger decline in gross margin than Hollowman can before it will cease to generate sufficient cash to pay its interest in full. The reason is that noncash depreciation charges represent a larger portion of Rock Solid's total operating expenses − 4.2 percent of $1.790 billion, versus 1.9 percent of $1.560 billion for Hollowman (Exhibit 8.4). This difference, in turn, indicates that Rock Solid's business is more capital-intensive than Hollowman's. Further inspection of the companies' financial statements would likely show Rock Solid to have a larger percentage of total assets concentrated in property, plant, and equipment.

EXHIBIT 8.4 Statements of Income ($000,000 omitted) Year Ended December 31, 2020

	Rock Solid Corporation	Hollowman, Inc.
Sales	$1,800.0	$1,575.0
Cost of goods sold	1,620.0	1,480.5
Depreciation and amortization	75.0	30.0
Selling, general, and administrative expense	115.0	130.0
Operating income	(10.0)	(65.5)
Interest expense	58.0	53.0
Income (loss) before income taxes	(68.0)	(118.5)
Provision (credit) for income taxes	(14.3)	(25.0)
Net income (loss)	(53.7)	(93.5)

In summary, conventionally measured fixed charge coverage is nearly identical for the two companies, yet they differ significantly in their probability of defaulting on interest payments in a cyclical downturn. Taking EBITDA into account enables analysts to discriminate between the two credits that look similarly risky by other measures. This is a second legitimate reason for the ratio's popularity, along with its usefulness in ensuring comparability of companies with dissimilar depreciation policies, when estimating the total enterprise values.

ABUSING EBITDA

Like many other financial ratios, EBITDA can provide valuable insight when used properly. It is potentially misleading, however, when applied in the wrong context. A tip-off to the possibility of abuse is apparent from the preceding illustration. By adding depreciation to the numerator, management can emphasize (legitimately, in this case) that although Rock Solid's operating profits make no contribution toward paying its 2020 interest bill, the company is generating 147 percent as much cash as it needs for that purpose.

In their perennial quest for cheap capital, LBO sponsors are keenly aware of the comfort that lenders derive from a fixed charge coverage ratio comfortably above 1X, sometimes paying too little attention to the means by which it is achieved. To exploit the effect as fully as possible, sponsors strive to steer credit analysts' focus away from traditional fixed charge coverage and toward EBITDA coverage of interest. Shifting investors' attention was particularly beneficial during the 1980s, when some buyouts were so highly leveraged that projected EBIT would not cover pro forma interest expense even in a good year. The sponsors reassured nervous investors by ballyhooing EBITDA coverage ratios that exceeded the psychologically critical threshold of 1.0 times. Meanwhile, the sponsors' investment bankers insinuated that traditionalists who fixated on sub-1.0X EBIT coverage ratios were hopelessly antiquated and self-defeatingly conservative in their analysis.

In truth, a bit of caution is advisable in the matter of counting depreciation toward interest coverage. The argument for favoring the EBITDA-based over EBIT-based fixed charge coverage rests on a hidden assumption. Adding depreciation to the numerator is appropriate only for the period over which a company can put off a substantial portion of its capital spending without impairing its future competitiveness.

Over a full operating cycle, the capital expenditures reported in a company's statement of cash flows are ordinarily at least as great as the depreciation charges shown on its income statement. The company must repair the physical wear and tear on its equipment. Additional outlays are required for the replacement of obsolete equipment. If anything, capital spending is likely to exceed depreciation over time, as the company expands its productive capacity to accommodate rising demand. Another reason that capital spending may run higher than depreciation is that newly acquired equipment may be costlier than the old equipment being written off, as a function of inflation.

In view of the ongoing need to replace and add to productive capacity, the cash flow represented by depreciation is not truly available for paying interest, at least not on any permanent basis. Rather, the D in EBITDA is a safety valve that the corporate treasurer can use if EBIT falls below I for a limited time. Under such conditions, the company can temporarily reduce its capital spending, freeing up some of its depreciation cash flow for interest payments. Delaying equipment purchases and repairs that are essential, but not urgent, should inflict no lasting damage on the company's operations, provided the profit slump lasts for only a few quarters. Most companies, however, would lose their competitive edge if they spent only the bare minimum on property, plant, and equipment, year after year. It was disingenuous for sponsors of the most highly leveraged buyouts of the 1980s to suggest that their companies could remain healthy while paying interest substantially greater than EBIT over extended periods.

Naturally, the sponsors were prepared with glib answers to this objection. Prior to the buyout, they claimed, management had been overspending on plant and equipment. The now-deposed chief executives allegedly had wasted billions on projects that were monuments to their egos, rather than economically sound corporate investments. In fact, the story went, investments in low-return projects were the cause of the stock becoming cheap enough to make the company vulnerable to takeover. Investors ought to be pleased, rather than alarmed, to see capital expenditures fall precipitously after the buyout. Naturally, this line of reasoning was less persuasive in cases where the sponsors teamed up with the incumbent CEO in a management-led buyout.

With the benefit of hindsight, the assumptions behind many of the LBOs' financial projections were extremely aggressive. Often, the projections optimistically assumed that the huge debt repayment obligations would be financed with the proceeds of asset sales. The sponsors declared that they would raise immense quantities of cash by unloading supposedly nonessential assets.

Still, the sponsors' arguments were not entirely unfounded. At least some of the vast, diversified corporations that undertook leveraged buyouts during the 1980s had capital projects that deserved to be canceled. Some of the bloated conglomerates owned deadweight assets that were well worth shedding.

The subsequent wave of LBO-related bond defaults,[1] however, vindicated analysts who had voiced skepticism about the new-styled corporate finance. Depreciation was not, after all, available as a long-run source of cash for interest payments. This was a lesson applicable not only to the extremely leveraged deals of the 1980s but also to the more conservatively capitalized LBOs of later years.

A MORE COMPREHENSIVE CASH FLOW MEASURE

Despite some shortcomings as a tool for quantifying credit risk, EBITDA has become a fixture in securities analysis. Many practitioners now consider the ratio synonymous with cash flow or, more formally, operating cash flow (OCF). The interchangeability in analysts' minds of EBITDA and OCF is troubling in light of a long tradition of empirical research linking genuine cash flow and bankruptcy risk.

In an influential 1966 study,[2] William H. Beaver tested various financial ratios as predictors of corporate bankruptcy. Among the ratios he tested was a definition of cash flow still widely used today. Cash flow (as defined by Beaver, 1966) is:

Net Income + Depreciation, Depletion, and Amortization

(Depletion, a noncash expense applied to natural resource assets, is ordinarily taken to be implicit in depreciation and amortization, hence the use of the acronym EBITDA, rather than EBITDDA.)

Beaver found that of all the ratios he tested, the best single predictor of bankruptcy was a declining trend in the ratio of cash flow to total debt. This relationship made intuitive sense. Practitioners reasoned that bankruptcy risk was likely to increase if net income declined or total debt increased, either of which would reduce the cash-flow-to-total-debt ratio. The empirical evidence indicated that by adding depreciation to the numerator, analysts improved their ability to predict which companies would go bust, relative to comparing total debt with net income alone.

Note that Beaver's definition of cash flow was more stringent than EBITDA, since he did not add back either taxes or interest to net income. Even so, bond analysts have developed a tradition of telescoping default risk into the single ratio of cash flow (by which they mean EBITDA) as a percentage of total debt, all based ultimately on Beaver's 1966 finding.[3]

In so doing, practitioners have institutionalized a method that Beaver never advocated and that subsequent experience has shown to be seriously flawed.

Beaver did not conclude that analysts should rely exclusively on the ratio of cash flow to debt ratio, but merely that it was the single best bankruptcy predictor. As he noted in his study, other academic researchers were already attempting to build bankruptcy models with greater predictive power by combining ratios into a **multivariate** analysis. As of 1966, no one had yet succeeded, but just two years later, Edward I. Altman introduced a multivariate model composed of five ratios[4] (see Chapter 13). The development of Altman's Z-Score and other multivariate models has demonstrated that no single financial ratio predicts bankruptcy as accurately as a properly selected combination of ratios.

Since 1968, there has been no excuse for reducing bankruptcy risk to the sole measure of EBITDA to total debt. Nevertheless, that procedure remains common shorthand for credit risk. Similarly unjustifiable, on the basis of empirical evidence, is the widely used single-variable approach of ranking a sample of corporate borrowers according to their EBITDA coverage of interest.

Bizarrely, investment managers sometimes ask bond analysts to provide rankings of companies by their "actual credit risk," as opposed to Moody's, Standard & Poor's, or Fitch ratings. Asked to elaborate on this request, the investment managers reply that actual risk *obviously* means EBITDA coverage. Apparently, they consider it self-evident that the single ratio of cash flow (as they define it) to fixed charges predicts bankruptcy better than all of the rating agencies' quantitative and qualitative considerations combined. Little do the investment managers realize that they are setting credit analysis back by more than half a century!

Nearly as outmoded as exclusive reliance on a single EBITDA-based ratio is certain analysts' belief that they can derive a satisfactory measure of cash flow by simply selecting some version of earnings and adding back depreciation. It became apparent that neither EBITDA nor net income plus depreciation was a valid proxy for cash flow at least as far back as 1975, when W. T. Grant filed for bankruptcy. The department store chain's collapse showed that reliance on an earnings-plus-depreciation measure could cause analysts to overlook weakness at a company with substantial working capital needs. Many subsequent failures in the retailing and apparel industries have corroborated that finding.

At the time of its bankruptcy filing, W. T. Grant was the largest retailer in the United States. Up until two years before it went belly-up, the company reported positive net income (see Exhibit 8.5). Moreover, the department store chain enjoyed positive and stable cash flow (as defined by Beaver, in other words, net income plus depreciation). Bankruptcy therefore seemed

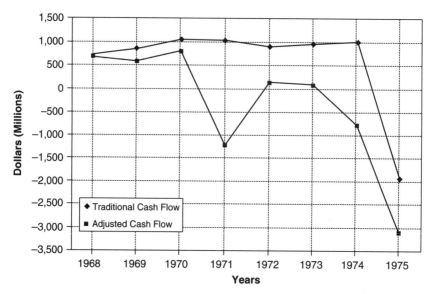

EXHIBIT 8.5   W. T. Grant Alternative Cash Flow Measures 1967–1975.
Sources: Clyde P. Stickney and Paul R. Brown, *Financial Reporting and Statement Analysis: A Strategic Perspective,* 4th ed. (Orlando, FL: Dryden), 106–123; James Largay, "Cash Flows, Ratio Analysis and the W. T. Grant Company Bankruptcy," *Financial Analysts Journal,* July–August 1980, 51–55.

a remote prospect, even though the company's net income failed to grow between the late 1960s and early 1970s. In 1973, W. T. Grant's stock traded at 20 times earnings, indicating strong investor confidence in the company's future. The board of directors reinforced that confidence by continuing to authorize dividends until mid-1974.

Investors would have been less sanguine if they had looked beyond the cash sources (earnings and depreciation) and uses (interest and dividends) shown on the income statement. It was imperative to investigate whether two balance sheet items, inventories and accounts receivable, were tying up increasing amounts of cash. If so, it became vital to determine whether the company could generate an offsetting amount of cash by expanding its accounts payable. Recognizing the need for this added level of analysis, the Financial Accounting Standards Board (FASB) eventually prescribed a more comprehensive definition of *operating cash flow,* as defined in SFAS 95, "Statement of Cash Flows."

Operating cash flow (as defined by FASB, 1987):

Net Income + Depreciation − Changes in Working Capital Requirements where:

$$\text{Working Capital Requirements} = \text{Accounts Receivable} + \text{Inventory}$$
$$- \text{Accounts Payable}$$

Note that this definition focuses on the elements of working capital that ordinarily grow roughly in proportion with the scale of operations. The FASB formulation excludes cash and marketable securities, as well as short-term debt.

WORKING CAPITAL ADDS PUNCH TO CASH FLOW ANALYSIS

Adding working capital to cash flow analysis frequently reveals problems that may not be apparent from observing the trend of EBITDA or net income plus depreciation. In fact, reported earnings often exceed true economic profits specifically as a function of gambits involving inventories or accounts receivable. Fortunately, such ploys leave telltale signs of earnings manipulation. Aside from seasonal variations, the amount of working capital needed to run a business represents a fairly constant percentage of a company's sales. Therefore, a material increase in inventories or receivables as a percentage of sales is a red flag. Analysts should strongly suspect that the company is dragging its feet on writing off unsalable merchandise or postponing write-offs off bad receivables, meaning that current earnings are overstated. Naturally, management invariably offers a more benign explanation.

Consider, for example, an apparel manufacturer that must produce its garments before knowing which new styles will catch the fancy of shoppers in the season ahead. Suppose that management guesses wrong about the fashion trend. The company now holds inventory that can be sold, if at all, only at knockdown prices. Instead of selling the unfashionable garments, which would force the manufacturer to recognize the loss in value, management may decide to retain them in its finished goods inventory. Accounting theory states that the company should nevertheless recognize the loss by writing down the merchandise. In practice, though, management may persuade its auditors that no loss of value has occurred. After all, judging what is fashionable is a subjective process. Furthermore, management can always argue that the goods remain in its warehouse only because of a temporary slowdown in orders. If the auditors buy the story, it will not alter the fact that the company has suffered an economic loss. Analysts focusing exclusively on EBITDA will have no inkling that earnings are down or that the company' cash resources may be starting to strain.

In contrast, analysts will recognize that something is amiss if they monitor a cash flow measure that includes working capital in addition to net income and depreciation. While the current season's goods remain in inventory, the company is producing clothing for the next season. Observe what happens to working capital requirements, bearing in mind the FASB 95 definition, as the new production enters inventory:

Working Capital Requirements = Accounts Receivable

+ Inventory − Accounts Payable

Inventory rises, causing working capital requirements to increase. According to the FASB definition, a rise in working capital requirements reduces operating cash flow. Analysts receive a danger signal, even though net income plus depreciation advances steadily.

A surge in accounts receivable, similarly, would reduce operating cash flow. The buildup in receivables could signal either of two types of underlying problems. On the one hand, management may be trying to prop up sales by liberalizing credit terms to its existing customers. Specifically, the company may be carrying financially strained businesses by giving them more time to pay. If so, average accounts receivable will be higher than in the past. That will soak up more cash and force the company to absorb financing costs formerly borne by its customers. Alternately, a buildup in receivables may result from extension of credit to new, less creditworthy customers that pay their bills comparatively slowly. To reflect the greater propensity of such customers to fail on their obligations, the company ought to increase its reserve for bad debts. Current-period reported income would then decline. Unfortunately, companies do not always do what they ought to, according to good accounting practice. If they do not, a cash flow measure that includes working capital requirements will reveal a weakness not detected by net income plus depreciation or EBITDA.

To be sure, management may attempt to mask problems related to inventory or receivables by pumping up the third component of working capital requirements, accounts payable. If the company takes longer to pay its own bills, the resulting rise in payables may offset the increase on the asset side. Fortunately for analysts, companies think twice before playing this card, because of potential repercussions on operations. Suppliers might view a slowdown in payments as a sign of financial weakness. Vital trade credit could dry up as a consequence.

In any case, analysts should use operating cash flow as one of many diagnostic tools. They should not rely on it exclusively, any more than they should limit their surveillance solely to tracking EBITDA. If a company resorts to stretching out its payables, other ratios detailed in Chapter 13 (receivables to sales and inventories to cost of goods sold) will nevertheless send out warning signals. Note, as well, that if the company does not finance the bulge in inventories and receivables by extending its payables or drawing down cash, it must add to its borrowings. Accordingly, a rising debt-to-capital ratio (see Chapter 13) can confirm an adverse credit trend revealed by operating cash flow.

CONCLUSION

Despite repeated demonstrations of the truism that no single measure encapsulates all of a company's pertinent financial traits, investors continue to search for the silver bullet. If a company's value is not a direct function of its net income, they tell themselves, the problem must be that net income is too greatly affected by incidental factors such as tax rates and financial leverage. The answer must be to move up the income statement to a measure that puts companies on a more even plane with one another. As former Merrill Lynch investment strategist Richard Bernstein points out,[5] operating earnings tend to be stabler than reported earnings, EBIT tends to be stabler than operating earnings, and EBITDA tends to be stabler than EBIT.

Companies welcome analytical migration toward less variable measures of performance, because investors reward stability with high price-earnings multiples. The trend of moving up the income statement reached its logical conclusion during the technology stock boom of the late 1990s. Investors latched onto the highest, most stable figure of all by valuing stocks on price-sales ratios. (To obscure what was going on, some companies actually resorted to discussing their earnings before expenses, or EBE.) As New Economy companies that report little if any GAAP income have become more prominent in the public equity market, multiples of sales have gained considerable respectability among analysts.

One thing that has not changed is the principle that reducing company analysis to a single financial ratio such as EBITDA, although alluring as a labor-saving device, is unwise. Once corporate managers find out which ratio analysts are single-mindedly focused on, they will devote massive time and energy to gaming that metric. Considering a variety of ratios may improve the analysis simply because companies' efforts to dress up the premier ratio will cause others to weaken, as when delayed write-offs of stale inventory flatter earnings but bloat the ratio of inventory to cost of goods sold.

CHAPTER 9

The Reliability of Disclosure and Audits

A naive observer might consider it overkill to scrutinize a company's financial statements for signs that management is presenting anything less than a candid picture. After all, extensive regulations compel publicly traded corporations to disclose material events affecting the value of their securities. Even if a company's management is inclined to finagle, investors have a second line of defense in the form of mandatory annual certification of the financials by highly trained auditors. The Securities and Exchange Commission's (SEC) Corporation Finance and Enforcement divisions provide an additional line of defense.

These arguments accurately portray how the system is supposed to work for the benefit of the users of financial statements. As in so many other situations, however, the gap between theory and practice is substantial when it comes to relying on legal mechanisms to protect shareholders and lenders. Up to a point, it is true, fear of the consequences of breaking the law keeps corporate managers in line. *Bending* the law is another matter, though, in the minds of many executives. If their bonuses depend on presenting results in an unfairly favorable light, they can usually see their way clear to adopting that course.

Getting the job done, in the corporate world's success-manual jargon, most definitely includes hard-nosed negotiating with auditors over the limits to which the accounting standards may be stretched. Technically, the board of directors appoints the auditing firm, but management is the point of contact in hashing out the details of presenting financial events for external consumption. A tension necessarily exists between standards of professional excellence (which, it must be acknowledged, matter a great deal to most accountants) and fear of the consequences of losing a client.

At some point, resigning the account becomes a moral imperative, but in the real world, accounting firms must be pushed rather far to reach that point. As a part of the seasoning process leading to a managerial role, accountants become reconciled to certain discontinuities between the bright, white lines drawn in college accounting courses and the fuzzy boundaries for applying the rules. Consequently, it is common for frontline auditors to balk at an aggressive accounting treatment proposed by a company's managers, only to be overruled by their senior colleagues.

Even if the auditors hold their ground against corporate managers who believe that everything in life is a negotiation, the outcome of the haggling will not necessarily be a fair picture of the company's financial performance. At the extreme, executives may falsify their results. Fraud is an unambiguous violation of accounting standards, but audits do not invariably catch it. Cost considerations preclude reviewing every transaction or examining every bin to see whether it actually contains the inventory attributed to it. Instead, auditors rely on sampling. If they happen to inspect the wrong items, falsified data will go undetected. Extremely clever scamsters may even succeed in undermining the auditors' efforts to select their samples at random, a procedure designed to foil concealment of fraud.

When challenged on inconsistencies in their numbers, companies sometimes blame error, rather than any intention to mislead the users of financial statements. Seasoned followers of the corporate scene are likely to be skeptical of such claims. They realize that companies are not always as forthcoming as investors might reasonably expect. The following examples illustrate that audit failure can indeed be real and costly to the unwary.

WHERE WAS THE CASH?

The stock of Wirecard AG, one of Germany's showcase fintech companies, was on a roll as 2019 began. The brokerage firm Bankhaus Metzler added the payments processor to its list of Top 10 stock picks, saying the company was likely to scale up its business further and outperform its peers. Wirecard was scheduled to appear at investor events hosted by financial powerhouses Guggenheim Partners and Commerzbank. CEO Markus Braun spoke encouragingly about Wirecard's fourth-quarter 2018 earnings at the DLD tech conference. By January 29, 2019, the company's stock was up by 26 percent since year-end, far outpacing the German DAX index's 6 percent gain.

Suddenly, Wirecard's fortunes took a turn for the worse. Its share price plunged by 13 percent on January 30. Early that day, the drop was attributed to margin weakness in the company's 4Q 2018 earnings report, but a more troubling development then emerged. The *Financial Times* reported that a Singapore-based executive in charge of accounting for the company's Asia-Pacific region was suspected of facilitating a number of suspicious transactions with forged and backdated contracts. Following the standard script in such situations, Wirecard denied any wrongdoing, charging that the *FT* story was not only false, inaccurate, misleading, and defamatory, but that it lacked any substance and was completely meaningless.

Germany's financial regulator, BaFin, responded by banning short-selling of Wirecard shares. Prosecutors in Munich, close to the company's headquarters in Aschheim, began investigating the *Financial Times* for possible violation of securities trading rules. At that point, prosecutors said there was no sign that Wirecard had engaged in improper accounting or violated German laws.

Over the remainder of 2019, Wirecard shares fluctuated as the *Financial Times* continued its investigative reporting of the company's accounting practices and Wirecard claimed that an external probe by a law firm delivered a clean bill of health. A company spokesperson dismissed the business daily's new revelations as nonsense on the grounds that all of Wirecard's numbers had been audited. Increasingly, though, the reliability of the audits by Ernst & Young was coming into question. Finally, on October 21, 2019, the company's management and supervisory board commissioned KPMG to perform an additional independent audit on its 2016 to 2018 results.

When KPMG delivered its report on April 28, 2020, Wirecard shares plummeted more than 26 percent as the special audit left key questions about the company's accounting practices unanswered. KPMG stated that Wirecard had not delivered all of the requested documents, or had taken several months to deliver them. Furthermore, nearly all the submitted documents were electronic copies and were therefore unverifiable. According to KPMG, lack of cooperation from three third-party processors of payments for Wirecard customers made it impossible to validate any underlying transactions for 2016–2018. Consequently, KPMG was unable to state one way or the other whether the reported sales revenue existed or was correct.

Wirecard's decline accelerated after that point. Its shares plunged by 37 percent on June 18, 2020, as Ernst & Young told the company that so far no adequate audit evidence could be found for €1.9 billion of cash, representing approximately one-quarter of Wirecard's balance sheet. There were indications that auditors had been deceived with spurious balance confirmations. CEO Braun resigned the next day and on June 22 Wirecard stated that the missing cash probably did not exist. Braun was arrested the next day on suspicion of falsifying revenue. By June 30, Wirecard shares had fallen to €5.73 from €94.56 a month earlier. In the interim the stock had closed as low as €1.28, on June 26, one day after the company filed for insolvency.

Familiar-Sounding Criticisms of the Wirecard Audit

As in previous accounting scandals, criticism rained down on the audit process in the wake of Wirecard's collapse. It turned out, according to *Financial Times* reporting, that just a few weeks before the insolvency Ernst & Young delivered a draft version of its official audit opinion. It reportedly rejected whistleblowers' allegations, as well as concerns raised in KPMG's special audit. Ernst & Young's draft reportedly stated that Wirecard's financial statements, including the balance sheet showing €1.9 billion cash that management later said was probably nonexistent, truly and fairly portrayed the company's net assets and financial position. According to the *Financial Times*, the draft opinion went on to say that Ernst & Young had found nothing problematic about the Asian business of TPA, Wirecard's third-party payment-transactions-acquiring business, which was shortly thereafter exposed as a sham.

The *Wall Street Journal* reported in 2020 that Ernst & Young had signed off on the company's 2016–2018 financial statements despite having raised questions about unorthodox arrangements whereby Wirecard's cash was held in bank accounts that it did not control. Ernst & Young rejected criticisms of its audit procedures, saying it had been duped along with everybody else. The firm also noted that it had refused to sign off on the 2019 statements after it received fake confirmations of the balances at trustee accounts at two banks that were supposedly holding Wirecard's money.[1]

Wirecard's perpetration of a massive fraud despite the scrutiny of a Big Four auditor had an all too familiar ring. In 2003 came the revelation that €3.9 billion of cash held in a bank account by an affiliate of the Italian food company Parmalat was a fabrication supported by a forged document. Deloitte, Parmalat's primary auditor since 1999, subsequently agreed to pay $149 million to the company and $8.5 million to investors. PwC was fined £1.4 million, then a record for a U.K. accounting firm, after JPMorgan Chase admitted in 2010 that for seven years it had mixed as much as $23 billion in client funds with its own in an unsegregated account. PwC had certified several times that the bank was handling the clients' money properly. In 2018 KPMG was sanctioned by the U.K.'s accounting regulator for "unacceptable deterioration" in audit quality in connection with its work for Carillon, a failed construction company.

Also familiar to longtime observers of financial reporting were the structural factors that Brooke Masters of the *Financial Times* viewed as the root cause of all of these incidents. Auditors are selected and paid by the companies they audit. The corporate clients want audits completed swiftly and inexpensively, enabling them to release their results and move on. Failing to satisfy management's desire for quick, no-hassle audits would be bad for business, because the clients are also prospects for highly profitable consulting and tax services. Most of the time the numbers are honest, so auditors tend to assume they will not be the unlucky guardians scorched by the fraudulent exception. Attempts have been made since the early 2000s to eliminate conflicts of interest in auditing, but with only limited success.[2]

How Outsiders Detected Improprieties

Considering the huge financial irregularities that escaped detection in yearly audits of Wirecard, it would have been surprising if outside analysts relying on the published statements had uncovered all of the hanky-panky. Only by finding sources within the company were investigative journalists able to obtain the facts that brought about the company's downfall. The January 30, 2019, *Financial Times* article that set in motion Wirecard's final decline was based on an internal presentation and other documents to which its reporters managed to gain access. Accounting irregularities in Singapore came to light through a whistleblower inside the company.

The remarkable thing is how long Wirecard was able to keep a lid on its misrepresentations. For example, more than a decade before its collapse, the company was fined by leading credit card companies for certain troubling practices. In 2008, according to a *Wall Street Journal* report,[3] Mastercard Inc. fined Wirecard £11 million for using the wrong merchant codes to process gambling transactions. The following year, the *WSJ* reported that Visa Inc. fined Wirecard's banking unit for incurring chargebacks totaling 15 percent of the unit's revenue in the quarter in question. (Visa considered anything greater than 1 percent of purchases a high rate.) Chargebacks are transactions that are disputed by cardholders. Sources cited by the *Wall Street Journal* said many of the disputed charges involved fraudulent use of credit cards on websites of Wirecard clients.

Information about the credit card company fines only came to light through *Wall Street Journal* reporting in 2020. Twelve years earlier, however, Wirecard's stock plunged by 24 percent on a single day (June 27, 2008) in response to rumors that the company was manipulating its balance sheet. CEO Braun responded by saying the company would ask BaFin to investigate possible manipulation of its stock by short sellers.

Wirecard succeeded over many years in concealing much of its skullduggery, even from its auditor. Intensive scrutiny of disclosures in the company's published financial statements did, however, expose some of its dubious dealings long before the company's collapse. For example, Zatarra Research & Investigations found evidence of *round-tripping* as far back as 2009. This scam consists of one company selling an asset to another company, while concurrently agreeing to buy back the same or similar assets. Scams associated with round-tripping include inflating the buyer/seller's market capitalization, overstating its profits, evading taxes, and laundering money. Zatarra, headed by analyst Matthew Earl, noted that the most notorious practitioner of round-tripping was Enron. (See Chapter 11.)

Wirecard bought E-Credit Plus Singapore in December 2009 for €12.8 million. In the two months preceding that transaction, Zatarra found, E-Credit's ownership changed hands three times. In late 2014, the entity that by then had been renamed Wirecard Asia was sold back to its original owner, Yoshio Tomiie. The sale price was officially €4.3 million, but €2.5 million of cash and cash equivalents, as well as €1.7 million of receivables net of liabilities, went with the business. In effect, Wirecard returned the company to its original owner for free.

While Zatarra ascertained these facts from public filings, doing so required a considerable amount of digging. Tomiie had taken great pains to hide his renewed ownership of E-Credit, burying it under three layers of holding companies. Further doubts that the 2009 and 2014 transactions were arms-length were raised by the fact, also uncovered by Zatarra, that six months before Wirecard acquired E-Credit, Wirecard Asia Pacific's vice president, Robert Lock, became an officer of an E-Credit subsidiary. Zatarra not unreasonably wondered whether Lock received any proceeds of the 2009 purchase of E-Credit.

Forensic accounting on the massive scale undertaken by organizations such as Zatarra is not feasible for most users of financial statements. Many of them have long lists of companies to follow and are hard pressed just to keep up with quarterly earnings reports and relevant corporate news. The Wirecard affair serves as a useful reminder, however, that suspicious-looking items may truly signal irregularities in financial statements. A leading auditor's signoff does not guarantee that everything is on the level.

SLOPPINESS CAN BE A RED FLAG

Sloppy financial reporting can be a sign of worse things to come, especially when it coincides with other classic red flags. A case in point is the foreshadowing of a sudden, sharp price drop in shares of American Realty Capital Properties. ARCP, a Phoenix-based commercial real estate investment trust (REIT), was founded by entrepreneur Nicholas Schorsch in 2010. Through a flurry of acquisitions it soon became the largest owner of single-tenant properties such as restaurants and drugstores, vaulting Schorsch to the billionaire ranks.

Things seemed to be going splendidly for ARCP as 2014 began. On January 28 Moody's Investors Service confirmed the company's investment grade Baa3 issuer debt rating and revised its rating outlook to "stable" from "review, direction uncertain." Moody's had previously signaled a potential rating change in October 2013 in reaction to a definitive merger agreement between ARCP and Cole Real Estate Investments, raising questions about how much debt ARCP would assume in the deal and how its credit metrics would be affected. In conjunction with the rating confirmation, Moody's said that it expected the REIT would successfully integrate its recent acquisitions, aim for more prudent growth going forward, improve its credit metrics, and maintain sufficient liquidity. Nothing but blue skies appeared to lie ahead for ARCP.

Before the year was over, the REIT was engulfed in thunderstorms. On October 29, 2014, ARCP announced that it had overstated adjusted funds from operations (AFFO), a commonly used measure of REIT performance, by $12 million in 2014's first quarter and by about $10.9 million in the second quarter. According to management, some amounts belonging to non-controlling interests were wrongly included in AFFO.

ARPC added that its audit committee believed certain financial reporting errors "were intentionally made" and "intentionally not corrected." In a conference call, CEO David S. Kay said the company had determined that the first-quarter overstatement was unintentional but that that the second-quarter number derived from a calculation made "in order to conceal the error from the first quarter."[4] Kay blamed the problems on bad judgment rather than bad people and eventually went so far as to portray the whole thing as a positive event, as it made ARPC a better, sounder company.

Immediately after the revelations of financial reporting errors Standard & Poor's placed the REIT's BBB– credit rating on watch for possible down-grade to the speculative grade range. ARCP's share price plunged by 19 percent on October 29. That loss was reduced from a 37 percent intraday decline by management's statement that the original error proceeded from a change in accounting method and did not reflect an intention to inflate earnings. Prices also fell by 2 percent to 14 percent on the shares of three other companies overseen by ARCP founder Nicholas Schorsch.

ARCP asked for and received the resignations of its chief financial officer and chief accounting officer. The company's auditor, Grant Thornton LLP, declined to comment. A person familiar with the matter stated that the Securities and Exchange Commission planned to initiate an inquiry into the accounting irregularities. The Federal Bureau of Investigation subsequently launched its own probe.

The company's troubles did not end with the October 29, 2014, disclosure of intentional misrepresentation of financial data. The stock dropped by 8.5 percent on December 15 in reaction to the surprise resignations of CEO David Kay and Chief Operating Officer Lisa Beeson, apparently at the behest of the company's independent auditors. Up until that point, Kay, who had taken over as CEO from Schorsch only in September, had adamantly insisted that he would remain in place. It was further disclosed that on December 12 Schorsch had resigned as chairman. He had retained that title following the earlier, long-planned handover of the CEO title to Kay. Schorsch consequently walked away from a compensation package totaling approximately $100 million.

On December 16 Moody's downgraded ARCP to the speculative grade rating of Ba1 and stated that the outlook remained negative. Standard & Poor's, for its part, cut the company's corporate-credit level rating from BBB– to BB. The rating agency highlighted the ongoing management's limited experience in running a public company. By this time, ARCP's share price was down by 38 percent from its level just prior to the October 29 disclosures.

Barely a week later, on December 24, ARCP discontinued its quarterly dividend until it could generate accurate third-quarter 2014 financials. The company further stated that its reported results as far back as 2013 could no longer be relied upon and that it had hired outside auditors and counsel to investigate.

When ARCP's internal investigation wrapped up in March 2015, the company restated earnings for several earlier periods. Investors breathed a sigh of relief that the investigation found no misstatement of the value of the REIT's real estate holdings. The report did, however, highlight inappropriate payments of at least $8.5 million to a management company controlled by Schorsch. It also stated that agreements involving stock awards to Schorsch and another former executive contained provisions that rendered them more generous to the awardees than what the company's compensation committee had authorized. ACRP sought to distance itself from its troubled past in July 2015 by renaming itself Vereit.

In November 2017 former CFO Block was convicted of deceiving investors by inflating the REIT's financial statements and was sentenced to 18 months in prison. Prosecutors had calculated that non-binding federal sentencing guidelines called for a 105-year sentence, based on the more than $3 billion decline in ARCP's market value after the misstatements came to light. Former chief accounting officer Lisa McAlister cooperated with prosecutors and pleaded guilty to related charges. She was sentenced only to time served.

Schorsch and Block agreed in July 2019 to pay more than $60 million to settle SEC charges that they had wrongfully profited from their roles in two REIT mergers. In September 2019, the now restyled Vereit, Schorsch's American Realty Capital, Brian Block, and Grant Thornton settled a shareholder class action for a total of $1 billion.

Naturally, shareholders would have preferred to avoid being victimized by ARCP's financial reporting fraud and spending nearly five years trying to recover their losses through litigation. As it happened, there were clouds on the horizon well before the storm commenced on October 19, 2014. Heeding similar, early signs of trouble could help scrutinizers of financial statements steer clear of future debacles.

On June 3, 2014, Marcato Capital Management LP, holder of 2.4 percent of the REIT's common shares, announced that on the previous day it sent a letter to ARCP's lead independent director.[5] Marcato's letter focused largely on its displeasure with the company's recent issuance of equity at $12 a share. Only a month earlier, Executive Chairman Schorsch had stated that selling stock at that price, a bit below where ARCP shares were trading at the time, would severely undervalue the company.

The most worrisome signs of looming trouble that Marcato's letter pointed out were two financial reporting errors. The first occurred in ARCP's May 20, 2014, 8-K filing. (This mandatory Securities and Exchange Commission report addresses unscheduled material events or corporate changes.) The filing presented pro forma financial statements for 2014's first quarter that used an inaccurate share count, necessitating a subsequent amendment advising investors to disregard the previous filing. ARCP then made a mistake in the prospectus for the abovementioned issuance. The company stated that the fees associated with its recent purchase of a $1.5 billion real estate portfolio from the Red Lobster restaurant chain totaled an improbably high $108 million. On May 29 ARCP filed an 8-K reducing that figure by 90 percent to the correct amount, $10.8 million.

Marcato attributed these errors to disorder in the company's financial controls, brought about by a rapid succession of major transactions. These included not only the aforementioned Red Lobster deal and equity issuance, but three acquisitions and the sale of a multi-tenant retail portfolio. The events of October 2014, however, suggested there was more to the story than too many deals in too short a period overwhelming the company's financial reporting system.

Indeed, ARCP's 2014 experiences upholds the "cockroach theory." The name derives from the popular belief that seeing one of these pests means many more are present. This bit of market wisdom holds that when a company discloses bad news on the financial reporting front, other, potentially worse news is likely to follow.

On the eve of the October 29 bombshell ACRP's share price was trailing the Bloomberg REIT index, −3.7 percent to 20 percent, for the year, yet the stock had barely reacted to the May 29 8-K disclosure of a financial reporting error. There was similarly little market response the following day, when eyebrows were raised by FPL Associates's analysis of ACRP's "outperformance"-based executive compensation plan. A senior managing director at the consulting firm said the size of the compensation pool, which stood to pay Schorsch as much as $94.1 million over the succeeding five years, was the largest that FPL had observed in the REIT sector. The plan had drawn criticism from proxy advisory services Institutional Shareholders Services and Glass, Lewis & Co. (ACRP shares did fall by 5 percent the day after the May 20 8-K filing.)

Consistent with the cockroach theory, investors could have avoided the large losses that followed five months later if they had regarded May 2014's developments as signs of worse to come. The other lesson to be drawn from the ACRP affair is that audits should not be considered definitive. Subsequent revisions can substantially affect securities valuations.

See Preface for a discussion to learn why CEOs may avoid culpability for financial reporting irregularities, despite the intentions of the Sarbanes-Oxley Act of 2002.

HOW MANIPULATION EVADES DETECTION

The gambits described elsewhere in this book are not just hypothetical accounting tricks that the auditors have gotten wise to and protect investors from in all instances. In fact, in the last few years the Securities and Exchange Commission's enforcement division has used novel data analytics to extract penalty settlements from three public companies on charges of EPS manipulation that went undetected by the auditors. As reported by the *Wall Street Journal* in 2021,[6] the securities law violations that the SEC personnel set out to uncover included making unsupported adjustments to items such as stock-based compensation accounts and recording loss contingencies in the wrong quarters. The three companies that came under fire, Interface Inc., Fulton Financial Corp., and Healthcare Services Group Inc., all settled without admitting or denying the charges and paid fines ranging from $1.5 million to $6 million.

How could the SEC investigators find manipulation that the auditors missed? Their method derived from 2009 research by Nadya Malenko, former SEC commissioner Joseph Grundfest, and Yao Shen.[7] Those researchers found improbably low appearances of the numeral "4" in the reported earnings per share of many companies' quarterly reports.

As a simple function of probability, "4" ought to appear in the tenths place of a company's unrounded EPS in about one out of ten quarters. An abnormally low incidence of that numeral raises suspicions that management is improperly rounding up the earnings figure. Indeed, Malenko et al. found a strong correlation between companies with unusually low usage of "4" and future restatements of financial reports.

Frequently, the tricks employed to bump EPS higher are small. As a result, they do not reach a materiality threshold used by auditors to determine which quarterly adjustments to examine. The auditors focus on higher-level reviews, testing companies' internal controls and questioning corporate officers on the rationales for large or unusual journal entries. According to sources consulted by the *Wall Street Journal*, more charges of earnings manipulation may be generated by the SEC's newly adopted investigative technique.

SYSTEMATIC PROBLEMS IN AUDITING

No system for auditing companies' books will ever work perfectly. Updating of accounting standards will inevitably lag business innovations that generate new types of transactions, giving companies leeway in how they are to be reported. Indeed, companies devote vast energy specifically to finding gray areas and loopholes in existing standards. Moreover, even crystal-clear accounting rules cannot fully protect the users of financial statements from corporate executives who violate them. Regrettably, the most respected auditing firms are bound to have a few bad apples (i.e., individuals willing to accept bribes to facilitate management's misrepresentations rather than faithfully fulfill their role as protectors of financial statement users). As with other types of crime, it is not feasible for the government to devote enough resources to law enforcement to deter would-be perpetrators through near certainty of getting caught.

Acknowledging that no perfect system can be designed, however, is quite different from saying that existing provisions for issuing financial accounting standards, conducting audits, and policing fraud are as good as real-world conditions permit. The present system is not the product of objective analysis by panels of experts driven solely by a desire to provide accurate and transparent financial statements to the public. On the contrary, the design of the rule-making bodies and the rules they issue are outcomes of fierce political struggles. Auditing firms are profit-maximizing businesses that face unavoidable conflicts between upholding professional standards on the one hand, and retaining clients and controlling costs on the other. Given these facts, individual cases of audit failure cannot be viewed as isolated incidents. A systematic component perpetuates financial misreporting, despite reforms that periodically emerge in reaction to exceptionally shocking accounting scandals.

The system's response to the financial reporting megascandals of 2001–2002, involving prominent companies such as Enron, Global Crossing, Tyco International, and WorldCom, illustrates the intractability of the problem. Critics of the accounting profession highlighted the conflict of interest that had grown over the years between the provision of audits and the sale of consulting services to the same clients. Was an auditor likely to stand firm in a dispute over accounting policy, they asked, if the company's management could dangle lucrative consulting contracts as an inducement to back down?

Popular outrage over the post–Tech Wreck accounting scandals created political momentum to eliminate the auditing-consulting conflict. A *Wall Street Journal* analysis of the companies constituting the Dow Jones Industrial Average[8] found, however, that two years after the Securities and Exchange Commission began to crack down on the practice, 62 percent of fees paid to auditors were for nonauditing services. Furthermore, the decline from 75 percent in the preceding year (2001) was overstated. The new rules on auditor independence expanded the definition of what could be considered part of the audit fee. Services that were reclassified from non-auditing to auditing included statutory audits, reviews of documents filed with the Securities and Exchange Commission, and consultations on taxes and accounting to the extent they were needed to comply with generally accepted auditing standards. To some extent as well, the relative decline in the auditing-related portion of total fees reflected an average 10 percent to 15 percent year-over-year increase in the cost of audits, reflecting the increased complexity of accounting standards and expanded use of specialists to deal with derivatives contracts. According to Barbara Roper, director of investor protection at the Consumer Federation of America, "The conflict looks less without anything having changed."[9]

The response to the 2001–2002 accounting scandals illustrates the way lobbyists for reporting companies and their auditors can block more thoroughgoing reforms. Advocates for the users of financial statements, such as the Chartered Financial Analysts Institute, are outgunned by corporate and auditing interests. Those groups commit substantial resources to participating in hearings and requests for comments that influence the deliberations of the Financial Accounting Standards Board and the SEC. As the reform process drags on, popular anger over accounting issues tends to subside, as the public's attention shifts to new controversies in other areas of legislation and regulation. With attention diverted from reform of the accounting system, persistent lobbying by corporations and auditors waters down the original sweeping proposals.

Systematic problems in the audit process arise not only from the regulatory structure but also from the business strategies of profit-maximizing accounting firms.[10] The problem dates back to the 1970s, when the American Institute of Certified Public Accountants lifted a ban on auditors advertising their services, soliciting rival firms' clients unless invited, and participating in competitive bids for business. This change resulted from a federal government crackdown on such rules within professions, deeming them anticompetitive and threatening to launch antitrust suits to abolish them. Bidding wars resulted, and over time, audits became a service that accounting firms offered at a knockdown rate to compete for the more profitable consulting business. Increasingly, auditing was offered at a flat fee, making it imperative to hold down costs. Under pressure to limit the hours devoted to an audit, firms were not consistently able to devote the resources needed to uncover improper reporting.

In the 1990s, risk-based audits emerged as a means of keeping a lid on costs. Firms abandoned their traditional bottom-up approach of examining all components of the financial statements. Instead of focusing on details of individual transactions, they identified the areas that in their judgment presented the greatest risk of error or fraud, such as complex derivatives. Incredibly, these judgments in some cases were based on management's advice. For instance, when Ernst & Young audited the 2002 accounts of HealthSouth (see Chapter 11 for details of that company's massive accounting fraud), the audit team asked the company's executives whether they were aware of any significant instances of fraud, to which the executives naturally answered no. The auditors accepted management's assertion on the grounds that they considered HealthSouth's management ethical and its system for generating financial data reliable. On that basis, the Ernst & Young audit team performed many fewer tests of HealthSouth's numbers than they would have at a company they deemed to have a higher risk of improper accounting.

The detrimental impact of the shift toward risk-based audits was also apparent in the accounting fraud of telecommunications giant WorldCom. For a period during 2002, investors seriously wondered if any company's financial statements were reliable, considering what lay beneath the WorldCom financials that, according to Arthur Andersen, were prepared in accordance with generally accepted accounting principles (GAAP). All told, WorldCom racked up $10.6 billion of fraudulent profits on the way to becoming, in 2002, the largest corporate bankruptcy up to that time.

In WorldCom's early days, Arthur Andersen audited the company in a meticulous, bottom-up way. It reviewed thousands of individual transactions and confirmed them in the company's general ledger. As the company grew, however, Andersen migrated toward a risk-based process. The auditors used sophisticated software to analyze WorldCom's statements and met to brainstorm about ways in which management might be fudging the numbers. Once they identified an area of high risk, they assessed the adequacy of the internal controls by reviewing procedures with employees and running sample tests to determine whether the procedures were being followed.

If a question arose about controls or procedures, Andersen relied on the answers provided by management. This was problematic for two reasons. First, Andersen's software had identified WorldCom as a maximum-risk client. Second, the relationship between Andersen and WorldCom's management was not conducive to asking tough questions or being skeptical about the answers. In its proposal to the company for the 2000 audit, Andersen characterized itself as "a committed member of [WorldCom's] team."[11] Imagine a football referee calling himself a member of a team in a game at which he was officiating!

Andersen's auditors regularly asked WorldCom managers whether they had made any unusual top-side adjustments (i.e., general ledger accounting entries that were recorded after the books had closed for the quarter). The executives consistently replied that they had not, and according to a report by the company's bankruptcy examiner, Andersen did no tests to confirm their claims. As a supposed safeguard, the auditors looked for large swings in items on WorldCom's consolidated balance sheet. Finding none, they concluded that no follow-up procedures were needed. As it turned out, however, management had manipulated the statements precisely to ensure that there would be no unusual variances. WorldCom's top-side adjustments reversed liabilities and reclassified expenses as assets to delay the recognition of costs. If Andersen's people had drilled down to specific journal entries in the old-fashioned way, they would have discovered hundreds of large entries of suspiciously round numbers and no supporting documentation. One post-quarter-end entry for $239 million was documented solely by a sticky note showing the number "$239,000,000."

Going to the trouble of checking such items, however, would have added to the cost of auditing WorldCom. That was not something Arthur Andersen was keen on, given that it had already spent more on the company's audit than it had billed. As a result of competitive pressures, the audit had become a loss leader that Andersen used to obtain profitable consulting business from WorldCom.

Obsessive cost control similarly hamstrung the auditors' backup to protecting users of financial statements, the Securities and Exchange Commission.[12] Congress was stingy in funding the SEC's efforts to check filings such as 10-Ks, 10-Qs, and initial public offering prospectuses. Between 1981 and 2001, the number of filings that the commission's Corporation Finance Division was called on to review grew by 81 percent, but the staff expanded by only 29 percent. A report by management consultant McKinsey & Co. found that to meet numerical targets for reviewing filings, the overstretched Corporation Finance employees gamed the system, selecting smaller, easy-to-review filings and avoiding more complex ones. Furthermore, the emphasis on volume deterred the surveillance people from exercising their option of ordering deeper reviews. A further indication of tightfistedness in funding the SEC was loss of staff, as salaries fell behind private-sector pay levels. In 1999 and 2000, SEC personnel quit at twice the average rate within the federal government.

Congress's unwillingness to give the SEC the resources it needed to do its job reflected more than competing claims on the federal budget. From an ideological standpoint, many members of Congress opposed strict controls on business. One manifestation of this attitude was a 1995 proposal for a five-year freeze on the SEC's budget, a cutback in the number of commissioners from five to three, and a requirement that the agency justify the cost of any regulatory change. Fortunately for users of financial statements, these proposals were not accepted. In October 2000, SEC Chairman Arthur Levitt and enforcement chief Richard Walker presented evidence of auditors agreeing to turn a blind eye to accounting irregularities rather than risk losing profitable consulting business. Levitt wanted to restrict firms' ability to provide auditing and consulting to the same clients, but Senate Banking Committee Chairman Phil Gramm denounced the plan as "too draconian."[13] The SEC had to settle for merely requiring companies to disclose the amounts they paid auditors for consulting work.

Lynn Turner, former chief accountant at the SEC, said that the relentless assault from Congress affected the commission's agenda and reforms. In addition, Congress's tight rein on the purse strings had an adverse effect at the ground level of enforcement. Between 1991 and 2001, the cases opened by the Enforcement Division grew by 65 percent while the staff expanded by only 27 percent. According to former SEC official Richard Sauer, resources were too stretched to leave time to prospect for new infractions. There was already a backlog of items that clearly constituted violations. These constraints signaled to corporate management that there was a good chance that cheating would go undetected.

As a demonstration of the impact of Congress's frugality, in 1999, the enforcement staff followed up on an investment newsletter tip regarding financial misreporting at Tyco International. Responding to a request for documents, Tyco submitted pages that blacked out entries related to Chairman Dennis Kozlowski's borrowings under an employee loan program, saying those items were irrelevant to the SEC's request. It later turned out that Kozlowski had borrowed extensively for personal expenses, even though the program was intended to help executives cover taxes on stock grants. Fearful that a wider probe would absorb too much of their limited resources, SEC personnel did not question the blackouts or request the full company ledger. They shut down their investigation with no action. New York State prosecutors later charged Kozlowski with looting $600 million from Tyco.

One final line of defense for users of a company's financial statements is the audit committee of its board of directors. This protection has not proven infallible over the years. In a study of financial frauds that came to light between 1987 and 1997, the Securities and Exchange Commission found that the audit committees of many of the companies involved met only once a year or so. Some had no audit committees. In one of the few encouraging notes of recent years, the SEC has imposed a financial literacy requirement on audit committee members. This might seem too obvious a criterion to necessitate a specific regulation, but readers should bear in mind that former football star and convicted armed robber O.J. Simpson once served on the audit committee of Infinity Broadcasting Corporation.[14]

CONCLUSION

If the horror stories recounted in this chapter were isolated incidents, it might be valid to argue that in most cases, the combined impact of corporate disclosure requirements, external audits, and regulatory backup ensures a high level of reliability in financial statements. Intense analysis of the statements by the users would then seem superfluous. Many companies, however, are either stingy with information or slippery about the way they present it. Rather than laying down the law (or GAAP), auditors typically wind up negotiating with management to arrive at a point where they can convince themselves that the bare minimum requirements of good practice have been satisfied. Taking a harder line may not produce fuller disclosure for investors but merely mean sacrificing the auditing contract to another firm with a more accommodating policy. Given the observed gap between theory and practice in financial reporting, users of financial statements must provide themselves with an additional layer of protection through tough scrutiny of the numbers.

CHAPTER 10

Mergers-and-Acquisitions Accounting

Business combinations attract vast attention beyond the investment world for a variety of reasons. Consolidation of smaller enterprises into larger ones often produces economies of scale and scope that contribute to economic efficiency and growth. In some instances, though, the antitrust authorities seek to block a proposed merger or acquisition, alleging that it will cause an industry to become overly concentrated. That could enable the combined company to extract monopolistic profits, a detriment rather than a benefit to the economy. Fees from advising on M&A transactions are an important revenue source for investment banks. Hollywood occasionally puts the drama of takeover battles onscreen.

Investors often attribute value to companies, over and above what is justified by their earnings prospects and risks, based on their perceived attractiveness as acquisition candidates. In these transactions, the acquirer typically pays a substantial premium to the target company's prevailing share price. The acquiring company's shareholders can benefit when an M&A deal genuinely creates **synergy**, but they must be on guard against corporate managers' efforts to produce the illusion of value creation through financial reporting gimmickry.

Inflating reported earnings in the context of M&A has a long history. **Pooling-of-interests** accounting was a favorite device of 1960s conglomerates, which were popularly described as operating on the $2 + 2 = 5$ principle. In a transaction that qualified for pooling treatment, the cost of paying a premium to the acquired company's prevailing stock price conveniently disappeared.

Reform was slow in coming, thanks is no small part to lobbying by companies that liked the latitude afforded by the M&A accounting rules then in place. In 2000, three decades after first lambasting pooling-of-interests in an article titled "Dirty Pooling," *Barron's* took aim at Cisco's burying of costs associated with its frequent acquisitions.[1] Accounting watchdog Abraham J. Briloff calculated that in the case of the networking solutions company's acquisition of GeoTel Communications for $2 billion in Cisco stock, just $41 million of that cost went onto Cisco's balance sheet.

In 1997, four years before Briloff's Cisco critique, the *Wall Street Journal* reported that FASB was at long last considering restricting or abolishing the use of pooling-of-interests.[2] FASB spokesperson Deborah Harrington explained that allowing the option of pooling treatment prevented investors from comparing economically similar acquisitions that were accounted for differently. The issuers of financial statement, true to form, overwhelmingly preferred the method that made it difficult to compare deals booked as poolings to those recorded through **purchase accounting**. According to Securities Data Co, poolings had outnumbered purchase-accounting-method deals by a ratio of ten to one over the preceding five years. Chief SEC accountant Mike Sutton reported that over 40 percent of his staff's time was absorbed by tussles over which mergers qualified for pooling.

Not until 2001, four years after the news arrived that the accounting rule-maker was taking up the issue, did Financial Account Standard No. 141 finally go into effect. The new standard required the use of purchase accounting for all mergers and acquisitions.

Investors should not have been lulled into thinking that reform put an end to M&A accounting gimmickry. In 2003, the *Financial Times* noted an interesting pattern in industrial components maker Danaher's financial statements.[3] The prevailing rules enabled companies to write up the value of goodwill created in an acquisition after fully evaluating the transaction. *FT* contributor John Dizard found that following its frequent acquisitions, Danaher wrote up the goodwill while at the same time writing down the value of tangible assets such as inventories and receivables.

Danaher's management declined to answer Dizard's questions about the rationales for deciding that the acquired companies' tangible assets were worth less than they had been carried at on the acquired companies' books. He could therefore only hypothesize how this process could be abused to fabricate earnings. As Dizard explained, a company could game the accounting rules and bolster the earnings that support its stock valuation by writing down supposedly unsalable inventories and allegedly uncollectable receivables. Upward revaluation of goodwill would more than offset those losses. Subsequently, the company could find that those purportedly unsalable inventories were salable after all and, lo and behold, the ostensibly uncollectable receivables were in fact collectable. The profits resulting from the associated sales and collections would be greater than if the assets had not been sharply written down in the post-acquisition phase.

FASB further refined the M&A accounting standards in 2007 by replacing purchase accounting with **purchase acquisition accounting**. Despite continuing reforms in financial reporting standards, however, analysts still need to keep their guard up when gauging the earnings impact of business combinations.

In 2019 *MarketWatch* reported that the Securities and Exchange Commission had stepped up its efforts to discourage acquisition-related adjustments for deferred revenue that was written off under GAAP. Some acquisitive companies were adding back this "ghost revenue" in calculating adjusted revenue numbers commonly used by analysts. In June 2019, for example, Ribbon Communications responded to an SEC comment letter by agreed to drop its acquisition-related revenue adjustment from future filings.[4]

The two following case studies highlight financial signals that can help investors dodge nasty M&A-related shocks.

GOODWILL GOES BAD

"When one door closes, another one opens," said Alexander Graham Bell. Acquisition-happy companies did not fail to see the door that FASB opened for would-be abusers of financial reporting rules at the same time that it closed the door on pooling-of-interests accounting. At that point, the accounting rule-maker also ended the requirement for annual amortization of goodwill. Since then, public companies have been required only to examine their goodwill at least once a year and take a write-down if they find that its value has been impaired. That change removed some of the pre-2001 purchase accounting method's disincentive to paying an excessive premium over an acquired company's net value. Under the old standard, the more goodwill that was created in an acquisition, the greater was the annual hit to earnings from mandatory goodwill amortization. Now, companies could buy earnings through acquisitions at rich prices with relative impunity.[5]

Not total impunity, mind you. In 2015, General Electric paid $10.1 billion for the French company Alstom's energy businesses. Those operations had a book value of –$7.2 billion. GE booked the difference between the two figures as goodwill, justifying the price it paid by synergies that it could achieve by such means as cross-selling complementary product lines to generate incremental revenues. The resulting, greater-than-100-percent ratio of goodwill to acquisition price was a rarity. That ratio averaged just 65 percent in the preceding five years' industrial-sector acquisitions.[6]

On October 1, 2018, GE announced that it would write off $23 billion from the value of its power equipment business. The charge was mostly related to the ill-fated acquisition of the Alstom energy businesses. On the following day, GE fired its CEO after just 14 months in that position and Standard & Poor's downgraded the company's credit rating from A to BBB+. The company's disclosure that it would miss its 2018 earnings and cashflow goals was a contributing factor in both of those developments.

GE's stock actually rose on October 1, reflecting investor enthusiasm for the executive chosen as the company's new CEO, Larry Culp. As Jack Cieselski of *Analyst's Accounting Observer* noted, the power business' troubles were well known by then and were already incorporated in the share price. The outgoing CEO, John Flannery, had acknowledged in 2017 that if he had it to do over again, he would pay a substantially lower price for the Alstom Assets. Between the November 2, 2015, close of the Alstom deal and the October 1, 2018, write-down of the former Alstom businesses and other power division assets, GE's stock plunged by 36 percent while the S&P 500 climbed by 39 percent. In short, the market imposed a large penalty on shareholders well before the company officially conceded that the goodwill it recorded in the Alstom deal was illusory.

DOUBLE TROUBLE

On November 20, 2012, Hewlett-Packard announced that it would take an $8.8 billion write-down on the UK software company Autonomy Corp. that it acquired on October 3, 2011. HP's share place dropped by 12 percent on the day of the announcement while the S&P 500 edged 0.7 percent higher. The wide-ranging technology company stated that more than $5 billion of the Autonomy write-down was related to financial reporting improprieties that it discovered only after the acquisition closed. According to HP, the fraudulent accounting went undetected by the leading auditing firms that scrutinized Autonomy prior to the acquisition but came to light when a whistleblower stepped forward.

Controversy arose immediately. Autonomy co-founder Mike Lynch denied the claims of improper accounting. He blamed the loss of value on post-acquisition mismanagement by Hewlett-Packard. The stock market's previous assessment of HP management lent some support to that notion. In the five years preceding the Autonomy write-down, HP's stock price declined by 67 percent.

Some commentators were skeptical that with a balance sheet of just $3.5 billion shortly before being acquired, Autonomy could have created as much as $5 billion of false value through financial reporting improprieties.

They suggested that as in the GE-Alstom affair discussed earlier, the underlying problem was a too-high price paid in the acquisition.

Lynch hotly denied that Autonomy misrepresented any financial reporting data under his leadership. In a 2010 speech, however, he had recounted that in the company's startup phase he placed a sign reading "Authorized Personnel Only" on an office door. Behind that door, he told visitors, were 500 engineers working on top-secret projects. In reality, it was a door to a broom closet. Autonomy's colorful CEO gave the company's conference rooms names drawn from James Bond movies and at one point filled the office fish tank with pirhanas.[7]

Nine years after Hewlett-Packard's $8.8 billion write-down, the issues it raised were still not fully resolved. Autonomy's former CFO was convicted of falsifying financial statements in 2018, but in October 2021 Lynch was still awaiting a decision on a $5 billion lawsuit brought against him by Hewlett-Packard, the largest-ever U.K. fraud trial. More important for analysts than the apportionment of blame for the $23 billion write-down are lessons that can be drawn from the debacle. By learning those lessons, investors may avoid huge losses of value in future M&A transactions. Leaving aside issues of quality of management, which require study of corporate strategy and execution, the lessons to derive from this case study fall into two categories – financial reporting matters and valuation of acquisition targets.

Financial Reporting

Australian investor John Hempton labeled Autonomy's financial reporting "perverse" in light of the norms of its industry.[8] He explained that software companies ordinarily have very few receivables because they sell their products upfront and for cash. At the same time, they have obligations to service their software for a long period after they sell it. Consequently, software companies' unearned income is typically a multiple of receivables. Autonomy's balance sheet, on the other hand, showed large receivables. This was the result of booking sizable income for which the company had not received cash, while booking no obligation for future services. Hempton emphasized that these facts could all be ascertained by examining Autonomy's balance sheet.

Renowned short seller James Chanos stated that in early 2011, several months before Autonomy's acquisition, the software maker was his largest European short position. Chanos's firm, Kynikos Associates, criticized the company's financial reporting in a report of July 2009. The payment of an unusually large premium for Autonomy was a factor in Chanos's naming of Hewlett-Packard as an "ultimate value trap" at the July 2012 Delivering Alpha Conference sponsored by CNBC and Institutional Investor.[9]

An October 31, 2009, article in the *Daily Telegraph* maintained that the length of Autonomy's **cash conversion cycle** "should ring alarm bells for investors." One implication of this divergence from the industry norm was that the company was generating growth through acquisitions rather than organic growth. In July 2010 an analyst at KBC Peel Hunt cited concerns about increased capitalization of research and development costs at Autonomy.[10]

In summary, outside analysts pointed out signs of potential financial reporting chicanery at Autonomy well before HP signed on the dotted line to buy the company. It was later reported that HP personnel studying the potential acquisition heard talk of accounting irregularities and looked into it. In the end, though, the company accepted documentation from Autonomy that refuted the allegations.[11]

Valuation

It was not solely with 20/20 hindsight that some financially astute individuals judged the price paid by Hewlett-Packard to be excessive. Oracle CEO Larry Ellison stated that in April 2011 his company turned down a chance to acquire Autonomy. At a **market capitalization** at the time of $6 billion, Oracle's M&A head and its president told Lynch that Autonomy was already extremely overvalued. Six months later HP paid $11.7 billion.[12]

Within HP, Chief Financial Officer Cathie Lesjak reportedly opposed the Autonomy acquisition because she considered it too expensive. According to reporting by *Fortune*, she pointed out that HP was proposing to pay 11 times revenue while similar companies were trading at three times revenue.[13] At the time as well, according to the *New York Times*, board member Meg Whitman complained to other directors about the price tag on Autonomy.[14] Shortly after the deal was struck, Whitman became HP's CEO and in that role defended the acquisition. Technology analyst Toni Sacconaghi of Sanford C. Bernstein said that in the days following the acquisition announcement he spoke to many of HP's major shareholders and not one thought the company should go ahead with the transaction.[15] (See Chapter 14 for metrics commonly used in valuing companies' stocks.)

Analytical Takeaways

For analysts, the key question about Hewlett-Packard's ill-fated Autonomy acquisition is not how the blame of the $8.8 billion Autonomy write-down should be allocated among financial reporting improprieties, an excessive acquisition price, and post-acquisition missteps by HP management. Instead, the point is to identify signs of potential trouble in future M&A deals that can be identified in advance from financial data available to outsiders. The financial reporting red flags spied by critics of Autonomy and of its acquisition by HP included Autonomy's unfavorable comparisons with peers on the level of receivables and the length of the cash conversion cycle. Similarly pointing to trouble were valuation metrics that were out of line with those of comparable companies.

CONCLUSION

A consistent theme through financial history has been corporations' efforts to boost reported earnings and therefore their stock prices by exploiting weaknesses in accounting standards for business combinations. Over time, reforms of those standards have shifted the specific tactics employed by issuers of financial statements. The rule changes have not, however, completely insulated investors from nasty surprises when the artificiality of much M&A-based value creation comes to light. Analysts should study each new blowup to determine whether earlier financial statements contained clues that trouble was brewing. That process will enable them to develop a checklist to aid in spotting potential for massive value destruction in the future.

CHAPTER 11

Is Fraud Detectable?

This chapter addresses the most difficult challenge to an analyst of financial statements. It is the case of a company that does not merely bend the rules, but intentionally breaks them. Sometimes the auditor actively participates in the fraud, thereby disabling one of the analyst's key defenses against deception. Analysts who uncover a major, flagrant violation of financial reporting standards can avert huge investment losses or produce large gains by selling short. They also can make their reputations in the process.

Frauds as colossal as some discussed in this chapter have become rarer in the United States since passage of the Sarbanes-Oxley Act of 2002, popularly referred to as "Sarbox." That legislation required chief executive officers to sign their companies' financial statements, making them more prosecutable and less able to shift responsibility for accounting fraud than formerly. For analysts specifically looking for stocks to sell short for large profits, however, good opportunities continue to appear in other countries.

Furthermore, financial reporting fraud has not completely disappeared in the United States. As explained in the Preface, chief executives of some companies that intentionally misrepresented their results have successfully shielded themselves from Sarbox-based prosecution via subcertification of the statements they signed.

In 2016, though, the *Financial Times* reported that the U.S. Securities and Exchange Commission had initiated a new crackdown on financial reporting practices.[1] As reporter David J. Lynch detailed, the energy industry was a particular focus of the SEC's increased scrutiny in the wake of a 75 percent plunge in oil prices over the preceding two years. One investigation led to a settlement of accounting fraud charges with Miller Energy Resources' former chief executive officer, chief financial officer, and external accountant. The three had valued certain Alaskan oil wells at $480 million, more than 100 times the price the company paid to acquire them.

Former CEO David Hall and CFO Paul Boyd were both fined $125,000 and banned for five years from serving as officers or directors of publicly traded companies. External accountant Carlton Vogt was barred for three years from appearing before the SEC. The Miller Energy affair was less spectacular than the pre-Sarbox frauds detailed in this chapter, but the older cases remain instructive on techniques for finding clues that something is amiss in companies' financial reporting.

The following discussion of outright fraud begins with "Telltale Signs of Manipulation," the findings of systematic studies of financial statements of companies that misrepresented their results. Four case studies of fraudulent reporting follow, involving Enron, HealthSouth, Parmalat, and Luckin Coffee. These studies explain how the frauds were perpetrated and also explore the extent to which analysts did or did not succeed in detecting the wrongdoing before investors suffered massive losses.

TELLTALE SIGNS OF MANIPULATION

The aggressive accounting practices detailed in the preceding chapters may not win awards for candor, but neither will most of them land corporate managers in prison. There are many ways for companies to pull the wool over investors' eyes without fear of legal retribution. Sometimes, however, corporate executives step over the line into illegality.

Outright misrepresentation falls into a category entirely separate from the mere exploitation of financial reporting loopholes. Moreover, the gravity of such misconduct is not solely a matter of temporal law. In 1992, the Roman Catholic Church officially classified fraudulent accounting as a sin. A catechism unveiled in that year listed cooking the books in a series of so-called new transgressions, that is, offenses not known in 1566, the time of the last previous overhaul of church teachings.

Neither fear of prosecution nor concern for spiritual well-being, however, entirely deters dishonest presenters of financial information. Audits, even when conducted in good faith, sometimes fail to uncover dangerous fictions. Financial analysts must therefore strive to protect themselves from the consequences of fraud.

No method is guaranteed to uncover malfeasance in financial reporting, but neither are analysts obliged to accept an auditor's clean opinion as final. Even without the resources that are available to a major accounting firm, it is feasible to find valuable clues about the integrity of financial statements.

Messod Daniel Beneish, professor of accounting and information systems at the Kelley School of Business at Indiana University, has developed a model for identifying companies that are likely to manipulate their earnings, based on numbers reported in their financial statements.[2] (Beneish defines *manipulation* to include both actual fraud and the management of earnings or disclosure within generally accepted accounting practices [GAAP]. In either case, his definition specifies that the company subsequently must have been required to restate results, write off assets, or change its accounting estimates or policies at the behest of its auditors, an internal investigation, or a Securities and Exchange Commission [SEC] probe.) Beneish finds, by statistical analysis, that the presence of any of the following five factors increases the probability of earnings manipulation:

1. Increasing days' sales in receivables.
2. Deteriorating gross margins.
3. Decreasing rates of depreciation.
4. Decreasing asset quality (defined as an increase in the ratio of noncurrent assets other than property, plant, and equipment to total assets).
5. Growing sales.

Note that Beneish does not characterize these indicators as irrefutable evidence of accounting malfeasance. Indeed, it would be disheartening if every company registering high sales growth were shown to be achieving its results artificially. Nevertheless, Beneish's data suggest a strong association between the phenomena he lists and earnings manipulation.

Evidence of financial reporting manipulation can also be found outside the financial statements. A paper published by the Rock Center for Corporate Governance[3] focuses on the conference calls that corporate senior executives make in connection with quarterly earnings releases. Professor David F. Larcker and doctoral candidate Anastasia A. Zakolyukina of the Stanford Graduate School of Business identified verbal cues of financial reporting hanky-panky by analyzing the question-and-answer sections of the transcripts of 29,663 conference calls.

Based on which companies subsequently restated their results, as well as a set of criteria for identifying especially serious accounting problems, Larcker and Zakolyukina label each Q&A section "truthful" or "deceptive." Their methodology produces significantly better than random results, classifying 50 percent to 65 percent of the Q&A sections correctly. They also find that judgments based on the words used by chief executive officers and chief financial officers are more accurate than a model based on discretionary accruals.

Relative to the answers given by truthful executives, the replies of deceptive executives contain more references to general knowledge (such as the phrase "you know"), fewer nonextreme positive emotions ("solid" or "respectable"), and fewer references to shareholder value and value creation. Furthermore, deceptive CEOs make fewer references to themselves and more to impersonal third parties, saying "the team" or "the company," rather than "I." They use more extreme positive emotions ("fantastic," for example) and fewer extreme negative emotions, as well as fewer words conveying anxiety.

Another systematic approach to detecting fraudulent reporting derives from a Sarbanes-Oxley provision requiring public companies' auditors to report on and attest to management's assessment of internal controls on financial reporting. A 2017 study by accounting professors Dain C. Donelson, Matthew S. Ege, and John M. McInnis[4] compared auditor reports on this matter during 2004–2007 with SEC reports of financial fraud and Justice Department Enforcement actions of 2005–2010. It turned out that auditors had found material weaknesses in financial reporting controls at 30 percent of companies that later faced legal actions in which fraud was revealed. In view of Donelson et al.'s findings, it behooves users of financial statements to watch for auditors' citations of material weaknesses in financial reporting controls as a sign that accounting fraud may eventually come to light.[5]

One additional tipoff of financial reporting fraud can be found outside the financial statements themselves, according to research by Paul Calluzzo, Wei Wang, and Serena Wu of Queen's University.[6] They documented a statistical tendency of companies with suspect financial statements to relocate their corporate headquarters so as to come under the jurisdiction of regional SEC offices with histories of lesser intensity in scrutinizing local firms. After relocating, companies that are motivated by scrutiny avoidance exhibit higher scores on a model designed to predict the likelihood of misstatement. They are also more likely than peer companies to restate their earnings.

In another example of the intellectual firepower being trained on detecting financial reporting fraud, some researchers are utilizing the 1938 finding of a physicist and known as Benford's Law.[7] It states that counterintuitively to most people, lists of numbers contain many more low digits than high digits. In 2014 Columbia University accounting professor Dan Amiram, along with co-authors Zahn Bozanic of Ohio State University and Ethan Rouen, a doctoral candidate at Columbia, demonstrated to the Securities and Exchange Commission a method of applying Benford's Law to public companies' financial statements. According to their analysis, the statements of Enron (see "Enron: A Media Sensation") displayed a clear variation from the Benford-predistribution on digits.[8]

The SEC's interest in advanced methodologies for ferreting out financial reporting fraud was also evident in its 2012 adoption of a computer program known as the "Accounting Quality Model." Nicknamed "Robo-Cop" by the media, the program searches for outliers and other red flags in companies' financial statements. The Accounting Quality Model underwent extensive revision subsequent to its launch. David Woodcock, head of the SEC's financial reporting and audit task force, commented that while quantitative tools would only get better over time, developing viable enforcement cases would always require human judgment.[9] With that in mind, let us see how human ingenuity fared in detecting some of the most famous financial reporting frauds.

FRAUDSTERS KNOW FEW LIMITS

Companies that cross the line from earnings management to outright fraud sometimes go to great lengths to cover their tracks. This may include enlisting the auditors to be coconspirators against, rather than protectors of, the users of financial statements. The evidence of criminal misrepresentation often appears obvious after the fact, yet not even the most skilled analysts definitively identified some of the most famous frauds until the schemes became unsustainable and the companies collapsed.

The following four case studies – Enron, HealthSouth, Parmalat, and Luckin Coffee – are cautionary tales. What appears to be a run-of-the-mill instance of aggressive reporting may prove to be something far more malevolent. It may turn out to be a case of no bona fide assets supporting the claims of creditors and shareholders. In studying these notorious frauds, readers should pay close attention not only to the suspicious financial statement items but also to the behavior of senior managers as the validity of their stated profits is challenged.

ENRON: A MEDIA SENSATION

In October 2000, *Fortune* published a list of the world's most admired companies, based on evaluations by executives and securities analysts. The business magazine wrote about one of these elite corporations, "No company illustrates the transformative power of innovation more dramatically than Enron."[10] Over the preceding decade, *Fortune* continued, Enron had transformed itself from an Old Economy pipeline operator to a **New Economy** trading powerhouse and increased its revenues from $200 million to $40 billion by inventing entirely new businesses. As it turned out, Enron's inventing had more to do with its reported earnings. The company filed for bankruptcy on December 2, 2001, only a little more than a year after being ranked among the 25 most admired companies in the world.

Enron's spectacular fall was an extraordinary media event. For more than a year, newspaper headlines dealt with a single company's accounting practices, a subject rarely given such attention. The affair spawned a best-selling book, *The Smartest Guys in the Room,* by Bethany McLean and Peter Elkind, which was adapted into a film directed by Alex Gibney. Lucy Prebble's satirical play, *Enron,* was a runaway hit in London, but the New York production closed after just three weeks, adding the backers' $3.6 million to the collateral damage from the company's sorry history.[11]

More important from the standpoint of investors and lenders, Enron raised the bar for financial statement analysts. The company did not merely take liberties with accounting standards in ways that standard ratio analysis would reveal. Instead, the secretive management kept many of the most important sources of reported earnings off the balance sheet and did its best to intimidate anyone who complained about inadequate disclosure. As a result, some portfolio managers and analysts came to mistrust management long before any serious misrepresentation came to light. Outsiders' inability to model the company's earnings added to their discomfort. Restatements announced in late 2001 covered annual reports beginning in 1997, but not until a few days before Enron's collapse did security analysts openly proclaim that the company's financial statements were unreliable.

Company Background

Enron was the product of the 1979 acquisition of Houston Natural Gas by InterNorth, the holding company for Northern Natural Gas, founded in Omaha, Nebraska, in 1932. Shortly after the formation of HNG/InterNorth, former HNG Chief Executive Officer Kenneth Lay became CEO and renamed the company Enteron. After business cards and stationery were printed, management learned that the new name closely resembled the Greek word for intestines, so Enron was substituted.

Lay took Enron far beyond its original activities: natural gas pipelines and the generation and distribution of electricity and natural gas. He developed a vast trading business dealing in diverse products that included oil transportation, electric power, steel, paper, broadband, weather, and wastewater, as well as a variety of commodity futures. In 1999, the company launched an Internet-based trading business, EnronOnline. President and Chief Operating Officer Jeffrey Skilling built this operation into America's leading gas and electricity wholesaler and succeeded Lay as CEO.

Enron rode high on the trend of energy deregulation. In 2000, revenues more than doubled, earnings soared by 25 percent, and the company's share price rose by 89 percent. In 2001, however, everything began to unravel. In August, Skilling suddenly stepped down as CEO, forcing Lay, who had continued as chairman, to take back the reins. Lay commented, "I can honestly say the company is in the strongest shape it's ever been in."[12] Unexpected turnover in senior management is a classic warning sign of financial misrepresentation, and trouble was signaled again with the departure of Chief Financial Officer Andrew Fastow in October.

At the same time that he was a senior executive of Enron, Fastow had been the managing member of LJM Cayman, a private investment partnership that engaged in derivatives transactions ostensibly designed to manage Enron's trading risk. Shareholders saw a conflict of interest in Fastow's dual role and worried about the vagueness of disclosure regarding LJM and related partnerships. In response to this criticism, Enron terminated its relationship with the partnerships. The associated write-down of a promissory note produced a $1.2 billion decline in shareholders' equity, which Enron did not even mention in its earnings release for the quarter ending September 30, 2001.

When CEO Lay later alluded to the write-down in a conference call with analysts, investors became alarmed about the lack of clarity regarding the partnerships. They feared that Enron might have used them to hide losses in its core trading business. Investors were not alone in their confusion. In August, when asked about details of Fastow's complex transactions, Lay had replied that the questions were getting way over his head. Now, the two individuals who did appear to understand the deals – Skilling and Fastow – were gone from the company. Investor anxiety mounted as the Securities and Exchange Commission launched an investigation into Enron's financial reporting.

Ominously as well, the supposedly highly profitable company was facing a possible cash squeeze. Enron drew down a $3.3 billion bank line of credit and faced the possibility that its debt would be downgraded to speculative grade. Already, Enron's bonds were trading at yields comparable to others in that category. The company faced the problem that a fall to speculative grade might compel it to issue tens of millions of shares of stock to cover the $3.3 billion of loans it had guaranteed, driving down its share price through **dilution**. Downgrading could also cripple Enron's trading business by inducing other traders to cease doing business with it.

As the situation deteriorated, Enron struck a deal to be acquired by Dynegy for stock of the rival energy trader worth $9.80 per Enron share. A year earlier, Enron had traded at $83. The transaction, which included a cash infusion by Dynegy's 27 percent owner, ChevronTexaco, hinged on Enron avoiding a downgrade to speculative grade.

Enron's case for remaining investment grade was not helped by a $591 million downward restatement of earnings for the period 1997 through 2001. Most of the revision arose from including in earnings the results of two special purpose partnerships formerly treated as independent and of a subsidiary of the LJM partnership previously run by Fastow. The remainder, $92 million, consisted of changes that Enron's auditor, Arthur

Andersen, had recommended but backed down on, accepting the company's argument that the amounts involved were immaterial.

A spokesman for Arthur Andersen called it "an unfortunate situation."[13] This proved to be a massive understatement. The firm, one of the nation's five largest auditors, was forced out of the accounting business after being convicted of obstruction of justice for shredding documents related to the Enron audit.

Enron at long last conceded that it was overly indebted. Management tried to restructure existing debt, arrange additional borrowings, obtain equity infusions, and raise cash by selling overseas assets. On November 19, 2001, the company told investors that it had $9.15 billion in debt coming due by the end of 2002 and only about $1.75 billion of cash and credit lines available. This disclosure came in the 10-Q for the quarter ending September 30, which was filed five days late – another classic warning sign of financial reporting malfeasance.

On November 21, Fitch stated that its Enron rating of BBB–, the lowest in the investment grade tier, depended on the Dynegy acquisition being consummated. The rating agency warned that if the deal broke down, a bankruptcy filing was highly possible. For the next few days, Standard & Poor's, Moody's Investors Service, and Fitch kept their ratings in the investment grade category as the company attempted to negotiate a restructuring of its bank debt. On November 28, the talks broke down, and all three agencies lowered Enron to speculative grade. Dynegy terminated its proposed acquisition, and on December 2, Enron became, by a wide margin, the biggest corporate bankruptcy ever, up to that time.

In congressional hearings on December 12, Arthur Andersen CEO Joseph P. Berardino suggested that Enron might have violated securities laws. Fastow pleaded guilty to wire and securities fraud. Lay and Skilling were convicted of fraud and conspiracy, although Lay's conviction was rescinded when he died shortly before he was to begin his prison sentence.

How Enron Misled Investors

One key to Enron's concealment of its true financial condition was simply a lack of forthrightness. Many of Enron's disclosures met the letter of the law, but according to a *Wall Street Journal* article, some top-flight professors of accounting said they could not make heads or tails of Enron's transactions with Fastow or the company's reasons for entering into them. Another article in the same publication stated that most securities analysts readily conceded that they did not know how Enron made money.

The company's description of its business shed no light and instead spread confusion. Enron derived more than 90 percent of its reported revenue from trading, which it called "wholesale services." It explained that business as follows:

> *Enron builds wholesale businesses through the creation of networks involving selective asset ownership, contractual access to third-party assets, and market-making activities.*

This statement, wrote Dan Ackman on Forbes.com, read "like something written in German, translated to Chinese and back to English by way of Polish."[14]

Enron also misled investors by aggressively exploiting wiggle room in the accounting rules. The company booked revenue from its energy-related derivatives contracts on the basis of gross value, rather than net value, as is the norm for other securities transactions. For instance, if a brokerage firm trades 10,000 shares of a $50 stock for a customer, it books as revenue either its commission or the spread between the bid and asked price, which might total $500. Trading an energy contract with the same gross value of $500,000 and a similarly small commission or spread, Enron booked revenue of $500,000 – a thousand times what a brokerage firm would record. This accounting treatment enabled Enron to double its reported revenue in 2000, leapfrogging companies with far greater economic impact to call itself the "seventh largest company in America."

Excessive liberties with **mark-to-market accounting** rules constituted yet one more element of Enron's misrepresentation. Under GAAP, it was legitimate to include in current earnings the profits on energy-related contracts and other derivatives that it expected to earn over future periods that could be as long as 20 years. At the end of each quarter, the company estimated the fair value of each open contract to buy or sell electricity or natural gas at a stated price. A subsequent change in the value of a contract would be added to or subtracted from earnings. The potential for abuse arose from the fact that quoted market prices were available only for contracts extending out a few years. No such independent basis for valuation existed for longer-dated contracts. In such cases, Enron was allowed to generate its own valuations, using undisclosed assumptions and pricing models.

Naturally, Enron Chief Accounting Officer Richard Causey assured investors that the company's valuation estimates were conservative. He also maintained that the unrealized gains were not heavily concentrated in long-term contracts, where uncertainty regarding valuation was greatest. Analysts nevertheless worried about Enron's disclosure that it booked $747 million in unrealized gains in the second quarter of 2001. That figure exceeded the company's **EBITDA** of $609 million. (For competitors that did not disclose a comparable number, analysts made quarterly comparisons of the changes in values of net assets from risk management activities.)

President Jeffrey Skilling went further than Causey in discouraging skepticism about the veracity of Enron's reported earnings, venturing into outright intimidation. On a conference call dealing with Enron's earnings, analyst Richard Grubman complained that the company was unique in refusing to include a balance sheet in its earnings release. Skilling replied, "Well thank you very much, we appreciate that ... [obscene epithet]."[15]

Another hint regarding Enron's deceptive methods emerged as the company was attempting to save itself through a sale to Dynegy. Floyd Norris of the *New York Times* reported that on October 23, 2001, the day before the company forced out Chief Financial Officer Andrew Fastow, the Financial Accounting Standards Board's (FASB) Emerging Issues Task Force received a rush question: A hypothetical "Big Energy Corporation" has a natural gas pipeline subsidiary and an energy trading subsidiary. May the company report profits earned in one subsidiary but not report losses incurred at the other?

Just as Enron's income statement concealed the nature of its reported earnings, its balance sheet misrepresented the reality of its financial position. From the outset of Ken Lay's transformation of a trading natural gas utility into a trading powerhouse, massive amounts of debt had been required. Off-balance-sheet entities kept debt off the company's books, based on accounting rules under which Enron could assert that it did not exert control. Experienced credit analysts ignored the accounting technicalities and added back Enron's proportionate share of the off-balance-sheet entities' debt. Still, the off-balance-sheet vehicles, combined with nontransparent disclosures, enabled the company to make itself look less debt-laden than it really was. From heavy reliance on off-balance-sheet financing, it was not a wholly surprising progression to Fastow's lucrative and conflicted partnerships.

Enron also disguised the magnitude of its debt burden by extensive use of a derivatives trade called a "prepaid swap." Unlike an ordinary swap, this transaction required Enron's counterparty to make its payments upfront, while Enron's payments were spread over a multiyear period. The spokesman for one bank that engaged in a prepaid swap noted that the cash flows replicated a floating-rate loan. Therefore, he said, the bank booked the transaction as a loan. Enron, in contrast, treated it as a swap.

While Enron grossly misled investors by stretching the rules, a large part of its deception consisted of outright violation of basic accounting standards, with the acquiescence of its auditor. Among the objections that Arthur Andersen agreed to waive on grounds of immateriality was a $172 million addition to shareholders' equity in 2000. The amount represented a note receivable that the company received in exchange for shares of stock that it issued to four special purpose entities. Under GAAP, when a company issues stock, it can record equity only when it receives cash. When Enron revised its financial statements in October 2001, it blithely labeled this violation of GAAP an accounting error.

Another violation of GAAP improperly enabled Enron to keep debt of an affiliate off its balance sheet. In testimony before Congress, Arthur Andersen CEO Berardino said that Enron failed to disclose to its auditor that it had guaranteed half of a 3 percent investment by a financial institution in its special purpose entity, Chewco Investments. Under GAAP, that arrangement meant Enron failed to meet a test for avoiding consolidation of Chewco.

As the Enron scandal continued to generate headlines, reports emerged of grossly fraudulent activities. Employees claimed that in 1998, management took them to an empty trading floor and had them pretend to be salespeople busily engaged in selling energy contracts, all to impress visiting securities analysts. Equally crude was a scheme in which Enron reportedly borrowed $500 million from a bank and bought Treasury bills. A few days later, it sold the Treasury bills and repaid the bank, reporting the proceeds from the meaningless transaction as operating cash flow.

Did Analysts Detect the Fraud?

The high profile of Enron's collapse spelled fame and fortune for anyone who could legitimately claim to have spotted the fraud in advance. Investors were sure to flock to anyone with a methodology deemed likely to uncover future faked profits. The record indicates, however, that not even diligent scrutinizers of Enron's financial statements recognized the depths of the fraud. Management successfully concealed the worst of its misdeeds until most of the investors' money had been lost.

To be sure, the lack of transparency in Enron's financial statements attracted notice well before the debacle. On September 20, 2000, the *Wall Street Journal* raised concerns about the year-to-date near-doubling of Enron's share price to $84.875, some 60 times earnings. The article drew attention to the major contribution of unrealized, noncash gains to the reported earnings of Enron and other companies with large energy-trading units. "There could be a quality-of-earnings issue," said Michigan State University accounting professor Tom Linsmeier. "There certainly might be great volatility that could cause what now looks like a winning, locked-in gain to not arise sometime in the future."[16] The opacity of Enron's fair value assumptions was a major concern. "Ultimately they're telling you what they think the answer is, but they're not telling you how they got to that answer," Business Valuation Services analyst Stephen Campbell complained. "That is essentially saying 'trust me.'"[17]

The *Wall Street Journal*'s detailed discussion of the mark-to-market accounting issue alerted short seller James Chanos of Kynikos Associates to the potential downside in Enron's stock. Renowned for his skill as a dissector of financial statements, Chanos was modest about his discoveries when he later discussed Enron's fall. Up until the summer of 2001, Chanos stated, he suspected nothing worse than a case of overstated earnings. "That is all you could tell from [Enron's] documents," he said.[18] Chanos thought that the stock price would decline but not that it would plunge to pennies a share.

Others who pored over the financials achieved similar results. For instance, in May 2001, Off Wall Street Consulting recommended a short sale of Enron, then trading around $59. The analytical firm cited two factors identifiable from the financial statements, namely, the mark-to-market on nontraded assets and related-party transactions with private partnerships. When Enron fell to $26, a little below Off Wall Street Consulting's $30 target price, the firm removed its sell recommendation. That proved astute in the short run, as the stock rallied to $36 before entering its final death spiral. If Off Wall Street had known the full scope of Enron's deception, however, it presumably would have set a target price well below $30.

In August 2001, BNP Paribas analyst Daniel Scotto issued a report titled "All Stressed Up and No Place to Go," which urged investors to sell Enron's stock and bonds no matter what. Ten months earlier, Scotto suspended his ratings on all companies conducting business in California, including Enron. That action, however, was based on his concern that the companies would not be fully compensated by regulators for deferred energy accounts under the state's deregulation plan. In short, Scotto deserved credit for advising investors to bail out before some of the biggest losses, but his warning came long after the $90 peak of August 2000.

Another purported instance of advance detection of Enron's misreporting involved the Cayuga Fund, managed with the assistance of students at the Cornell University Johnson Graduate School of Management. On December 1, 2000, a year and a day before the bankruptcy filing, the fund liquidated its entire Enron position at $67.38. That enabled the fund to book a return of 129 percent on shares it had purchased much more cheaply.

Feidhlim Boyle and Tyger Park, the students who advocated a 100 percent sale, noted that the Beneish financial model indicated a possibility of earnings manipulation. In addition, the student-analysts observed a lack of clarity in the earnings generated by the energy trading business. Finally, they could not understand the footnotes in the annual report, and their professor likewise found them obscure. Park recalled a remark by master investor Warren Buffett that if you cannot understand the footnotes, it is because management does not want you to.

The Cornell students did not detect Enron's fraud, however. In fact, they downplayed the importance of the Beneish model's signal. The students recommended a sale based on the stock's prevailing price but rated Enron neutral over the long term, which they surely would not have done if they suspected massive falsification.

McCullough Research did an excellent job of spotting inconsistencies in Enron's financials. Enron Online's quarterly earnings report for the nine months ending September 30, 2001, claimed $544 billion of notional revenue (representing electricity and gas transmitted), yet its Federal Energy Regulatory Commission filing for the same period showed only $693 *million* of energy purchases and sales. McCullough also found a discrepancy between reported earnings less dividends and additions to retained earnings. Finally, the firm noted that Enron's reported cash flow included customer deposits in California that had to be repaid at a later point. Net of that item, cash flow was negative. This was all solid financial statement analysis, but the problems came to light only in the month before Enron's bankruptcy filing.

Finally, Egan-Jones Ratings Company gained widespread recognition for being swifter to downgrade Enron's bonds to speculative grade than larger competitors such as Moody's and Standard & Poor's. The BB rating to which Egan-Jones lowered the debt, however, connoted only about a 1 percent probability of default within one year. Moreover, the downgrade occurred just 37 days before Enron filed for bankruptcy, although the company's misrepresentations dated back to at least 1997. Egan-Jones deserved credit for its analytical rigor, but like the others, it cannot truly claim that it unearthed a fraud deep enough to destroy the company.

Lessons for Financial Analysts

Enron's success in sustaining its fraud over a long period represents a cautionary tale of the limitations of financial statement analysis. The auditors' failure to curb flagrant abuses of GAAP posed a huge obstacle to analysts. On top of that, the company did its best to make its financial reports unfathomable. "They're not very forthcoming about how they make their money," said John Olson, who headed research at Sanders, Morris & Harris. "I don't know an analyst worth his salt who can seriously analyze Enron."[19]

In a case of this sort, the most diligent investigation of the numbers may not turn up a smoking gun before the company collapses. Accordingly, analysts should be especially wary when a strong likelihood of financial manipulation, as indicated by tools such as the Beneish model, coincides with nontransparent financial reporting. There are many companies to invest in without risking capital on those that fail the smell test.

HEALTHSOUTH'S EXCRUCIATING ORDEAL

After working as a physical therapist and a junior executive of a small Texas hospital chain, 30-year-old Richard Scrushy (pronounced "SCROO-shee") founded HealthSouth in 1984. The business proved highly successful, thanks in large measure to a generous Medicare reimbursement policy for physical rehabilitation of an aging population keen on sports and exercise. Over two decades, Scrushy built the Birmingham, Alabama, company into the largest chain of its kind in the United States, with 1,500 rehabilitation hospitals.

In the process, Scrushy amassed immense wealth, becoming known as the Donald Trump of Birmingham. He acquired seven corporate jets, which he frequently piloted. Several philanthropies that benefited from Health-South's generosity named buildings after Scrushy. He also captured attention as the lead singer of his own country music band. Famed athletes John Smoltz and Dan Marino were hired to speak at a children's road show sponsored by HealthSouth.

Scrushy's ascent proceeded without a hitch until 1997, when Congress sharply cut back Medicare reimbursements to hospitals. During the next two years, HealthSouth's operating margins and profits plummeted. Scrushy responded by slashing salaries and divesting unprofitable sidelines. When those measures failed to revive profits, he tightened operations, cutting average patient's stays from 21.5 to 17.5 days. Still, the company struggled to meet Wall Street securities analysts' lofty earnings estimates.

In the end, HealthSouth met the analysts' expectations only by stretching the truth. On March 19, 2003, the Securities and Exchange Commission charged that HealthSouth had overstated earnings by $1.4 billion since 1999. Prosecutors later raised the figure to nearly $2.5 billion. PriceWaterhouseCoopers, the new auditor chosen after the scandal broke, eventually added to this total $500 million in incorrect accounting for goodwill and other acquisition-related items in the period 1994 through 1999, plus $800 million to $1.6 billion in "aggressive accounting" from 1992 to March 2003. In 2005, HealthSouth restated its results for 2001–2002, reducing revenue by about $1.5 billion and changing its originally reported $481 million of earnings for the two years to $555 million of losses.

According to the SEC's complaint, HealthSouth's falsification began shortly after the company went public in 1986. The securities regulator also claimed that Chairman and Chief Executive Officer Scrushy had personally profited from the fraud by selling at least 7.8 million of his own shares and by receiving a $6.5 million bonus based on the false profits. Scrushy, who was placed on leave following the SEC bombshell and fired soon thereafter, had only recently returned to his CEO post after a six-month investigation of insider trading allegations.

Regarding the new charges, his lawyers commented, "Mr. Scrushy was shocked and surprised at the unexpected actions taken by the government over the past two days."[20] Even after all five chief financial officers who worked under Scrushy during the company's history confessed to participating in the fraud, the defense team maintained that Scrushy was unaware of the financial statement manipulation. "I'm not an accountant," the defendant stated in a later civil trial related to the allegations.

Flat denial by Scrushy, regardless of the evidence that emerged, was a consistent theme as the HealthSouth story unfolded. Scrushy disavowed any culpability in an interview on the *60 Minutes* network television program, but when asked to repeat his declaration of innocence in a congressional hearing, he invoked his Fifth Amendment right against self-incrimination. Later, during his trial for fraud, Scrushy said that if acquitted, he would try to regain his position as chief executive officer of HealthSouth, notwithstanding a Securities and Exchange Commission enforcement action pending against him. A woman who worked as a personal shopper for Scrushy's wife said of the couple, "Their life was about as uninhibited by reality as one could imagine."[21]

In a monumental case of unfortunate timing, a book hailing Health-South's phenomenal success reached bookstores shortly before the SEC filed its allegations. *The Story of HealthSouth,* by Jeffrey L. Rodengren, was published by Write Stuff Syndicate, a firm specializing in corporate histories. Senators Orrin Hatch of Utah and Tom Harkin of Iowa had contributed an admiring foreword, unaware of the impending storm. (The two senators also participated in Scrushy's 1997 wedding, with Hatch writing a song for the occasion.)

Methods of Misrepresentation

According to HealthSouth whistleblower Weston L. Smith, Scrushy regularly convened so-called family meetings in which he directed company executives to inflate reported earnings to meet securities analysts' estimates. The fake accounting entries were called "dirt."[22] Smith, who pleaded guilty to four federal criminal charges, had been HealthSouth's chief financial officer until August 2002, before switching to head of inpatient operations. The complaint stated that when HealthSouth officials and accountants urged Scrushy to cease inflating profits, he replied, in effect, "Not until I sell my stock."[23]

Among the false filings Smith admitted to was a certification that financial statements sent to the SEC were true. Doing so was a violation of the Sarbanes-Oxley Act, enacted in 2002 following massive financial reporting frauds at Enron and WorldCom. The Sarbox provision requiring CFOs and CEOs to attest to the accuracy of financial statements gave prosecutors a powerful weapon to wield against falsifiers, but HealthSouth's fraud dispelled any notion that the tough new law would end financial misreporting altogether.

HealthSouth exaggerated its earnings by understating the gap between the cost of a treatment and the amount that the patient's insurance would cover. That enabled the company to set aside an unrealistically small allowance for uncollectable accounts. Each time the company overstated its net revenue and earnings in this way, it made a corresponding balance sheet adjustment, raising the value of an asset such as property, plant, and equipment. Another HealthSouth executive who pleaded guilty to participating in accounting fraud said the company overbooked certain reserve accounts referred to internally as "socks," then later "bled them out" into revenue.[24]

To avoid detection, HealthSouth made no large, concentrated adjustments but instead spread them over several different categories, including inventory, intangible assets, and property, plant, and equipment (PP&E). Knowing that the auditors would question an addition to fixed assets only if it was greater than a certain dollar amount, the company officials were careful not to exceed that threshold.

By mid-2002, using this little-by-little approach, the company managed to overstate its PP&E by more than 50 percent. Lehman Brothers accounting analyst Robert Willens later commented, "They were smart enough to realize that, as long as the increases weren't dramatic, the auditors were not going to deviate from the sampling approach they typically take."[25] If the auditors did question an accounting entry, HealthSouth executives reportedly created a phony document to validate the item.

HealthSouth also propped up profits by failing to write off receivables with little chance of being collected. That classic dodge accounted for most of the $500 million of questionable accounting uncovered by an internal investigation, separate from PriceWaterhouseCoopers' study of outright falsification. In addition, the company did not recognize losses when it sold assets that had declined in value. Also, in one instance, the financial statements treated arm and leg braces bearing the HealthSouth logo as inventory, even though the company would generate no revenue from handing them out free at its medical centers.

Securities holders paid a heavy price for HealthSouth's financial hankypanky. Following the SEC's initial accusation of financial reporting violations on March 19, 2003, HealthSouth lost access to a $1.25 billion line of credit. With a $354 million convertible bond coming due in a little over a week, it appeared doubtful that the company could arrange a new loan to cover the debt maturity without first filing for bankruptcy.

(As post-bankruptcy lenders, the banks would get first claim on Health-South's assets.) According to Premila Peters of KDP Investment Advisors, the company owed $3.5 billion in total, but based on its cash flow, its value was only $2.4 billion.[26]

Shareholders and bondholders were initially trapped in their positions because trading in the company's securities was suspended on March 19. (Bond market participants who misinterpreted the suspension made a few trades on March 20, but the SEC nullified those transactions.) When trading in the company debt resumed on March 21, the convertible **subordinated** bonds closed at 20, down from as high as 98 earlier in the week. Health-South's senior bonds were down from the mid-80s to about 44. Additional bad news for bondholders arrived as bankers blocked the company from making the April 1 principal repayment on the convertible bonds. As for the stock, trading resumed on an over-the-counter basis, and the shares ended March at 8.5 cents, down from $3.91 before the trading halt.

The People versus Scrushy

By October 15, 2003, a total of 15 HealthSouth executives had pleaded guilty to involvement in fraudulent reporting. Several had testified that Scrushy knew about or directed the accounting fraud. "The dominoes are falling, and they are falling fast," said one person involved in the investigation. "It's an investigator's dream."[27] Former SEC attorney Christopher Bebel added, "Scrushy's prospects look bleak."[28]

Compounding Scrushy's legal problems, federal prosecutors disclosed in July 2003 that they had uncovered evidence of tax fraud, obstruction of justice, witness intimidation, money laundering, and public corruption. It also emerged that the Federal Bureau of Investigation was looking into the suicide of William Massey Jr., who managed an umbrella company for Scrushy's personal businesses. Two months before taking his own life, Massey made a hasty business trip to the Bahamas. The FBI suspected Scrushy of setting up offshore bank accounts as a tax dodge.

On November 4, 2003, federal prosecutors charged Richard Scrushy with 85 charges related to a false accounting slammed, including conspiracy, securities fraud, mail and wire fraud, and money laundering. Perjury and obstruction of justice were added the following year, when a revised indictment consolidated the charges into a total of 58. The 2003 indictment made Scrushy the first CEO accused of violating the Sarbanes-Oxley Act because he had signed the financial statements. He pleaded not guilty to all charges, claiming that notwithstanding his reputation as a micromanager, he was oblivious to the massive fraud. Even though several of the 15 Health-South executives who pleaded guilty had implicated him, Scrushy's attorney brushed off the prosecutors' evidence. "They don't have much," he said. "Their primary case is weak."[29]

In his seemingly uphill battle to beat the rap, Scrushy capitalized on the confident prosecutors' decision not to seek a change in venue from Birmingham, where he was admired as a local boy who made good. Scrushy pushed this advantage by hosting a new television series on a Birmingham station. He claimed that the purpose was not to present his own side of the case against him, but he reserved the right to counter "blatantly wrong" statements.[30] The program was taped at Word of Truth Productions, part of the outreach ministry of a predominantly Black church that Scrushy joined in 2003.

Both his membership in the congregation and the TV show raised speculation that he hoped to win sympathy from jurors in a city where African Americans constituted 73 percent of the population. Scrushy played the religion card by becoming a nondenominational preacher and delivering guest sermons at several local churches. A former business associate of Scrushy's commented that he had never observed any Black executives at HealthSouth and added, "The first time I heard religion and Richard Scrushy mentioned in the same sentence was when I read about him going to Guiding Light Church."[31] According to other accounts, Scrushy was deeply involved in Christianity as a youth but later drifted away. Scrushy remained steadfast in the face of criticism: "I am innocent of the accusations against me," he said, "and have been blessed by the Lord in having the resources to confront my accusers."[32]

During the trial, Scrushy and his lawyers insisted they had nothing to do with another locally telecast program, *The Scrushy Trial with Nikki Preede*. This program aired on a station owned by Scrushy's son-in-law, and its host had done public relations work for Scrushy's law firm. A former Scrushy attorney was a frequent commentator on the show, and the station's general manager had played guitar and fiddle in Scrushy's country-western band. The judge felt obliged to instruct the jury not to watch any television programs dealing with Scrushy and HealthSouth.

Scrushy's defense also employed more conventional tactics, such as attacking one government witness for marital infidelity. His lawyers hammered at the light sentences meted out to HealthSouth executives who confessed and testified against Scrushy. Perhaps effective as well was the lead defense attorney's appearance in a necktie decorated with an image of rats eating cheese, echoing his description of a key prosecution witness's character. In the prosecutors' view, Scrushy benefited as well from the judge's habit of cracking jokes during long stretches of accounting-related testimony, arguing that it may have caused some jurors to take the proceedings less seriously than they ought.

In any event, on June 28, 2005, Richard Scrushy was acquitted of all charges. "It was venue," said former federal prosecutor George B. Newhouse Jr.[33] He echoed a number of legal experts who asserted that the defendant would have been convicted had prosecutors tried him anyplace other than Birmingham.

Scrushy's acquittal did not end his legal troubles, however. Four months later, he was indicted on charges of bribing the former governor of Alabama to appoint him to the state board responsible for approving hospital construction. In addition, he faced a shareholder suit and SEC civil charges arising from the accounting fraud. Scrushy eventually settled the SEC case without admitting guilt, agreeing to give up $77.5 million in stock gains and pay a $3.5 million penalty. The judge in the shareholder suit ordered him to pay $2.8 billion. Finally, Scrushy was convicted of the bribery charge and sentenced to 10 years and six months in prison. The judge rejected his plea that if he were incarcerated, his good work as a minister would suffer.

Audit Failure at HealthSouth

The most dismaying aspect of the performance of HealthSouth's auditor, Ernst & Young, was its failure to challenge a sudden, large increase in cash. The Justice Department claimed that the company's reported $545 million **cash balance** in 2002's second quarter, a jump of more than 50 percent from the preceding quarter, was overstated by more than $300 million. Lehman Brothers accounting analyst Willens noted that auditors were supposed to confirm cash balances by obtaining a sample. "It's one of the easiest things to audit and it does seem amazing," said Willens. "But a sample may have led them to conclude that everything was in order."[34]

Other red flags apparently were ignored. Michael Vines, a bookkeeper who left HealthSouth's accounting department in March 2002, warned Ernst & Young about accounting fraud, but the auditing firm concluded that the company's accounting was legitimate. Additionally, a HealthSouth internal auditor told Ernst & Young that she could not get full access to the company's books. The independent auditor took no action in response to that disturbing statement, according to another partner.

In the view of experts in the field, internal checks and balances also broke down at HealthSouth. The board's audit committee met only once during 2001, three times less than the minimum recommended by the SEC. That should have alerted the company's independent auditor that the company's internal controls were not adequately supervised and might be unreliable. Such infrequent convening of the audit committee meant it was "nonexistent, for all practical purposes," according to Columbia University accounting professor Itzhak Sharav.[35]

Other reasons existed for questioning whether HealthSouth's board was sufficiently independent to fulfill its watchdog responsibilities. "There has been so much sleeping on the job at the HealthSouth board that it could rise to gross negligence," asserted Paul Lapides, head of the Corporate Governance Center.[36] Particularly troubling were directors' transactions with HealthSouth and Scrushy. One director earned $250,000 a year in consulting fees from the company, and another received a $5.6 million contract to install glass at a hospital constructed by HealthSouth. Another director bought a $395,000 resort property in conjunction with Scrushy. Six directors and a seventh's wife were participants (in some instances through related entities) in an online medical supply venture to which HealthSouth directed more than $174 million in business. Moreover, for several years, a single board committee oversaw both corporate audit and compensation. Corporate governance experts could find no parallel at another major company for this arrangement, which was especially problematic considering that the audit failure fattened Scrushy's pay package.

Early Warning Signs

In 1999–2000, when Scrushy instituted an assembly-line-like process to move patients through the system more swiftly, operating earnings skyrocketed by 143 percent. Sales, however, inched up by just 3 percent. Investigators later concluded that this implausibly large gap was a product of fabricated profit numbers. Users of financial statements should be skeptical of such wide disparities between changes in revenue and profit.

Negative surprises can also be a warning sign, as HealthSouth demonstrated. The SEC complaint claimed that when Scrushy told investors on August 27, 2002, that a change in Medicare reimbursements would cost the company $175 million annually, he was overstating the true impact by about $150 million. According to the SEC, other HealthSouth executives were worried that under the newly enacted Sarbanes-Oxley Act, the requirement to certify the company's false financial statements meant they might face prison sentences. The executives claimed that to lower security analysts' expectations and thereby relieve the pressure to falsify, they persuaded Scrushy to abandon the reporting fraud and give securities analysts a bogus profit warning. In response, HealthSouth's stock plunged 44 percent in a single day.

A large stock sale by Scrushy three months before that precipitous drop aroused the SEC's suspicions of insider trading. That trail ultimately led in the unexpected direction of financial reporting fraud. For users of financial statements, the lesson is that a management that appears untrustworthy on other grounds may be tampering with the books as well.

MILK AND OTHER LIQUID ASSETS

Parmalat SpA's rise to the rank of Italy's largest food producer and the world's largest dairy company began in 1961, when Calisto Tanzi inherited a ham and salami business. Two years later, Tanzi created the Parmalat milk brand. He built it into an industry leader by importing technology for packaging milk in distinctive rectangular cartons and preserving it for up to six months without refrigeration. By 1970, the brand was internationally known as the "milk of champions," and the company started sponsoring ski events. Tanzi expanded the product line to desserts, sauces, cookies, and fruit juices and the corporate sponsorship to auto racing and soccer. In the 1990s, Parmalat went public and launched a series of acquisitions in Italy, the United States, Latin America, and Asia. The company's well-known brands included Archway cookies, Pomi pasta sauces, and Sunnydale Farms milk. Along the way, Tanzi became a major contributor to political campaigns and received a knighthood from the Italian state.

On December 19, 2003, Bank of America said documents indicating a $4.7 billion balance in a Parmalat account were not authentic. Standard & Poor's promptly downgraded Parmalat's debt to D, indicating default. Four days later, holding company Parmalat Finanziaria SpA announced plans to file for bankruptcy. As evidence of financial fraud emerged, Tanzi was arrested. He estimated the hole in Parmalat's balance sheet at $10 billion, said he had been falsifying the financial statements for at least a decade, and admitted that he had unlawfully shifted at least $640 million from Parmalat to money-losing travel businesses controlled by his family. Tanzi ultimately received a 10-year prison sentence.

As it turned out, the fraud extended beyond the phantom liquidity on Parmalat's balance sheet. A preliminary report issued in January 2004 revealed that the company had net debt of approximately $18 billion, almost $16 billion of which had not been disclosed previously. PriceWaterhouseCoopers also found that the company's revenues for the nine months ended September 30, 2003, were only €4 billion, rather than the reported €5.4 billion. Reported as €651 million, EBITDA was actually just €121 million, according to the accounting firm, which was brought in to investigate after the scandal broke. Parmalat's market capitalization prior to the scandal exceeded €2 billion, but according to a report by Enrico Bondi, the special administrator appointed by the Italian government, actual assets totaled less than €1 billion at the end of 2003. In a bizarre touch, company executives attempted to destroy a computer used in the fraud by smashing it with a hammer.

Investors had little official warning of trouble until the month before Parmalat's collapse. As late as October 2003, Deutsche Bank's equity research group rated the company's stock a buy, highlighting its strong reported cash flow, and Citibank put out an optimistic report in November. Furthermore, the company's debt carried an investment grade rating until nine days before the bankruptcy filing. Earlier on, however, there were classic warning signs that may indicate trouble even if a company outwardly appears successful.

A major red flag was Parmalat's voracious appetite for debt, despite claiming to have a huge cash balance. When challenged on this point, Chief Financial Officer Fausto Tonna consistently replied that the company was on the acquisition trail and that its liquid balances were earning good returns. Union officials at the company's main milk plant received a similar answer and were threatened with a lawsuit if they made any public suggestion of financial improprieties. In a similar vein, Calisto Tanzi charged that financial institutions, including Lehman Brothers, were spreading rumors of accounting irregularities to drive down the price of its stock. This sort of response is typical of companies engaged in financial fraud. One investment banker who had declined to deal with Parmalat told *Business Week* that things had "been strange" at the company since the mid-1980s. "It smelled bad," he confided.[37]

Suspiciously high profitability constituted a danger sign to some observers. A Milan banker noted that a very well-managed company in Parmalat's business would achieve an operating margin of 6 to 7 percent, yet Parmalat was reporting 12 percent.[38] Lack of transparency in financial reporting was another warning. "Parmalat was an 'avoid' recommendation," said BarCap high yield bond analyst Robert Jones. "There simply wasn't enough information to form a fundamental credit view."[39] Not everybody steered clear, however. "Everyone who did their research knew this wasn't the cleanest company," commented RBS consumer products analyst Rob Orman, "but many people looked at the spread[40] and thought, how far wrong can you go with a dairy company?"[41]

The 2002 financial statements of Parmalat's Brazilian unit, Parmalat Participacoes do Brasil Ltda., included evidence that Parmalat was prettying up its balance sheet through elaborate financial engineering. Deep in the footnotes of the Brazilian subsidiary's statements was a disclosure that on January 18, 2002, the subsidiary issued a €500 million security convertible into company shares. Unlike the owner of a standard convertible bond, for whom conversion is optional, the buyer of this instrument "made an irrevocable commitment to convert" into shares at the 2008 maturity. Parmalat Participacoes do Brasil Ltda. accounted for the transaction (in U.S. dollars) as $523.8 million of "funds for capital increase," part of an undifferentiated $764 million balance sheet entry encompassing minority interest, funds for capital increase, and shareholders' equity.

When this item was consolidated at the parent level, it was simply part of shareholders' equity. Furthermore, analysts suspected that the buyer of the convertible security was another Parmalat unit. On the same day that the convertible was issued, Parmalat Finance Corp. BV issued a €300 million bond. This would mean that by selling debt in one unit and buying it in another, the company increased its shareholders' equity. Management declined to comment when the transaction subsequently came to light, and unfortunately, the Brazilian subsidiary's financial statement was not a public document, so outsiders could not have used it to get wind of Parmalat's hanky-panky. Behind the scenes as well was the information that Parmalat units engaged in currency hedges with related parties. The economic impact of such a transaction does not truly constitute a hedge.

Additional straws in the wind for attentive investors appeared in selected brokerage firm research reports. In December 2002, Merrill Lynch analysts Joanna Speed and Nic Sochovsky downgraded Parmalat to sell, saying that the company's frequent recourse to the bond market, while reporting high cash balances, threw into question its cash-generating ability. The analysts also presciently viewed Parmalat's exceptionally large cash balance as a negative. They appropriately argued that maintaining vast amounts of debt while holding cash that generated a lower interest rate, rather than using the cash to reduce debt, represented "inefficient balance sheet management."[42] The explanation for this uneconomic behavior turned out to be that the cash was fictitious. On January 24, 2003, an analyst at Auerbach Grayson & Co. estimated that Parmalat's net financial debt was $4.5 billion, rather than the $2.3 billion reported by the company.[43] Special administrator Bondi contended that Parmalat's true financial condition was easily determinable by comparing its published debt totals with independently produced data on the amount of bonds it had issued.

Another hazard signal emerged on February 26, 2003, when Parmalat suddenly canceled its plan to sell 30-year bonds. Potential buyers of the issue were voicing uneasiness about the company's need to borrow at the same time that it claimed to have $5.3 billion in cash. The company said it would instead issue bonds with maturities of just seven years, suggesting the market had less confidence in Parmalat's long-run stability than management had thought. This news triggered a fall in the company's stock price to a seven-year low. On February 28, Parmalat called off the seven-year issue.

In the last two months before the bankruptcy filing, the signs of trouble multiplied. On November 6, Consob, the Italian stock market regulator, requested details on how Parmalat had invested €3.5 billion and how it planned to pay back bonds scheduled to mature by the end of 2004. On November 11, auditor Deloitte & Touche disclosed that it was unable to confirm that Parmalat had accounted correctly for a $135 million gain on a currency-related derivatives contract. A classic danger sign, senior management turnover, surfaced on November 14 with the second resignation within a year by a chief financial officer. Next, on November 27, the company announced that it had sold its stake in a hedge fund based in the Cayman Islands for $589.9 million but on December 8 revealed that the proceeds were not recoverable. By that time, it was clear that the company was facing a liquidity squeeze. On December 9, Parmalat failed to pay a €150 million bond maturity. The company made the required principal payment on December 12, but by then, Standard & Poor's had downgraded its debt to speculative grade.

Oddly, the person who achieved the greatest renown for early recognition of the Parmalat's house of cards was not a financial analyst, but a comedian. During a theater presentation in September 2002, more than a year before the bankruptcy filing, the popular Italian entertainer Beppe Grillo recounted to his audience that a Parmalat executive had told him the company had €13 billion in debts and €13 billion in assets. Grillo, an acerbic critic of Italian government and business practices, quipped about Parmalat: "In a normal country, it would collapse, bankrupt."[44] A videotape of Grillo's one-man show was broadcast on Italian television after his joke became reality.

Grillo claimed his anecdote was true but declined to name his informant. Later, though, he was called to testify in the judicial investigation of the Parmalat scandal. Asked to explain how he had managed to foresee the bankruptcy, he stated that anyone could have seen the holes in Parmalat's balance sheet, given that the financial reports were easily accessible. Grillo had a bit of an advantage over the average citizen, however. Prior to becoming a comedian, he earned a degree in accounting. He later founded a political party that captured 25.5 percent of the popular vote in the 2013 Italian parliamentary election.

TROUBLE WAS BREWING AT LUCKIN

Luckin Coffee, a coffee shop operator based in Xiamen, China, commenced operations in 2017. The company took aim at U.S.-based Starbucks, the Chinese market's dominant competitor, with technology designed to reduce labor costs, deliver coffee swiftly, and undercut Starbucks's prices. Luckin's bold plans attracted substantial financial backing from venture capital firms, the state-run China International Capital Corp., Singapore's sovereign wealth fund, and investment giant BlackRock.

The company swiftly grew to more than 4,500 coffee shops, overtaking Starbucks on that measure. Luckin went public in 2019, less than two years after its founding. It followed up its $645 million initial public offering (IPO) by raising $865 million in convertible bonds and additional stock in January 2020.

Public market investors probably should have been concerned that some of Luckin's early investors cashed out their holdings in the IPO. On March 31, 2020, the company disclosed that an internal investigation had revealed that executives including its chief operating officer fabricated 2.2 billion ($310 million) of transactions from the second to fourth quarters of 2019. Luckin's stock plunged by 75 percent on the news. Management said that its 2019 financial statements could not be relied upon and that it was also looking into its earlier financial disclosures.

On May 11, facing possible delisting by the NASDAQ exchange, Luckin fired Chief Executive Officer Jenny Qian and Chief Operating Officer Jian Liu. Liu acknowledged that his management style might have been too aggressive but denied that he had set out to deceive investors. Following a six-week suspension, Luckin's American depositary shares (ADRs) resumed trading, only to continue their previous slide. On May 27, the shares closed at $2.50, down from a peak of $50.02 on January 17.

Spotting Trouble before the Collapse

Luckin's share price did not collapse completely without warning. On January 31, 2020, Muddy Waters, a firm specializing in short selling, announced that it had shorted Luckin after receiving an anonymous 89-page report alleging accounting irregularities and a broken business model at Luckin. Muddy Waters called the report credible. The shares promptly dropped by 11 percent. On cue, Luckin categorically denied the allegations against it, labeling the report's methodology flawed, its evidence unsubstantiated, and its interpretation of events malicious.

The unidentified author(s) of the report did not uncover evidence of accounting irregularities solely by analyzing the Luckin's financial statements. Consider, for example, the claim that the daily number of items sold per Luckin store was overstated by at least 69 percent in 3Q 2019 and by 88 percent in the 4Q 2019. According to the report, these estimates derived from video surveillance and tabulation of traffic on 981 store days at a representative sample of Luckin's directly operated coffee shops. Amassing this huge volume of data required the mobilization of 92 full-time and 1,418 part-time staff. Clearly, only highly resourced organizations can undertake this kind of research.

Scrutiny of financial statements did play a role in the report's claim that management overstated its 3Q 2019 advertising expenses by more than 150 percent. According to the author(s), the discrepancy was uncovered by comparing the reported expenditures with media revenues tracked by a third party. The report speculated that Luckin inflated its advertising outlays in order to recycle the amounts into overstatement of revenue and store-level profit.

Subsequent investigative reporting by the *Wall Street Journal*[45] drew on the proverbial "people familiar with" Luckin's operations. Even before the 2019 IPO, according to the article, employees began generating fake transactions, using individual accounts registered with cellphone numbers. The business daily's exposé also depended on obtaining internal documents.

According to reporter Jing Yang, assisted by colleague Zhou Wei, Luckin escalated its exaggeration of revenues following the IPO by selling vouchers redeemable for tens of millions of cups of coffee to companies linked to chairman and controlling shareholder Charles Lu. Public documents – not company financial statements but corporate registration records – established the connections between buyers of the vouchers and two of Lu's previous ventures. Some of the voucher-purchasing companies had the same addresses as branches of those businesses, CAR Inc. and Ucar.

Two lessons emerge from this incident. One is that nearly two decades after Sarbanes-Oxley reduced (not eliminated) outright fraud in financial reporting by U.S. companies, securities of certain other countries continued to pose major hazards to users of financial statements. The second takeaway is that in some instances, even a meticulous examination of the issuer's financial statements will not bring the malfeasance to light. In such cases, exposing the deceptive reporting depends on some combination of whistleblowers, access to non-public documents, and large-scale surveillance efforts.

CONCLUSION

Each of these financial reporting episodes had a theatrical aspect. The downfall of Enron's management contained elements of tragedy that made it adaptable to the stage. Richard Scrushy made a farce of the legal proceedings against him, while Beppe Grillo lent a comic twist to the Parmalat case. The revelation of Luckin Coffee's fraud unfolded like a whodunit. Even though outright fraud is rarer in the United States than it was prior to passage of the Sarbanes-Oxley Act, analysts who learn the lessons of events that foreshadowed the revelation of these frauds may become the heroes of future financial reporting dramas. Note that the opportunities for such heroism remain abundant in many non-U.S. jurisdictions.

PART Four

Forecasts and Security Analysis

CHAPTER 12

Forecasting Financial Statements

Analysis of a company's current financial statements, as described in Chapters 2 through 4, is enlightening, but not as enlightening as the analysis of its *future* financial statements. After all, it is future earnings and dividends that determine the value of a company's stock (see Chapter 14) and the relative likelihood of future timely payments of debt service that determines credit quality (see Chapter 13). To be sure, investors rely to some extent on the past as an indication of the future. Because already-reported financials are available to everyone, however, studying them is unlikely to provide any significant advantage over competing investors. To capture fundamental value that is not already reflected in securities prices, the analyst must act on the earnings and credit quality measures that will appear on future statements.

Naturally, the analyst cannot know with certainty what a company's future financial statements will look like. Neither are financial projections mere guesswork, however. The process is an extension of historical patterns and relationships, based on assumptions about future economic conditions, market behavior, and managerial actions.

Financial projections will correspond to actual future results only to the extent that the assumptions prove accurate. Analysts should therefore energetically gather information beyond the statements themselves. They must constantly seek to improve the quality of their assumptions by expanding their contacts among customers, suppliers, and competitors of the companies they analyze.

A TYPICAL ONE-YEAR PROJECTION

The following one-year projection works through the effects of the analyst's assumptions on all three basic financial statements. There is probably no better way than following the numbers in this manner to appreciate the interrelatedness of the income statement, the cash flow statement, and the balance sheet.

Exhibit 12.1 displays the current financial statements of a fictitious company, Colossal Chemical Corporation. The historical statements constitute a starting point for the projection by affirming the reasonableness of assumptions about future financial performance. We will assume throughout the commentary on the Colossal Chemical projection that the analyst has studied the company's results over not only the preceding year but also over the past several years.

Projected Income Statement

The financial projection begins with an earnings forecast (Exhibit 12.2). Two key figures from the projected income statement, net income and depreciation, will later be incorporated into a projected statement of cash flows. The cash flow statement, in turn, will supply data for constructing a projected balance sheet. At each succeeding stage, the analyst will have to make additional assumptions. The logical flow, however, begins with a forecast of earnings, which will significantly shape the appearance of all three statements.

Immediately following is a discussion of the assumptions underlying each line in the income statement, presented in order from top (sales) to bottom (net income).

Sales The projected $9,617 million for 2021 represents an assumed rise of 4 percent over the actual figure for 2020 shown in Exhibit 12.1. Of this increase, higher shipments and higher prices will each account for 2 percent.

To arrive at the projected 2021 sales, the analyst builds a forecast from the ground up, using the historical segment data shown in Exhibit 12.3. Sales projections for the company's business – basic chemicals, plastics, and industrial chemicals – can be developed with the help of such sources as trade publications, trade associations, and firms that sell econometric forecasting models. Certain assumptions about economic growth (increase in gross domestic product) in the coming year underlie all such forecasts. The analyst must be careful to ascertain the GDP forecaster's underlying assumptions and judge whether they seem realistic.

If the analyst is expected to produce an earnings projection that is consistent with an in-house economic forecast, then it will be critical to establish a historical relationship between key indicators and the shipments of the company's various business segments. For example, a particular segment's shipments may have historically grown at 1.5 times the rate of industrial production or have fluctuated in essentially direct proportion to housing starts.

EXHIBIT 12.1   Financial Statements

Financial Statements of Colossal Chemical Corporation Year Ended December 31, 2020 ($000,000 omitted)

Income statement		Statement of cash flows	
Sales	$ 9,247		
Cost of goods sold	6,380	Cash flows from operating	
Selling, general, and		activities	
administrative expense	1,387	Net income	$ 295
Depreciation	684	Depreciation	684
Research and development	231	Deferred income taxes	36
		Working capital changes,	(107)
Total costs and expenses	8,683	excluding cash	
		marketable securities	
		Total operating cash flows	908
Operating income	564		
Interest expense	188		
Interest (income)	3	Cash flows from investing	
		activities	
Earnings before income taxes	373	Additions to property,	719
		plant, and equipment	
Provision for income taxes	78	Total investing cash flows	719
Net income	$ 295		
		Cash flows from financing	
		activities	
EBITDA	1,246	Increase (decrease) in notes	0
		payable	
		Increase (decrease) in	(95)
		long-term debt	
EBITDA/interest expense	6.63	Dividends	(98)
		Total cash flows from	(193)
		financing activities	
Long-term debt/EBITDA	3.8		
Total debt/EBITDA	4.1	Net change in cash	$ (4)
Balance sheet			
Cash and marketable	203	Notes payable	171
securities			
Accounts receivable	1,017	Accounts payable	925
Inventories	1,664	Current portion of	225
		long-term debt	
Total current assets	2,885	Total current liabilities	1,321
Property, plant, and	9,133	Long-term debt	4,680
equipment			
		Deferred income taxes	599
Total assets	$12,018	Shareholders' equity	5,418
		Total liabilities and SE	$12,018

EXHIBIT 12.2   Earnings Forecast

Colossal Chemical Corporation Projected Income Statement ($000,000 omitted)

	2021
Sales	$9,617
Cost of goods sold	6,636
Selling, general, and administrative expense	1,442
Depreciation and amortization	731
Research and development	240
Total costs and expenses	9,049
Operating income	568
Interest expense	178
Interest income	2
Earnings before income taxes	389
Provision for income taxes	82
Net income	307
EBITDA	1,298

Similarly, price increases should be linked to the expected inflation level. Depending on the product, this will be represented by either the Consumer Price Index or the Producer Price Index.

Basic industries such as chemicals, paper, and capital goods tend to lend themselves best to the macroeconomic-based approach described here. In rapidly growing technology sectors and hits-driven businesses such as motion pictures and toys, the connection between sales and the general economic trend will tend to be looser. Forecasting in such circumstances depends largely on developing contacts within the industry being studied. The objective is to make intelligent guesses about the probable success of a company's new products.

A history of sales by geographic area (Exhibit 12.4) provides another input into the sales projection. An analyst can modify the figures derived from industry segment forecasts to reflect expectations of unusually strong or unusually weak economic performance in a particular region of the globe. Likewise, a company may be experiencing an unusual problem in a certain region, such as a dispute with a foreign government. The geographic sales breakdown can furnish some insight into the magnitude of the expected impact of such occurrences.

Cost of Goods Sold The $6,636 million cost-of-goods-sold figure in Exhibit 12.2 represents 69 percent of projected sales. That corresponds to a gross margin of 31 percent, unchanged from the previous year.

EXHIBIT 12.3 Colossal Chemical Corporation Results by Industry Segment ($000,000 omitted)

	2016	2017	2018	2019	2020
Sales					
Basic chemicals	$3,650	$3,748	$4,078	$4,277	$4,528
Plastics	1,732	1,718	1,853	1,960	2,011
Industrial chemicals	2,141	2,206	2,466	2,536	2,708
Total	$7,524	$7,673	$8,397	$8,773	$9,247
Operating income					
Basic chemicals	$209	$184	$231	$291	$333
Plastics	92	145	89	57	85
Industrial chemicals	99	110	99	124	145
Total	$401	$440	$419	$472	$564
Depreciation					
Basic chemicals	$264	$264	$287	$293	$316
Plastics	109	115	126	144	155
Industrial chemicals	178	178	201	207	213
Total	$552	$558	$615	$644	$684
Identifiable assets					
Basic chemicals	$4,618	$4,632	$5,077	$5,290	$5,570
Plastics	2,117	2,151	2,412	2,528	2,672
Industrial chemicals	3,124	3,131	3,494	3,631	3,775
Total	$9,860	$9,915	$10,983	$11,449	$12,018

The projected gross margin for a company in turn reflects expectations about changes in costs of labor and material. Also influencing the gross margin forecast is the expected intensity of industry competition, which affects a company's ability to pass cost increases on to customers or to retain cost decreases.

In a capital-intensive business such as basic chemicals, the projected capacity utilization percentage (for both the company and the industry) is a key variable. At full capacity, fixed costs are spread out over the largest possible volume, so unit costs are minimized. Furthermore, if demand exceeds capacity so that all producers are running flat out, none will have an incentive to increase volume by cutting prices. When such conditions prevail, cost increases will be fully (or more than fully) passed on, and gross margins will widen. That will be the result, at least, until new industry capacity is built, bringing supply and demand back into balance. Conversely, if demand were expected to fall rather than rise in 2021, leading to a decline in capacity utilization, Exhibit 12.2's projected gross margin would probably be lower than in 2020, rather than higher. (For further discussion of the interaction of fixed and variable costs, see Chapter 3.)

EXHIBIT 12.4 Colossal Chemical Corporation Results by Geographic Area ($000,000 omitted)

	2016	2017	2018	2019	2020
Sales					
North America	$4,055	$4,161	$4,496	$4,733	$5,002
Europe	2,443	2,559	2,791	2,889	3,014
Latin America	478	460	418	404	474
Far East	548	492	692	748	757
Total	$7,524	$7,673	$8,397	$8,773	$9,247
Operating income					
North America	$89	$114	$103	$128	$153
Europe	184	167	216	220	273
Latin America	60	85	60	57	92
Far East	67	74	39	67	46
Total	$401	$440	$419	$472	$564

As with sales, the analyst can project cost of goods sold from the bottom up, segment by segment. Since the segment information in Exhibit 12.3 shows only operating income, and not gross margin, the analyst must add segment depreciation to operating income, then make assumptions about the allocation of selling, general, and administrative (SG&A) expense and research and development (R&D) expense by segment. For example, operating income by segment for 2020 works out as shown in Exhibit 12.5, if SG&A and R&D expenses are allocated in proportion to segment sales.

EXHIBIT 12.5 Colossal Chemical Corporation Operating Income by Segment – 2020

	Basic Chemicals	Plastics	Industrial Chemicals	Total
Operating income	$333	$85	$145	$564
Plus: depreciation	316	155	213	684
Plus: SG&A	680	301	406	1,387
Plus: R&D	113	50	68	231
Equals: gross margin	$1,442	$591	$832	$2,866
Sales	$4,528	$2,011	$2,708	$9,247
Gross margin percentage	31.9%	29.4%	30.7%	31.0%
Memo: segment sales as percentage of total:	49.0%	21.7%	29.3%	100.0%

By compiling the requisite data for a period of several years, the analyst can devise models for forecasting gross margin percentage on a segment-by-segment basis.

Selling, General, and Administrative Expense   The forecast in Exhibit 12.2 assumes continuation of a stable relationship in which SG&A expense has historically approximated 15 percent of sales. The analyst would vary this percentage for forecasting purposes if, for example, recent quarterly income statements or comments by reliable industry sources indicated a trend to a higher or lower level.

Depreciation   Depreciation expense is essentially a function of the amount of a company's fixed assets and the average number of years over which it writes them off. If, on average, all classes of the company's property, plant, and equipment (PP&E) are depreciated over ten years, then on a **straight-line basis**, the company will write off one-tenth (10.0 percent) each year. From year to year, the base of depreciable assets will grow to the extent that additions to PP&E exceed depreciation charges.

Exhibit 12.2 forecasts depreciation expenses equivalent to 8.0 percent of PP&E as of the preceding year-end, based on a stable ratio between the two items over an extended period. Naturally, a projection should incorporate any foreseeable variances from historical patterns. For example, a company may lengthen or shorten its average write-off period, either because it becomes more liberal or more conservative in its accounting practices or because such adjustments are warranted by changes in the rate of obsolescence of equipment. Also, a company's mix of assets may change. The average write-off period should gradually decline as comparatively short-lived assets, such as data-processing equipment, increase as a percentage of capital expenditures and as long-lived assets, such as bricks and mortar, decline.

Research and Development   Along with advertising, R&D is an expense that is typically budgeted on a percentage-of-sales basis. The R&D percentage may change if, for example, the company makes a sizable acquisition in an industry that is either significantly more, or significantly less, research-intensive than its existing operations. In addition, changing incentives for research, such as extended or reduced patent protection periods, may alter the percentage of sales a company believes it must spend on research to remain competitive. Barring developments of this sort, however, the analyst can feel fairly confident in expecting that the coming year's R&D expense will represent about the same percentage of sales as it did last year. Such an assumption (at 2.5 percent of sales) is built into Exhibit 12.2.

Operating Income The four projected expense lines are summed in Exhibit 12.2 to derive total costs and expenses. The total of $9,049 million is subtracted from projected sales to calculate projected operating income of $568 million.

Interest Expense Exhibit 12.6a displays information found in the notes to financial statements that can be used to estimate the coming year's interest expense. (Not every annual report provides the amount of detail shown here. Greater reliance on assumptions is required when the information is sketchier.)

The key to the forecasting method employed in Exhibit 12.6b is to estimate Colossal Chemical's embedded cost of debt, that is, the weighted average interest rate on the average outstanding amount of the company's existing long-term debt during the preceding year. The next step is to apply the embedded cost of 3.77 percent to Colossal's $4.728 billion projected 2021 average amount outstanding of long-term debt. This produces projected interest expense on long-term debt of $178.1 million.

To that figure, the forecaster must add $2.6 million of interest charges related to the short-term debt (notes payable). These projections are based on an average of the year-end 2020 and projected year-end 2021 outstanding balances, which comes to $171 million. The assumed average interest rate is 1.50 percent, based on an in-house interest rate forecast.

Bear in mind that the method described here for projecting interest expense involves a certain amount of simplification. Applied retroactively, it will not necessarily produce the precise interest expense shown in the historical financial statements. For one thing, paydowns of long-term debt will not come uniformly at midyear, as implicitly assumed by the estimation procedure for average amounts of long-term debt outstanding. Certainly, analysts should recognize and adjust for major, foreseeable changes in interest costs, such as refinancing of high-coupon bonds with cheaper borrowings. By the same token, forecasters should not go overboard in seeking precision on this particular item. For Colossal Chemical, projected interest for 2021 comes to only 1.9 percent of sales, so a 10 percent error in estimating the item will have little impact on the net earnings forecast. Analysts should reserve their energy for projecting interest expense for more highly leveraged companies. Their financial viability may depend on the size of the interest expense nut they must cover each quarter.

Interest Income Exhibit 12.2 incorporates a forecast of interest income using the year-end balance of cash and marketable securities. Based on expectations of an average money market rate of return of 1.0 percent on corporate cash, the average balance of $203 billion will generate $2 million of interest income.

EXHIBIT 12.6a   Details of Long-Term Debt, Short-Term Debt, and
Interest Expense

		Colossal Chemical Corporation ($000,000 omitted)	
		December 31,	
Long-term debt		2019	2020
	Coupon		
2.5% notes due February 2021	2.50%	$ 225	$ 225
3.35% notes due March 2022	3.35%	197	197
3.75% notes due November 2023	3.75%	708	708
1.75% notes due July 2024	1.75%	1,005	1,005
4.75% notes due April 2025	4.75%	283	283
7.5% debentures due April 2025	7.50%	53	–
7.375% debentures due April 2025	7.375%	42	–
4.6% notes due April 2029	4.60%	467	467
4.90% notes due February 2040	4.90%	453	453
4.55% notes due July 2045	4.55%	1,342	1,342
Total		$4,775	$4,680
Short-term debt			
Average interest for the year	1.50%		
Commercial paper and short-term borrowings	171		
Credit facilities borrowings	0		
Total	171		

Total borrowing			
Borrowings due within one year	225		
Long-term borrowing	4,775	4,680	
Reduction in long-term debt	95		

Annual maturities of long-term debt for the next five years are as follows:

2021	225
2022	197
2023	708
2024	1,005
2025	283

(These numbers are found in companies' Notes to Financial Statements.)

Provision for Income Taxes   Following the deduction of interest expense and the addition of interest income, earnings before income taxes stand at $387 million. The forecast reduces this figure by the **statutory tax rate** of 21 percent, based on Colossal's effective rate having historically approximated the statutory rate. For other companies, effective rates could vary widely as a result of tax loss carryforwards and investment tax credits, among other items.

EXHIBIT 12.6b

266

Calculation of Embedded Cost of Long-Term Debt

Colossal Chemical Corporation ($000,000 omitted)

	2019		2020	Average amount outstanding			@Rate		Estimated interest charges on long-term debt
2.5% notes due February 2021	225	+	225	÷2	=	225	2.50%	=	5.63
3.35% notes due November 2022	197	+	197	÷2	=	197	3.35%	=	6.60
3.75% notes due March 2023	708	+	708	÷2	=	708	3.75%	=	26.55
1.75% notes due July 2024	1005	+	1005	÷2	=	1005	1.75%	=	17.59
4.75% notes due April 2025	283	+	283	÷2	=	283	4.75%	=	13.44
7.50% debentures due April 2025	53	+	0	÷2	=	27	7.50%	=	1.99
7.375% debentures due April 2025	42	+	0	÷2	=	21	7.375%	=	1.55
4.6% notes due April 2029	467	+	467	÷2	=	467	4.60%	=	21.48
4.90% notes due February 2040	453	+	453	÷2	=	453	4.90%	=	22.20
4.55% notes due July 2045	1342	+	1342	÷2	=	1342	4.55%	=	61.06
	$4,775		$4,680					Total	178.08

Interest charges on long-term debt

178.08

Average amount of total long-term debt outstanding		Embedded cost of long-term debt
[(4775+4680)/2]	4,728	3.77%

Interest charges on short-term debt   171   1.50%

Interest charges on long-term debt	178.1
Interest charges on short-term debt	2.6
Total interest charges (interest expense)	181

Management will ordinarily be able to provide some guidance regarding major changes in the effective rate, and changes in the statutory rate are widely publicized by media coverage of federal tax legislation.

Projected Statement of Cash Flows

The completed income statement projection supplies the first two lines of the projected statement of cash flows (Exhibit 12.7). Net income of $305 million and depreciation of $731 million come directly from Exhibit 12.2 and largely determine the total sources (funds provided by operations) figure. The other two items have only a small impact on the projections.

Deferred Income Taxes This figure can vary somewhat unpredictably from year to year, based on changes in the gap between tax and book depreciation and miscellaneous factors such as leases, installment receivables, and unremitted earnings of foreign subsidiaries. Input from company management may help in the forecasting of this figure. The $38 million figure shown in Exhibit 12.7 represents 46 percent of the projected provision for taxes, the same percentage observed in the actual 2020 income statement in Exhibit 12.1.

EXHIBIT 12.7   Projected Statement of Cash Flows, 2021

	Colossal Chemical Corporation ($000,000 omitted)
Statement of cash flows	
Net income	307
Depreciation	731
Deferred income taxes	38
Working capital changes, excluding cash and marketable securities	(71)
Cash flows from operating activities	1,005
Additions to property, plant, and equipment	(767)
Cash flows from investing activities	(767)
Increase (decrease) in notes payable	(4)
Increase (decrease) in long-term debt	(128)
Dividends	(102)
Cash flows from financing activities	(234)
Increase in cash	4

Working Capital Changes (Excluding Cash and Borrowings) Details of the derivation of the –$10 million projection appear at the bottom of Exhibit 12.7. The forecast assumes that each working capital item remains at the same percentage of sales shown in the historical statements in Exhibit 12.1. Accounts receivable, for example, at approximately 11 percent of sales, rise from $1,017 million to $1,058 million, an increase of $41 million, as sales grow from $9,247 million in 2020 to a projected $9,617 million in 2021.

Before assuming a constant-percentage relationship, the analyst must verify that the most recent year's ratios are representative of experience over several years. Potential future deviations from historical norms must likewise be considered. For example, a sharp drop in sales may produce involuntary inventory accumulation or a rise in accounts receivable as the company attempts to stimulate its sales by offering easier credit terms.

Additions to Property, Plant, and Equipment The first and largest of the uses on this cash flow projection is capital expenditures. A company may provide a specific capital spending projection in its annual report and then, as the year progresses, update its estimate in its quarterly statements or 10-Q reports and in press releases. Even if the company does not publish a specific number, its investor-relations officer will ordinarily respond to questions about the range or at least the direction (up, down, or flat) for the coming year.

Dividends The $102 million figure shown assumes that Colossal will continue its stated policy of paying out in dividends approximately one-third of its sustainable earnings (excluding extraordinary gains and losses). Typically, this sort of guideline is interpreted as an average payout over time, so that the dividend rate does not fluctuate over a normal business cycle to the same extent that earnings do. A company may even avoid cutting its dividend through a year or more of losses, borrowing to maintain the payout if necessary. This practice often invites criticism and may stir debate within the board of directors, where the authority to declare dividends resides.

Until the board officially announces its decision, an analyst attempting to project future dividends can make only an educated guess. In a difficult earnings environment, moreover, a decision to maintain the dividend in one quarter is no assurance that the board will decide the same way three months later.

Paydown of Notes Payable and Long-Term Debt After including in the cash flow projection a $4 million addition to Cash and Marketable Securities as a function of projected sales growth, we calculate that on a net basis Colossal Chemical will generate $130 million in 2021. Based on management comments we assume in this projection that Colossal Chemical will apply its surplus to debt reduction.

This projection assumes that any net cash generated will be applied to debt retirement. A net cash use, on the other hand, will be made up through drawing down short-term bank lines. Underlying these assumptions about the company's actions are management's stated objectives and some knowledge of how faithfully management has stuck to its plans in the past.

Other assumptions might be more appropriate in other circumstances. For example, a net provision or use of cash might be offset by a reduction or increase in cash and marketable securities. A sizable net cash provision might be presumed to be directed toward share repurchase, reducing shareholders' equity, if management has indicated a desire to buy in stock and is authorized to do so by its board of directors. Instead of making up a large cash shortfall with short-term debt, a company might instead fund the borrowings as quickly as possible (add to its long-term debt). Alternatively, a company may have a practice of financing any large cash need with a combination of long-term debt and equity, using the proportions of each that are required to keep its ratio of debt to equity at a desired, constant level.

The allocation of debt reduction between notes payable and long-term debt is based on the ending balances shown in the projected balance sheet that follows.

Projected Balance Sheet

With the exception of the allocation of debt reduction between notes payable and long-term debt, constructing the projected balance sheet (Exhibit 12.8) requires no additional assumptions beyond those made in projecting the income statement and statement of cash flows. The analyst simply updates the historical balance sheet in Exhibit 12.1 on the basis of information drawn from the other statements.

EXHIBIT 12.8 Colossal Chemical Corporation Projected Balance Sheet
December 31, 2021 ($000,000 omitted)

Cash and marketable securities	207	Notes payable	161
Accounts receivable	1,058	Accounts payable	962
Inventories	1,731	Current portion of long-term debt	197
Total current assets	$2,996	Total current liabilities	$1,320
		Long-term debt	4,584
Property, plant, and equipment	9,169	Deferred income taxes	637
		Shareholders' equity	5,624
Total assets	12,165	Total liabilities and shareholders' equity	$12,165

Most of the required information appears in the projected statement of cash flows (Exhibit 12.7). Accounts receivable, inventories, and accounts payable, for example, reflect the projected changes in working capital. This projection maintains those items at the same percentages of sales as they represented in 2020. Property, plant, and equipment rises from the prior year's level of $895 million by $767 million of additions, less $731 million of depreciation. The projected cash flow statement also furnishes the increases in deferred income taxes and the change in shareholders' equity (net income less dividends).

The ending balances of notes payable and long-term debt, as well as the corresponding figures in the projected cash flow statement, are worked out as a small puzzle. First, the $225 million current portion of long-term debt in the 2020 balance sheet is replaced by the $197 million of debt coming due with 12 months of December 31, 2021, as shown in Exhibit 12.6b.

Naturally, the $225 million of notes maturing in 2021 must be replaced with new debt. Plodding through each step of paydowns and new issuance, however, is an unnecessary time drain. The net of it all is that the debt in the three categories shown on the liabilities side of the balance sheet must sum to $12,165 million less accounts payable, deferred income taxes, and shareholders' equity. That comes to $4,942 million. The $197 million current portion of long-term debt, already filled in, leaves $4,745 million to be divided between notes payable and long-term debt. Allocate the amount in the same proportions to each other as in the 2020 balance sheet and the projected balance sheet is complete. To derive the corresponding amounts on the projected cash flow statement, subtract the 2020 balance sheet amounts from the projected 2021 amounts. Puzzle solved.

SENSITIVITY ANALYSIS WITH PROJECTED FINANCIAL STATEMENTS

Preparing a set of projected financial statements provides a glimpse at a company's future financial condition, given certain assumptions. The analyst can study the projected statements using the same techniques discussed in Chapters 2 through 4 for the historical statements and also use them to calculate the ratios employed in credit analysis (Chapter 13) and equity analysis (Chapter 14). Based on the historical and projected data in Exhibits 12.1 through 12.8, Colossal Chemical's credit quality measures will improve in 2021 (Exhibit 12.9). Total debt will decline, not only in absolute terms but also as a percentage of total capital—from 46 percent to 44 percent. Similarly, cash provided as a percentage of total debt will rise from 20.0 percent to 21.6 percent. Alternatively, as shown in the exhibit, the

EXHIBIT 12.9   Trend of Credit Quality Measures – Base Case

Colossal Chemical Corporation ($000,000 omitted)

	2020 (Actual)**	2021 (Projected)*
Total debt		
Notes payable	$ 171	$ 161
Current portion of long-term debt	225	197
Long-term debt	4,680	4,584
Total debt	5,076	4,942
Deferred income taxes	599	637
Shareholders' equity	5,418	5,624
Total capital	$11,093	$11,203
Total debt as a percentage of total capital	46%	44%
Cash provided by operations (before working capital changes)	1,015	934
Total debt	$ 5,076	$ 4,942
Total debt as a multiple of cash provided by operations	5.00	5.29
EBITDA	1,246	1,298
Total debt/EBITDA	4.1	3.81
Operating cash flow	908	1,005
Capital expenditures	(719)	(767)
Free cash flow (OCF – CAPX)	190	238

*From Exhibits 12.7 and 12.8
**From Exhibit 12.1

reciprocals indicate debt as a multiple of cash provided falling from 1.97X to 1.61X. As explained in Chapter 13, these trends indicate reduced financial risk. Naturally, the projected ratios are only as reliable as the assumptions underlying the projected statements that generated them. Logical though they may seem, the assumptions rest heavily on macroeconomic forecasting, which is far from an exact science, to put it charitably. Typically, the analyst must modify the underlying economic assumptions, and therefore the projections, several times during the year as business activity diverges from forecasted levels.

Knowing that conditions can, and in all likelihood will, change, wise investors and lenders will not base their decisions entirely on a single set of projections, or point forecast. Instead, they will assess the risks and potential rewards in light of a range of possible outcomes.

Exhibit 12.10 illustrates how the analyst can modify the underlying assumptions and then observe the extent to which projected ratios will be altered. This process is known as **sensitivity analysis**. In the example, the

EXHIBIT 12.10   Sensitivity Analysis Projected Financial Statements

Colossal Chemical Corporation

Year Ended December 31, 2021 ($000,000 omitted)
Reduce Base Case (Exhibit 12.2) Sales Growth Assumption from 4% to 1%
(No improvement in gross margin over preceding year)

Income statement		Statement of cash flow	
Sales	$ 9,339		
Cost of goods sold	6,444	**Cash flows from operating activities**	
Selling, general, and administrative expense	1,401	Net income	$ 276
		Depreciation	731
Depreciation	731	Deferred income taxes	34
Research and development	233	Working capital changes, excluding cash and marketable securities	18
Total costs and expenses	8,809		
		Cash flows from operating Activities	$ 1,023
Operating income	530	**Cash flows from investing activities**	
Interest expense	178	Additions to property, plant, and equipment	(767)
Interest income	3	**Cash flows from investing activities**	$ (767)
Earnings before income taxes	349	**Cash flows from financing activities**	
Provision for income taxes	73	Increase (decrease) in notes payable	(8)
		Increase (decrease) in long-term debt	(159)
Net income	276	Dividends	(91)
		Cash flows from financing activities	$ (258)
EBITDA	1,258		
		Increase in cash	$ 2

		Balance sheet		
Cash and marketable securities	$ 205	Notes payable	$ 165
Accounts receivable	1,027	Accounts payable	934
Inventories	1,681	Current portion of long-term debt	197
Total current assets	$ 2,913	Total current liabilities	$ 1,296
Property, plant, and equipment	9,169	Long-term debt	4,550
		Deferred income taxes	633
		Shareholders' equity	5,603
Total assets	$12,082	Total liabilities and shareholders' equity	$12,082

analyst projects a sales increase over the preceding year of just 1 percent. That is three percentage points below the rate assumed in the base case (the most probable scenario) represented by Exhibit 12.2. The less optimistic sales forecast implies a less robust economy than assumed in the base case. For example, the analyst may assume no real growth and a 1 percent inflation rate. In the revised scenario, the analyst assumes that Colossal will manage to maintain the gross margins achieved in the preceding year. In another instance, particularly a sales decline, that assumption might not be justified, due to the fixed component of cost of goods sold. Keeping the other assumptions intact, the revised projections show smaller increases, relative to the base case, in net income and shareholders' equity. Cash provided by operations is actually higher than in Exhibit 12.7 due to the smaller need to add to working capital excluding cash and marketable securities. Long-term debt consequently declines more rapidly under the new assumptions.

Using Exhibit 12.10's revised statements, the analyst can recalculate Exhibit 12.9's credit quality measures as shown in Exhibit 12.11. Under

EXHIBIT 12.11 Trend of Credit Quality Comparison

Colossal Chemical Corporation

Year Ended December 31, 2021 (Projected) ($000,000 omitted)

	Pessimistic case*	Base case**
Total debt		
Notes payable	$ 165	$ 171
Current portion of long-term debt	197	225
Long-term debt	4,550	4,680
	4,912	5,076
Deferred income taxes	633	599
Shareholders' equity	5,603	5,418
Total capital	$11,148	$11,093
Total debt as a percentage of total capital	44.1%	45.8%
Funds provided by operations (before working capital changes)	1,041	1,015
Total debt	4,912	5,076
Cash provided as a percentage of total debt	21.2%	20.0%
EBITDA	1,258	1,246
Total debt/EBITDA	3.91	4.07
Operating cash flow	1,023	908
Capital expenditures	(767)	(719)
Free cash flow (OCF – CAPX)	256	189

*From Exhibit 12.10.
**From Exhibit 12.1

the new, more pessimistic sales growth and gross margin assumptions, projected cash provided by operations represent 21.2 percent of total debt. The improvement over 2020 is indicated by the lower 20.0 percent ratio projected in the base case. Total debt as a percentage of total capital declines modestly under the changed assumptions, to 44.1 percent from 45.8 percent in the base case. Although the addition to retained earnings (and hence growth in shareholders' equity) is smaller in the pessimistic case, so is the need for new working capital to support increased sales. The borrowing need is therefore reduced, offsetting the slower growth in equity.

To complete the analysis, an investor or lender will also want to project financial statements on an optimistic, or best-case, scenario. Sample assumptions for a three-scenario sensitivity analysis might be:

	Assumed Sales Growth	Assumed Gross Margin
Optimistic case (best realistic scenario)	6%	33%
Base case (most likely scenario)	4%	31%
Pessimistic case (worst realistic scenario)	1%	31%

Note that the assumptions need not be symmetrical. The optimistic case in this instance assumes sales only two percentage points higher than the base case, whereas the pessimistic case reduces base case sales by three percentage points. The analyst simply believes that the most range of possible outcomes involves more downside than upside.

Other assumptions can be modified as well, recognizing the interaction among the various accounts. Colossal Chemical may have considerable room to cut its capital spending in the short run if it suffers a decline in cash provided by operations. A projection that ignored this financial flexibility could prove overly pessimistic. Conversely, the assumption that a company will apply any surplus funds generated to debt reduction may produce an unrealistic projected capital structure. Particularly in a multiyear projection for a strong cash generator, the ratio of debt to capital may fall in the later years to a level that the company would consider excessively conservative. In such cases, it may be appropriate to alter the assumption from pure debt retirement to maintenance of a specified leverage ratio. Surplus cash will thus be applied to stock repurchase to the extent that not doing so would cause the debt component of capital to fall below a specified percentage.

In addition to creating a range of scenarios, sensitivity analysis can also enable the analyst to gauge the relative impact of changing the various assumptions in a projection. Contrast, for example, the impact of a 1 percent change in gross margins with the impact of a 1 percent change in the tax rate on Colossal Chemical's income statement. Exhibit 12.12 shows the effects of these two changes in assumptions on the projected income statement in Exhibit 12.2, holding all other assumptions constant. The sensitivity of net income to a 1 percent decrease in gross margin is $76 million ($307 million minus $231 million, all other things being equal. A 1 percent change in the tax rate, on the other hand, affects net income by just $4 million ($307 million minus $303 million), once again holding everything else constant.

This type of analysis is popular among investors. They may, for example, estimate the impact on a mining company's earnings, and hence on its stock price, of a 10-cent rise in the price of a pound of copper. Another application is to identify which companies will respond most dramatically to some expected economic development, such as a drop in interest rates. A rate decline will have only a minor impact on a company for which interest costs represent a small percentage of expenses. The impact will be greater

EXHIBIT 12.12   Sensitivity Analysis: Impact of Changes in Selected Assumptions on Projected Income Statement

Colossal Chemical Corporation
Year Ended December 31, 2021
($000,000 omitted)

	Base case	1% decline in gross margin	1% rise in tax rate
Sales	$ 9,617	$ 9,617	$ 9,617
Cost of goods sold	6,636	6,732	6,636
Selling, general, and administrative expense	1,442	1,442	1,442
Depreciation	731	731	731
Research and development	240	240	240
Total costs and expenses	9,049	9,145	9,049
Operating income	568	472	568
Interest expense	178	178	178
Interest income	2	2	2
Earnings before income taxes	389	292	389
Provision for income taxes	82	61	86
Net income	$ 307	$ 231	$ 303

Base case is Exhibit 12.2.

on a company with a large interest cost component and with much of its debt at floating rates. (This assumes the return on the company's assets is not similarly rate sensitive.)

Appealing though it may be, sensitivity analysis is a technique that must be used with caution. As suggested, it generally isolates a single assumption and proceeds on the assumption that all other things remain equal. In the real world, this is rarely the case. As previously noted, when sales fall, typically, so do gross margins. For one thing, cost per unit rises as fixed costs of production get spread over a smaller number of units. In addition, declining capacity utilization throughout the industry puts downward pressure on prices. Similarly, rising interest rates do not affect only interest expense and interest income. Higher rates depress the level of investment in the economy, which can eventually depress the company's sales.

PROJECTING FINANCIAL FLEXIBILITY

Just as projected statements can reveal a company's probable future financial profile, they can also indicate the likely direction of its financial flexibility, a concept discussed in Chapter 4. For example, the projected statement of cash flows shows by how comfortable a margin the company will be able to cover its dividend with internally generated funds. Likewise, the amount by which debt is projected to rise determines the extent to which nondiscretionary costs (in the form of interest charges) will increase in future income statements.

There is one important aspect of financial flexibility, continuing compliance with loan covenants, for which projections are indispensable. As Exhibit 12.13 illustrates, debt covenants may require the borrower to maintain a specified level of financial strength. Compliance may be measured either by absolute dollar amounts of certain items or by ratios.[1] Sanctions against an issuer that commits a technical default (violation of a covenant, as opposed to failure to pay interest or principal on schedule) can be severe. The issuer may be barred from paying further dividends or compelled to repay a huge loan at a time when refinancing may be difficult. Curing the default may necessitate unpleasant actions, such as a dilution of shareholders' interests by the sale of new equity at a time when the stock price is depressed. Alternatively, the borrower can request that its lenders waive their right to accelerate payment of the debt. The lenders, however, are likely to demand some quid pro quo along the lines of reducing management's freedom to act without consulting them.

EXHIBIT 12.13   Sample Debt Restriction Disclosures

Certain of our debt financing agreements (including our term loans, revolving credit facilities and spare engine EETCs) contain loan to value (LTV) ratio covenants and require us to appraise the related collateral annually. Pursuant to such agreements, if the LTV ratio exceeds a specified threshold or if the value of the appraised collateral fails to meet a specified threshold, as the case may be, we are required, as applicable, to pledge additional qualifying collateral (which in some cases may include cash or investment securities), or pay down such financing, in whole or in part.

Specifically, we are required to meet certain collateral coverage tests on an annual basis for our Credit Facilities, as described below.

At 31, 2019, we were in compliance with the applicable collateral coverage tests as of the most recent measurement dates.

—American Airlines Inc. (AAL) 2019 10K

The 2018 Coty Credit Agreement contains affirmative and negative covenants. The negative covenants include, among other things, limitations on debt, liens, dispositions, investments, fundamental changes, restricted payments and affiliate transactions. With certain exceptions as described here, the 2018 Coty Credit Agreement, as amended, includes a financial covenant that requires us to maintain a Total Net Leverage Ratio (as defined here), equal to or less than the ratios shown for each respective test period.

Quarterly test period ending	Total net leverage ratio[a]
June 30, 2019, through December 31, 2021	5.25 to 1.00
31-Mar-22	5.00 to 1.00
30-Jun-22	4.75 to 1.00
30-Sep-22	4.50 to 1.00
31-Dec-22	4.25 to 1.00
March 31, 2023, through June 30, 2023	4.00 to 1.00

[a]Total Net Leverage Ratio means, as of any date of determination, the ratio of: (a) (i) Total Indebtedness minus (ii) unrestricted cash and Cash Equivalents of the Parent Borrower and its Restricted Subsidiaries as determined in accordance with GAAP to (b) Adjusted EBITDA for the most recently ended Test Period (each of the defined terms used within the definition of Total Net Leverage Ratio have the meanings ascribed to them within the 2018 Coty Credit Agreement, as amended).

—Coty Inc. (COTY) 2019 10K

The Secured Revolving Facility contains fixed charge coverage and debt to EBITDA financial covenants. The Company is required to maintain a fixed charge coverage ratio of not less than 1.75 to 1.00 and a consolidated debt to consolidated EBITDA ratio not exceeding 4.00 to 1.00 for the

(*Continued*)

EXHIBIT 12.13   *(Continued)*

---

most recent four-quarter period. Additionally, the Secured Revolving Facility provides that investments and restricted payments may be made, without limitation on amount, if (a) at the time of and after giving effect to such investment or restricted payment, the ratio of consolidated debt to consolidated EBITDA for the most recent four-quarter period is less than 3.50 to 1.00 and (b) no default or event of default exists. As of February 1, 2020, the Company was in compliance with both of its financial covenants, and the ratio of consolidated debt to consolidated EBITDA was less than 3.50 to 1.00.

—L Brands (LB) 2019 10K

The Credit Agreement has a financial covenant that requires the Company to maintain a minimum fixed charge coverage ratio of 1.00 to 1.00 (i) on any date on which availability under the Senior Secured Revolving Credit Facility is less than $200,000 or (ii) on the third consecutive business day on which availability under the Senior Secured Revolving Credit Facility is less than $250,000 and, in each case, ending on and excluding the first day thereafter, if any, which is the 30th consecutive calendar day on which availability under the revolver is equal to or greater than $250,000. As of February 29, 2020, the Company's fixed charge coverage ratio was greater than 1.00 to 1.00 and the Company was in compliance with the Credit Agreement's financial covenant. The Credit Agreement also contains covenants which place restrictions on the incurrence of debt, the payments of dividends, the making of investments, sale of assets, mergers and acquisitions and the granting of liens.

—Rite Aid Corporation (RAD) 2019 10K

The continued availability of the revolving credit agreement requires U.S. Cellular to comply with certain negative and affirmative covenants, maintain certain financial ratios and make representations regarding certain matters at the time of each borrowing.

The revolving credit agreement includes the following financial covenants:

Consolidated Interest Coverage Ratio may not be less than 3.00 to 1.00 as of the end of any fiscal quarter.

Consolidated Leverage Ratio may not be greater than the ratios indicated as of the end of any fiscal quarter for each period specified:

Period	Ratios
From the agreement date of May 10, 2018, through June 30, 2019	3.25 to 1.00
From July 1, 2019, and thereafter	3.00 to 1.00

– U.S. Cellular Corp (USM) 2019 10K

PRO FORMA FINANCIAL STATEMENTS

Another way that the analyst can look forward with financial statements is to construct pro forma statements that reflect significant developments, prior to reflection of those developments in subsequent published statements. It is unwise to base an investment decision on historical statements that antedate a major financial change such as a major (non-routine) stock repurchase, write-off, acquisition, or divestment. By the same token, it can be important to determine quickly whether news that flashes across the screen will have a material effect on a company's financial condition. For example, will a just-announced plan to repurchase 5 million shares materially increase financial leverage? To answer the question, the analyst must adjust the latest balance sheet available, reducing shareholders' equity by the product of 5 million and an assumed purchase price per share, then reduce cash or increase debt as the accounting offset.

Pro Forma Statements for Acquisitions

Pro forma statements are not limited to analysts' rough-and-ready modifications of previously released financial reports, generated in response to corporate announcements. The category also includes detailed income statements and balance sheets that companies provide in connection with major corporate transactions. These unaudited statements contain new disclosures and are filed with the Securities and Exchange Commission on to notify investors of material, unscheduled events. It is imperative to read them in conjunction with the accompanying notes.

Exhibit 12.14 is the pro forma combined income statement for retail pharmacy operator CVS Health's proposed $77 billion cash and stock acquisition of healthcare insurer Aetna, announced on December 3, 2017. CVS Health had become the second-largest player in the pharmacy benefits management (PBM) business in 2006 by acquiring Caremark Rx for $21 billion. Its offer to buy Aetna was seen as a defensive move against PBM heavyweight UnitedHealth Group and expected competition in the pharmacy business from online retailing giant Amazon.

The planned combination promised to produce a substantial synergy, since CVS Health earned $6.713 billion of pharmacy and clinical services revenues from Aetna in the nine months ending September 30, 2017. Accordingly, the notes to the pro forma income statement detail the elimination of the related cost of revenues and administrative fees from selling, general, and administrative expenses.

EXHIBIT 12.14 Unaudited Pro Forma Condensed Combined Statement of Income for the Nine Months Ended September 30, 2017

	CVS Health	Aetna	Pro Forma Adjustments (Note 6)	Pro Forma Combined
	(Millions, except per common share data)			
Revenues:				
Pharmacy, consumer products, and other:				
Net revenues	$ 134,185	$ –	$ (6,713) (j)	$ 127,472
Insurance:				
Premiums (i)	2,195	40,810	–	43,005
Fees and other revenue	–	4,142	–	4,142
Net investment income	–	730	(87) (k)	643
Total net revenues	136,380	45,682	(6,800)	175,262
Operating costs and expenses:				
Pharmacy, consumer products, and other:				
Cost of revenues	113,807	–	(6,627) (j)	107,180
Insurance:				
Benefit costs (i)	1,932	33,428	–	35,360
	115,739	33,428	(6,627) (j)	142,540
Selling, general and administrative expenses	14,232	9,193	1,153 (l)	24,578
Total operating costs and expenses	129,971	42,621	(5,474)	167,118
Operating income	6,409	3,061	(1,326)	8,144
Interest expense, net	744	349	1,357 (m)	2,450

EXHIBIT 12.14 (Continued)

	CVS Health	Aetna	Pro Forma Adjustments (Note 6)	Pro Forma Combined
		(Millions, except per common share data)		
Loss on early extinguishment of debt	–	246	–	246
Other expense (income)	206	–	(129) (n)	77
Income from continuing operations before income tax provision	5,459	2,466	(2,554)	5,371
Income tax provision	2,115	815	(996) (o)	1,934
Income from continuing operations	3,344	1,651	(1,558)	3,437
(Income) loss from continuing operations attributable to noncontrolling interest	(1)	9	–	8
Income from continuing operations attributable to CVS Health	$ 3,343	$ 1,660	$ (1,558)	$ 3,445
Earnings per share from continuing operations attributable to CVS Health:				
Basic	$ 3.26	$ 4.95		$ 2.65 (q)
Diluted	$ 3.25	$ 4.92		$ 2.63 (q)
Weighted average shares:				
Basic	1,022	335	(61)	1,296 (p)
Diluted	1,026	338	(56)	1,308 (p)

See the accompanying notes to the unaudited pro forma condensed combined financial statements, which are an integral part of these statements. The pro forma adjustments shown above are explained in *Note 6. Income Statement Pro Forma Adjustments*, beginning on page 53 of this joint proxy statement/prospectus.

Among other pro forma income statement adjustments, CVS Health reclassified insurance premiums from CVS Health's SilverScript Insurance Company Medicare Part D prescription plan and presented them separately from net revenues from pharmacy, consumer products, and other. These reclassifications were made to conform with Aetna's insurance-related presentation. CVS Health also adjusted the pro forma income statement for forgone interest income associated with adjusting the amortized cost of Aetna's debt securities investment portfolio to fair value as of the merger's completion.

In addition, CVS Health's first-quarter 2017 early adoption of Accounting Standards Update 2017-07, *Improving the Presentation of Net Periodic Pension Cost and Net Periodic Postretirement Benefit Cost* necessitated the restatement of certain Aetna selling, general, and administration expenses to other expense (income) to conform to CVS Health's accounting policy. Furthermore, interest expense was increased to reflect expected debt issuance to fund the Aetna deal and reduced interest income to reflect the use of some of CVS Health's balance sheet cash for the transaction. The interest expense adjustment also took into account amortization of the estimated fair value adjustment to Aetna debt that was to be assumed by CVS Health. CVS Health quantified how sensitive its interest expense adjustments were to an increase or decrease of interest rates from those assumed in the pro forma income statement.

The pro forma income statement incorporated applicable statutory income tax rates in effect on September 30, 2017, generally 39 percent. CVS Health based its projection of combined basic and diluted earnings per share from continuing operations on the combined weighted average basic and diluted common shares of CVS Health and Aetna. Aetna's historical weighted average basic and diluted shares were assumed to be replaced by the shares that CVS Health expected to issue as part of the consideration to Aetna shareholders.

Exhibit 12.15 is the pro forma combined balance sheet for the CVS Health-Aetna deal. It reflects the use of available cash for partial funding of the transaction, elimination of trade receivables and payables between the two companies, elimination of Aetna's historical goodwill, and creation of an estimate of goodwill for the acquisition. Additionally, the pro forma balance sheet adjusts Aetna's intangible assets and other assets for their estimated fair value. The statement also adjusts accrued expenses and other current liabilities to accrue estimated acquisition-related transaction costs and reduce current tax liabilities related to estimated tax-deductible acquisition-related transaction costs.

As for debt, the pro forma balance sheet reflects the issuance of CVS Health long-term debt and related debt issuance costs, eliminates Aetna debt

EXHIBIT 12.15 Unaudited Pro Forma Condensed Combined Balance Sheet, as of September 30, 2017

	CVS Health	Aetna	Pro Forma Adjustments (Note 7)	Pro Forma Combined
		(Millions)		
Assets:				
Cash and cash equivalents	$ 2,485	$ 5,928	$ (3,197) (r)	$ 5,216
Investments	75	2,869	–	2,944
Accounts receivable, net	12,440	4,965	(778) (s)	16,627
Inventories	14,147	–	–	14,147
Other current assets	776	2,672	–	3,448
Total current assets	29,923	16,434	(3,975)	42,382
Long-term investments	–	21,507	–	21,507
Property and equipment, net	9,914	581	–	10,495
Goodwill	38,169	10,683	38,861 (t)	87,713
Intangible assets, net	13,303	1,273	26,572 (u)	41,148
Separate account assets	–	4,335	–	4,335
Other assets	1,544	2,570	(1,216) (v)	2,898
Total assets	$ 92,853	$ 57,383	$ 60,242	$ 210,478
Liabilities and equity:				
Pharmacy claims and discounts payable	$ 9,807	$ –	$ –	$ 9,807
Health care costs payable and other insurance liabilities	–	7,562	(778) (s)	6,784
Accrued expenses and other current liabilities	16,303	10,087	413 (w)	26,803
Short-term debt and current portion of long-term debt	2,403	1,998	–	4,401
Total current liabilities	28,513	19,647	(365)	47,795
Long-term debt	23,386	8,161	45,653 (x)	77,200
Deferred income taxes	4,442	72	9,353 (y)	13,867

EXHIBIT 12.15 (*Continued*)

284

	CVS Health	Aetna	Pro Forma Adjustments (Note 7)	Pro Forma Combined
		(Millions)		
Separate account liabilities	–	4,335	–	4,335
Other long-term insurance liabilities	–	7,475	–	7,475
Other long-term liabilities	1,644	1,875	–	3,519
Total liabilities	57,985	41,565	54,641	154,191
Shareholders' equity:				
Common stock and capital surplus	32,026	4,707	(4,707) (z)	32,026
Treasury stock and shares held in trust	(37,795)	–	21597 (aa)	(16,198)
Retained earnings	40,779	12,037	(12,450) (bb)	40,366
Accumulated other comprehensive income (loss)	(147)	(1,161)	1161 (cc)	(147)
Total shareholders' equity	34,863	15,583	5,601	56,047
Noncontrolling interest	5	235	–	240
Total equity	34,868	15,818	5,601	56,287
Total liabilities and equity	$ 92,853	$ 57,383	$ 60,242	$ 210478

(1)On an historical basis, share information of CVS Health is as follows: 3.2 billion common shares authorized; 1.7 billion common shares issued and 1.0 billion shares outstanding. On a pro forma combined basis, share information is as follows: 3.2 billion common shares authorized; 2.0 billion common shares issued and 1.287 billion common shares outstanding.

See the accompanying notes to the unaudited pro forma condensed combined financial statements, which are an integral part of these statements. The pro forma adjustments shown above are explained in *Note 7. Balance Sheet Pro Forma Adjustments*, beginning on page 57 of this joint proxy statement/prospectus.

issuance costs that have no future economic benefit, and adjusts Aetna's debt to an estimate of fair value. Aetna's deferred income tax liabilities (assets) are adjusted for items such as intangible assets, tax-deductible goodwill, and capitalized software, among others.

Aetna's historical common shares and additional paid-in capital are eliminated and CVS Health shares are issued from treasury stock to record the stock portion of the acquisition. Aetna's historical retained earnings are eliminated and the estimated after-tax portion of acquisition-related transaction costs projected to be incurred after September 30, 2017, are recorded. Finally, Aetna's historical accumulated other comprehensive income is eliminated.

The CVS Health-Aetna amalgamation obtained antitrust clearance in September 2018. The Justice Department approved the deal on condition that CVS Health sell Aetna's Medicare prescription drug-plan business. Nearly a year later a federal judge approved the settlement. Fully integrating the two businesses took still longer. Questions on this point lingered in investors' minds in February 2020 when the former Aetna Chief Executive Officer resigned from CVS Health's board and said the integration was "far from over." CVS's CEO, in contrast, called the integration "successful."[2] The lesson to draw is that pro forma statements may meticulously detail the accounting ramifications of a business combination, but they cannot fully capture the uncertainties inherent in trying to make two previously independent companies mesh.

MULTIYEAR PROJECTIONS

So far, this chapter has focused on one-year projections and pro forma adjustments to current financial statements. Such exercises, however, represent nothing more than the foundation of a complete projection. A fixed-income investor buying a 30-year bond is certainly interested in the issuer's financial prospects beyond a 12-month horizon. Similarly, a substantial percentage of the present value of future dividends represented by a stock's price lies in years beyond the coming one. Even if particular investors plan to hold the securities for one year or less, they have an interest in estimating longer-term projections. Their ability, 6 or 12 months hence, to sell at attractive prices will depend on other investors' views at the time of the issuer's prospects.

The inherent volatility of economic conditions makes long-term projections a perilous undertaking. In the late 1970s, prognosticators generally expected then-prevailing tightness in energy supplies to persist and worsen, resulting in continued escalation of oil prices. The implications of this scenario included large profits for oil producers and boom conditions for manufacturers of oil exploration supplies, energy-conservation products, and alternative-energy equipment. By the early 1980s, the energy picture had changed from scarcity to glut, and many companies that had expected prosperity instead suffered bankruptcy. In subsequent years, numerous other discontinuities have forced companies to revise their long-range plans. They have included:

- A wave of sovereign debt defaults by less developed countries in Latin America.
- A stock market crash on October 19, 1987.
- A huge wave of leveraged buyout bankruptcies.
- A war in the Persian Gulf.
- A boom and bust in Internet stocks.
- A financial crisis in Asia.
- The September 11, 2001, terrorist attacks on the Pentagon and World Trade Center, followed by new wars in the Persian Gulf and Afghanistan.
- The most severe financial crisis and recession since the 1930s, lasting from 2007 to mid-2009 and leading to reduced expectations for longer-run economic growth.
- Beginning in 2020, the COVID-19 pandemic, the deadliest such event in 100 years, triggered a deep recession that could not have been foreseen even shortly before it began.

The frequency of such shocks makes it difficult to have high confidence in projections covering periods even as short as five years.

Notwithstanding their potential for badly missing the mark, multiyear projections are essential to financial analysis in certain situations. For example, some capital-intensive companies such as paper manufacturers have long construction cycles. They add to their capacity not in steady, annual increments but through large, individual plants that take several years to build. While a plant is in construction, the company must pay interest on the huge sums borrowed to finance it. This increased expense depresses earnings until the point, several years out, when the new plant comes onstream and begins to generate revenues. To obtain a true picture of the company's long-range financial condition, the analyst must somehow factor in the income statements for the fourth and fifth years of the construction project. These are far more difficult to forecast than first- or second-year results, which reflect cyclical peak borrowings and interest costs.

Radical financial restructurings also necessitate multiyear projections. Examples include leveraged buyouts, megamergers, and massive stock buybacks. The short-term impact of these transactions is to increase financial risk sharply. Often, leverage rises to a level investors are comfortable with only if they believe the company will be able to reduce debt to more customary levels within a few years. Sources of debt repayment may include both cash flow and proceeds of planned asset sales. Analysts must make projections to determine whether the plan for debt retirement rests on realistic assumptions. A lender cannot prudently enter into a highly leveraged transaction without making some attempt to project results over several years, notwithstanding the uncertainties inherent in such long-range forecasts.

Fortunately for analysts, today's sophisticated financial modeling tools make it feasible to run numerous scenarios for proposed transactions. Analysts can vary the underlying economic assumptions and deal terms as they change from day to day. Once the company's financial structure becomes definitive, the analyst can input the final numbers into the spreadsheet. From that point, the critical task is to monitor the restructured company's quarter-by-quarter progress, comparing actual results with projections.

Financial modeling tools are helpful in analyzing conventionally capitalized companies, as well as highly leveraged transactions. In projecting the financials of companies with already-strong balance sheets, however, analysts should not assume that all excess cash flow will be directed toward debt retirement. Conservatively capitalized companies generally do not seek to reduce their financial leverage below some specified level. Instead, they use surplus funds to repurchase stock or make acquisitions.

Essentially, multiyear projections involve the same sorts of assumptions described in the one-year Colossal Chemical projection (Exhibits 12.1 through 12.12). When looking forward by as much as five years, though, the analyst must be especially cognizant of the impact of the business cycle. Many companies' projected financial statements look fine as long as sales grow like a hockey stick (sloping upward). Their financial strength dissipates quickly, however, when sales turn downward for a year or two.

Notwithstanding the many uncertainties that confront the financial forecaster, carefully constructed projections can prove fairly accurate. The results can be satisfying even when the numbers are strongly influenced by hard-to-predict economic variables. The detailed projections reproduced as Exhibit 12.16 was generated by independent high-yield bond analyst Stan Manoukian.[3] This exhibit shows how the bottom-up approach illustrated in the fictitious Colossal Chemical example can be applied in real life to companies outside the basic industry sphere.

EXHIBIT 12.16 Hertz Corporation Historical and Near-Term Projected Data

Outstanding Debt Summary

Senior 1st-lien term loan	$656	HVF II U.S. ABS program	$10,893
Senior 1st-lien revolver	$615	Donlen U.S.ABS program	$1,592
Total 1st-lien debt	$1,271	U.S. vehicle RCF	$93
Senior 2nd-lien notes	$350	European vehicle notes	$794
Total secured debt	$1,621	European ABS program	$650
Senior unsecured notes	$2,700	Canadian securitization	$251
Promissory unsecured notes	$27	Donlen Canadian securitization	$27
Total non-vehicle debt	$4,348	Australian securitization	$149
Cash	$900	New Zealand revolver	$46
Net parent debt	$3,448	U.S. facility	$229
		Total vehicle debt	$14,724

What's the Problem?

When things were doing well, Hertz was able to gradually increase the number of rental cars in the U.S. from 500,000 in 2014 to 535,000 in 2019 (7 percent increase). However, revenue per day has not materially increased from 2014; it has actually declined from $46.07 in 2014 to $43.73 in 2019. At the same time, Avis, the closest competitor, has been able to grow the number of U.S. cars by 18 percent and revenue per day by 38 percent. And looking at these differences, it is difficult not to draw a conclusion about the quality of management at both companies. The issue is all about the efficiency of utilization of each car. This efficiency has clearly been superior at Avis.

U.S. statistics	2014	2019	Changes
HTZ average fleet	499,100	534,879	7%
CAR average	369,015	434,570	18%
HTZ rev/day	$46.07	$43.73	−5%
CAR rev/day	$41.33	56.94	38%

When the economy started sinking, Hertz needed to materially shrink its fleet, which needs a technical OK by ABS debt holders, since the fleet reduction cannot negatively affect asset-backed securities (ABS) debtholders (see below). If Hertz can sell its cars efficiently, its EBITDA will decline in full correlation with the decline in the total number of cars. And in order to return to the normalized level operations, say in 2022, Hertz will need to (a) get access to new ABS tranches and (b) demonstrate superior operating performance, which is only possible if it can keep its market share. We highly doubt that these steps will be possible to accomplish by 2022.

EXHIBIT 12.16   (*Continued*)

ABS Debt in Financial Statements

Almost $11 billion of the U.S. ABS debt is reflected in the financial statements through the following items:

1. Depreciation of the revenue-earning equipment;
2. Interest on vehicle debt;
3. Fleet capital expenditure (capex) purchases;
4. Fleet capex disposals.

The company's corporate EBITDA reported in financial statements already incorporates all expense associated with the acquisition and financial maintenance of all U.S. cars. Almost 100 percent of the U.S. fleet is financed by ABS tranches. The Parent company makes lease payments, depreciation payments, and interest payments to HVF II and it distributes it to holders of ABS debt.

How to Shrink the Fleet?

Instead of fighting for the right to reject leases, Hertz has agreed to pay ABS debtholders $650mm in 6 equal tranches through the end of 2020 and to reduce its fleet by 182,521 cars by December 31, 2020:

Program vehicle to be sold	27,618
Non-program vehicles to be sold	154,903
Total vehicles to be sold	182,521

Hertz has committed to cover the difference to ABS debt. In exchange, Hertz can pocket $900 per car sold. It is unclear if the demand for used cars will continue as robust as it is today. It is also unclear when the travel rate starts normalizing to the pre-crisis level.

	95%	100%
U.S cars on March 31, 2020	518,580	518,580
Cars est. on June 1, 2020	492,521	492,521
Cars to be sold between		
June 1 & Dec. 31, 2020	182,521	182,521
Cars est. on Dec. 31, 2020	310,000	310,000
Parent keeps per vehicle sold	$900	$900
Target proceeds from car sales (bn)	$4,146	$4,146
Average price/car	$22,715	$22,715
Guaranteed proceeds from sales	$3,939	$3,939
Implied average price/car	$21,579	$21,579
Minus parent retention	($164)	($164)
Distribution to HVF II Series 2013	$3,774	$3,982
Remaining 2013 Series on 12/31/2020	$1,081	$873

EXHIBIT 12.16 (*Continued*)

Balance Sheet & Operations

The Parent company's first lien debt is paid the interest during the bankruptcy. The interest on the 2nd-lien debt and unsecured debt accrues.

The balance of the ABS debt as of May 31, 2020, was $10,172mm versus $10,893mm as of May 20, 2020. It is clear that Hertz has been aggressively selling its fleet. The company states that LTV ratio as of May 31, 2020, was 89.1 percent, with $975mm of the over-collateralization:

	05/31/20	Sell cars	Gain on sale	ABS book depreciation	Casu-alty	Collected cash	Lease Interest payment	Pro Forma 12/31/2020
Total vehicles	492,521	(182,521)						310,000
Fleet asset balance	$11,147	($3,864)		($1,466)	($112)	($415)		$5,290
ABS debt	$10,172	($3,864)	($282)			($415)	($650)	$4,961
Over collateralization	$975							
LOC	$275					($110)		$165
LTV	89.9%							90.9%

The next major issue is that Hertz intends to sell its most expensive cars to maximize debt reduction under the ABS pool. That means that cars left will generate smaller revenues per day. An average selling price in the U.S, after the expiration of the 18-month lease is between $17,000 and $18,000. That is materially different from the expected sales per car of $22,715. We have also looked at prices of Hertz and its other brands at Expedia. We have found that Hertz has the most expensive prices at all major U.S. hubs. That implies that the company has been losing the market share to Avis. This loss is one of the most important hurdles for the company to return to the pre-Covid-19 EBITDA generation any time soon. Moreover, the dispute on lease rejection still needs to be finalized, and it is unclear if Hertz will not have any deficiency claims when it emerges from bankruptcy.

EXHIBIT 12.16 (*Continued*)

	Coupon	Maturity	Face value	*Market price*	Market value	Cash interest
Cash as of 5/20/2020			$900			
Vehicle debt						
U.S. ABS HVF II Series 2013-A	2.71%	Mar-22	$4,855	100.0%	$4,855	$131.6
U.S. HVF II Series 2015-1	2.93%	Mar-20	$0			
U.S. HVF II Series 2015-3	3.10%	Sep-20	$371	100.0%	$371	$11.5
U.S. HVF II Series 2016-2	3.41%	Mar-21	$595	100.0%	$595	$20.3
U.S. HVF II Series 2016-4	3.09%	Jul-21	$424	100.0%	$424	$13.1
U.S. HVF II Series 2017-1	3.38%	Oct-20	$450	100.0%	$450	$15.2
U.S. HVF II Series 2017-2	3.57%	Oct-22	$370	100.0%	$370	$13.2
U.S. HVF II Series 2018-1	3.41%	Feb-23	$1,058	100.0%	$1,058	$36.1
U.S. HVF II Series 2018-2	3.80%	Jun-21	$213	100.0%	$213	$8.1
U.S. HVF II Series 2018-3	4.15%	Jul-23	$213	100.0%	$213	$8.8
U.S. HVF II Series 2019-1	3.85%	Mar-22	$745	100.0%	$745	$28.7
U.S. HVF II Series 2019-2	3.51%	May-24	$799	100.0%	$799	$28.0
U.S. HVF II Series 2019-3	2.91%	Dec-24	$800	100.0%	$800	$23.3
			$10,893		$10,893	$338
Donlen U.S.						
HFLF Series 2013-2	2.56%	Mar-21	$485	100.0%	$485	$12.4
HFLF Series 2016-1	4.89%	Feb-20	$0			
HFLF Series 2017-1	2.54%	May-21	$155	100.0%	$155	$3.9
HFLF Series 2018-1	2.78%	Sep-22	$374	100.0%	$374	$10.4
HFLF Series 2019-1	2.41%	Nov-22	$578	100.0%	$578	$13.9
			$1,592		$1,107	$28

(*Continued*)

EXHIBIT 12.16 (*Continued*)

	Coupon	Maturity	Face value	*Market price*	Market value	Cash interest
Other vehicle debt						
U.S. vehicle RCF	3.61%	Jun-21	$93	100.0%	$93	$3.4
European ABS	1.60%	Nov-21	$650	100.0%	$650	$10.4
Hertz Canadian securitization	3.10%	Mar-21	$251	100.0%	$251	$7.8
Donlen Canadian securitization	2.59%	Dec-22	$27	100.0%	$27	$0.7
Hertz Netherlands Sr. unsec. notes	4.125%	Oct-21	$246	88.0%	$216	$10.1
Hertz Netherlands Sr. unsec. notes	5.50%	Mar-23	$548	88.0%	$482	$30.1
Australian securitization	2.11%	Jun-21	$149	100.0%	$149	$3.1
New Zealand RCF	3.82%	Jun-21	$46	100.0%	$46	$1.8
U.K. facility	2.59%	Sep-22	$229	100.0%	$229	$5.9
Other vehicle debt	3.82%	Nov-24	$0	100.0%	$0	$0.0
Total vehicle debt			$14,724		$14,144	$440
Non-vehicle debt						
Senior RCF	3.99%	Jun-23	$615	90.0%	$554	$24.5
Senior TL L+2.75%	3.74%	Jun-23	$656	90.0%	$590	$24.5
2nd-lien notes	7.625%	Jun-22	$350	80.0%	$280	$26.7
Sr. unsecured notes	6.25%	Oct-22	$500	39.0%	$195	$31.3
Sr. unsecured notes	5.50%	Oct-24	$800	39.0%	$312	$44.0
Sr. unsecured notes	7.125%	Aug-26	$500	39.0%	$195	$35.6
Sr. unsecured notes	6.00%	Jan-28	$900	39.0%	$351	$54.0
Sr. unsecured promissory notes	7.00%	Jan-28	$27	39.0%	$11	$1.9
Other debt	5.70%	NA	$21	39.0%	$8	$1.2
Total non-vehicle debt			$4,369		$2,496	$244
Total debt			$19,093		$16,639	$683
Equity	142.1	Shares	$1.50		$213.2	
Minority interests					$119.0	
Enterprise value					$18,525.2	

EXHIBIT 12.16 (*Continued*)

We present our updated financial forecast that incorporates information on estimated car sales through the end of 2020. According to this analysis, our best case 2022 corporate EBITDA should not exceed the $350mm level.

2022 Corp. EBITDA	$150	$250	$325
Multiple	6.0x	6.0x	6.0x
EV	$900	$1,500	$1,950
Cash on May 20, 2020	$900	$900	$900
Equity from car sales	$200	$225	$250
Cash burn though bankruptcy	($400)	($350)	($300)
Exit cash	$700	$775	$850
Total EV	$1,600	$2,275	$2,800
1st-lien debt	$1,271	$1,271	$1,271
Recovery 1st-lien debt	100.0%	100.0%	100.0%
Available for 2nd-lien debt	$329	$1,004	$1,529
2nd-lien debt	$350	$350	$350
Recovery 2nd-lien debt	94.0%	100.0%	100.0%
Available for unsec. pool	$0	$654	$1,179
Face value unsec. notes	$2,727	$2,727	$2,727
Unsec. prepetition claims	$390	$390	$390
Total unsecured claims	$3,117	$3,117	$3,117
Recovery for unsec. claims	0.0%	21.0%	37.8%

(*Continued*)

EXHIBIT 12.16 (*Continued*)

	2016	2017	2018	Q1 2019	Q2 2019	Q3 2019	Q4 2019	2019	Q1 2020	Q2 2020e	Q3 2020e	Q4 2020e	2020e	2021e	2022 low	2022 high
U.S. operations rental revenues	$6,038	$5,994	$6,480	$1,520	$1,751	$1,962	$1,705	$6,938	$1,381	$615	$680	$760	$3,436	$3,608	$4,100	$4,662
Change	-3.1%	-0.7%	8.1%	6.6%	9.2%	5.4%	7.3%	7.1%	-9.1%	-64.9%	-65.3%	-55.4%	-50.5%	5.0%	13.6%	29.2%
Transaction days (000s)	142,268	140,382	149,463	35,582	41,173	41,399	37,705	155,859	31,564	15,000	17,000	20,000	83,564	88,000	100,000	111,000
Change	2.7%	-1.3%	6.5%	4.0%	6.3%	4.2%	2.6%	4.3%	-11.3%	-63.6%	-58.9%	-47.0%	-46.4%	5.3%	13.6%	26.1%
Revenue per day	$42.44	$42.06	$42.67	$41.90	$42.54	$46.67	$43.81	$43.73	$42.74	$41.00	$40.00	$38.00	$41.12	$41.00	$41.00	$42.00
Change	-5.6%	-0.9%	1.5%	2.4%	2.8%	1.0%	1.3%	2.5%	2.0%	-3.6%	-14.3%	-13.3%	-6.0%	-0.3%	0.0%	2.4%
Average fleet	484,800	484,700	506,900	501,767	554,794	566,229	534,879	534,879	443,819	353,185	310,000	406,396	320,000	370,000	400,000	
Fleet efficiency	80.4%	79.3%	80.8%	77.9%	81.6%	80.3%	76.6%	79.8%	66.9%	37.1%	52.9%	70.1%	56.3%	75.3%	74.0%	76.0%
RPU/month	$1,037.9	$1,030.5	$1,065.3	$1,009.8	$1,052.0	$1,155.0	$1,062.5	$1,080.9	$887.7	$461.9	$641.8	$817.2	$704.6	$939.6	$923.4	$971.3
Change	-2.1%	-0.7%	3.4%					1.5%	-12.1%	-56.1%	-44.4%	-23.1%	-34.8%	33.4%	-1.7%	3.4%
Direct exp./car/month	$626.7	$627.7	$659.9	$648.4	$632.1	$647.0	$635.0	$645.9	$622.9	$518.2	$613.5	$645.2	$596.5	$690.1	$608.1	$599.0
Available car days	177,437	176,916	185,019	45,661	50,486	51,527	47,557	195,231	47,191	40,388	32,140	28,520	148,238	116,800	135,050	146,000
Rev. per avail. car/day	$34.03	$33.88	$35.02	$33.29	$34.68	$38.08	$35.85	$35.54	$29.26	$15.23	$21.16	$26.65	$23.18	$30.89	$30.36	$31.93
Percentage of cars available	36.6%	36.5%	36.5%	36.4%	36.4%	36.4%	35.6%	36.5%	36.4%	36.4%	36.4%	36.8%	36.5%	36.5%	36.5%	36.5%
International operations rental revenues	$2,097	$2,169	$2,276	$433	$564	$702	$470	$2,169	$368	$254	$341	$360	$1,323	$1,680	$1,785	$2,010
Change	-9.6%	3.4%	4.9%	-7.5%	0.5%	-4.1%	-8.7%	-4.7%	-15.0%	-55.1%	-51.4%	-23.4%	-39.0%	27.0%	6.3%	19.7%
Transaction days (000s)	48,627	50,301	50,417	10,127	13,125	15,631	11,256	50,139	8,863	6,500	8,750	9,000	33,113	40,000	42,000	46,750
Change	1.6%	3.4%	0.2%	1.5%	-0.8%	-1.5%	-0.8%	-0.6%	-12.5%	-50.5%	-44.0%	-34.0%	-34.0%	20.8%	5.0%	16.9%
Revenue per day	$40.74	$40.18	$43.49	$42.56	$42.97	$45.67	$43.72	$43.73	$42.35	$39.00	$39.00	$40.00	$39.95	$42.00	$42.50	$43.00
Change	-15.9%	-1.4%	8.2%	-2.0%	1.2%	1.4%	1.0%	0.6%	-0.5%	-9.2%	-14.6%	-8.5%	-8.7%	5.1%	1.2%	2.4%
Average fleet	173,400	178,100	180,400	152,747	186,881	213,294	180,723	183,411	147,987	135,000	130,000	134,497	125,000	160,000	170,000	170,000
Fleet efficiency	76.8%	77.4%	76.6%	72.9%	77.2%	80.5%	67.7%	74.9%	65.8%	52.9%	74.0%	78.3%	67.5%	73.1%	71.9%	75.3%
RPU/month	$1,007.8	$1,014.9	$1,051.4	$944.9	$1,006.0	$1,097.1	$866.9	$985.5	$828.9	$625.9	$875.0	$960.0	$819.6	$933.3	$929.7	$985.4
Change	-12.0%	0.7%	3.6%					-6.3%	-12.3%	-37.8%	-20.2%	10.7%	-16.8%	13.9%	-0.4%	5.6%
Direct exp./car/month	$603.6	$595.6	$603.3	$619.8	$588.6	$603.2	$575.5	$596.1	$596.9	$543.2	$615.4	$680.0	$607.2	$611.1	$617.2	$612.7
Available car days	63,464	65,007	65,846	13,900	17,006	19,410	15,648	65,964	13,467	12,285	11,830	11,509	49,091	54,750	58,400	62,050
Rev. per avail. car/day	$33.04	$33.37	$34.57	$31.15	$33.16	$36.17	$30.04	$32.88	$27.33	$20.63	$28.85	$31.28	$26.94	$30.68	$30.57	$32.40
Percentage of cars available	36.6%	36.5%	36.5%	36.4%	36.4%	36.4%	34.6%	36.0%	36.4%	36.4%	36.4%	36.8%	36.5%	36.5%	36.5%	36.5%

EXHIBIT 12.16   (*Continued*)

	2016	2017	2018	Q1 2019	Q2 2019	Q3 2019	Q4 2019	2019	Q1 2020	Q2 2020e	Q3 2020e	Q4 2020e	2020e	2021e	2022 low	2022 high
U.S. Car rental sales	$6,114	$5,994	$6,480	$1,520	$1,784	$1,962	$1,672	$6,938	$1,381	$615	$680	$760	$3,436	$3,608	$4,100	$4,662
Direct expenses	$3,646	$3,651	$4,014	$976	$1,052	$1,099	$1,019	$4,146	$969	$690	$650	$600	$2,909	$2,650	$2,700	$2,875
Percentage of sales	59.6%	60.9%	61.9%	64.2%	59.0%	56.0%	60.9%	59.9%	70.2%	112.2%	95.6%	78.9%	84.7%	73.4%	65.9%	61.7%
SG&A	$397	$392	$466	$121	$119	$125	$125	$490	$115	$95	$90	$85	$385	$365	$370	$380
Percentage of sales	6.5%	6.5%	7.2%	8.0%	6.7%	6.4%	7.5%	7.1%	8.3%	15.4%	13.2%	11.2%	11.2%	10.1%	9.0%	8.2%
Dep. of rev. earning veh.	$1,753	$1,904	$1,678	$386	$411	$420	$439	$1,656	$463	$350	$290	$220	$1,323	$990	$1,075	$1,200
D&A/per fleet unit/month	$301	$327	$276	$256	$247	$247	$274	$258	$298	$263	$274	$237	$271	$258	$242	$250
Other	$0	$3	($96)	($30)	($46)	($49)	($41)	($166)	($33)	$15	$15	$15	$12	$15	$15	$15
Adjusted EBITDA U.S.	$318	$50	$226	$7	$156	$269	$48	$480	($199)	($505)	($335)	($130)	($1,169)	($382)	($30)	$222
Inter. car rental sales	$2,097	$2,169	$2,276	$433	$560	$702	$474	$2,169	$368	$254	$341	$360	$1,323	$1,680	$1,785	$2,010
Direct expenses	$1,256	$1,273	$1,306	$284	$330	$386	$312	$1,312	$265	$220	$240	$255	$980	$1,100	$1,185	$1,250
Percentage of sales	59.9%	58.7%	57.4%	65.6%	58.9%	55.0%	65.8%	60.5%	72.0%	86.8%	70.3%	70.8%	74.1%	65.5%	66.4%	62.2%
SG&A	$215	$223	$248	$54	$55	$60	$52	$221	$48	$45	$50	$50	$193	$180	$190	$200
Percentage of sales	10.3%	10.3%	10.9%	12.5%	9.8%	8.5%	11.0%	10.2%	13.0%	17.8%	14.7%	13.9%	14.6%	10.7%	10.6%	9.9%
Dep. of rev. earning veh.	$389	$416	$448	$97	$106	$126	$111	$440	$89	$75	$75	$77	$316	$320	$340	$360
D&A/per fleet unit/month	$187	$195	$207	$212	$189	$197	$205	$200	$200	$185	$192	$205	$196	$178	$177	$176
Other	$0	($22)	($43)	($11)	($13)	($15)	($10)	($49)	($11)	$0	$0	$0	($111)	$0	$0	$0
Adjusted EBITDA Inter.	$237	$235	$231	($13)	$56	$115	($11)	$147	($45)	($87)	($24)	($22)	($177)	$80	$70	$200
Equipment rental & other	$592	$640	$748	$154	$167	$172	$179	$672	$174	$110	$120	$125	$529	$575	$600	$640
Direct expenses	$22	$40	$37	$6	$7	$7	$8	$28	$7	$6	$6	$6	$25	$26	$26	$26
Percentage of sales	3.7%	6.3%	4.9%	3.9%	4.2%	4.1%	4.5%	4.2%	4.0%	5.5%	5.0%	4.8%	4.7%	4.5%	4.3%	4.1%
SG&A	$40	$35	$37	$7	$7	$8	$13	$35	($4)	$6	$6	$6	$14	$30	$35	$37
Percentage of sales	6.8%	5.5%	4.9%	4.5%	4.2%	4.7%	7.3%	5.2%	-2.3%	5.5%	5.0%	4.8%	2.6%	5.2%	5.8%	5.8%
Dep. of rev. earning veh.	$459	$478	$564	$109	$117	$121	$122	$469	$125	$100	$110	$110	$445	$445	$445	$445
Other	$0	($13)	($28)	($10)	($12)	($12)	($6)	($40)	($22)	($10)	($10)	($10)	($52)	($40)	($40)	($40)
Adjusted EBITDA Equipm	$71	$74	$82	$22	$24	$24	$30	$100	$24	($12)	($12)	($7)	($7)	$34	$54	$92
Adjusted EBITDA Corp.	($255)	($92)	($106)	($20)	($29)	($16)	($13)	($78)	($23)	($20)	($10)	($8)	($61)	($70)	($70)	($70)
Adjusted EBITDA Total	$371	$267	$433	($4)	$207	$392	$54	$649	($243)	($624)	($381)	($167)	($1,414)	($338)	$24	$444

EXHIBIT 12.16 (*Continued*)

Hertz	Q1 2019	Q2 2019	Q3 2019	Q4 2019	2019	Q1 2020	Q2 2020e	Q3 2020e	Q4 2020e	2020e	2021e	2022e	2022e
Car rental revenues	$1,953.0	$2,344.0	$2,664.0	$2,146.0	$9,107.0	$1,749.0	$868.5	$1,021.3	$1,120.0	$4,758.8	$5,288.0	$5,885.0	$6,672.3
Change	3.1%	5.7%	3.1%	4.1%	4.0%	-10.4%	-62.9%	-61.7%	-47.8%	-47.7%	11.1%	11.3%	26.2%
Number of transactions (000s)													
Domestic transaction days	35,582	41,173	41,399	37,705	155,859	31,564	15,000	17,000	20,000	83,564	88,000	100,000	111,000
International transaction days	10,127	13,125	15,631	11,256	50,139	8,863	6,500	8,750	9,000	33,113	40,000	42,000	46,750
Worldwide transaction days	45,709	54,298	57,030	48,961	205,998	40,427	21,500	25,750	29,000	116,677	128,000	142,000	157,750
Domestic revenue per day	$41.90	$42.54	$46.67	$41.88	$43.73	$42.74	$41.00	$40.00	$38.00	$41.12	$41.00	$41.00	$42.00
International revenue per day	$42.56	$42.97	$45.67	$44.88	$42.98	$42.35	$39.00	$39.00	$40.00	$39.95	$42.00	$42.50	$43.00
Global revenue per day	$42.05	$42.65	$46.40	$42.58	$43.73	$43.26	$40.40	$39.66	$38.62	$40.79	$41.31	$41.44	$42.30
Average domestic fleet	501,767	554,794	566,229	534,879	534,879	518,580	443,819	353,185	310,000	406,396	320,000	370,000	400,000
Average international fleet	152,747	186,881	213,294	183,411	183,411	147,987	135,000	130,000	125,000	134,497	150,000	160,000	170,000
Average global fleet	654,514	741,675	779,523	718,290	718,290	666,567	578,819	483,185	435,000	540,893	470,000	530,000	570,000
Domestic capacity utilization	77.9%	81.6%	80.3%	77.5%	79.8%	66.9%	37.1%	52.9%	70.9%	56.3%	75.3%	74.0%	76.0%
International capacity utilization	72.9%	77.2%	80.5%	67.4%	74.9%	65.8%	52.9%	74.0%	79.1%	67.5%	73.1%	71.9%	75.3%
Global capacity utilization	76.7%	80.5%	80.4%	74.9%	78.6%	66.6%	40.8%	58.6%	73.3%	59.1%	74.6%	73.4%	75.8%
Domestic car rental revenues	$1,490.9	$1,751.5	$1,932.1	$1,641.2	$6,815.7	$1,349.0	$615.0	$680.0	$792.0	$3,436.0	$3,608.0	$4,100.0	$4,662.0
Change	2.4%	2.8%	1.0%	0.7%	6.9%	-9.5%	-64.9%	-64.8%	-51.7%	-49.6%	5.0%	13.6%	13.7%
International car rental revenues	$431.0	$564.0	$713.9	$446.1	$2,155.0	$375.3	$253.5	$341.3	$352.7	$1,322.8	$1,680.0	$1,785.0	$2,010.3
Change	-7.5%	0.5%	-4.1%	-8.7%	-1.7%	-12.9%	-55.1%	-52.2%	-21.0%	-38.6%	27.0%	6.3%	12.6%
Total car rental revenues calculated	$1,921.9	$2,315.5	$2,646.0	$2,087.4	$8,970.7	$1,724.4	$868.5	$1,021.3	$1,144.6	$4,758.8	$5,288.0	$5,885.0	$6,672.3
Change					4.7%	-10.3%	-62.5%	-61.4%	-45.2%	-47.0%	11.1%	11.3%	13.4%
Other car rental revenues	$31.1	$28.5	$18.0	$58.6	$136.3	$24.6	$0.0	$0.0	$0.0	$0.0	$0.0	$0.0	$0.0
Total car rental sales	$1,953.0	$2,344.0	$2,664.0	$2,146.0	$9,107.0	$1,749.0	$868.5	$1,021.3	$1,120.0	$4,758.8	$5,288.0	$5,885.0	$6,672.3
Change					4.0%	-10.4%	-62.9%	-61.7%	-47.8%	-47.7%	11.1%	11.3%	13.4%
Equipment rental	$0.0	$0.0	$0.0	$0.0	$0.0	$174.0	$110.0	$120.0	$125.0	$529.0	$575.0	$600.0	$640.0
Other sales	$154.0	$167.0	$172.0	$179.0	$672.0	$0.0	$0.0	$0.0	$0.0	$0.0	$0.0	$0.0	$0.0
Total sales	$2,107.0	$2,511.0	$2,836.0	$2,325.0	$9,779.0	$1,923.0	$978.5	$1,141.3	$1,245.0	$5,287.8	$5,863.0	$6,485.0	$7,312.3
Change	2.1%	5.1%	2.8%	1.4%	2.9%	-8.7%	-61.0%	-59.8%	-46.5%	-45.9%	10.9%	10.6%	12.8%

EXHIBIT 12.16 (*Continued*)

Hertz	Q1 2019	Q2 2019	Q3 2019	Q4 2019	2019	Q1 2020	Q2 2020e	Q3 2020e	Q4 2020e	2020e	2021e	2022e	2022e
Expenses													
Direct operating expense	$1,266.0	$1,388.0	$1,492.0	$1,340.0	$5,486.0	$1,241.0	$916.0	$896.0	$861.0	$3,914.0	$3,776.0	$3,911.0	$4,151.0
Percentage of total sales	*60.1%*	*55.3%*	*52.6%*	*57.6%*	*56.1%*	*64.5%*	*93.6%*	*78.5%*	*69.2%*	*74.0%*	*64.4%*	*60.3%*	*56.8%*
Dep. of revenue/earning equip.	$592.0	$634.0	$667.0	$672.0	$2,565.0	$677.0	$525.0	$475.0	$407.0	$2,084.0	$1,755.0	$1,860.0	$2,005.0
Percentage of sales	28.1%	25.2%	23.5%	28.9%	26.2%	35.2%	53.7%	41.6%	32.7%	39.4%	29.9%	28.7%	27.4%
SG&A	$234.0	$258.0	$232.0	$245.0	$969.0	$208.0	$201.0	$201.0	$211.0	$821.0	$850.0	$765.0	$777.0
Percentage of total sales	11.1%	10.3%	8.2%	10.5%	9.9%	10.8%	20.5%	17.6%	16.9%	15.5%	14.5%	11.8%	10.6%
Net interest	$183.0	$199.0	$204.0	$219.0	$805.0	$175.0	$200.0	$200.0	($131.0)	$444.0	$320.0	$335.0	$365.0
Taxes	$1.0	$4.0	$74.0	($16.0)	$63.0	($4.0)	$0.0	$0.0	$4.0	$0.0	$0.0	$0.0	$0.0
Impairment charges	($20.0)	($12.0)	($6.0)	$38.0	$0.0	($18.0)	$0.0	$0.0	$18.0	$0.0	$0.0	$0.0	$0.0
Minority interest	$0.0	$0.0	$4.0	($63.0)	($59.0)	$0.0	$0.0	$0.0	$0.0	$0.0	$0.0	$0.0	$0.0
Net income	($149.0)	$40.0	$169.0	($110.0)	($50.0)	($356.0)	($863.5)	($630.8)	($125.0)	($1,975.3)	($838.0)	($386.0)	$14.3
Cash EBITDA adjustments	$58.0	$161.0	$96.0	$144.0	$459.0	$86.0	$0.0	$0.0	($86.0)	$0.0	$0.0	$0.0	$0.0
Cash EBITDA	$665.0	$1,026.0	$1,208.0	$884.0	$3,783.0	$560.0	($138.5)	$44.3	$87.0	$552.8	$1,237.0	$1,809.0	$2,384.3
Percentage of total sales	31.6%	40.9%	42.6%	38.0%	38.7%	29.1%	-14.2%	3.9%	7.0%	10.5%	21.1%	27.9%	32.6%
Non-fleet Capex	($54.0)	($64.0)	($52.0)	($54.0)	($224.0)	($59.0)	($40.0)	($35.0)	($40.0)	($174.0)	($180.0)	($190.0)	($200.0)
Fleet Capex purchases	($3,973.0)	($4,974.0)	($2,589.0)	($2,178.0)	($13,714.0)	($4,346.0)	($250.0)	($250.0)	($250.0)	($5,096.0)	($9,500.0)	($10,500.0)	($11,100.0)
Fleet Capex disposals	$2,153.0	$2,059.0	$1,981.0	$3,293.0	$9,486.0	$2,212.0	$1,616.0	$1,457.0	$1,400.0	$6,685.0	$6,000.0	$7,850.0	$8,350.0
Other Capex items	$19.0	$2.0	$0.0	$6.0	$27.0	$96.0	$0.0	$0.0	$0.0	$96.0	$0.0	$0.0	$0.0
Cash interest	($116.0)	($237.0)	($160.0)	($190.0)	($703.0)	($129.0)	($111.0)	($105.0)	($95.0)	($440.0)	($360.0)	($375.0)	($385.0)
Cash taxes	($6.0)	($9.0)	$3.0	($9.0)	($21.0)	($5.0)	$0.0	$0.0	$0.0	$0.0	$0.0	$0.0	$0.0
Changes in working capital	($29.0)	($240.0)	$128.0	($18.0)	($159.0)	$23.0	($100.0)	($150.0)	($75.0)	($302.0)	$250.0	$0.0	$0.0
Cash flow proxy	($1,341.0)	($2,437.0)	$519.0	$1,734.0	($1,525.0)	($1,648.0)	$976.5	$961.3	$1,027.0	$1,316.8	($2,553.0)	($1,406.0)	($950.7)
Cash flow from operations	$514.0	$540.0	$1,179.0	$667.0	$2,900.0	$449.0	($349.5)	($210.8)	($78.0)	($189.3)	$1,127.0	$1,434.0	$1,999.3
Cash flow from investments	(1,855.0)	(2,977.0)	(660.0)	$1,067.0	(4,425.0)	(2,097.0)	1,326.0	1,172.0	1,110.0	1,511.0	(3,680.0)	(2,840.0)	(2,950.0)
Cash flow from financing	937.0	2,085.0	(478.0)	($1,069.0)	1,475.0	1,697.0	(976.5)	(961.3)	(1,081.0)	(1,321.8)	2,553.0	1,406.0	950.8

EXHIBIT 12.16 (*Continued*)

Hertz	Q1 2019	Q2 2019	Q3 2019	Q4 2019	2019	Q1 2020	Q2 2020e	Q3 2020e	Q4 2020e	2020e	2021e	2022e	2022e
Cash	1,006.0	654.0	695.0	1,360.0	1,360.0	1,409.0	900.0	900.0	900.0	900.0	900.0	900.0	900.0
Receivables	1,563.0	1,698.0	1,966.0	1,840.0	1,840.0	2,095.0							
Days receivables	67.5	61.5	63.1	72.0	67.7	99.1							
Inventories	0.0	0.0	0.0	0.0	0.0	0.0							
Days inventory													
Other current assets	1,107.0	926.0	830.0	689.0	689.0	1,121.0							
Accounts payable	1,279.0	1,369.0	870.0	943.0	943.0	998.0							
Days payable	91.9	89.8	53.1	64.0	61.9	73.2							
Other AP	$4,489.0	$4,568.0	$4,641.0	$4,707.0	$4,707.0	$4,599.0							
Debt	$17,257.0	$19,347.0	$18,041.0	$17,089.0	$17,089.0	$18,754.0	$17,777.5	$16,816.3	$15,735.3	$15,735.3	$18,288.3	$19,694.3	$20,645.0
Net debt	16,251.0	18,693.0	17,346.0	15,729.0	15,729.0	17,345.0	16,877.5	15,916.3	14,835.3	14,835.3	17,388.3	18,794.3	19,745.0
EBITDA reconciliation													
Net income	($149.0)	$40.0	$169.0	($110.0)	($50.0)	($356.0)	($863.5)	($630.8)	($125.0)	($1,975.3)	($838.0)	($386.0)	$14.3
Full D&A	$690.0	$738.0	$779.0	$561.0	$2,768.0	$730.0	$570.0	$520.0	$462.0	$2,282.0	$1,955.0	$2,060.0	$2,205.0
Net interest	$183.0	$199.0	$204.0	$219.0	$805.0	$175.0	$200.0	$200.0	$131.0	$444.0	$320.0	$335.0	$365.0
Taxes	$1.0	$4.0	$74.0	($14.0)	$65.0	($4.0)	$0.0	$0.0	$4.0	$0.0	$0.0	$0.0	$0.0
Company's EBITDA	$725.0	$981.0	$1,226.0	$656.0	$3,588.0	$545.0	($93.5)	$89.3	$210.0	$750.8	$1,437.0	$2,009.0	$2,584.3
Car rental fleet interest	($112.0)	($127.0)	($92.0)	($163.0)	($494.0)	($103.0)	($90.0)	($80.0)	($77.0)	($350.0)	($320.0)	($320.0)	($320.0)
Car rental fleet depreciation	($641.0)	($688.0)	($727.0)	($509.0)	($2,565.0)	($677.0)	($525.0)	($475.0)	($407.0)	($2,084.0)	($1,755.0)	($1,860.0)	($2,005.0)
Non-cash expenses	$3.0	$0.0	$0.0	($3.0)	$0.0	$0.0	$0.0	$0.0	$0.0	$0.0	$0.0	$0.0	$0.0
Other	$21.0	$41.0	($15.0)	$73.0	$120.0	($8.0)	$0.0	$0.0	$8.0	$0.0	$0.0	$100.0	$100.0
Corporate EBITDA	($4.0)	$207.0	$392.0	$54.0	$649.0	($243.0)	($708.5)	($465.8)	($266.0)	($1,683.3)	($638.0)	($71.0)	$359.3
Corporate EBITDA car rental	($6.0)	$212.0	$384.0	$37.0	$627.0								
Corporate EBITDA equipment	$22.0	$24.0	$24.0	$30.0	$100.0								
Other	($20.0)	($29.0)	($16.0)	($13.0)	($78.0)								
Corporate EBITDA	($4.0)	$207.0	$392.0	$54.0	$649.0								

EXHIBIT 12.16 (*Continued*)

Disclosure

> *The views expressed about the debt securities that are the subject of this research report accurately reflect the personal views, as of the report's publication date, of the Independent Credit Research, LLC ("ICR") analyst primarily responsible for drafting the report. No part of the analyst's compensation was, is, or will be, directly or indirectly, related to the specific recommendations or views expressed by him in this research report. The analyst's evaluation of the subject debt securities may change subsequent to the publication of this report. Neither the analyst nor ICR assumes any duty to update the information contained in this report. This research report is for informational purposes only and does not provide individually tailored tax, legal, or investment advice. It has been prepared without regard to the individual financial circumstances and objectives of persons who receive it. The debt instruments discussed in this research report may not be suitable for all investors. ICR strongly recommends that investors independently evaluate particular investments and strategies, and encourages investors to seek the advice of a financial adviser. The appropriateness of a particular investment or strategy will depend on an investor's individual circumstances and objectives. Therefore, any decisions you make based upon any information contained in this research report are your sole responsibility. Under no circumstances is this report to be used or considered as an offer to sell or a solicitation of any offer to buy any equity or debt security or any options, futures or other derivatives related to such securities.*

> *ICR, its officers and affiliates do not hold securities covered by this report.*

CONCLUSION

Of the various types of analysis of financial statements, projecting future results and ratios requires the greatest skill and produces the most valuable findings. Looking forward is also the riskiest form of analysis, since there are no correct answers until the future statements appear. Totally unforeseeable events may invalidate the assumptions underlying the forecast; economic shocks or unexpected changes in a company's financial strategies may knock all calculations into a cocked hat.

The prominence of the chance element in the forecasting process means that analysts should not be disheartened if their predictions miss the mark, even widely on occasion. They should aim not for absolute prescience but rather for a sound probabilistic model of the future. The model should logically incorporate all significant evidence, both within and external to the historical statements. An analyst can then judge whether a company's prevailing valuations (e.g., stock price, credit rating) are consistent with the possible scenarios and their respective probabilities.

By tracking the after-the-fact accuracy of a number of projections, an analyst can gauge the effectiveness of these methods. Invariably, there will be room for further refinement, particularly in the area of gathering information on industry conditions. No matter how refined the methods are, however, perfection will always elude the modeler since no business cycle precisely recapitulates its predecessor. That is what ultimately makes looking forward with financial statements such a challenging task. The lack of a predictable, recurring pattern is also what makes financial forecasting so valuable. When betting huge sums in the face of massive uncertainty, it is essential that investors understand the odds as fully as they possibly can.

CHAPTER 13

Credit Analysis

Credit analysis is one of the most common uses of financial statements, reflecting the many forms of debt that are essential to the operation of a modern economy. Merchants who exchange goods for promises to pay need to evaluate the reliability of those promises. Commercial banks that lend the merchants the funds to finance their inventories likewise need to calculate the probability of being repaid in full and on time. The banks must in turn demonstrate their creditworthiness to other financial institutions that lend to them by purchasing their certificates of deposit and bonds. In all of these cases, financial statement analysis can significantly influence a decision to extend or not to extend credit.

As important as financial statements are to the evaluation of credit risk, however, the analyst must bear in mind that other procedures also play a role. Financial statements tell much about a borrower's *ability* to repay a loan but disclose little about the equally important *willingness* to repay. Accordingly, a thorough credit analysis may have to include a check of the subject's past record of repayment, which is not part of a standard financial statement. Moreover, to assess the creditworthiness of the merchant in this example, the bank must consider, along with the balance sheet and income statement, the competitive environment and strength of the local economy in which the borrower operates. Lenders to the bank will in turn consider not only the bank's financial position but also public policy. Believing that a sound banking system benefits the economy as a whole, national governments empower central banks to act as lenders of last resort. As a result, fewer bank failures occur than would be the case under pure, unrestrained competition.

An even more basic reason that analyzing a company's financial statements may not be sufficient for determining its credit quality is that the borrower's credit may be supported, formally or informally, by another entity.

Many municipalities obtain cost savings on their financings by having their debt payments guaranteed by bond insurers with premier credit ratings. For holders of these municipal bonds, the insurer's creditworthiness, not the municipality's financial condition, is the basis for determining the likelihood of repayment. Corporations, too, sometimes guarantee the debt of weaker credits. Even when the stronger company does not take on a legal obligation to pay if the weaker company fails on its debt, implicit support may affect the latter's credit quality. If a company is dependent on raw materials provided by a subsidiary, there may be a reasonable presumption that it will stand behind the subsidiary's debt, even in the absence of a formal guarantee.

Keeping in mind that the final judgment may be influenced by other information as well, the analyst can begin to extract from the financial statements the data that bear on credit risk. Each of the basic statements – the balance sheet, income statement, and statement of cash flows – yields valuable insights when studied through ratio analysis techniques, as well as when used in the evaluation of fixed-income securities. In each case, the analyst must temper any enthusiasm generated by a review of historical statements with caution based on a consideration of financial ratios derived from projected statements for future years.

BALANCE SHEET RATIOS

The most immediate danger faced by a lender is the risk that the borrower will suffer illiquidity – an inability to raise cash to pay its obligations. This condition can arise for many reasons, one of which is a loss of ability to borrow new funds to pay off existing creditors. Whatever the underlying cause, however, illiquidity manifests itself as an excess of current cash payments due, over cash currently available. The current ratio gauges the risk of this occurring by comparing the claims against the company that will become payable during the current operating cycle (current liabilities) with the assets that are already in the form of cash or that will be converted to cash during the current operating cycle (current assets). Referring to capital goods manufacturer Illinois Tool Works's balance sheet (Exhibit 13.1), the company's current ratio as of December 31, 2019, was 2.90:

$$\text{Current ratio} = \frac{\text{Current assets}}{\text{Current liabilities}} = \frac{\$6,253}{\$2,154} = 2.90$$

Analysts also apply a more stringent test of liquidity by calculating the quick ratio, or acid test, which considers only cash and current assets that

EXHIBIT 13.1 Illinois Tool Works Inc. Balance Sheet

Statement of Financial Position – USD ($) in Millions	Dec. 31, 2019
Current assets:	
Cash and equivalents	$1,981
Trade receivables	2,461
Inventories	1,164
Prepaid expenses and other current assets	296
Assets held for sale	351
Total current assets	6,253
Net plant and equipment	1,729
Goodwill	4,492
Intangible assets	851
Deferred income taxes	516
Other assets	1,227
Total assets	15,068
Current liabilities:	
Short-term debt	4
Accounts payable	472
Accrued expenses	1,217
Cash dividends payable	342
Income taxes payable	48
Liabilities held for sale	71
Total current liabilities	2,154
Noncurrent liabilities:	
Long-term debt	7,754
Deferred income taxes	668
Noncurrent income taxes payable	462
Other liabilities	1,000
Total noncurrent liabilities	9,884
Common stock (par value of $0.01 per share):	
Issued – 550.0 shares in 2019 and 2018 outstanding – 319.8 shares in 2019 and 328.1 shares in 2018	6
Additional paid-in-capital	1,304
Retained earnings	22,403
Common stock held in treasury	(18,982)
Accumulated other comprehensive income (loss)	(1,705)
Noncontrolling interest	4
Total stockholders' equity	3,030
Total liabilities and stockholders' equity	$15,068

Source: 10K.

can be most quickly converted to cash (marketable securities and receivables). Illinois Tool Works's quick ratio on December 31, 2019, was 2.06:

$$\text{Quick ratio} = \frac{\text{Quick assets}}{\text{Current liabilities}} = \frac{\$1,981 + 2,461}{\$2,154} = 2.06$$

Besides looking at the ratio between current assets and current liabilities, it is also useful, when assessing a company's ability to meet its near-term obligations, to consider the difference between the two, which is termed *working capital*. Referring once again to Exhibit 13.1, working capital is $4.099 billion.

$$\text{Working capital} = \text{Current assets} - \text{Current liabilities}$$
$$\$4,099 \quad = \quad \$6,253 \quad - \quad \$2,154$$

Analysis of current assets and current liabilities provides warnings about impending illiquidity, but lenders nevertheless periodically find themselves saddled with loans to borrowers that are unable to continue meeting their obligations and are therefore forced to file for bankruptcy. Recognizing that they may one day find themselves holding defaulted obligations, creditors wish to know how much asset value will be available for liquidation to pay off their claims.[1] The various ratios that address this issue can be grouped as measures of financial leverage.

A direct measure of asset protection is the ratio of total assets to total liabilities, which in the example shown in Exhibit 13.1 comes to:

$$\frac{\text{Total assets}}{\text{Total liabilities}} = \frac{\$15,068}{\$2,154 + 9,884} = 1.25$$

Note that total liabilities (short-term and long-term) of $12.038 billion are equivalent to total assets less shareholders' equity. Looking at it another way, Illinois Tool Works's assets of $15.068 billion could decline in value by 20 percent before proceeds of a liquidation would be insufficient to satisfy lenders' claims. The greater the amount by which asset values could deteriorate, the greater the equity cushion (*equity* is, by definition, total assets minus total liabilities), and the greater the creditor's sense of being protected.

Lenders also gauge the amount of equity "beneath" them (junior to them in the event of liquidation) by comparing it with the amount of debt outstanding. For finance companies, where the ratio is typically greater than 1.0, it is convenient to express the relationship as a debt-equity ratio:

$$\frac{\text{Total debt}}{\text{Total equity}}$$

Conventionally capitalized industrial corporations (as opposed to companies that have undergone *leveraged buyouts*), generally have debt-equity ratios of less than 1.0. The usual practice is to express their financial leverage in terms of a total-debt-to-total-capital ratio:

$$\frac{\text{Total debt}}{\text{Total debt} + \text{Minority interest} + \text{Total equity}}$$

Banks' capital adequacy is commonly measured by the ratio of equity to total assets:

$$\frac{\text{Total equity}}{\text{Total assets}}$$

Many pages of elaboration could follow on the last few ratios mentioned. Their calculation is rather less simple than it might appear. The reason is that aggressive borrowers frequently try to satisfy the letter of a maximum leverage limit imposed by lenders without fulfilling the conservative spirit behind it. The following discussion of definitions of leverage ratios addresses the major issues without laying down absolute rules about correct calculations. As explained later in the chapter, ratios are most meaningful when compared across time and across borrower. Consequently, the precise method of calculation is less important than the consistency of calculation throughout the sample being compared.

What Constitutes Total Debt?

At one time, it was appropriate to consider only long-term debt in leverage calculations for industrial companies, since short-term debt was generally used for seasonal purposes, such as financing Christmas-related inventory. A company might draw down bank lines or issue commercial paper to meet these funding requirements, then completely pay off the interim borrowings when it sold the inventory. Even today, a firm that zeros out its short-term debt at some point in each operating cycle can legitimately argue that its true leverage is represented by the permanent (long-term) debt on its balance sheet. Many borrowers have long since subverted this principle, however, by relying heavily on short-term debt that they neither repay on an interim basis nor fund (replace with long-term debt) when it grows to sufficient size to make a bond offering cost-effective. Such short-term debt must be viewed as permanent and included in the leverage calculation. (Current maturities of long-term debt should also enter into the calculation of total debt, based on a conservative assumption that the company will replace maturing debt with new long-term borrowings.)

As an aside, the just-described reliance on short-term debt is not necessarily as dangerous a practice as in years past, although it should still raise a caution flag for the credit analyst. Two risks are inherent in depending on debt with maturities of less than one year. The first is potential illiquidity. If substantial debt comes due at a time when lenders are either unable to renew their loans (because credit is tight) or unwilling to renew (because they perceive the borrower as less creditworthy than formerly), the borrower may be unable to meet its near-term obligations. This risk may be mitigated, however, if the borrower has a revolving credit agreement, which is a longer-term commitment by the lender to lend (subject to certain conditions, such as maintaining prescribed financial ratios and refraining from significant changes in the business). The second risk of relying on short-term borrowings is exposure to interest-rate fluctuations. If a substantial amount of debt is about to come due, and interest rates have risen sharply since the debt was incurred, the borrower's cost of staying in business may skyrocket overnight.

Note that exposure to interest rate fluctuations can also arise from long-term **floating-rate debt.** Companies can limit this risk by using **financial derivatives.** One approach is to cap the borrower's interest rate, that is, set a maximum rate that will prevail, no matter how high the market rate against which it is pegged may rise. Alternatively, the borrower can convert the floating-rate debt to **fixed-rate debt** through a derivative known as an interest-rate swap. (The forces of supply and demand may make it more economical for the company to issue floating-rate debt and incur the cost of the swap than to take the more direct route to the same net effect, that is, to issue fixed-rate debt.) Public financial statements typically provide only general information about the extent to which the issuer has limited its exposure to interest rate fluctuations through derivatives.

Borrowers sometimes argue that the total debt calculation should exclude debt that is convertible, at the lender's option, into common equity. Hard-liners on the credit analysis side respond: "It's equity when the holders convert it to equity. Until then, it's debt." Realistically, though, if the conversion value of the bond rises sufficiently, most holders will in fact convert their securities to common stock. This is particularly true if the issuer has the option of calling the bonds for early retirement, which results in a loss for holders who fail to convert. Analysts should remember that the ultimate objective is not to calculate ratios for their own sake but to assess credit risk. Therefore, the best practice is to count convertible debt in total debt but to consider the possibility of conversion when comparing the borrower's leverage with that of its peer group.

Preferred stock[2] is a security that further complicates the leverage calculation. From a legal standpoint, preferred stock is clearly equity; in liquidation, it ranks junior to debt. Preferred stock pays a dividend rather than interest, and failure to pay the dividend does not constitute a default. On the other hand, preferred dividends, unlike common dividends, are contractually fixed in amount. An issuer can omit its preferred dividend but not without also omitting its common dividend. Furthermore, many preferred dividends are **cumulative**, meaning that the issuer must repay all preferred dividend arrearages before resuming common stock dividends. Furthermore, companies are reluctant to omit preferred dividends because doing so sends an unwanted signal of financial strain to the market.

For these reasons, treating preferred stock purely as equity for credit analysis purposes would understate financial risk. A formal way to take this risk into account is to calculate the ratio of total fixed obligations to total capital:[3]

$$\frac{\text{Total debt} + \text{Preferred stock} + \text{Preference stock}}{\text{Total debt} + \text{Minority interest} + \text{Preferred stock} + \text{Preference stock} + \text{Common equity}}$$

Off-Balance-Sheet Liabilities

In their quest for methods of obtaining the benefits of debt without suffering the associated penalties imposed by credit analysts, corporations have by no means limited themselves to the use of leases. Like leases, the other popular devices may provide genuine business benefits, as well as the cosmetic benefit of disguising debt. In all cases, the focus of credit-quality determination must be economic impact, which may or may not be reflected in the accounting treatment.

A corporation can employ leverage yet avoid showing debt on its consolidated balance sheet by entering joint ventures or forming partially owned subsidiaries. At a minimum, the analyst should attribute to the corporation its proportionate liability for the debt of such ventures, thereby matching the cash flow benefits derived from the affiliates. (Note that cash flow is generally reduced by unremitted earnings – the portion not received in dividends – of affiliates that are not fully consolidated.) In some cases, the affiliate's operations are critical to the parent's operations, as in the case of a jointly owned pulp plant that supplies a paper plant wholly owned by the parent. There is a strong incentive, in such instances, for the parent to keep the jointly owned operation running by picking up the debt service commitments of a partner that becomes financially incapacitated, even though it may have no legal obligation to do so. (In legal parlance, this arrangement is known as a *several* obligation, in contrast to a *joint* obligation in which each partner is compelled to back up the other's commitment.) Depending on the particular circumstances, it may be appropriate to attribute to the parent more than its proportionate share – up to 100 percent – of the debt of the joint venture or unconsolidated subsidiary.

Surely one of the most ingenious devices for obtaining the benefits of debt without incurring balance sheet recognition was described by *The Independent* in 1992. According to the British newspaper, the Faisal Islamic Bank of Cairo had provided $250 million of funding to a troubled real estate developer, Olympia & York. As an institution committed to Islamic religious principles, however, the bank was not allowed to charge interest. Instead, claimed *The Independent,* Faisal Islamic Bank in effect had acquired a building from Olympia & York, along with an option to sell it back. The option was reportedly exercisable at $250 million plus an amount equivalent to the market rate of interest for the option period. Because the excess was not officially classified as interest, said *The Independent,* the $250 million of funding did not show up as a loan on Olympia & York's balance sheet.

The Independent noted a denial by an Olympia & York spokesperson that "any such *loan* existed" (emphasis added). If, however, the account was substantially correct, then the religious-prohibition-of-interest gambit succeeded spectacularly in diverting attention from a transaction that had all the trappings of a loan. Barclays Bank, one of Olympia & York's most important lenders, commented that it had never heard of the Faisal Islamic Bank transaction.[4]

Of a somewhat different character within the broad category of off-balance-sheet liabilities are employee benefit obligations. Under Statement of Financial Accounting Standards (SFAS) 87, balance sheet recognition is now given to pension liabilities related to employees' service to date. Similarly, SFAS 106 requires recognition of postretirement health care benefits as an on-balance-sheet liability. Additional requirements are set out in SFAS 158. Projected future wage increases are still not recognized, although they affect the calculation of pension expense for income statement purposes. Unlike some other kinds of hidden liabilities, these items arise exclusively in furtherance of a business objective (attracting and retaining capable employees), rather than as a surreptitious means of leveraging shareholders' equity.

Generally speaking, pension obligations that have been fully funded (provided for with investment assets set aside for the purpose) present few credit worries for a going concern. Likewise, a modest underfunding that is in the process of being remediated by an essentially sound company is no more than a small qualitative factor on the negative side. On the other hand, a large or growing underfunded liability can be a significantly negative consideration – albeit one that is hard to quantify explicitly – in assessing a deteriorating credit. In bankruptcy, it becomes essential to monitor details of the Pension Benefit Guaranty Corporation's efforts to assert its claim to the company's assets, which, if successful, reduce the settlement amounts available to other creditors.

Are Deferred Taxes Part of Capital?

Near the equity account on many companies' balance sheets appears an account labeled "Deferred Income Taxes." This item represents the cumulative difference between taxes calculated at the statutory rate and taxes actually paid. The difference reflects the tax consequences, for future years, of the differences between the tax bases of assets and liabilities and their carrying amounts for financial reporting purposes.

Many analysts argue that net worth is understated by the amount of the deferred tax liability, since it will in all likelihood never come due and is therefore not really a liability at all. (As long as the company continues to pay taxes at less than the statutory rate, the deferred tax account will continue to grow.) Proponents of this view adjust for the alleged understatement of net worth by adding deferred taxes to the denominator in the total-debt-to-total-capital calculation, thus:

$$\frac{\text{Total debt}}{\text{Total debt} + \text{Deferred taxes} + \text{Minority interest} + \text{Total equity}}$$

In general, this practice is sound. Analysts must, however, keep in mind that the precise formula for calculating a ratio is less important than the assurance that it is calculated consistently for all companies being evaluated. The caveat is that many factors can contribute to deferred taxes, and not all of them imply a permanent deferral. A defense contractor, for example, can defer payment of taxes related to a specific contract until the contract is completed. The analyst would not want to add to equity the taxes deferred on a contract that is about to be completed, although in such situations specific figures may be hard to obtain.

The Importance of Management's Attitude toward Debt

As the preceding discussion has established, companies use numerous gambits in their quest to enjoy the benefits of aggressive financial leverage without suffering the consequences of low credit ratings and high borrowing costs. Analysts should note that corporations' bag of tricks is not confined to accounting gimmicks. Some management teams also rely on a bait-and-switch technique.

The ploy consists of announcing that management has learned the hard way that conservative financial policies serve shareholders best in the long run. Never again, vows the chief executive officer, will the company undergo the financial strain that it recently endured as a result of excessive borrowing a few years earlier. To demonstrate that they truly have gotten religion, the managers institute new policies aimed at improving cash flow and pay down a slug of short-term borrowings. On the strength of the favorable impression that these actions create among credit analysts who rely heavily on trends in financial ratios, the company floats new long-term bonds at an attractive rate. Once the cash is in the coffers, management loses its motivation to present a conservative face to lenders and reverts to the aggressive financial policies that so recently got the company into trouble.

Not everybody is taken in by this ruse. Moody's and Standard & Poor's place heavy emphasis on management's attitude toward debt when assigning bond ratings (see "Relating Ratios to Credit Risk" later in this chapter). They strive to avoid upgrading companies in response to balance sheet improvements that are unlikely to last much beyond the completion of the next public offering. As a reward for such vigilance, the agencies are routinely accused of being backward-looking. The corporations complain that the bond raters are dwelling unduly on past, weaker financial ratios. In reality, the agencies are thinking ahead. Based on their experience with management, they are inferring that the recent reduction in financial leverage reflects expediency, rather than a long-term shift in debt policy. In general, credit analysts should assume that the achievement of higher bond ratings is a secondary goal of corporate management. If a company's stock has been languishing for a while, management will not ordinarily feel any urgency about eliminating debt from the capital structure, an action that reduces return on shareholders' equity (see Chapter 14). Similarly, the typical chief executive officer, being only human, finds it difficult to resist a chance to run a substantially bigger company. Therefore, if a mammoth acquisition opportunity comes along, the CEO is likely to pursue it, even if it means borrowing huge amounts of money and precipitating a rating downgrade, rather than the hoped-for upgrade.

Like other types of financial statement analysis, finding meaning in a company's balance sheet requires the analyst to look ahead. When management's probable future actions are taken into account, the company's prospects for repaying its debts on schedule may be better or worse than the ratios imply. The credit analyst cannot afford to take management's representations at face value, however. When a chief executive officer claims that obtaining a higher bond rating is the corporation's overriding objective, it is essential to ask for specifics: What are the elements of the company's action plan for achieving that goal? Which of the steps have been achieved so far?

Above all, the credit analyst must listen closely for an escape clause, typically uttered while the company is engaged in a debt offering. It can be heard when a prospective buyer asks whether management will stay on course for a rating upgrade come hell or high water. The CEO casually replies, "Of course, if a once-in-a-lifetime major acquisition opportunity were to come along, and it required us to borrow, we would have to delay our plans for debt reduction temporarily." The credit analyst can generally assume that shortly after the bond deal closes, the once-in-a-lifetime opportunity will materialize.

INCOME STATEMENT RATIOS

Although an older approach to credit analysis places primary emphasis on liquidity and asset protection, both of which are measured by balance sheet ratios, the more contemporary view is that profits are ultimately what sustain liquidity and asset values. High profits keep plenty of cash flowing through the system and confirm the value of productive assets such as plant and equipment. In line with this latter view, the income statement is no longer of interest mainly to the equity analyst but is essential to credit analysis as well.

A key income statement focus for credit analysis is the borrower's profit margin (profit as a percentage of sales). The narrower the margin, the greater the danger that a modest decline in selling prices or a modest increase in costs will produce losses, which will in turn begin to erode such balance sheet measures as total debt to total capital by reducing equity.

Profit can be measured at several levels of the income statement, either before or after deducting various expenses to get to the bottom line, net income. The most commonly used profit margins are the following:

$$\text{Gross margin} = \frac{\text{Sales} - \text{Cost of goods sold}}{\text{Sales}}$$

$$\text{Operating margin} = \text{Net income} + \text{Income taxes} + \text{Interest expense}$$

$$\frac{\text{Interest income} - \text{Other income}}{\text{Sales}}$$

$$\text{Pretax margin} = \frac{\text{Net income} + \text{Income taxes}}{\text{Sales}}$$

$$\text{Net margin} = \frac{\text{Net income}}{\text{Sales}}$$

Applying these definitions to Illinois Tool Works's income statement (Exhibit 13.2), the company's profit margins in 2019 were:

$$\text{Gross margin} = \frac{\$14,109 - 8,187}{\$14,109} = 42.0\%$$

$$\text{Operating margin} = \frac{\$2,521 + 767 + 221 - 107}{\$14,109} = 24.1\%$$

$$\text{Pretax margin} = \frac{\$2,521 + 767}{\$14,109} = 23.3\%$$

$$\text{Net income} = \frac{\$2,521}{\$14,109} = 17.9\%$$

Note that in connection with the operating margin calculation, Illinois Tool Works's income statement shows "operating revenue" and "cost of revenue" in lieu of the "sales" and "cost of goods sold" terms shown in the formula definitions, above. In addition, the company's income statement contains no separate line entry for interest income. A practical aspect of ratio analysis is that presentations are not uniform across all companies' financial

EXHIBIT 13.2   Illinois Tool Works Inc. Income Statement

Statement of Income – USD ($) in Millions	12 Months Ended Dec. 31, 2019
Income statement [abstract]	
Operating revenue	$14,109
Cost of revenue	8,187
Selling, administrative, and research and development expenses	2,361
Legal settlement (income)	0
Amortization and impairment of intangible assets	159
Operating income	3,402
Interest expense	(221)
Other income (expense)	107
Income before taxes	3,288
Income taxes	767
Net income	$ 2,521
Net income per share:	
Basic (in dollars per share)	$ 7.78
Diluted (in dollars per share)	$ 7.74

Source: 10K.

statements. Some differences are merely semantic, but others are substantive. This fact does not negate the value obtainable from calculating and comparing ratios. It is just one of several reasons why, as detailed later in this chapter, ratio-based analysis must be supplemented with other analyses to arrive at valid conclusions.

High profit margins give creditors confidence that a company is successful and can therefore continue attracting new capital from investors. The ability to maintain a funding capability is an essential component of a strong credit profile. Credit analysts must delve into the numbers to confirm that management is continuing to reinvest in the business in order to preserve long-run profitability. The risk is that management will instead cut investment spending, thereby elevating near-term profits in hopes of boosting the stock price.

Observe that for some companies, deducting other income, as called for by the operating margin formula, will result in an addback of a negative figure. In some instances, an after-tax nonoperating item can produce a disparity between the numerators in the pretax and operating margins, as calculated from the bottom up in accordance with the formula, and the corresponding figure derived by working from the top down. For example, the cumulative effect of a change in accounting procedures will appear below the line, that is, after income taxes have already been deducted. The sum of net income and provision for income taxes will then differ from the pretax income figure that appears in the income statement. To ensure comparability across companies, analysts should take care to follow identical procedures in calculating each company's margins, rather than adopting shortcuts that may introduce distortion.

The various margin measures reflect different aspects of management's effectiveness. Gross margin, which is particularly important in analyzing retailers, measures management's skill in buying and selling at advantageous prices. Operating margin shows how well management has run the business – buying and selling wisely and controlling selling and administrative expenses – before taking into account financial policies (which largely determine interest expense) and the tax rate (which is outside management's control).[5] These last two factors are sequentially added to the picture by calculating pretax margin and net margin, with the latter ratio reflecting all factors, whether under management's control or not, that influence profitability.

In calculating profit margins, analysts should eliminate the effect of extraordinary gains and losses to determine the level of profitability that is likely to be sustainable in the future.

Fixed-charge coverage is the other category of income statement ratios of keen interest to credit analysts. It measures the ability of a company's earnings to meet the interest payments on its debt, the lender's most direct concern. In its simplest form, the fixed-charge coverage ratio indicates the multiple by which operating earnings suffice to pay interest charges:

$$\text{Fixed-charge coverage} = \frac{\text{Net income} + \text{Income taxes} + \text{Interest expense}}{\text{Interest expense}}$$

The rise of leveraged buyouts in the 1980s helped popularize an alternative measure of fixed charge coverage. It adds two noncash charges, depreciation and amortization, to the numerator of the original version. The modified ratio is known as "EBITDA coverage," with the acronym signifying earnings before interest, taxes, depreciation, and amortization. The previous formula is now commonly called "EBIT coverage."

$$\text{EBITDA coverage} = \frac{\begin{array}{c}\text{Net income} + \text{Income taxes} \\ + \text{Interest expense} + \text{Depreciation} + \text{Amortization}\end{array}}{\text{Interest expense}}$$

Leveraged buyouts of the 1980s and beyond loaded up on debt and hence interest expense. They aimed to minimize rather than maximize net income, thereby incurring as little income tax as possible. Analysts put strong emphasis on EBITDA coverage because they did not want to underestimate LBO companies' near-term ability to cover their interest charges, to which the amounts represented by noncash charges could be applied.

EBITDA coverage is now widely used for conventionally financed, as well as highly leveraged companies. It provides useful insight into companies' short- to intermediate-term ability to stay current on interest payments. Analysts should bear in mind, however, that over the longer run companies do need to use cash to replace the tangible and intangible assets that give rise to depreciation and amortization. EBIT coverage is therefore a truer measure of how well a company can meet its interest obligations over the long term.

The basic interest coverage formulas require several refinements. As with profit margins, extraordinary items should be eliminated from the calculation to arrive at a sustainable level of coverage. Two other important adjustments involve capitalized interest and payments on operating leases.

Capitalized Interest

Under SFAS 34, a company may be required to capitalize, rather than expense, a portion of its interest costs. The underlying notion is that like the actual bricks and mortar purchased to construct a plant, the cost of the money borrowed to finance the purchase provides benefits in future periods and therefore should not be entirely written off in the first year. Whether it is expensed or capitalized, however, all interest incurred must be covered by earnings and should therefore appear in the denominator of the fixed-charge coverage calculation. Accordingly, the basic formula can be rewritten to include not only the interest expense shown on the income statement but also capitalized interest, which may appear either on the income statement or in the notes to financial statements. (If the amount is immaterial, capitalized interest will not be shown at all, and the analyst can skip this adjustment.) The numerator should not include capitalized interest, however, for the amount is a reduction to total expenses and consequently reflected in net income. Including capitalized interest in the numerator would therefore constitute double counting:

$$\text{Fixed-charge coverage (adjusted for capitalized interest)} = \frac{\text{Net income} + \text{Income taxes} + \text{Income expense}}{\text{Interest expense} + \text{Capitalized interest}}$$

Lease Expense

As mentioned above, off-balance-sheet operating leases have virtually the same economic impact as on-balance-sheet debt. Just as credit analysts should take into account the liabilities represented by these leases, they should also factor into coverage calculations the annual fixed charges associated with them.

One approach to taking the impact of leases into account simply adds the total current-year rental expense from notes to financial statements to both the numerator and denominator of the fixed-charge coverage calculation. An alternate method includes one-third of rentals (as shown in the following calculation) on the theory that one-third of a lease payment typically represents interest that would be paid if the assets had been purchased with borrowed money, and two-thirds is equivalent to principal repayment:

$$\text{Fixed-charge coverage (adjusted for capitalized interest and operating leases)} = \frac{\text{Net income} + \text{Income taxes} + \text{Income expense} + \frac{1}{3}\text{ Rentals}}{\text{Interest expense} + \text{Capitalized interest} + \frac{1}{3}\text{ Rentals}}$$

Two complications arise in connection with incorporating operating lease payment into the fixed-charge coverage calculation. First, the SEC does not require companies to report rental expense in quarterly statements. The analyst can therefore only estimate where a company's fully adjusted coverage stands, on an interim basis, in relation to its most recent full-year level. (Capitalized interest, by the way, presents the same problem, although some companies voluntarily report capitalized interest on an interim basis.) Second, retailers in particular often negotiate leases with rents that are semifixed, tied in part to revenues of the leased stores. Some argue that the variable portion – contingent rentals – should be excluded from the fixed-charge coverage calculation. That approach, however, results in a numerator that includes income derived from revenues in excess of the threshold level, while omitting from the denominator charges that were automatically incurred when the threshold was reached. A better way to recognize the possible avoidance of contingent lease payments is by capitalizing only the mandatory portion when calculating the balance sheet ratio of total debt to total capital.

Interest Income

A final issue related to fixed-charge coverage involves interest income. Companies sometimes argue that the denominator should include only net interest expense: the difference between interest expense and income derived from interest-bearing assets, generally consisting of marketable securities. They portray the two items as offsetting, with operating earnings having to cover only the portion of interest expense not automatically paid for by interest income. Such treatment can be deceptive, however, when a company holds a large but temporary portfolio of marketable securities. In this situation, fixed-charge coverage based on net interest expense in the current year can greatly overstate the level of protection that may be expected in the succeeding year, after the company has invested its funds in operating assets. If, however, a company's strategy is to invest a substantial portion of its assets indefinitely in marketable securities (as some pharmaceutical manufacturers do, to capture certain tax benefits), analysts should consider the associated liquidity as a positive factor in their analysis.

STATEMENT OF CASH FLOWS RATIOS

Ratios related to sources and uses of funds measure credit quality at the most elemental level – a company's ability to generate sufficient cash to pay its bills. These ratios also disclose a great deal about financial flexibility; a company that does not have to rely on external financing can take greater operating risks than one that would be forced to retrench if new capital suddenly became scarce or prohibitively expensive. In addition, trends in sources-and-uses ratios can anticipate changes in balance sheet ratios. Given corporations' general reluctance to sell new equity, which may dilute existing shareholders' interest, a recurrent cash shortfall is likely to be made up with debt financing, leading to a rise in the total-debt-to-total-capital ratio.

For capital-intensive manufacturers and utilities, a key ratio is cash flow to capital expenditures:

$$\frac{\text{Cash flow from operations}}{\text{Capital expenditures}}$$

The higher this ratio, the greater the financial flexibility implied. It is important, though, to examine the reasons underlying a change in the relationship between internal funds and capital outlays. It is normal for a capital-intensive industry to go through a capital-spending cycle, adding capacity by constructing large-scale plants that require several years to complete. Once the new capacity is in place, capital expenditures ease for a few years until demand growth catches up and another round of spending begins. Over the cycle, the industry's ratio of cash falls. By definition, the down leg of this cycle does not imply long-term deterioration in credit quality. In contrast, a company that suffers a prolonged downtrend in its ratio of cash flow to capital expenditures is likely to get more deeply into debt and therefore become financially riskier with each succeeding year. Likewise, a rising ratio may require interpretation. A company that sharply reduces its capital budget will appear to increase its financial flexibility, based on the cash-flow-to-capital-expenditures ratio. Cutting back on outlays, however, may impair the company's long-run competitiveness by sacrificing market share or by causing the company to fall behind in technological terms.

Although the most recent period's ratio of cash flow to capital expenditures is a useful measure, the credit analyst is always more interested in the future than in the past. One good way of assessing a company's ability to sustain its existing level of cash adequacy is to calculate depreciation as a percentage of cash flow:

$$\frac{\text{Depreciation}}{\text{Cash flow from operations}}$$

Unlike earnings, depreciation is essentially a programmed item, a cash flow assured by the accounting rules. The higher the percentage of cash flow derived from depreciation, the more predictable a company's cash flow and the less dependent its financial flexibility on the vagaries of the marketplace.

Also important among the ratios derived from the statement of cash flows is the ratio of capital expenditures to depreciation:

$$\frac{\text{Capital expenditures}}{\text{Depreciation}}$$

A ratio of less than 1.0 over a period of several years raises a red flag, since it suggests that the company is failing to replace its plant and equipment. Underspending on capital replacement amounts to gradual liquidation of the firm. By the same token, though, the analyst cannot necessarily assume that all is well simply because capital expenditures consistently exceed depreciation. For one thing, persistent inflation means that a **nominal dollar** spent on plant and equipment today will not buy as much capacity as it did when the depreciating asset was acquired. (Technological advances in production processes may mitigate this problem because the cost in real terms of producing one unit may have declined since the company purchased the equipment now being replaced.) A second reason to avoid complacency over a seemingly strong ratio of capital expenditures to depreciation is that the depreciation may be understated with respect either to wear and tear or to obsolescence. If so, the adequacy of capital spending will be overstated by the ratio of capital spending to depreciation. Finally, capital outlays may be too low even if they match in every sense the depreciation of existing plant and equipment. In a growth industry, a company that fails to expand its capacity at roughly the same rate as its competitors may lose essential economies of scale and fall victim to a **shakeout**.

Credit analysts carry further the concept underlying the ratio of capital expenditures to depreciation by bringing other cash flow items and dividends into the picture and calculating free cash flow as follows:

$$\text{Free Cash Flow} = \text{Cash Flow from Operating Activities} \\ - \text{Capital Expenditures} - \text{Dividends}$$

Some credit analysts who focus on debt of highly leveraged companies put primary emphasis on a company's ability to generate positive free cash flow. They reason that as long as a company has sufficient cash flow to replace its fixed assets and satisfy shareholders' demands for payout of a portion of profits, it will not be dependent on outside financing. Management will have the option of retiring debt and thereby reducing financial risk. The key question, naturally, is whether the profitability underlying the cash flow from operating activities is sustainable.

COMBINATION RATIOS

Each of the financial ratios discussed so far in this chapter is derived from numbers collected from just one of the three basic financial statements. In financial analysis, these rudimentary tools are analogous to the simple machines – the wedge, the lever, the wheel, and the screw – that greatly increased the productivity of their prehistoric inventors. How much more remarkable an advance it was, however, when an anonymous Chinese person combined two simple machines, a lever and a wheel, to create a wheelbarrow! In similar fashion, combining numbers from different financial statements unleashes vast new analytical power.

Rate-of-Return Measures

One of the most valuable types of combination ratios combines earnings with balance sheet figures. Such ratios measure the profit that an enterprise is generating relative to the assets employed or the capital invested in it. This kind of measure provides a link between credit analysis and the economic concept of productivity of capital.

To illustrate, consider Companies A, B, and C, all of which are debt-free. If we look only at net margin, a ratio derived solely from the income statement, Company A is superior to both its direct competitor, Company B, and Company C, which is in a different business. Looking at the combination ratio of return on equity, however, we find that Company C ranks highest, notwithstanding that sales margins tend to be narrower in its industry:

	Company A	Company B	Company C
Sales	$1,000,000	$1,000,000	$2,000,000
Net income	50,000	40,000	60,000
Equity	500,000	500,000	500,000
Net margin $\left(\dfrac{\text{Net Income}}{\text{Net Sales}} \right)$	5.0%	4.0%	3.0%
Return on equity $\left(\dfrac{\text{Net Income}}{\text{Equity}} \right)$	10.0%	8.0%	12.0%

To an economist, this result suggests that investors earning 8 percent to 10 percent in Company A and Company B's industry will seek to shift their capital to Company C's industry, where 12 percent returns are available. The credit implication of this migration of capital is that Companies A and B will have greater difficulty raising funds and therefore less financial flexibility. The credit impact on Company C, conversely, is favorable.

There are several variants of the rate-of-return combination ratio, each with a specific analytical application. Return on equity, which has already been alluded to, measures a firm's productivity of equity and therefore provides an indication of its ability to attract a form of capital that provides an important cushion for the debtholders:

$$\text{Return on equity} = \frac{\text{Net income}}{\text{Common equity} + \text{Preferred equity}}$$

In calculating this ratio, analysts most commonly use as the denominator equity as of the final day of the year in which the company earned the income shown in the numerator. This method may sometimes produce distortions. A company might raise a substantial amount of new equity near the end of the year. The denominator in the return-on-equity calculation would consequently be increased, but the numerator would not reflect the benefit of a full year's earnings on the new equity because it was employed in the business for only a few days. Under these circumstances, return on equity will compare unfavorably (and unfairly) with that of a company that did not abruptly expand its equity base.

The potential for distortion in the return-on-equity calculation can be reduced somewhat by substituting for end-of-year equity so-called average equity:

$$\frac{\text{Return on}}{\text{average equity}} = \frac{\text{Net income}}{\dfrac{(\text{Equity at beginning of year} + \text{Equity at end of year})}{2}}$$

(Some analysts prefer this method to the year-end-based calculation, even when sudden changes in the equity account are not an issue.)

Another limitation of combination ratios that incorporate balance sheet figures is that they have little meaning if calculated for portions of years. Suppose that in 2018 a company earns $6 million on year-end equity of $80 million, for a return on equity of 7.5 percent. During the first half of 2019, its net income is $4 million, of which it pays out $2 million in dividends, leaving it $82 million in equity at June 30, 2019. With the company having earned in half a year two-thirds as much as it did during all of 2018, it is illogical to conclude that its return on equity has fallen from 7.5 percent to 4.9 percent ($4 million ÷ $82 million).

To derive a proper return on equity, it is necessary to annualize the earnings figure. Merely doubling the first half results can introduce some distortion, though, since the company's earnings may be seasonal. Even if not, there is no assurance that the first-half rate of profitability will be sustained in the second half. Accordingly, the best way to annualize earnings is to calculate a trailing 12-months' figure:

$$\frac{\text{Net income for second half of 2018} + \text{Net income for first half of 2019}}{\text{Equity at June 30, 2019}}$$

If the analyst is working with the company's 2018 annual report and 2019 second-quarter statement, 2018 second-half earnings will not be available without backing out some numbers. For ease of calculation, the numerator in the preceding ratio can be derived as follows:

Net income for full year 2018.

Less: Net income for first half of 2018.

Plus: Net income for first half of 2019.

For the credit analyst, return on equity alone may be an insufficient or even misleading measure. The reason is that a company can raise its return on equity by increasing the proportion of debt in its capital structure, a change that reduces credit quality. In Exhibit 13.3, Company Y produces a higher return on equity than the more conservatively capitalized Company X, even though both have equivalent operating margins.

Note that Company Y enjoys its edge despite having to pay a higher interest rate on account of its riskier financial structure.

Income statement ratios such as net margin and fixed-charge coverage, which point to higher credit quality at Company X, serve as a check against return on equity, which ranks Company Y higher. A later section of this chapter explores systematic approaches to reconciling financial ratios that give contradictory indications about the relative credit quality of two or more companies. The more immediately relevant point, however, is that other combination ratios can also be used as checks against an artificially heightened return on equity. Using the same figures for Companies X and Y, the analyst can calculate return on total capital, which equalizes for differences in capital structure. On this basis, Company Y enjoys only a negligible advantage related to its slower growth in retained earnings (and hence in capital):

$$\text{Return on total capital} = \frac{\text{Net income} + \text{Income taxes} + \text{Interest expense}}{\text{Total debt} + \text{Total equity}}$$

Company X	Company Y

$$\frac{9.6 + 4.9 + 2.0}{25.0 + 81.4} = \frac{16.5}{106.4} = 15.5\% \qquad \frac{7.9 + 4.1 + 4.5}{50.0 + 55.3} = \frac{16.5}{105.3} = 15.7\%$$

EXHIBIT 13.3 Effect of Debt on Return on Equity ($000,000 omitted)

	Company X		Company Y	
	12/31/2018	12/31/2019	12/31/2018	12/31/2019
Total debt	$ 25.00 25%	$ 25.00 23%	$ 50.00 50%	$ 50.00 47%
Total equity	$ 75.00 75%	$ 81.40 77%	$ 50.00 50%	$ 55.30 53%
Total capital	$ 100.00 100%	$ 106.40 100%	$ 100.00 100%	$ 105.30 100%
Debt/equity	33%	31%	100%	90%
2019 results		Company X		Company Y
Sales		125.00		125.00
Operating expenses		108.50[1]		108.50[1]
Operating income		16.50		16.50
Interest expense		0.75[2]		2.00[3]
Pretax income		15.75		14.50
Income taxes		3.31[4]		3.05[4]
Net income		12.44		11.45
Dividends		4.11[5]		3.78[5]
Additions to retained earnings		8.34		7.67
Operating margin		13.2%		13.2%
Net margin		10.0%		9.2%
Return on equity		15.3%		20.7%
Fixed-charge coverage		22.0		8.3
Return on total capital		15.5%		15.7%

[1] At 86.8% of sales
[2] At 3% average interest rate
[3] At 4% average interest rate
[4] At 21 % of pretax income
[5] At 33% of net income

Total debt in this calculation includes short-term debt, current maturities of long-term debt, and long-term debt, for reasons described earlier under "What Constitutes Total Debt?" Similarly, total equity includes both preferred and preference stock. If there is a minority interest, the associated income statement item should appear in the numerator and the balance sheet amount in the denominator.

Turnover Measures

In addition to measuring return on investment, a particular type of combination ratio known as a turnover ratio can provide valuable information about asset quality. The underlying notion of a turnover ratio is that a company requires a certain level of receivables and inventory to support a given volume of sales. For example, if a manufacturer sells its goods on terms that require payment within 30 days, and all customers pay exactly on time, accounts receivable on any given day (barring seasonality in sales) will be $30 \div 365$, or 8.2 percent of annual sales. Coming at the question from the opposite direction, the analyst can calculate the average length of time that a receivable remains outstanding before it is paid (the calculation uses the average amount of receivables outstanding during the year):

$$\text{Average days of receivables} = \frac{\dfrac{(\text{A/R beginning of year} + \text{A/R end of year})}{2}}{\times 365 \text{ Annual sales}}$$

This ratio enables the analyst to learn the company's true average collection period, which may differ significantly from its stated collection period.

By inverting the first portion of the average days of receivables calculation, one can determine how many times per year the company turns over its receivables:

$$\text{Receivables turnover} = \frac{\text{Annual sales}}{\dfrac{(\text{ARBY} + \text{AREY})}{2}}$$

where: ARBY = Accounts receivable at beginning of year
AREY = Accounts receivable at the end of year

As long as a company continues to sell on the same terms, its required receivables level will rise as its sales rise, but the ratio between the two should not change. A decline in the ratio may signal that the company's customers are paying more slowly because they are encountering financial difficulties. Alternatively, the company may be trying to increase its sales by liberalizing its credit standards, allowing its salespeople to do more business with less financially capable customers. Either way, the ultimate collectability of the accounts receivable shown on the balance sheet has become less certain. Unless the company has reflected this fact by increasing its allowance for doubtful receivables, it may have to write off a portion of receivables against income at some point in the future. The analyst should therefore adjust the company's total-debt-to-total-capital ratio for the implicit overstatement of equity.

Another asset quality problem that can be detected with a combination ratio involves unsalable inventory. A fashion retailer's leftover garments from the preceding season or an electronics manufacturer's obsolete finished goods can be worth far less than their balance sheet values (historical cost). If the company is postponing an inevitable write-off, it may become apparent through a rise in inventory without a commensurate rise in sales, resulting in a decline in inventory turnover:

$$\text{Receivables turnover} = \frac{\text{Annual sales}}{\dfrac{(\text{IBY} + \text{IEY})}{2}}$$

where: IBY = Inventory at beginning of year
        IEY = Inventory at end of year

A drop in sales is another possible explanation of declining inventory turnover. In this case, the inventory may not have suffered a severe reduction in value, but there are nevertheless unfavorable implications for credit quality. Until the inventory glut can be worked off by cutting back production to match the lower sales volume, the company may have to borrow to finance its unusually high working capital, thereby increasing its financial leverage. Profitability may also suffer as the company cuts its selling prices, accepting a lower margin to eliminate excess inventory.

One objection to the preceding inventory-turnover calculation involves the variability of selling prices. Suppose that the price of a commodity chemical suddenly shoots up as the result of a temporary shortage. A chemical producer's annual sales – and hence its inventory turnover – may rise, yet the company may not be physically moving its inventory any faster than before. Conversely, a retailer may respond to a drop in consumer demand and cut its prices to avoid a buildup of inventory. The shelves and back room have no more product than previously, yet the ratio based on annual sales indicates that turnover has declined.

To prevent such distortions, the analyst can use the following variant ratio:

$$\text{Inventory turnover} = \frac{\text{Annual cost of goods sold}}{\dfrac{(\text{IBY} + \text{IEY})}{2}}$$

This version should more closely capture the reality of a company's physical turnover. Cost of goods sold and inventory are both based on historical cost, whereas selling prices fluctuate with market conditions, causing a mismatch between the numerator and denominator of the turnover calculation.

To see how combination ratios involving working capital items can in turn be combined to gain further insights, see **cash conversion cycle** in the Glossary.

Total-Debt-to-Cash-Flow Ratio

A final combination ratio that is invaluable in credit analysis is the ratio of total debt to cash flow:

$$\frac{\text{Total debt}}{\text{to cash flow}} = \frac{\text{Short-term debt} + \text{Current maturities} + \text{Long-term debt}}{\text{Cash flow from operations}}$$

A less precise, but commonly used variant substitutes EBITDA for true operating cash flow:

$$\text{Total debt to EBITDA} = \frac{\begin{array}{c}\text{Short-term debt} + \text{Current maturities} \\ + \text{Long-term debt}\end{array}}{\begin{array}{c}\text{Net income} + \text{Income taxes} + \text{Interest expense} \\ + \text{Depreciation} + \text{Amortization}\end{array}}$$

The total debt to cash flow ratio expresses a company's financial flexibility in a most interesting way. If, for the sake of illustration, a company has total debt of $60 million and cash flow from operations of $20 million, it has the ability to liquidate all its debt in three years by dedicating 100 percent of its cash flow to that purpose. This company clearly has greater financial flexibility than a company with $80 million of debt and a $10 million annual cash flow, for an eight-year debt-payback period. In the latter case, flexibility would be particularly limited if the company's debt had an average maturity of significantly less than eight years, implying the possibility of significant refinancing pressure under tight credit conditions.

All very interesting, one might say, but in reality, how many companies dedicate 100 percent of their cash flow to debt retirement? The answer is very few, but total debt to cash flow is still a good ratio to monitor for credit quality. It enjoys distinct advantages over some of the more frequently invoked credit-quality measures, which are derived from the balance sheet or income statement alone. The total-debt-to-total-capital ratio has the inherent flaw that equity may be understated or overstated relative to its economic value. After all, the accounting rules do not permit a write-up of assets unless they are sold, nor do the rules require a write-down until someone makes the possibly subjective determination that the assets have fallen in value. In comparison, total debt is an objective number, a dollar amount that must contractually be repaid. Fixed-charge coverage, too, has a weakness, for it is based on earnings, which are subject to considerable manipulation. Cash flow eliminates one major opportunity for manipulation: under-depreciation. If a company inflates its reported earnings by writing down its fixed assets more slowly than economic reality dictates, it is merely taking money out of one cash flow pocket and putting it into the other. Cash flow, then, puts companies on equal footing, whatever their depreciation policies.

Built from two comparatively hard numbers, the ratio of total debt to cash flow provides one of the best single measures of credit quality. Analysts should not worry about whether its literal interpretation – the period required for a total liquidation of debt – is realistic but instead focus on its analytical value.

RELATING RATIOS TO CREDIT RISK

The discussion of financial ratios up to this point has sidestepped an obvious and critical question: How does an analyst who has calculated a ratio know whether it represents good, bad, or indifferent credit quality? Somehow, the analyst must relate the ratio to the likelihood that the borrower will satisfy all scheduled interest and principal payments in full and on time. In practice, this is accomplished by testing financial ratios as predictors of the borrower's propensity not to pay (to default). For example, a company with high financial leverage is statistically more likely to default than one with low leverage, all other things being equal. Similarly, high fixed-charge coverage implies less default risk than low coverage. After identifying the factors that create high default risk, the analyst can use ratios to rank all borrowers on a relative scale of propensity to default.

Many credit analysts conduct their ratio analyses within ranking frameworks established by their employers. Individuals engaged in processing loan applications may use criteria derived from the lending institution's experience over many years in recognizing the financial characteristics that lead to timely payment or to default. In the securities field, bond ratings provide a structure for analysis. Exhibits 13.4 and 13.5 show the rating definitions of two leading bond-rating agencies, Moody's Investors Service and Standard & Poor's. (The following discussion uses the rating notations and their corresponding spoken equivalents interchangeably – AAA and Triple-A, AA and Double-A, and so on.)

EXHIBIT 13.4 Moody's Bond Ratings (Definitions)

Long-Term Obligation Ratings

Moody's long-term ratings are opinions of the relative credit risk of financial obligations with an original maturity of one year or more. They address the possibility that a financial obligation will not be honored as promised. Such ratings use Moody's Global Scale and reflect both the likelihood of default and any financial loss suffered in the event of default.

Aaa	Obligations rated Aaa are judged to be of the highest quality, with minimal credit risk.
Aa	Obligations rated Aa are judged to be of high quality and are subject to very low credit risk.
A	Obligations rated A are considered upper-medium grade and are subject to low credit risk.
Baa	Obligations rated Baa are subject to moderate credit risk. They are considered medium grade and as such may possess certain speculative characteristics.
Ba	Obligations rated Ba are judged to have speculative elements and are subject to credit risk.
B	Obligations rated B are considered speculative and are subject to high credit risk.
Caa	Obligations rated Caa are judged to be of poor standing and are subject to very high credit risk.
Ca	Obligations rated Ca are highly speculative and are likely in, or very near, default, with some prospect of recovery of principal or interest.
C	Obligations rated C are the lowest rated class and are typically in default, with little prospect for recovery of principal or interest.

Note: Moody's appends numerical modifiers 1, 2, and 3 to each generic rating classification from Aa through Caa. The modifier 1 indicates that the obligation ranks in the higher end of its generic rating category; the modifier 2 indicates a mid-range ranking; and the modifier 3 indicates a ranking in the lower end of that generic rating category.
Source: Moody's Investors Service.

Because much credit work is done in the context of established standards, the next order of business is to explain how companies can be ranked by ratios on a relative scale of credit quality. Bond ratings are the standard on which the discussion focuses, but the principles are applicable to in-house credit-ranking schemes that analysts may encounter. Following a demonstration of the use of credit rating standards, this chapter concludes with an examination of the methods underlying the construction of standards to show readers how financial ratios are linked to default risk.

EXHIBIT 13.5 Standard & Poor's Bond Ratings (Definitions)

S&P's global rating scale provides a benchmark for evaluating the relative credit risk of issuers and issues worldwide.

Investment Grade

AAA	Extremely strong capacity to meet financial commitments. Highest rating.
AA	Very strong capacity to meet financial commitments.
A	Strong capacity to meet financial commitments, but somewhat susceptible to adverse economic conditions and changes in circumstances.
BBB	Adequate capacity to meet financial commitments, but more subject to adverse economic conditions.
BBB−	Considered lowest investment-grade by market participants.

Speculative Grade

BB+	Considered highest speculative-grade by market participants.
BB	Less vulnerable in the near-term but faces major ongoing uncertainties to adverse business, financial and economic conditions.
B	More vulnerable to adverse business, financial, and economic conditions but currently has the capacity to meet financial commitments.
CCC	Currently vulnerable and dependent on favorable business, financial, and economic conditions to meet financial commitments.
CC	Highly vulnerable: default has not yet occurred, but is expected to be a virtual certainty.
C	Currently highly vulnerable to non-payment, and ultimate recovery is expected to be lower than that of higher rated obligations.
D	Payment default on a financial commitment or breach of an imputed promise; also used when a bankruptcy petition has been filed or similar action taken.

Ratings from "AA" to "CCC" may be modified by the addition of a plus (+) or minus (−) sign to show relative standing within the major rating categories.

Source: Standard & Poor's.

Note that in much the same way as financial ratios can be related to credit risk, analysts can analyze risk premiums on corporate bonds and tradable loans. The process involves ranking debt issuers not by their agency ratings but by their obligations' yield premiums over U.S. Treasury bonds, which are conventionally deemed to be free of default fault risk. Investors' most direct concern is not whether a company's debt is rated correctly. They care above all whether the issuer's debt is priced properly, as determined by comparing its yield premium with yield premiums of companies that measure up similarly in terms of their key financial ratios.

The following analysis focuses primarily on estimating the probability that a borrower will pay interest and principal in full and on time. It does not address the percentage of principal that the lender is likely to recover in the event of default. Certainly, expected recoveries have an important bearing on the decision to extend or deny credit, as well as on the valuation of debt securities. Bankruptcy analysis, however, is a huge topic by itself. It goes well beyond comparing the actual value (as opposed to book value) of the defaulted company's assets with the amount of its liabilities, although that is part of the relevant analysis. A comprehensive estimation of creditors' recoveries depends on a detailed knowledge of the relevant legislation and a thorough understanding of the dynamics of the negotiations between creditors and the management of a company in Chapter 11 **reorganization** proceedings. Such matters are beyond the scope of this book. For the securities of highly rated companies, moreover, the potential percentage recovery of principal tends to be a comparatively minor valuation factor. Over the short to intermediate term, the probability of a bankruptcy filing by such a company is small.

Although the reader will not find a complete guide to bankruptcy analysis in these pages, Chapter 14 is relevant from the standpoint of determining the failed firm's equity value, a key step in the reorganization or liquidation of the company. In addition, the bibliography includes books that discuss bankruptcy in extensive detail.

Comparative Ratio Analysis

The basic technique in assigning a relative credit ranking is to compare a company's ratio with those of a peer group. Size and line of business are the key criteria for identifying a company's peers.

On the matter of size, a manufacturer with $5 billion in annual sales will ordinarily be a better credit risk than one with similar financial ratios but only $50 million in sales. As a generalization, bigger companies enjoy economies of scale and have greater leverage with suppliers by virtue of their larger purchasing power. A big company can spread the risks of obsolescence and competitive challenges over a wide range of products and customers, whereas a smaller competitor's sales are likely to be concentrated on a few products and customers. Particularly vulnerable is a company with just a single manufacturing facility. An unexpected loss of production could prove fatal to such an enterprise. Lack of depth in management is another problem commonly associated with smaller companies.

Unquestionably, some very large companies have failed in the past. There is ample evidence, as well, of inefficiency in many large, bureaucratic organizations. The point, however, is not to debate whether big corporations are invincible or nimble, but to determine whether they meet their obligations with greater regularity, on average, than their pint-size peers.

Statistical models of default risk confirm that they do. Therefore, the bond-rating agencies are following sound methodology when they create size-based peer groups.

Line of business is another basis for defining a peer group. Because different industries have different financial characteristics, ratio comparisons across industry lines may not be valid. A machinery manufacturer's sales may fluctuate substantially over the capital goods cycle. In contrast, a personal care products manufacturer derives its revenues from essential products that are in demand year in and year out. The personal care products company therefore has greater predictability of earnings and cash flow. It can tolerate a higher level of fixed charges, implying a larger proportion of debt in its capital structure, than the machinery manufacturer. The rating agencies may assign Single-A ratings to a manufacturer of personal care products with a ratio of total debt to total capital that would earn a machinery maker with similar ratio ratings no higher than Triple-B.

For this reason, a ratio comparison between companies in different industries can be misleading. One company can look superior based on a particular ratio, yet still be excessively leveraged in view of the operating risks in its industry. Comparability problems become even more pronounced when ratio analysis crosses boundaries of broadly defined sectors of the economy (e.g., industrial, financial, utility, and transportation).

Carrying this principle to its logical conclusion, however, requires a peer group of companies with virtually identical product lines. Operating risk varies to some extent even among closely allied businesses. Strictly speaking, a producer of coated white paper is not comparable to a producer of kraft linerboard, nor a producer of facial tissue to a producer of fine writing paper.

Too zealous an effort to create homogeneous peer groups, though, narrows the field to such an extent that ratio comparisons begin to suffer from having too few data points. At the extreme, a comparison with only one other peer company is not terribly informative. The company being evaluated may rank above its lone peer, but the analyst does not know whether the peer is strong or weak.

On the other hand, suppose that with respect to a particular financial ratio, a company ranks fourth among a peer group of 10 companies, with eight in the group tightly distributed around the median and with one outlier each at the high and low ends. It is valid to say that the company has average risk within its peer group, at least in terms of that one ratio.

There are two techniques for resolving the trade-off between strict comparability and adequate sample size. Both consist of peer group comparisons. By employing both approaches, the analyst can achieve a satisfactory assessment of relative credit risk.

The first technique is to compare the company against a reasonably homogeneous industry peer group, such as the personal and household products companies shown in Exhibit 13.6. Credit analysts can use this type of analysis to slot a company within its industry. The ratios in the 23-company sample comparison are averages, computed over three years. Averaging minimizes the impact of unrepresentative results that any company may report in a single year.

Note that the following discussion deals with *company* credit ratings. The rating on a particular obligation of a company will depend on its priority within the capital structure. Examples, from highest to lowest priority, include secured loans, senior unsecured bonds, subordinated bonds, and preferred stocks.

Standard & Poor's conducts far more analysis in assigning the ratings indicated in the table, but the exhibit provides some insight into how well two basic financial ratios sort the companies by rating. (In both comparisons, a higher ratio indicates superior credit quality.) All companies rated AA or A rank in the top third by free cash flow as a percentage of total debt. Conversely, all those rated B or CCC place in the bottom half. Companies rated in the middle range, BBB or BB, are more widely scattered.

Less efficient at sorting the companies is EBITDA/interest expense, even though this ratio is so popular among practitioners that some regard it as shorthand for a company's credit quality. Ranked by EBITDA coverage, AA and A companies are found in both the top and bottom half. EBITDA coverage does at least place the group's lowest-rated issuer, CCC– Revlon, at the very bottom of the heap.

Avon Products ranks last or next to last in these ratio comparisons despite a mid-range rating of BB–. That seeming anomaly is explained by financial support that has been provided by the company's majority owner, Natura & Co., which was rated Ba2 by Moody's and BB by Standard & Poor's as of 2021. Even though Natura does not formally guarantee Avon's debt, the rating agencies perceived, as of this book's going to print, that it would continue to provide support if required. This concept of implicit support, mentioned near the beginning of this chapter, is one more example of credit analysts needing to look beyond the financial ratios to form a complete picture.

The second technique of comparative ratio analysis that is useful in evaluating credit quality is ranking a company within a rating peer group. As noted, it is not appropriate to compare companies in disparate sectors of the economy, such as industrials and utilities. A rating peer group can, however, legitimately include a variety of industries within a broadly defined economic sector. The expanded sample available under this approach enables

EXHIBIT 13.6 Comparative Ratio Analysis: Personal & Household Products Companies, Annual Average 2018–2020

EBITDA/interest expense			Free cash flow as a percentage of total debt		
Company name	Times	Rating	Company name	Percentage	Rating
The Procter & Gamble Company	28.7	AA−	The Procter & Gamble Company	38.5	AA−
The Estee Lauder Companies	23.1	A+	Allegion U.S. Holding Company	37.8	AA−
Kimberly-Clark Corporation	16.9	A	Colgate-Palmolive Company	37.8	AA−
Church & Dwight Co., Inc.	14.7	BBB+	Church & Dwight Co., Inc.	35.7	BBB+
Whirlpool Corporation	12.2	BBB	The Clorox Company	34.4	A−
Fortune Brands Home & Security Inc.	11.4	BBB+	The Estee Lauder Companies	34.0	A+
Hasbro Inc.	7.0	BBB−	Kimberly-Clark Corporation	25.0	A
Acco Brands Corporation	6.6	BB−	Fortune Brands Home & Security Inc.	22.0	BBB+
Tempur Sealy International	6.6	BB	Central Pet & Garden Company	21.4	BB
Edgewell Personal Care Co.	6.3	BB	The Scotts Miracle-Gro Company	17.8	BB
The Scotts Miracle-Gro Company	6.3	BB	Tempur Sealy International	17.6	BB
Central Pet & Garden Company	5.7	BB	Acco Brands Corporation	14.4	BB−
Newell Brands Inc.	4.5	B	Edgewell Personal Care Co.	13.4	BB
Allegion U.S. Holding Company	4.4	AA−	Whirlpool Corporation	13.2	BBB
Colgate-Palmolive Company	4.4	AA−	Vista Outdoor Inc.	13.2	B+
Coty Inc.	3.5	B−	Newell Brands Inc.	11.5	B
Vista Outdoor Inc.	3.2	B+	Hasbro Inc.	9.5	BBB−
Energizer Holdings	2.9	BB−	Energizer Holdings	6.8	BB−
Spectrum Brands Inc.	2.7	B	Spectrum Brands Inc.	4.6	B
The Clorox Company	2.5	A−	Mattel Inc.	0.6	B+
Mattel Inc.	2.5	B+	Coty Inc.	−0.6	B−
Avon Products Inc.	1.8	BB−	Revlon Consumer Products Corporation	−4.4	CCC−
Revlon Consumer Products Corporation	1.1	CCC−	Avon Products Inc.	−8.4	BB−

Based on Standard & Poor's long-term local issuer credit ratings

Sources: Bloomberg; ICE Indices, LLC.

EXHIBIT 13.7 Median Ratios by Bond-Rating Category (North American Industrials, 2020)

Median ratios	AA	A	BBB	BB	B	CCC
Operating EBITDA margin (%)	29.0	20.8	20.5	18.0	15.6	10.1
Free cash flow margin (%)	5.5	8.1	6.4	6.0	3.1	0.9
Total debt with equity credit/operating EBITDA (x)	0.6	2.1	2.7	3.7	4.9	8.1
Funds from operations interest coverage (x)	26.9	11.7	8.2	5.0	2.8	1.3
Operating EBITDA/interest paid (x)	32.8	14.1	9.6	5.8	3.1	1.2
Funds from operations leverage (x)	0.7	2.6	3.0	4.1	4.9	7.8

Source: Fitch Ratings.

the analyst to fine-tune the slotting achieved via the industry peer group comparisons.

Exhibit 13.7 shows the medians of six financial ratios by the letter grades assigned by Fitch Ratings. The sample consists of 700 issuers versus just 23 in the preceding exercise of slotting by industry group. For ratios involving margins and interest coverage, the medians decline as ratings decline. For ratios that measure financial leverage, the medians rise as ratings decline. The discontinuity on the free cash flow margin line is likely attributable to the small sample size (six) of companies rated AA.

Exhibit 13.8 illustrates one more way to compare companies' credit ratios. It displays the cutoffs for the best and worst quartiles, as well as the medians, for three standard ratios. The table covers companies with Single-A composite ratings (based on the ratings of Moody's, Standard & Poor's, Fitch, and DBRS.) This analysis enables the analyst to slot a company within a letter-grade rating category. As noted in Exhibits 13.4 and 13.5, the

EXHIBIT 13.8 Average Ratios for Single-A Industrials 2018–2020

	Pretax interest coverage (x)*	Funds from operations to debt (%)	Total debt to total capital (%)
Best quartile	20.80	70.30	32.11
Median	13.92	41.49	47.59
Worst quartile	8.41	32.43	71.69

*Defined as (Pretax income + Total interest incurred)/Total interest incurred
Source: Bloomberg.

rating agencies add modifiers (1, 2, and 3 or + and –) to indicate whether a company ranks in the high, middle, or low zone within the categories from Aa/AA to Caa/CCC.

The three forms of comparative ratio analysis described here are helpful in assessing the credit quality of a company not rated by any of the leading rating agencies. Analysts can characterize a nonrated company by establishing which rating category its credit file most resembles, and where it ranks within that category, based on ratio comparisons. In such exercises, analysts should keep in mind the size criterion, previously discussed, for creation of peer groups.

Comparative ratio analysis is also useful in assessing the credit impact of a major transaction, such as a debt-financed acquisition or a major stock repurchase. The analyst can calculate ratios based on pro forma financial statements (see Chapter 12) and slot the company in a grid of median ratios by rating category, as in Exhibit 13.7. In view of changes in the peer group ratios that arise from fluctuations in business conditions, it is important to use data as up to date as possible for the exercise.

Analysts should also bear in mind that a company can potentially avert a downgrade implied by the pro forma ratios, provided management's credibility with the rating agencies is high. The key is to present a plausible plan for restoring financial leverage to its pre-transaction level within a few years. Note, however, that the company will merely delay the downgrade if it does not quickly begin to make palpable progress toward the long-range target. The rating agencies tend to be skeptical about a company's ability to implement a three-year plan entirely in the third year.

Ratio Trend Analysis

Comparative ratio analysis is an effective technique for assessing relative credit risk, yet it leaves the analyst exposed to a major source of error. Suppose two companies in the same industry posted an identical fixed-charge coverage of 3.5 times last year. On a ratio comparison, the two appear to be equally risky. Suppose, however, that one company had coverage of 5.0 times five years ago and has steadily declined to 3.5 times. Imagine, as well, that the other company's coverage has improved over the same period from 2.0 times to 3.5 times. If the two companies' trends appear likely to continue, based on analysis of their operations, then the happenstance that both covered their interest by 3.5 times last year should have little bearing on the credit assessment. The company that will have stronger coverage in the future is the better risk.

A further complication is that improving or deteriorating financial ratios can have different implications for different companies. In some cases, a declining trend over several years signals that a company has genuinely fallen to a new, lower level of credit quality. For other companies, negative year-over-year comparisons merely represent the down legs of their normal operating cycles.

Certain industries enjoy fairly stable demand, year in and year out. Small-ticket nondurables such as food, beverages, and beauty aids are not items that consumers cease to buy during recessions. At worst, people trade down to cheaper products within the same categories. In contrast, consumers tend to postpone purchases of big-ticket durable goods when credit is tight or when they have misgivings about the economic outlook. Producers of automobiles, houses, and major appliances are among the businesses that experience wide swings in demand between peaks and troughs in the economy. Profits typically fluctuate even more dramatically in these industries, due to the high fixed costs entailed in capital-intensive production methods.

In evaluating the long-range creditworthiness of cyclical companies, the rating agencies historically focused on cycle-to-cycle, rather than year-to-year, trends. Their notion was that a cycle-to-cycle pattern of similar highs and similar lows (Exhibit 13.9) did not imply a true impairment of financial strength. Deterioration was indicated only when a company displayed a trend of successively lower highs and lower lows (Exhibit 13.10).

The rating agencies label this traditional approach "rating through the cycle." Although it still influences the agencies' analysis, they have somewhat de-emphasized the concept over time. They are more likely than formerly to assume that an extended upturn or downtrend in a company's ratios represents a longer-lived shift. The agencies must also respond to fixed income investors' preferences regarding the optimal time horizon embedded in ratings.

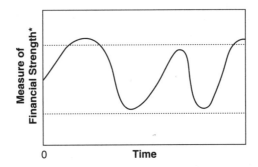

EXHIBIT 13.9   Cycle-to-Cycle Stability (Similar Highs and Lows).
*Examples: Operating margin, fixed charge coverage, ratio of cash flow to total debt.

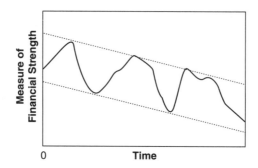

EXHIBIT 13.10 Cycle-to-Cycle Deterioration (Successively Lower Highs and Lower Lows).

Even in years past, when the agencies adhered more closely to the doctrine of rating through the cycle, it was often difficult to distinguish a normal, cyclical decline from more permanent deterioration, without the benefit of hindsight. There was always a danger that a company's management was portraying a permanent reduction in profitability as a routine cyclical slump. Then, as now, an analyst had to look beyond the financial statements to make an informed judgment about the likely persistence of an improvement or deterioration in financial measures.

Looking Beyond the Ratios

In addition to looking outside the financial statements, a thorough credit analysis requires scrutinizing the statements for items that raise questions about quality of financial reporting. Noble Group Ltd.'s decline during 2015–2018 provides an object lesson on this point.

The Hong Kong-based commodities trading firm was the subject of a February 15, 2015, report by Iceberg Research that highlighted its "remarkable ability to spot accounting loopholes."[6] Among other things, the report criticized Noble's accounting for related companies. For example, Noble held a 13 percent stake in Yancoal, a listed Australian company. Asserting that it had "significant influence" over the coal miner, a claim that Iceberg vigorously disputed, Noble classified Yancoal as an "associate" on its balance sheet. That classification ordinarily requires equity ownership between 20 percent and 50 percent.

Noble's dubious accounting treatment enabled it to carry its Yancoal stake at initial cost, adjusted for subsequent gains or losses (the "equity method"). On that basis, Noble showed the value of its holding at $614 million versus a market value of its shares of just $11 million. Noble would have had to show the smaller value on its balance sheet if it had followed standard accounting for an equity stake of less than 20 percent, namely, classifying Yancoal as a long-term investment.

The $603 million gap between the stated value of Noble's Yancoal investment and the market value represented 11 percent of Noble's stated shareholders' equity. Moreover, Noble had inflated the value of its Yancoal holding, as Iceberg detailed, by not calculating its initial cost in the customary way. Instead of basing it on the price it paid for the shares, Noble put them on its books at five times their market value, based on its cash flow projections for Yancoal.

Iceberg's report noted that other analysts had previously commented on Noble's valuation of its Yancoal stake, but went on to discuss similarly aggressive accounting for a new associate as of the fourth quarter 2014 statements, Noble Agri Ltd. A subsequent Iceberg report contended that the commodity trader's treatment of ongoing operations was even more disturbing than its handling of so-called associates.

Fixed income investors would have been wise to focus on the weakness of Noble's financial reporting quality, which Iceberg identified by looking beyond standard financial ratios. The company's 6.75 percent bond due in 2020 was quoted at 101.750 at the time of February 15, 2015, report. Standard & Poor's rated the company BBB– at the time. With its true financial condition more precarious than its balance sheet indicated, Noble took a beating amid falling commodity prices. By the end of 2015 its 6.75 percent bond was down by 33 percent, to 68.50. Over the same interval, the benchmark now known as the ICE BofA Asian Dollar Investment Grade Index was down by just 3 percent. On January 7, 2016, Standard & Poor's downgraded Noble to speculative grade, at BB+.

By then, a penetrating *Wall Street Journal* "Heard on the Street" column of July 2, 2015,[7] had highlighted the credit risk inherent in Noble's increase in debt of nearly $1 billion, to $4.9 billion, in the year's first quarter. That figure did not include the debt of associate Agri Ltd. Furthermore, wrote journalist Abheek Bhattacharya, who cited CreditSight's Andy DeVries in his article, Noble's leverage was understated by virtue of the company counting as equity a $400 million perpetual bond. Granted, the permanence of this debt capital made it somewhat equity-like, but unlike common stock dividends, interest payments on bonds cannot be omitted without triggering a default and potentially casting the borrower into bankruptcy.

Bhattacharya further pointed out that Noble faced $2.26 billion of debt maturities through March 2016, including $500 million in the form of five-year bonds coming due in August 2015. The choices for making those principal redemptions were mostly unattractive. Issuing new five-year bonds would be expensive in view of Noble's reduced credit rating. Cheaper interest rates were available on shorter-dated debt, but choosing that route that would postpone a potential refinancing problem only briefly.

At first blush, Noble had $928 million of cash that it could apply to debt redemption, but on closer examination, all but $499 million of that amount was tied up with brokers, in futures trading or otherwise. The company did have $3 billion in unused, committed credit facilities, but tapping that source would sacrifice some future financial flexibility. In any case, management appeared less concerned about reining in debt than attempting to shore up its stock price by buying back shares, thereby further increasing its financial leverage. Bhattacharya reported that during June 2015 Noble had spent $69.1 million on share repurchases, through the 29th. He warned that inattention to the balance sheet could cause creditors to desert the company.

Noble managed to dodge the bullet at that point, but its financial condition continued to deteriorate. By the end of 2017 its 6.75 percent bond was down to 37. Standard & Poor's downgraded the issue to CC on January 30, 2018. On March 13, amid plans for a financial restructuring, Noble failed to pay the coupon on a bond maturing in 2022. Over the next week the company said it would miss interest principal and interest payments on two other bonds and Standard & Poor's reduced its rating to D for default.

This case history demonstrates why credit analysts must do more with financial statements than mechanically calculate ratios. Certainly, Noble's financial ratios worsened as its bond prices plummeted, but investors hope to exit securities before, not concurrently with, major losses. Iceberg Research's analysis, at a time when Noble's 6.75 percent bond was trading above par, focused not on ratios but on management's exploitation of accounting loopholes. Those gambits enabled the company to understate its ratio of total debt to total capital, for example. The lesson for analysts hoping to add value in fixed income investment is that staying abreast of a company's ratios is essential, but not always sufficient.

Default Risk Models

As noted, comparative ratio analysis and ratio trend analysis are techniques for placing companies on a relative scale of credit quality. Many analysts have no need to look more deeply into the matter, but it is impossible to cover the topic of credit analysis satisfactorily without discussing two more fundamental issues. First, there is the question of how to set up a ranking scheme such as bond ratings in the first place. Second, there is the problem of conflicting indicators. How, for example, should an analyst evaluate a company that ranks well on fixed-charge coverage but poorly on financial leverage? A rigorous approach demands something more scientific than an individual analyst's subjective opinion that coverage should be weighted twice as heavily as leverage, or vice versa.

The solution to both of these problems lies in establishing a statistical relationship between financial ratios and default probability. This requires, first of all, collecting data on the default experience in a given population. Next, statistical methods are employed to determine which financial ratios have historically predicted defaults most reliably. Using a model derived from the best predictors, the analyst can then rank companies on the basis of how closely their financial profiles resemble the profiles of companies that defaulted.

One example of the various models that have been devised to predict defaults is Edward I. Altman's Z-Score model, which takes the following form:

$$Z = 1.2x_1 + 1.4x_2 + 3.3x_3 + 0.6x_4 + 1.0x_5$$

where: x_1 = Working capital/Total assets (%, e.g., 0.20, or 20%)
x_2 = Retained earnings/Total assets (%)
x_3 = Earnings before interest and taxes/Total assets (%)
x_4 = Market value of equity/Total liabilities (%)
x_5 = Sales/Total assets (number of times, e.g., 2.0 times)

In this model, scores below 1.81 signify serious credit problems, whereas a score above 3.0 indicates a healthy firm.

A refinement of the Z-Score model, the Zeta model developed by Altman and his colleagues,[8] achieved greater predictive accuracy by using the following variables:

x_1 = Earnings before interest and taxes (EBIT)/Total assets

x_2 = **Standard error of estimate** of EBIT/Total assets (normalized) for 10 years

x_3 = EBIT/Interest charges

x_4 = Retained earnings/Total assets

x_5 = Current assets/Current liabilities

x_6 = Five-year average market value of equity/Total capitalization

x_7 = Total tangible assets, normalized

Quantitative models such as Zeta, as well as others that have been devised using various mathematical techniques, have several distinct benefits. First, they are developed by objectively correlating financial variables with defaults. They consequently avoid guesswork in assigning relative weights to the variables. Second, the record of quantitative models is excellent from the standpoint of classifying as troubled credits most companies that subsequently defaulted. In addition, the scores assigned to non-defaulted companies by these models correlate fairly well with bond ratings. This suggests that although Moody's, Standard & Poor's, and Fitch Ratings originally developed their rating methods along more subjective lines, their conclusions are at least partially vindicated by statistical measures of default risk. Therefore, the credit analyst can feel comfortable about using methods such as ratio trend analysis to slot companies within the ratings framework. One may quarrel with the rating agencies' assessments of specific companies or industries, but there is strong statistical support for the notion that in the aggregate, ratings provide a valid, if rough, assessment of default risk. The lower a company's present rating, the higher its probability of defaulting over the next year, next two years, and so on up to 20 years.[9]

Useful as they are, though, quantitative default models cannot entirely replace human judgment in credit analysis.

For one thing, quantitative models tend to classify as troubled credits not only most of the companies that eventually default but also many that do not default.[10] Often, firms that fall into financial peril bring in new management and are revitalized without ever failing in their debt service. If faced with a huge capital loss on the bonds of a financially distressed company, an institutional investor might wish to assess the probability of a turnaround – an inherently difficult-to-quantify prospect – instead of selling purely on the basis of a default model.

The credit analyst must also bear in mind that companies can default for reasons that a model based solely on reported financial data cannot pick up. For example, U.S. Brass entered Chapter 11 proceedings in 1994 in an effort to resolve litigation involving defective plastic plumbing systems that it had manufactured. Dow Corning's 1995 bankruptcy filing offered a possible means of resolving massive litigation that arose from silicone gel breast implants sold by the company, which were alleged to cause autoimmune disease and other maladies. In 1999, Gulf States Steel, Inc. of Alabama filed for bankruptcy to address, among other matters, pending litigation with the Environmental Protection Agency and other potential environmentally related claims.[11] Purdue Pharma's 2019 bankruptcy filing was as a consequence of litigation related to prescriptions of opioids involved in numerous fatal overdoses. Typically, in such cases, neither the company's balance sheet nor its income statement signals an impending collapse. Eljer Industries, U.S. Brass's parent company, specifically indicated that the bankruptcy filing did not result from a cash flow shortfall. The problems were apparent in the company's notes to financial statements, but default models based entirely on financial statement data do not deal with contingent liabilities.

In the case of the Zeta model, the default hazard posed by a company's environmental or product liability litigation may be picked up, at least in part, by the ratio of market value of equity to total capitalization. Stock market investors consider such risks in determining share prices.

Some default risk models downplay statement data in favor of reliance on the equity market's wisdom. The best known model of this sort is marketed by Moody's KMV. BondScore, a product of CreditSights, combines quantitative analysis based on equity pricing with traditional credit analysis. Underlying these approaches is the observation that a company's debt and equity both derive their value from the same assets. Equity holders have only a residual claim after bondholders have been paid. Therefore, if the market value of a company's assets falls below the value of its liabilities, the stock becomes worthless. At that point, the company becomes bankrupt, its liabilities exceed its assets. Extending the logic, a declining stock price indicates that the company is getting closer to bankruptcy. In theory, then, credit analysts can skip the financial statement work and monitor companies' default risk simply by watching their stock prices.

Like the quantitative models consisting of financial ratios, the default risk models based on stock prices provide useful, but not infallible, signals. For example, when a company dramatically increases its total-debt-to-total-capital ratio by borrowing money to repurchase stock, its default risk clearly rises. At the same time, its stock price may also rise, reflecting the positive impact on earnings per share of increased financial leverage and a reduction in the number of shares outstanding. According to the theory underlying the stock-based default risk models, however, a rising share price indicates declining default risk. This is one of several caveats typically accompanying credit opinions derived from stock-based models.

Even if share prices were perfect indicators of credit risk, credit analysts would not escape the rigors of tearing apart financial statements. To begin with, not every company's shares trade in the public market. The producers of stock-based models attempt to get around this problem by using share prices of industry peers to create surrogates for private companies' unobservable equity values. This method, however, cannot capture the sort of company-specific risks that led to the above-listed bankruptcies that were triggered by massively costly lawsuits. Neither can stock-based default risk models relieve the analyst of such tasks as creating pro forma financial statements to gauge the impact of a potential merger or major asset sale. At most, incorporating stock prices into credit analysis is a useful complement to plumbing the financial statements for meaning with time-tested ratio calculations.

CONCLUSION

Default risk models can provide a solid foundation for credit analysis but must be used in conjunction with the analyst's judgment on matters too complex to be modeled. Much the same applies to all of the quantitative techniques discussed in this chapter. A lender should not offer credit before first running the numbers. By the same token, it is a mistake to rely solely on the numbers to sidestep a difficult decision. This can take the form of rejecting a reasonable risk by inflexibly applying quantitative criteria. Alternatively, it can wind up being costly to approve a credit against one's better judgment, while counting on financial ratios that are technically satisfactory as a defense against criticism if the loan goes bad.

As other chapters in this book demonstrate, financial statements are vulnerable to manipulation, much of which is perfectly legal. Often, the specific aim of the manipulators is to outfox credit analysts who mechanically calculate ratios without pausing to consider whether accounting ruses have defeated the purpose. Another danger in relying too heavily on quantitative analysis is that a company may unexpectedly and radically alter its capital structure to finance an acquisition or defend itself against a hostile takeover. Such action can render ratio analysis on even the most recent financial statements largely irrelevant. In the end, credit analysts must equip themselves with all the tools described in this chapter yet not be made complacent by them.

CHAPTER 14

Equity Analysis

Countless books have been written on the subject of picking stocks. The approaches represented in their pages cover a vast range. Some focus on technical analysis, which seeks to establish the value of a common equity by studying its past price behavior. Others take as their starting point the efficient market hypothesis, which in its purest form implies that no sort of analysis can identify values not already recognized and properly discounted by the market.

This chapter does not attempt to summarize or criticize all the methods employed by the legions who try to outperform the market. Rather, the discussion focuses primarily on the use of financial statements in **fundamental analysis.** This term refers to the attempt to determine whether a company's stock is fairly valued, based on its financial characteristics.

Certain elements of fundamental analysis do *not* rely entirely, or even primarily, on information found in the financial statements. For example, a company may appear to be a good candidate for a bust-up, or hostile takeover, premised on selling portions of the company to realize value not reflected in its stock price. As discussed later in this chapter, the analyst can estimate the firm's ostensible breakup value by studying its annual report. The feasibility of a hostile raid, however, may hinge on the pattern of share ownership, the availability of financing for a takeover, or laws applicable to tender offers. All these factors lie outside the realm of financial statement analysis, but may have a major bearing on the valuation process.

Note as well that **GAAP** earnings play a central role in traditional equity analysis, as detailed here. GAAP expenses items such as advertising and research and development (R&D) that create enduring values in many **New Economy** companies. Creating enduring value is the definition of producing an asset, a process that GAAP validates in the case of traditional manufacturing companies by capitalizing the expenditures on plant and equipment that produce the enduring value. In contrast, GAAP treats as current costs the outlays that produce (for example) long-term subscribers to Internet-based services. As a result, a New Economy company may create immense, sustainable value that the stock market will affirm, even as GAAP accounting shows that current costs more than fully offset the company's revenues. That leaves no earnings to which to apply a price-earnings multiple, as described in this chapter. Analysts following such companies may rely on other, operationally oriented metrics to judge the appropriateness of their stock prices.

Certainly, not all departures from relating stock prices to financial statement data qualify as sound practices. In 2021, online communities of novice investors, many of them sidelined from sports gambling by the COVID-19 pandemic's curtailment of sporting events, bid up so-called meme stocks in efforts to squeeze short-sellers who considered them overpriced. The sheer force of collective action rendered conventional notions of intrinsic value irrelevant, at least in the short run. We mention this phenomenon to reinforce the point that financial statement analysis coexists with other modes of stock selection.

A final point about the following material is that it should be read in conjunction with Chapter 12, "Forecasting Financial Statements." A company's equity value lies wholly in its future performance. Strictly speaking, therefore, historical financial statements aid the analysis only to the extent that they provide a basis for projecting future results. Into the formulas detailed in this chapter, the analyst must plug earnings and cash flow forecasts derived by the techniques described in Chapter 12.

THE DIVIDEND DISCOUNT MODEL

Several methods of fundamental common stock analysis have been devised over the years, but few match the intuitive appeal of regarding the stock price as the discounted value of expected future dividends. (See "Net Present Value" entry in the Glossary.) This approach is analogous to the yield-to-maturity calculation for a bond and therefore facilitates the comparison of different securities of a single issuer. Additionally, the method permits the analyst to address the uncertainty inherent in forecasting a noncontractual flow[1] by varying the applicable discount rate.

To understand the relationship between future dividends and present stock price, consider the following fictitious example: Hemidemi Semiconductor's annual common dividend rate is currently $2.10 a share. Because the company's share of a nonexpanding market is neither increasing nor decreasing, it will probably generate flat sales and earnings for the indefinite future and continue the dividend at its current level. Hemidemi's long-term debt currently offers a yield of 3 percent, reflecting the company's credit rating and the prevailing level of interest rates. Based on the greater uncertainty of the dividend stream relative to the contractual payments on Hemidemi's debt, investors demand a risk premium of four percentage points – a return of 3 percent + 4 percent = 7 percent – to own the company's common stock rather than its bonds.

The stock price that should logically be observed in the market, given these facts, is the price at which Hemidemi's annual $2.10 payout equates to a 10 percent yield, or algebraically:

$$P = \frac{D}{K}$$

$$P = \frac{\$2.10}{0.07}$$

$$P = \$30.00$$

where: P = Current stock price
D = Current dividend rate
K = Required rate of return

If the analyst agrees that 7 percent is an appropriate discount rate, based on a financial comparison between Hemidemi and other companies with similar implicit discount rates, then any price less than $30 a share indicates that the stock is undervalued. Alternatively, suppose the analyst concludes that Hemidemi's future dividend stream is less secure than the dividend streams of other companies to which a 7 percent discount rate is being applied. The analyst might then discount Hemidemi's stream at a higher rate, say 10 percent, and recalculate the appropriate share price as follows:

$$P = \frac{\$2.10}{0.10}$$

$$P = \$21.00$$

A market price of $30.00 a share would then indicate an overvaluation of Hemidemi Semiconductor.

Dividends and Future Appreciation

When initially introduced to the dividend-discount model, many individuals respond by saying, "Dividends are not the only potential source of gain to the stockholder. The share price may rise as well. Shouldn't any evaluation reflect the potential for appreciation?" It is in responding to this objection that the dividend-discount model displays its elegance most fully. The answer is that there is no reason for the stock price to rise in the future unless the dividend rises. In a no-growth situation such as Hemidemi Semiconductor, the valuation will look the same five years hence (assuming no change in interest rates and risk premiums) as today. There is consequently no fundamental reason for a buyer to pay more for the stock at that point. If, on the other hand, the dividend payout rises over time (the case that immediately follows), the stock *will* be worth more in the future than it is today. The analyst can, however, incorporate the expected dividend increases directly into the present-value calculation to derive the current stock price, without bothering to determine and discount back the associated future price appreciation. By thinking through the logic of the discounting method, the analyst will find that value always comes back to dividends.

Valuing a Growing Company

No-growth companies are simple to analyze, but in practice most public corporations strive for growth in earnings per share, which, as the ensuing discussion demonstrates, will lead to gains for shareholders. In analyzing growing companies, a somewhat more complex formula must be used to equate future dividends to the present stock price:

$$P = \frac{D(1+g)^1}{(1+K)^1} + \frac{D(1+g)^2}{(1+K)^2} + \cdots \frac{D(1+g)^n}{(1+K)^n}$$

where: P = Current stock price
D = Current dividend rate
K = Required rate of return
g = Growth rate

A number of dollars equivalent to P, if invested at an interest rate equivalent to K, will be equal, after n periods, to the cumulative value of dividends paid over the same interval, assuming the payout is initially an amount equivalent to D and increases in each period at a rate equivalent to g.

Fortunately, from the standpoint of ease of calculation, if n, the number of periods considered, is infinite, the preceding formula reduces to the simpler form:

$$P = \frac{D}{K - g}$$

In practice, this is the form ordinarily used in analysis, since companies are presumed to continue to operate as going concerns, rather than to liquidate at some arbitrary future date.

EXHIBIT 14.1   Selected Financial Data for Wolfe Food Company

Net income available to common shareholders	$45,000,000
Dividends to common shareholders	$15,000,000
Common shares outstanding	10,000,000
Expected annual growth in earnings	7%
Investors' required rate of return, given predictability of Wolfe's earnings	9%

Figures projected from the financial statements of the fictitious Wolfe Food Company (Exhibit 14.1) illustrate the application of the dividend-discount model. Observe that the company is expected to pay out $33\frac{1}{3}$ percent of its earnings to shareholders in the current year:

$$\text{Dividend payout ratio} = \frac{\text{Dividends to common shareholders}}{\text{Net income available to common shareholders}}$$

$$= \frac{\$15,000,000}{\$45,000,000}$$

$$= 33\frac{1}{3}\%$$

If Wolfe maintains a constant dividend **payout ratio**, it follows that the growth rate of dividends will equal the growth rate of earnings, which is expected to be 6 percent annually. On a per share basis, the initial dividend comes to $1.50:

$$\text{Dividend rate} = \frac{\text{Dividends to common shareholders}}{\text{Common shares outstanding}}$$

$$= \frac{\$15,000,000}{10,000,000}$$

$$= \$1.50 \text{ per share}$$

With these numbers, the analyst can now use the valuation formula to derive a share price of $75 for Wolfe:

$$P = \frac{D}{K - g}$$

$$P = \frac{\$1.50}{0.09 - 0.07}$$

$$P = \frac{\$1.50}{0.02}$$

$$P = \$75$$

The execution of this model rests heavily on the assumptions underlying the company's projected financial statements. To estimate the future growth rate of earnings, the analyst must make informed judgments both about the growth of the company's markets and about the company's ability to maintain or increase its share of those markets. Furthermore, the company's earnings growth rate may diverge from its sales growth due to changes in its operating margins that may or may not reflect industrywide trends.

Because of the uncertainties affecting such projections, the analyst should apply to equity valuation the same sort of sensitivity analysis discussed in connection with financial forecasting (see Chapter 12). For instance, if Wolfe Foods ultimately falls short of the 7 percent growth rate previously projected by one percentage point, then the $75 valuation will prove in retrospect to have been $25.00 too high:

$$P = \frac{D}{K - g}$$

$$P = \frac{\$1.50}{0.09 - 0.06}$$

$$P = \frac{\$1.50}{0.03}$$

$$P = \$50$$

Therefore, an analyst whose forecast of earnings growth has a margin of error of one percentage point should not put a strong buy recommendation on Wolfe when it is trading at $60 a share. By the same token, a price of $43, which implies a 5.5 percent growth rate, can safely be regarded as an undervaluation, provided the other assumptions are valid.

Earnings or Cash Flow?

Intuitively appealing though it may be, relating share price to future dividends through projected earnings growth does not jibe perfectly with reality. In particular, highly cyclical companies do not produce steady earnings increases year in and year out, yet the formula $P = D/K - g$ demands a constant rate of growth. If, as assumed previously, the company's dividend payout ratio remains constant, the pattern of its dividends will plainly fail to fit neatly into the formula.

What saves the dividend discount method from irrelevance is that companies generally do not strive for a constant dividend payout ratio at all costs. More typically, they attempt to avoid cutting the amount of the payout, notwithstanding declines in earnings. For example, a company that aims to pay out 25 percent of its earnings over a complete business cycle might record a payout ratio of 15 percent in a peak year and 90 percent or 100 percent in a trough year. Indeed, a company that records net losses may maintain its dividend at the established level, at least for a few years, resulting in a meaningless payout ratio calculation. (If losses persist, financial prudence will usually dictate cutting or eliminating the dividend to conserve cash.) As a rule, a cyclical company will not increase its dividend on a regular, annual basis. Nevertheless, the board will ordinarily endeavor to raise the payout over the longer term. In all of these cases, the $P = D/K - g$ formula will work reasonably well as a valuation tool, with the irregular pattern of dividend increases recognized through adjustments to the discount rate (K).

Although the dividend discount model can accommodate earnings' cyclicality, the analyst must pay close attention to the method by which a company finances the continuation of its dividend at the established rate. A chronically money-losing company that borrows to pay dividends is simply undergoing slow liquidation. (It is replacing its equity, ultimately 100 percent of it, with liabilities.) In such circumstances, the key assumption that dividends will continue for an infinite number of periods becomes unsustainable.

On the other hand, a cyclical company may sustain losses at the bottom of a business cycle yet never reach the point at which its funds from operations, net of capital expenditures required to maintain long-term competitiveness, fail to cover the dividend. Maintaining the dividend under these circumstances poses no financial threat. Accordingly, many analysts argue that cash flow, rather than earnings, is the true determinant of dividend-paying capability. By extension, they contend that projected cash flow, rather than earnings-per-share forecasts, should be the main focus of equity analysis.

Certainly, analysts need to be acutely conscious of changes in a company's cash-generating capability that are not paralleled by changes in earnings. For example, a company may for a time maintain a given level of profitability even though its business is becoming more capital-intensive. Rising plant and equipment requirements might transform the company from a self-financing entity into one that is dependent on external financing. Return on equity (ROE), defined as Net Income divided by Shareholders' Equity, will not reflect the change until, after several years, either the resulting escalation in borrowing costs or the increase in the equity base required to support a given level of operating earnings becomes material. Furthermore, as detailed in Chapters 6 and 7, reported earnings are subject to considerable manipulation. In fact, that is the flaw that helped to popularize the use of cash flow analysis in the first place. Cash generated from operations, which is generally more difficult for companies to manipulate than earnings, can legitimately be viewed as the preferred measure of future dividend-paying capability.

Notwithstanding these arguments, earnings per share forecasts remain the single most important focus of equity research. Stock prices often drop sharply in response to *earnings misses*, that is, when companies announce earnings lower than analysts' consensus forecasts. Similar reactions occur when companies lower their *earnings guidance*, that is, their expectations with respect to the next quarterly earnings announcement. Misses on consensus sales expectations can also affect stock prices, but earnings continue to occupy center stage. Nowadays, the number on which market participants lavish so much attention is likely to be *adjusted*, rather than GAAP earnings. Among the adjustments are elimination of events deemed one-time events, by common agreement if not by GAAP. Investors should approach adjusted (sometimes loosely referred to as "pro forma") earnings cautiously. Many companies promote versions of adjusted earnings designed to divert attention from inconvenient but genuine drags on their performance, often with the cooperation of Wall Street analysts who act more like cheerleaders than objective judges of value.

One other version of earnings employed by practitioners is **EBITDA.** This measure first became popular in the analysis of speculative-grade debt and leveraged buyouts, but it has gained some traction in equity analysis of conventionally capitalized companies. In many cases, though, the components of EBITDA other than net income are highly predictable over the near term. This is particularly true of depreciation. By accurately forecasting the more variable component, earnings, an investor can get a fairly good handle on EBITDA as well.

To some extent, the unflagging focus on earnings probably reflects institutional inertia. Portfolio managers measure the accuracy of brokerage houses' equity analysis in terms of earnings per share (EPS) forecasts. Investment strategists use aggregate earnings per share forecasts, among other inputs, to gauge the attractiveness of the stock market as a whole. Analysts who lack an EPS forecast would have a hard time getting into the discussion. Despite the entrenched position of earnings forecasts, however, a mechanism is available for adjusting a stock evaluation when the quality of the forecasted earnings is questionable due to aggressive accounting practices. Investors can reduce the earnings multiple, as explained in the following section.

THE PRICE-EARNINGS RATIO

Although the dividend discount model is an intuitively satisfying approach to valuing a common stock, it is not the most convenient method of comparing one stock's value with another's. Better suited to that task is the price-earnings ratio, alternately known as the P/E ratio or earnings multiple:

$$\text{Price-earnings ratio} = \frac{\text{Stock price}}{\text{Earnings per share}}$$

Based on this formula, Wolfe Food Company (see preceding section) has a price-earnings ratio of:

$$\text{Stock price} = \$75$$

$$\text{Net income available to common shareholders} = \$45,000,000$$

$$\text{Common shares} = 10,000,000$$

$$\text{Earnings per share} = \frac{\$45,000,000}{10,000,000}$$

$$= \$4.50$$

$$\text{Price-earnings ratio} = \frac{\$75}{\$4.50}$$

$$\text{Price-earnings ratio} = 16.7X$$

$$\text{Price-earnings ratio} = \frac{\$60}{\$3.60}$$

$$= 16.7X$$

To understand how the price-earnings ratio may be used to compare companies with one another, consider a competitor of Wolfe Food Company, Grubb & Chao (Exhibit 14.2). Grubb & Chao has the same expected earnings growth rate as Wolfe (6 percent) and is assigned the same required rate of return (9 percent). Its price-earnings ratio, however, is higher than Wolfe's (17.5X vs. 16.7X):

$$\text{Price-earnings ratio} = \text{Stock price}/\text{Earnings per share}$$

$$\text{Price-earnings ratio} = \$63 / \left(\frac{\$54,000,000}{15,000,000} \right)$$

$$= \frac{\$63}{\$3.60}$$

$$P/E = 17.5X$$

EXHIBIT 14.2   Selected Financial Data for Grubb & Chao

Net income available to common shareholders	$54,000,000
Dividends to common shareholders	$18,000,000
Common shares outstanding	15,000,000
Expected annual growth in earnings	7%
Investors' required rate of return, given predictability of company's earnings	9%
Current stock price	$63.00

Based on the information provided, an investor would regard Wolfe as a better value than Grubb & Chao. This conclusion proceeds from applying the dividend discount model to the latter's numbers:

$$P = D/(K - g)$$

$$P = \frac{\dfrac{\$18,000,000}{15,000,000}}{.09 - .07}$$

$$P = \frac{\$1.20}{.02}$$

$$P = \$60$$

The price thus derived is lower than the actual price of $63.00, implying an overvaluation by the market. Observe as well that the correct price for Grubb & Chao produces the same price-earnings ratio as calculated for Wolfe Food Company:

$$\text{Price-earnings ratio} = \frac{\$60}{\$3.60}$$

$$= 16.7X$$

Value comparisons based on P/E ratios can go well beyond this sort of company-to-company matchup. The analyst can rank all the companies within an industry (Exhibit 14.3), then judge whether the variations in price-earnings ratios appear justified, or whether certain companies seem out of line. Note that this table ranks companies on the basis of actual earnings over the preceding four quarters, rather than estimated earnings for the coming year, another typical format employed in P/E ratio comparisons. Earnings exclude extraordinary items (see Chapter 3). Earnings per share

EXHIBIT 14.3   Companies within an Industry

Ranked by price-earnings ratio: personal care industry December 31, 2019

Company	P/E
Estee Lauder Companies Inc	123.7
Inter Parfums, Inc.	59.2
Edgewell Personal Care Co	33.7
Mace Security International, Inc.	26.0
Procter & Gamble Co	25.8
Colgate-Palmolive Company	25.6
Kimberly Clark Corp	20.3
Nu Skin Enterprises, Inc.	14.7

Source: Stock Investor Pro and author calculations. Price to Earnings = Price / Diluted EPS, Forward 12 months.

are customarily calculated on a diluted basis by taking into account the possibility that new shares will be created through conversion of outstanding **convertible** securities or exercise of stock options or warrants.

Why P/E Multiples Vary

Justifications for differences in earnings multiples derive from the variables of the preceding valuation formulas. Consider the following two equations:

$$P = \frac{D}{K - g} \text{ and } P/E = \frac{P}{EPS}$$

where: P = Current stock price
 D = Current dividend rate
 K = Required rate of return
 g = Growth rate
 P/E = Price-earnings ratio
 EPS = Current earnings per share (annual)

Substituting $D/K - g$, which equals P, for the P in the other equation, produces the following expanded form:

$$P/E = \frac{\left(\frac{D}{(K-g)}\right)}{EPS}$$

Using this expanded equation permits the analyst to see quickly that an increase in the expected growth rate of earnings produces a premium multiple. For example, both Wolfe Food Company and Grubb & Chao have

7 percent growth factors, and both stocks currently trade at 16.7 times earnings. Suppose another competitor, Eatmore & Co., can be expected to enjoy 7.5 percent growth, by virtue of concentration in faster-growing segments of the food business. A substantially higher multiple results from this modest edge in earnings growth:

$$\frac{P}{E} = \left(\frac{D}{(K-g)} \right) / EPS$$

$$\frac{P}{E} = \frac{\dfrac{\$1.60}{0.09 - 0.075}}{\$4.80}$$

$$\frac{P}{E} = \frac{106.67}{\$4.80}$$

$$\frac{P}{E} = 22.2X$$

Eatmore & Co.'s earnings will not, however, command a premium (22.2X vs. 16.7X for its competitors) if the basis for its higher projected growth is subject to unusually high risks. For example, Eatmore's strategy may emphasize expansion in developing countries, where the rate of growth in personal income is higher than in the more mature economy of the United States. If so, Eatmore may be considerably more exposed than Wolfe or Grubb & Chao to the risks of nationalization, new restrictions on repatriation of earnings, protectionist trade policies, and adverse fluctuations in exchange rates. In that case, the market will raise its discount rate (K) on Eatmore's earnings. An increase of just half a percentage point (from 9.0 percent to 9.5 percent) drops Eatmore's earnings multiple below its competitors' 16.7X, reducing it from 22.2X to 13.3X:

$$\frac{P}{E} = \left(\frac{D}{(K-g)} \right) / EPS$$

$$\frac{P}{E} = \frac{\dfrac{\$1.60}{0.095 - 0.07}}{\$4.80}$$

$$\frac{P}{E} = 13.33X$$

In effect, the ability to vary the discount rate, and therefore assign a lower or higher multiple to a company's earnings, is the equity analyst's defense against earnings manipulation by management, as described in Chapter 3. A company may use liberal accounting practices and skimp on long-term investment spending, yet expect the resulting, artificially inflated earnings per share to be valued at the same multiple as its competitor's more legitimately derived profits. Indeed, the heart of many management presentations to analysts is a table showing that the presenting company's multiple is low by comparison with its peers. Typically, the chief executive officer cites this table as proof that the company is undervalued. The natural corollary is that in time investors will become aware of the discrepancy and raise the multiple and therefore the price of shares owned by those who are astute enough to buy in at today's dirt-cheap level.

These stories are sometimes persuasive, yet one must wonder whether such discrepancies in earnings multiples truly indicate inattention by analysts. In the case of a large-capitalization company, hundreds of Wall Street and institutional analysts are probably making the comparison on their own. If so, they are fully aware of the below-average multiple but consider it justified for one or more reasons, including the following:

- The company's earnings are more cyclical than those of its peer group.
- The company's earnings depend on a special tax break or other legislative or regulatory preference that could be rescinded as the political winds shift.
- The company has historically been prone to earnings surprises, which raise suspicions that the reported results reflect an exceptionally large amount of earnings management.
- Technological risk, in the form of potential disruption by novel business models or production methods, is unusually high.
- Management has a reputation for erratic behavior (e.g., abrupt changes in strategy, ill-conceived acquisitions) that makes future results difficult to forecast.

Analysts may be mistaken in these perceptions and may genuinely be undervaluing the stock. The low multiple is a conscious judgment, however, not a function of neglect. Even a small-capitalization company, which can more credibly claim that its stock is underfollowed by Wall Street, may have the multiple it deserves, notwithstanding that its competitors sport higher P/E ratios. It is appropriate to assign an above-average discount factor to the earnings of a company that competes against larger, better-capitalized firms. A small company may also be disadvantaged by a lack of depth in management and be at risk from concentration of its production in one or two plants.

Recognizing that qualitative factors may depress their multiples, companies often respond in kind, arguing that their low valuations are based on misperceptions. For example, a company in a notoriously cyclical industry may argue that it is an exception to the general pattern of its peer group. Thus, a manufacturer of automotive components may claim that its earnings are protected from fluctuations in new car sales by a heavy emphasis on selling replacement parts. Regardless of whether consumers are buying new cars, the reasoning goes, they must keep their existing vehicles in good repair. In fact, sales of replacement parts should rise if the existing fleet ages because fewer individuals buy new autos. Similarly, a building-materials manufacturer may claim to be cushioned against fluctuations in housing starts because of a strong emphasis in its product line on the remodeling and repair markets.

These arguments may contain a kernel of truth, but investors should not accept them on faith. Instead of latching on to the concept as a justification for immediately pronouncing the company's multiple too low, an analyst should independently establish whether an allegedly countercyclical business has in fact fit that description in past cycles. It is also important to determine whether the supposed source of earnings stability is truly large enough to offset a downturn of the magnitude that can realistically be expected in the other areas of the company's operations.

A good rule to remember is that a company can more easily create a new image than it can recast its operations. Analysts should be especially wary of companies that have tended to jump on the bandwagon of concepts associated with the hot stocks of the moment. When the Internet began revolutionizing industries in the 1990s, some relatively mundane companies projected more exciting images by doing little more than adding ".com" to their names. Investors were dazzled by the cost savings that could be realized with the help of new information management technology, but did not always pay close attention to the relative ability of companies to retain those savings rather than be forced by competition to pass them along to their customers. The day of reckoning arrived in March 2000, generally regarded as the bursting of the Dotcom Bubble. By no means, however, did that put an end to companies striving to present themselves as vehicles by which stock investors could express a view that came into vogue. For instance, when the COVID-19 pandemic struck in 2020, companies that could not credibly present a cutting-edge tech image instead sought to project themselves as "reopening plays" positioned to benefit especially well from resumption of normal economic activity.

Normalizing Earnings

Companies have strong incentives to obtain incremental increases in their earnings multiples, even at the cost of stretching the facts to the breaking point (or beyond). Accordingly, it is prudent to maintain a conservative

EXHIBIT 14.4 PPE Manufacturing
Corporation Earnings History Table

Year	Earnings per share
2016	$1.52
2017	1.63
2018	1.86
2019	2.04
2029	2.67 (estimated)

bias in calculating appropriate multiples. In addition to upping the discount rate (K) when any question arises about the quality of earnings, the analyst should normalize the earnings per share trend when its sustainability is doubtful.

Suppose, for example, that the fictitious PPE Manufacturing Corporation's earnings per share over the past five years are as shown in Exhibit 14.4. Customarily, PPE has commanded a multiple in line with the overall market, which is at present trading at 20 times estimated current-year earnings. By this logic, a price of 20 times $2.67, or approximately 53, seems warranted for PPE stock.

Exhibit 14.5 shows, however, that the current-year earnings estimate is well above PPE's historical trend line, making the sustainability of the current level somewhat suspect. As it turns out, the $2.67 estimate is bloated by special conditions that will probably not recur in the near future. Specifically, the customers for PPE's major product are stepping up their purchases

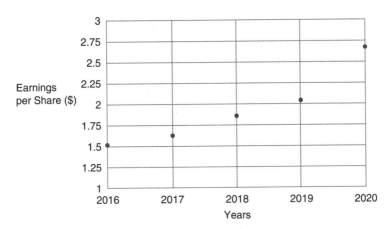

EXHIBIT 14.5 PPE Manufacturing Corporation Earnings History Graph.

in anticipation of an industrywide strike later in the year. A temporary shortage has resulted, causing buyers to raise their bids. With its plants running flat out (reducing unit costs to the minimum) and its price realizations climbing, PPE is enjoying profit margins that it has never achieved before – and probably never will again.

It hardly seems appropriate to boost PPE's valuation from 40.80 (20 times last year's earnings per share) to 53.40, a 31 percent increase, solely on the basis of an EPS hiccup that reflects no change in PPE's long-term earnings power. Accordingly, the analyst should normalize PPE's earnings by projecting the trend line established in preceding years. Exhibit 14.6 shows such a projection.

Least squares regression programs readily available on the Internet can be used to generate a graph like the one shown. The required x-value inputs are 1–5, corresponding to years 2016–2020 in this example. Corresponding to the x-values for those years are the y values, the EPS numbers shown in Exhibit 14.5. The regression program's output includes the formula for calculating the trendline EPS for each year:

$$y = 0.18x + 1.32$$

By this analysis, the trend-line solving for $x = 5$, we derive a current-year trend-line value of $2.22. Applying the market multiple of 20 produces an indicated stock price of 44.40. Some modest upward revision from this point may be warranted, for if nothing else, the company can reinvest its windfall profit in its business and generate a small, incremental earnings stream. By no means, though, should the company be evaluated on the basis of an earnings level that is not sustainable.

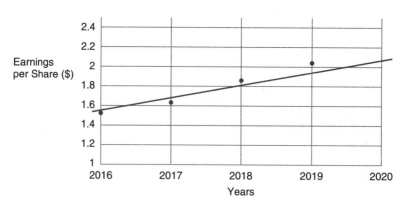

EXHIBIT 14.6 PPE Manufacturing Corporation Earnings Trend Sustainable Growth Rate.

Earnings sustainability is an issue not only in connection with unusual surges in earnings but also when it comes to determining whether a company's historical rate of growth in earnings per share is likely to continue. The answer is probably no if the growth has been fueled by anything other than additions to retained earnings per share.

Consider the following derivation of earnings per share:

$$\frac{\text{Asset}}{\text{turnover}} \times \frac{\text{Return on}}{\text{sales}} \times \text{Leverage} \times \frac{\text{Book value}}{\text{per share}} = \text{Earnings per share}$$

Or:

$$\frac{\text{Sales}}{\text{Assets}} \times \frac{\text{Net income}}{\text{Sales}} \times \frac{\text{Assets}}{\text{Net worth}} \times \frac{\text{Net worth}}{\text{Shares outstanding}}$$

$$= \frac{\text{Net income}}{\text{Shares outstanding}}$$

Earnings per share will not grow merely because sales increase. Any such increase will be canceled out in the preceding formula, given that the sales number appears in the denominator of return on sales as well as in the numerator of asset turnover. Only by an increase in one of the four terms on the left side of the equation, or by a reduction in the number of shares outstanding, will the product (earnings per share) rise. Aggressive management may boost asset turnover, but eventually the assets will reach the limits of their productive capacity. Return on sales, likewise, cannot expand indefinitely because too-fat margins will invite new competition. Leverage also reaches a limit because lenders will not continue advancing funds beyond a certain point as financial risk increases. This leaves only book value per share, which can rise unceasingly through additions to retained earnings, as a source of sustainable growth in earnings per share. As long as the amount of equity capital invested per share continues to rise, more income can be earned on that equity, and (as the reader can demonstrate by working through the preceding formula) earnings per share can increase.

A company's book value per share will not rise at all, however, if it distributes 100 percent of its earnings in dividends to shareholders. (This, by the way, is why an immediate increase in the dividend-payout ratio will not ordinarily cause a direct, proportionate rise in the stock price, as might appear to be the implication of the equation $P = D/K - g$.) Assuming the company can earn its customary return on equity on whatever profits it reinvests internally, raising its dividend-payout ratio reduces its growth in earnings per share (g). Such a move proves to be self-defeating, as both the numerator and the denominator (D and $K - g$, respectively) rise and P remains unchanged.

To achieve sustainable growth in earnings per share, then, a company must retain a portion of its earnings. The higher the portion retained, the more book value is accumulated per share and the higher can be the EPS growth rate. By this reasoning, the following formula is derived:

Sustainable growth rate = (Return on equity) × (Income reinvestment rate)

where: Income reinvestment rate = 1 − Dividend payout ratio

As mentioned, the one remaining way to increase earnings per share, after exhausting the possibilities already discussed, is to reduce the number of shares outstanding. Stock buybacks have valid corporate finance purposes. One is to prevent earnings dilution that would otherwise result from exercise of compensation-related stock options. In addition, returning capital to investors represents a better use of corporate funds than investing in projects that are unlikely to earn the corporation's cost of capital. Note, too, that from the shareholder's viewpoint, selling stock to the company – ideally at a higher price than the shareholder paid – is a more tax-efficient way of obtaining a cash distribution than receiving a dividend that will be taxed at ordinary income rates. More questionable is the use of a stock buyback as a short-run fix for a sagging share price, particularly if the repurchase seems timed to boost executive compensation that is tied to stock performance.

Between 1995 and 1999, International Business Machines spent $34.1 billion to repurchase shares, more than its $31.3 billion cumulative net income for the period. By reducing its shareholders' equity through stock purchases, IBM increased its **leverage** and, therefore, its financial risk. Moreover, the company intensified this effect by adding to its debt. Financial commentator James Grant quipped that if IBM continued to buy in shares, it would undergo a slow-motion leveraged buyout.[2] This approach to boosting EPS tends to be self-limiting, for as already noted, lenders refuse at some point to countenance increased indebtedness.

Analysts should note one subtlety in calculating the impact of stock repurchases on earnings per share. To the extent that the company funds the buybacks with idle cash, the increase in EPS is reduced by the amount of income formerly earned by parking the cash in short-term debt instruments. If a company has far more cash on its balance sheet than it can employ profitably in its operations, management cannot truly be accused of artificially inflating its per share income by buying in stock.

THE DU PONT FORMULA

The preceding discussion of sustainable growth introduced a formula that provided insight into earnings per share by disaggregating it into several simple financial ratios. Disaggregation can be applied in other beneficial ways in equity analysis, most notably in a technique known as the Du Pont Formula. (The idea is generally credited to Donaldson Brown, who developed the formula while at E. I. du Pont de Nemours, then applied it during the 1920s as vice president of finance at General Motors.) With the aid of the Du Pont Formula, the analyst can more readily perceive the sources of a firm's return on assets:

$$\text{Asset turnover} \times \text{Return on sales} = \text{Return on assets}$$

$$\frac{\text{Sales}}{\text{Assets}} \times \frac{\text{Income}}{\text{Sales}} = \frac{\text{Income}}{\text{Assets}}$$

This analysis can be expanded to ascertain the contribution of financial leverage to return on equity:

$$\text{Asset turnover} \times \text{Return on sales} \times \text{Financial Leverage} = \text{Return on Equity}$$

$$\frac{\text{Sales}}{\text{Assets}} \times \frac{\text{Income}}{\text{Sales}} \times \frac{\text{Assets}}{\text{Equity}} = \frac{\text{Income}}{\text{Equity}}$$

Note that "financial leverage" is not directly defined as a ratio of debt to assets or equity, as in most other contexts. Rather, it is the ratio of assets to equity. By definition, the excess of assets over equity consists of liabilities, not limited to debt. Conceptually, this version of financial leverage indicates how large an asset base is supported by the company's equity.

Like most ratio analysis, the Du Pont Formula is valuable not only for the questions it answers but also for the new ones it raises. If a company increases its return on assets by finding ways to reduce working capital without impairing competitiveness (thereby improving asset turnover), then it is likely to be able to perform at the higher level. On the other hand, cutting back on necessary capital expenditures will also have a positive effect – in the short run – on return on assets. Not only will the denominator decline in the asset turnover factor as a result of depreciation but also return on sales will rise as future depreciation charges are reduced by lower capital outlays in the current year. Underspending will eventually hurt competitiveness, and therefore the company's long-run return on assets, so analysts must probe to determine the true nature of shifts in these ratios.

A Du Pont analysis of the food processing industry (Exhibit 14.7) confirms the value of examining the components of return on equity. Based on ROE alone, for example, Campbell Soup (19.13 percent) and Pilgrim's Pride (18.05 percent) appear fairly similar. They achieved those numbers by very different methods, however. Campbell Soup turned over its assets only about half as frequently (0.62 times versus 1.29 times) and earned a lower margin on sales (2.60 percent versus 4.00 percent), resulting in a return on assets just one quarter as high (1.60 percent versus 6.42 percent). The higher return on

EXHIBIT 14.7 Du Pont Analysis of Food Processing Industry 2019 Results*

Company name	Asset turnover (x)	X	Return on sales (%)	=	Return on assets (%)	X	Financial leverage (x)	=	Return on equity
Campbell Soup Company	0.62		2.60%		1.60%		11.92		19.13%
Conagra Brands Inc.	0.43		7.11%		3.05%		3.01		9.19%
Darling Ingredients Inc.	0.63		9.29%		5.85%		2.08		12.18%
Flowers Foods, Inc.	1.30		3.99%		5.18%		2.52		13.02%
General Mills, Inc.	0.56		10.39%		5.82%		4.27		24.85%
Hershey Co.	0.98		14.40%		14.12%		4.68		66.11%
Hormel Foods Corp.	1.17		10.31%		12.07%		1.37		16.53%
Ingredion Inc.	1.03		6.65%		6.84%		2.22		15.18%
International Flavors & Fragrances	0.39		8.81%		3.41%		2.14		7.28%
J M Smucker Co.	0.47		6.53%		3.06%		2.10		6.42%
Kellogg Company	0.77		7.07%		5.47%		6.39		34.95%
Kraft Heinz Co.	0.25		7.75%		1.91%		1.97		3.75%
McCormick & Company, Incorporated	0.52		13.14%		6.78%		3.01		20.40%
Mondelez International Inc.	0.40		15.19%		6.09%		2.37		14.42%
Pilgrim's Pride Corporation	1.61		4.00%		6.42%		2.81		18.05%
Tyson Foods, Inc.	1.29		4.67%		6.01%		2.36		14.19%

*Calculations are subject to rounding errors.
Source: Stock Investor Pro and author calculations.

equity for Dean Foods is purely a consequence of using more than four times as much leverage (11.92 times versus 2.81 times).

Also noteworthy in Exhibit 14.7 is Hershey's extraordinarily high return on equity (66.11 percent). This ROE outlier results from the company's very low book value. Producers of branded food products typically derive their equity value primarily from consumer acceptance of their well-known brands, rather than the physical plants in which they produce their goods. Under generally accepted accounting principles (GAAP), the costs of these companies' product development and advertising, which create enduring value just as a factory or an oil well does, are expensed rather than capitalized. Unlike the accounting system, the financial markets recognize the economic value of brand names. Exhibit 14.8 shows that Hershey's book value is a mere 5.6 percent of its market value. The median **market-to-book** ratio within the group depicted is 3.86 times, underscoring how little investors regard accounting-based net worth as a measure of a company's economic value.

Branded food and consumer goods producers are not the only ones with value based largely on intellectual capital. Like those companies' expenditures aimed at building the economic value of their brands, the research and development outlays of technology and pharmaceutical companies are written off as incurred and consequently are assigned no asset value under GAAP. For these exemplars of the postindustrial economy, return on equity looks

EXHIBIT 14.8 Market Value to Book Value Ratios (2019) of Food Processing Industry

Company name	Market cap	Book value	Ratio
Hershey Co.	30,785.7	1,739.2	17.70
Campbell Soup Company	14,875.4	1,103.0	13.49
Kellogg Company	23,583.6	2,747.0	8.59
McCormick & Company, Incorporated	22,506.2	3,444.2	6.53
General Mills, Inc.	32,157.4	7,054.5	4.56
Hormel Foods Corp.	24,114.8	5,921.5	4.07
Flowers Foods, Inc.	4,600.3	1,263.4	3.64
Mondelez International Inc.	79,590.6	27,241.0	2.92
Tyson Foods, Inc.	33,047.5	13,950.0	2.37
Conagra Brands Inc.	15,202.6	7,384.6	2.06
J M Smucker Co.	11,777.1	7,970.5	1.48
Kraft Heinz Co.	39,230.7	51,623.0	0.76
Average			5.68

Source: Stock Investor Pro and author calculations.

less stratospheric when equity is viewed in terms of market capitalization rather than historical cost (see "Pros and Cons of a Market-Based Equity Figure" in Chapter 2).

VALUATION THROUGH RESTRUCTURING POTENTIAL

A subtler benefit of the Du Pont analysis is the insight it can provide into companies' potential for enhancing value through corporate restructuring. Whether initiated internally or imposed from outside, major revisions in operating and financial strategies can dramatically increase the price of a corporation's common shares. The analysis illustrated in Exhibit 14.7 helps to identify the type of restructuring that can unlock hidden value in a particular instance. Some companies have the potential to raise their share prices by utilizing their assets more efficiently, whereas others can increase their value by increasing their financial leverage.[3]

By way of background, corporate managers frequently find themselves at odds with stock market investors and speculators over issues of corporate policy. In general, managers prefer to maintain a certain amount of slack in their organizations, that is, a reserve capacity to deal with crises and opportunities. They tend to be less troubled than investors if their companies generate excess cash that remains on the balance sheet earning the modest returns available on low-risk, short-dated financial instruments. That cash may come in handy, they argue, if earnings and cash flow unexpectedly turn down or if an outstanding acquisition opportunity suddenly presents itself. Investors and speculators, in contrast, prefer to see the cash used to repurchase stock or returned to shareholders via dividends. Managers also tend to be more inclined than many shareholders are to believe that underperforming units can be rehabilitated. Their judgment is sometimes influenced by reluctance to admit that acquisitions in which they had a hand have worked out poorly.

Over the years, management–shareholder disputes over such operating- and financial-policy issues have featured a variety of tactics. As far back as 1927–1928, pioneer securities analyst Benjamin Graham waged a successful campaign to persuade the management of Northern Pipeline to liquidate certain assets that were not essential to the company's crude oil transportation business and distribute the proceeds to shareholders. Graham enlisted pivotal support for his effort from a major institutional holder, the Rockefeller Foundation. The outcome was unusual; both at the time and for many years afterward institutional investors generally sided with management. At most, institutions sold their shares if they became thoroughly dissatisfied with the way a company was being run.

Trying to use their stock ownership to spur change was not a widespread institutional practice. Therefore, management's main adversaries in battles over corporate governance were aggressive financial operators. During the 1950s, these swashbucklers attracted considerable attention by pushing for strategic redirection through proxy battles. Their modus operandi consisted of striving to obtain majority control of the board through the election of directors at the annual meeting of shareholders.

The 1970s brought a tactical shift to hostile takeovers, a type of transaction previously regarded as unsavory by the investment banks that acted as intermediaries in mergers and acquisitions. Hostile takeovers became especially prominent in the 1980s, fueled in part by the greatly increased availability of high-yield debt (informally referred to as *junk bond*) financing. High-yield bonds also financed scores of leveraged buyouts (LBOs), whose sponsors defended these controversial transactions in part by arguing that corporations could improve their long-run performance if they were taken private and thereby shielded from the public market's insatiable demand for short-run profit increases.

In the 1990s, institutional investors finally began to understand the influence they could wield in corporate boardrooms by virtue of their vast share holdings. Large institutional shareholders began to prod corporations to increase their share prices by such measures as streamlining operations, divesting unprofitable units, and using excess cash to repurchase shares. In some instances, where merely making their collective voice heard had no discernible effect, the institutions precipitated the ouster of senior management.

The shareholder activism of the 1990s flourished in an environment of comparatively high price-earnings ratios. Additionally, the period was characterized by a backlash against the previous decade's trend toward increased financial leverage. Conditions were not conducive to the sort of borrow-and-acquire transactions that drove much of the corporate restructurings of the 1980s.

Leveraged buyouts did not disappear, however. After the early-1990s wave of LBO bankruptcies, the buyout firms resumed their deal making. Under the banner of private equity, the LBO shops gained new prominence in the 2000s. It seemed clear that this category of alternative investments (those outside the traditional categories of public equities, bonds, and cash) had become a standard feature of the financial markets. A recurring boom-and-bust cycle in LBOs also appeared to have gotten ingrained into the investment landscape.

The prototypical leveraged buyout consists of gaining control of a company by buying its stock at a depressed price, then adding a large amount of debt to the capital structure. In the initial stage of the cycle, opportunities of this sort are abundant, because institutional investors are recovering from the previous bust. Absent the pressure of too many dollars chasing too few deals, it is feasible to extract value without creating undue bankruptcy risk, simply by increasing the ratio of debt to equity. The private equity firms emphasize the second factor in the modified Du Pont Formula – financial leverage.

In assessing a company's potential as a leveraged buyout candidate, private equity firms do not focus on traditional equity valuation techniques. Consider the fictitious Sitting Duck Corporation (Exhibit 14.9). Under conventional assumptions and given a prevailing earnings multiple of 17 on similar companies, Sitting Duck's equity will be valued at $1.122 billion, 2.2 times its book value of $502 million.

Leveraged buyout sponsors, however, would approach the valuation much differently. Their focus would not be on earnings, but on cash flow. After paying out approximately one-third of its earnings in dividends and more than offsetting depreciation through new expenditures for plant and equipment, Sitting Duck generated $31 million of cash in 2020. The incumbent management group used this cash to reduce an already

EXHIBIT 14.9   Sitting Duck Corporation

Year ended December 31, 2020
($000,000 omitted)

Balance sheet		Statement of cash flows	
Current assets	$ 611	Net income	$ 66
Property, plant, and equipment	418	Depreciation	38
Total assets	$1,029	Cash generated by operations	$ 104
Current liabilities	$ 360	Dividends	22
Long-term debt	167	Capital expenditures	41
Shareholder's equity	502	Increase in working capital	10
Total liabilities and equity	$1,000	Cash used in operations	73
		Net cash available	31
Income statement			
Sales	$1,253	Reduction of long-term debt	14
Cost of goods sold	1,048	Increase in cash and equivalents	$ 17
Selling, general, and adm. exp.	116		
Operating income	89		
Interest expense	5		
Pretax income	84		
Income taxes	18		
Net income	$ 66		

conservative (28 percent) year-end 2019 total-debt-to-total-capital ratio[4] and to add to the company's existing portfolio of marketable securities. To a buyout specialist, a more appropriate use of cash flow than reducing the total-debt-to-total-capital ratio to 25 percent would be to make it the basis for a takeover bid at the premium to Sitting Duck's prevailing stock price.

The arithmetic goes as follows: Assume lenders and bond buyers are currently willing to finance sound leveraged buyout projects that can demonstrate EBITDA coverage of 3.0 times. (The debt providers do not care about the company's book profits, but rather about its ability to repay debt. Cash generation is a key determinant of that ability.) Sitting Duck's operating income of $89 million, with $38 million of depreciation added back, produces EBITDA of $127 million. The amount of interest that $127 million can cover by 3.0 times is $42 million, an increase of $37 million over Sitting Duck's present $5 million interest expense. Assuming a blended borrowing cost of 6 percent on the LBO financing, a raider can load $700 million onto Sitting Duck, up from the present $167 million balance. (This example assumes that change-of-control covenants in Sitting Duck's existing debt require it to be redeemed in conjunction with the LBO.) If prevailing lending standards require equity of 50 percent in the transaction, the raider must put up an additional $700 million, for a total capitalization of $1.400 billion. By this arithmetic, the takeover artist can pay a premium of 25 percent ($1.400 billion ÷ $1.122 billion = 1.25) over Sitting Duck's present market capitalization. The purchase price equates to a multiple of 21 times earnings, rather than the 17 times figure currently assigned by the market. The LBO sponsor got to this number, however, through a measure of cash flow, rather than earnings. The EBITDA multiple of the bid is 11 times, close to the average level paid in large LBOs in 2020, as reported by S&P Global Markets Intelligence.[5] (As explained in Chapter 8, EBITDA is by no means the *best* measure of cash flow, but it can be fairly described as the standard in leveraged finance circles.)

Note that Sitting Duck's enlarged debt load greatly increases its credit risk. Prior to the LBO, its EBITDA covered interest expense by 25.4 times. By that ratio, the company would have fit the profile of a company rated AA, according to data presented in Exhibit 13.7 of the preceding chapter. The projected 3.0 times EBITDA/Interest ratio makes it look more like a B credit.

Stepping back from these calculations, one is bound to wonder whether the LBO sponsor can truly expect to earn a high return on investment after paying 25 percent above the prevailing price for Sitting Duck's shares. Many such transactions do prove highly profitable, with the new owners eventually exiting through sale of the company or an **initial public offering,** that is, returning the company to the public market. In some cases, the buyout sponsor takes out substantial dividends before exiting, adding to its profits. Although private equity firms downplay the role of timing in their success, buying companies when equity market valuations are low and selling when they are high is a winning formula. The only problem is that peaks in LBO activity – and EBITDA multiples – tend to be followed by recessions and bear markets in stocks. Late-cycle deals consequently become plagued by depressed earnings, making it difficult to cover the company's vastly increased interest charges at a time when exiting through an IPO is not feasible.

Rather than rely entirely on their ability to catch the highs and lows in the equity market, private equity firms try to enhance their probability of success by the following means:

1. *Profit Margin Improvement.* A leveraged buyout can bring about improved profitability for either of two reasons. First, a change in ownership results in a fresh look at the company's operations. The incoming managers may revise the company's model in a profit-enhancing way or institute best practices that increase operational efficiency. In addition, the newcomers may have less sentimental attachment to venerable product lines that no longer achieve hurdle rates of return. They can also more easily implement emotionally difficult steps to enhance profit margins, such as reducing the work force and outsourcing production. Second, management may obtain a significantly enlarged stake in the firm's success as the result of a buyout. With more skin in the game, managers may become less concerned about maintaining slack in their operations and more eager to squeeze every possible dollar of profit out of their company's assets. With an enhanced opportunity to participate in the benefits, managers may crack down on unnecessary costs that they formerly tolerated in the name of maintaining cordial relations with employees and suppliers. They may also pursue high-risk/high-potential-return projects more aggressively than in the past, particularly since much of the risk has been shifted to lenders. Regardless of how it comes about, however, improvement in profit margins means higher EBITDA. That, in turn, leads to a higher valuation and generates a profit for the LBO's equity investors.

   Analysts must watch out, however, for improvements in reported profit margins that represent nothing more than reduced investment in the company's fitness for the long run. Following an LBO, a company can report an immediate improvement in earnings by cutting back expenditures on advertising and research and development. Even though the accounting rules do not permit these outlays to be capitalized, they create benefits in future periods. Sharply reducing such expenditures, or delaying essential capital projects to conserve cash, can impair a company's future competitiveness, rendering the increase in current-period earnings illusory. Today's profit improvement can be a precursor of tomorrow's bankruptcy by a company that has economized its way to an uncompetitive state.

Regrettably, the income statement may provide too little detail to determine whether specific kinds of investment spending have been curtailed. Analysts must therefore query industry sources for evidence regarding the adequacy of the company's reinvestment in its business. If the company's customers report a drop in the quality of service following a leveraged buyout, it may indicate that important sales support functions have been eviscerated. Earnings may rise in the short run but soon begin to suffer as customers switch to other providers.

2. *Asset Sales*. As a function of the stock market's primary focus on earnings, a company's market capitalization may be far less than the aggregate value of its assets. For example, a subsidiary that contributes little to net income but generates substantial cash flow from depreciation has a potentially large value in the private market. In that realm, the unit would be priced on a multiple of EBITDA. Alternatively, a subsidiary might be unprofitable only because its scale is insufficient. A competitor might be willing to buy the unit and consolidate it with its own operations. The result would be higher combined earnings than the two operations were able to generate independently. An LBO sponsor who spies this sort of opportunity within a company may invest a small amount of equity and borrow the greater part of the purchase price, then liquidate the low-net-income operations to repay the borrowings. If carried out as planned, the asset sales will leave the acquirer debt-free and in possession of the remainder of the company, that is, the operations that previously contributed almost all of the net income. In the P/E-multiple-oriented stock market, that portion of the company will be worth as much as the entire company was previously. The LBO sponsor may then cash out by taking the company public again. After all the dust has settled, the sponsor should have cleared more than enough to cover the premium paid to original shareholders who sold into the buyout.

Unrealized earnings potential and EBITDA multiples are by no means the only valuation factors that come into play in corporate governance controversies. Proponents of policy changes in pursuit of enhanced shareholder value sometimes focus on the values of specific assets identified in the financial statements. For example, oil companies disclose the size of their reserves in their annual reports. Because energy companies frequently buy and sell reserves, and because the prices of larger transactions are widely reported, current market valuations are always readily at hand. If recent sales of reserves in the ground have occurred at prices that equate to $60 a barrel, then a company with 50 million barrels of reserves could theoretically liquidate those assets for $3 billion.[6] It may be that the sum of $3 billion and a P/E-multiple-based price for the company's refining, marketing, and transportation assets substantially exceeds the company's current market capitalization. If so, the so-called unrecognized value of the oil reserves can be the basis of an alternative method of evaluating the company's stock.

Would-be corporate restructurers also seek unrecognized value in other types of minerals, real estate, and long-term investments unrelated to a company's core business. Methods of realizing the value of such an asset include:

- Selling the asset for cash.
- Placing it in a separate subsidiary, then taking a portion of the subsidiary public to establish a market value for the company's residual interest.
- Placing the asset in a master limited partnership, interests in which are distributed to shareholders.

The key message to take away from this overview of- valuation via restructuring potential is that a focus on price-earnings multiples, the best-known form of fundamental analysis, is not the investor's sole alternative to relying on technicians' stock charts. There are in fact several approaches to fundamental analysis. A solid understanding of financial statements is essential to all of them, even though factors outside the financial statements also play a role in fundamental valuation.

ADVANCED EQUITY ANALYSIS

Using financial statements to value stocks is a vast topic that extends well beyond the basic concepts presented in this chapter. Numerous practitioners have developed sophisticated techniques to address such issues as the growing disconnect between companies' book values and the economic values of their net assets. Just a sampling of advanced approaches to equity analysis follows. The Bibliography provides references for further reading on the subject.

Credit Suisse's HOLT team argues that return on equity (ROE) is an unreliable measure of profitability, on several grounds. For one thing, as explained previously, companies are required under GAAP to write off expenditures on such items as marketing, research, and web services, rather than capitalize them as intangible assets. This is despite the fact that in today's economy, these outlays create enduring, quantifiable economic value no less than manufacturing companies' expenditures on factory construction. A **New Economy** company may consequently record an ROE below the going cost of equity capital for other, similar companies. According to traditional financial theory, that means its stock should trade at a discount to its book value per share. In reality, one routinely observes shares of such companies priced at substantial premiums to book value. This does not indicate that investors have mispriced a stock, but rather that they recognize value creation that GAAP dismisses.

A further shortcoming of ROE is its sensitivity to **financial leverage**. A debt-free company with ROE greater than its after-tax cost of debt can increase its ROE by adding debt to its capital structure. Adding debt and the associated interest expense, however, increases the company's fixed costs and therefore the volatility of its earnings. Investors assign less value to highly volatile earnings than to more stable earnings. In the marketplace, a given level of ROE achieved through aggressive leverage is not considered equivalent to the same level of ROE achieved with a low debt-to-capital ratio.

A way to bring equity analysis into line with market realities, while also improving comparability among companies, is to deemphasize ROE in favor of Return on Invested Capital (ROIC):

$$\text{ROIC} = \frac{\text{Net Income} + \text{Net Interest Paid} \times (1 - T_c)}{\text{Invested Capital}}$$

where:

T_c = The cash tax rate, i.e., Current Tax Expense
÷ Net Income Before Taxes

Invested Capital = Equity + Long-Term Debt
+ Short-Term Debt − Excess Cash

The numerator of the fraction shown here is also referred to as Net Operating Profit After Tax (NOPAT).

ROIC measures the return earned by all providers of capital and is unaffected by use of leverage. It has a weakness, however, in being influenced by the age of the company's assets. A company can boost its ROIC just by spending too little to keep its plant and equipment up to date.

The HOLT analysts therefore go further to obtain the best possible profitability measure. They undertake complex calculations to derive a company's Cash Flow Return on Investment (CFROI). This metric is defined as the weighted-average single-period **internal rate of return** on all of the firm's projects.

Turning to another departure from classic equity analysis, an influential 2020 article[7] by Baruch Lev and Anup Srivastava documented a decline over time in the success of **value investing** based on picking stocks with low market-to-book ratios. The two finance professors linked that decline to growing corporate investment in intangibles such as R&D, information technology, brand development, and human resources. Under GAAP, these investments are expensed, rather than capitalized. Therefore, they do not become part of companies' book value, unlike investment in tangibles such as plant and equipment. In economic terms, Lev and Srivastava contended, companies' book values became widely understated.

Up until the 1980s, tangibles such as plant and equipment dominated U.S. corporations' investment outlays. By the time Lev and Srivastava conducted their research, investment in intangibles were running twice the level of investment in tangibles. Equity investors in aggregate ascribed value to the intangibles that were absent from balance sheets, with the result that companies' market-to-book ratios rose relative to ratios observed in previous decades. Value investors who clung to stock selection criteria of earlier times avoided the shares of many companies that were doing an excellent job of creating bona fide economic value. In aggregate, consequently, money managers specializing in value investing lost the performance edge that their financial formulas had previously generated.

Lev and Srivastava asked whether the value investing strategy would fare better if market-to-book ratios were calculated by capitalizing the investments in intangibles that GAAP required companies to write off as incurred. Building on accounting methods developed in previous research, they capitalized companies' R&D expenditures, as well as a portion of selling, general, and administrative expense associated with such items as brands, information technology, business processes, and human resources. The authors then ranked companies by market-to-book ratio.

Next, they tested a value-style strategy of buying the bottom-ranked 30 percent ("value stocks") and shorting the top-ranked 30 percent ("glamour stocks"), first based on conventional GAAP accounting and then based on their revised book values. Many stocks assigned to the glamour category by conventional accounting qualified as value stocks when Lev and Srivastava's alternative accounting boosted their book values. In 34 out of the 39 years in the study's observation period, a value investing strategy based on bringing GAAP-discarded intangibles onto the balance sheet beat the strategy based on conventional accounting. The disparities widened after the 1970s, as companies' spending shifted increasingly toward intangibles. Lev and Srivastava also demonstrated superior results with a value-style strategy employing price-earnings ratios based on adding back to earnings the expenditures that create intangible assets. These findings underscore the loosening connection between data reported in financial statements and the values assigned by the market.

The HOLT and Lev–Srivastava analyses cannot be replicated as easily as the ratios described earlier in this chapter can be calculated. Those approaches do, however, point in helpful directions for equity investors hoping to prosper through rigorous financial statement analysis. While willing to venture outside the GAAP framework, HOLT and Lev–Srivastava do not rely on dubious "pro forma" or "adjusted" earnings that are simply attempts to portray companies' results in the most favorable light possible. These and other paths on the frontier of equity research are well worth exploration by analysts who have mastered the core principles presented in this chapter.

CONCLUSION

As noted at the outset of this chapter, valuations derived from financial statements represent only a portion of the analyses being conducted by millions of stock buyers and sellers during each trading session. Indeed, the split-second decision-making of traders on the exchange floors can scarcely be described as analysis of any kind. Rather, it amounts to a highly intuitive response to momentary shifts in the balance of supply and demand.

For the investor who takes a longer view, however, financial statement analysis provides an invaluable reference point for valuation. A stock may temporarily soar or plummet in frenzied reaction to a development of little ultimate consequence. Eventually, however, rationality usually reasserts itself. The share price then returns to a level that is justifiable on the basis of the company's long-range capacity to generate earnings and cash. Focusing not only on P/E, EBITDA, and market-to-book multiples, but also on breakup values, is consistent with this thesis. Equity analysts can delve more deeply into valuation by exploring refined techniques that improve companies' comparability and capture value creation unrecognized by GAAP. By studying the company's historical financial statements to forecast its future results, the analyst can derive an intrinsic value for a stock that is unaffected by the market's transitory moods.

CHAPTER 1 The Adversarial Nature of Financial Reporting

1. Howard M. Schilit, *Financial Shenanigans: How to Detect Accounting Gimmicks and Fraud in Financial Reports* (New York: McGraw Hill, 1993), 153.
2. Although this book focuses on for-profit companies, nonprofit companies and governmental entities also produce financial statements. Readers should not presume that those entities invariably eschew reporting trickery. Like their for-profit counterparts, nonprofit organizations seek to raise capital. They have incentives to portray their financial positions in as favorable a light as possible, when trying to borrow or to demonstrate their financial viability to providers of grants. On the other hand, nonprofits sometimes strive to make themselves appear less flush than they really are, to impress on donors the urgency of their appeal for funds. Governmental units sometimes resort to disingenuous reporting to avoid political fallout from the consequences of unsound fiscal policies. Anti-capitalist ideologues cannot truthfully contend that the profit motive alone leads to devious financial reporting.
3. "Mattel Completes Internal Investigation of Whistleblower Letter and Announces Remedial Actions." *Business Wire,* October 20, 2019.
4. Jean Eaglesham and Paul Ziobro, "Mattel, Auditor Hid Accounting Issues," *Wall Street Journal*, November 17, 2019, B1, B2.
5. "Fall Guy" – Josh Bramwell, "PwC Probably Did Celebrate When It Helped Mattel Cover Up an Accounting Error," *GoingConcern.com*, November 7, 2019.
6. Randall Smith, Steven Lipin, and Amal Kumar Naj, "Managing Profits: How General Electric Damps Fluctuations in Its Annual Earnings," *Wall Street Journal*, November 3, 1994, A1, A6.
7. In financial statements prepared for tax purposes, the corporation minimizes its taxable income by writing off fixed assets over the shortest allowable period. This is both a lawful and a customary practice. Companies are permitted to prepare separate sets of accounts for tax and financial reporting purposes. In the latter, they can make choices on discretionary accounting items that result in lower profits than shown in the former.
8. Senior executives typically own stock in their corporations, so to some extent they penalize their wealth by undercutting quality of earnings. Unless their stock holdings are very large, however, the direct benefits of increased bonuses more than fully offset the impact of reduced valuations on their shares.

9. Richard Zeckhauser, Jayendu Patel, Francois Degeorge, and John Pratt, "Reported and Predicted Earnings: An Empirical Investigation Using Prospect Theory." Project for David Dreman Foundation (1994).

10. Ibid.

11. Ciaral Linnane, "U.S. Companies Went Right Back to Heavy Use of Nonstandard Accounting Metrics During the Pandemic," *MarketWatch*, April 28, 2021.

12. Avi Salzman, "Boston Beer Loses Its Edge," *barrons.com*, February 25, 2017.

13. Ibid.

14. Heather Haddden and Annie Gasparro, "Whole Foods Wanted to Be More Than a Supermarket, and Therein Lies the Problem," *wsj.com*, April 12, 2017.

15. Ibid.

16. As December 31, 1999, approached, economic pundits warned of massive dislocations arising from a programming quirk whereby many computer systems would interpret the following date to be January 1, 1900. Many corporations attributed sluggish sales during the latter part of 1999 to customers' unwillingness to make major commitments in advance of impending chaos, fears of which proved to be greatly overstated.

17. See, for example, Michael C. Jensen and William H. Meckling, "Theory of the Firm: Managerial Behavior, Agency Costs and Ownership Structure," *Journal of Financial Economics* 3 (1976), 305–360.

CHAPTER 2   The Balance Sheet

1. For the record, the accounting profession defines *assets* as "probable future economic benefits obtained or controlled by a particular entity as a result of past transactions or events" (Statement of Financial Accounting Concepts No. 6, Financial Accounting Standards Board, Stamford, Connecticut, December 1985, 10).

2. Barry Libert and Barbara Sayre Casey, "Accounting for Value" (letter to editor), *Barron's*, December 11, 2000, 65.

3. Jonathan R. Laing, "The New Math: Why an Accounting Guru Wants to Shake Up Some Basic Tenets of His Profession," *Barron's*, November 20, 2000, 31–36.

4. Taylor Kuykendall, "U.S. Coal Companies Reduced Estimated Asset Value by at Least $1.80B in Q2," S&P Global Market Intelligence, September 10, 2020.

5. Henny Sender and Aline van Duyn, "Lack of Consistency in Lehman's Asset Valuations," *Financial Times*, March 15, 2010, 17.

6. Jonathan Ford, "Goodwill Witchcraft Led to GE's Monster $17bn Writedown," *Financial Times*, October 8, 2018, 4.

7. "Caterpillar Takes Action to Address Accounting Misconduct at Siwei, its Recently Acquired Company; Misconduct Results in a Fourth Quarter Non-Cash Charge of Approximately $580 Million and the Removal of Several Siwei Senior Managers," Bloomberg News (January 18, 2013). Source: Caterpillar Inc

8. Duncan Mavin, "Caterpillar's Wayward Path in China," *Wall Street Journal* (January 29, 2013), C10.

9. https://www.presciencepoint.com/wp-content/uploads/2018/04/Celadon-Group-CGI.pdf),

10. Richard H. Thaler, ed., *Advances in Behavioral Finance* (New York: Russell Sage Foundation, 1993).

CHAPTER 3 The Income Statement

1. Jack Hough, "Dining Out Is Back In. Servers Are Harder To Get in the Door," *Barron's* (May 24, 2021), 11.

2. There are a few exceptions to this generalization. Tax collectors, for example, examine a company's income statement to determine its tax liability. For them, next year is irrelevant because they can assess a tax only on what has already been earned.

3. Financial Accounting Standards: Original Pronouncements, as of June 1, 1980, Financial Accounting Standards Board, Stamford, Connecticut, 371–373. The APB opinion covering the issue became effective on October 1, 1973.

4. Emily Nelson, "P&G's One-Time Charges Make Critics Look Twice at Earnings," *Wall Street Journal*, April 4, 2001, C1–C2.

CHAPTER 4 The Statement of Cash Flows

1. Exhibit 4.2 and the accompanying narrative simplify the concept of cash flow to introduce it to the reader. Only the two major sources of cash, net income and depreciation, appear here, leaving to subsequent exhibits refinements such as deferred taxes, which arise from timing differences between the recognition and payment of taxes. Similarly, the uses of cash exclude a working capital factor, which is discussed in connection with Exhibit 4.9.

2. For a detailed rationale for the use of the EBITDA multiple to evaluate a firm, see "Valuation through Restructuring Potential" in Chapter 14. See also Chapter 8, "The Applications and Limitations of EBITDA."

3. Michael C. Jensen, "The Free Cash Flow Theory of Takeovers: A Financial Perspective on Mergers and Acquisitions and the Economy," in *The Merger Boom: Proceedings of a Conference*, ed. Lynn E. Browne and Eric S. Rosengren (Boston: Federal Reserve Bank of Boston, 1987), 102–137. This article provides the basis for the synopsis of the free cash flow argument described here, as well as the definition quoted.

4. Ibid.

CHAPTER 5 What Is Profit?

1. Jonathan Ford, "Accounting Has Become the Opposite of Useful for Users," *Financial Times*, March 11, 2019, 6.

2. Ibid.

3. Nikou Asgari, "Analysts Sceptical as 'Earnings before Coronavirus' Flatter Company Books," *Financial Times*, May 14, 2020, 1.

4. John Francis Fowler Jr., *Introduction to Wall Street: A Practical Guide Book for the Investor or Speculator* (New York: Harper & Brothers, 1930), 76.

5. This was probably even truer in 1930 than today, for it was only with the passage of the Securities Act of 1933 that it became a requirement for most U.S. public companies to have their financial statements audited by independent public accountants. Even then, financial reporting rules remained fairly loose while the federal government and accounting profession wrestled with the question of how best to establish standards.

CHAPTER 6   Revenue Recognition

1. "Gowex Exceeds Its Turnover Forecast and Reaches 182.8 Million Euros in 2013," Gowex via Globenewswire, March 20, 2014.

2. "Let's Gowex: A Pescanovan Charade," Gotham City Research LLC, July 1, 2014. https://ep00.epimg.net/descargables/2014/07/01/3728e3d1ea9446f8d3d1 3cad5ab7813d.pdf The report's title alludes to the 2013 collapse of Pescanova following the Spanish frozen fish producer's revelation of debts three times as great as than its audited statements had shown.

3. Tobias Buck, "Gowex Declares Bankruptcy and Admits Accounts Were Falsified," *Financial Times*, July 7, 2014, 15.

4. James Ludden, "Gowex Looking at Possible Legal Action Against Gotham, CEO Says," Bloomberg, July 1, 2014.

5. Messod D. Beneish, "The Detection of Earnings Manipulation," *Financial Analysts Journal*, September/October 1999, January 2004, 24–36.

6. Gardiner Harris, "Bristol-Myers Says Accounting Was 'Inappropriate,' Inflated Sales," *Wall Street Journal,* March 11, 2003, A2, A8.

7. Gardiner Harris, "At Bristol-Myers, Ex-Executives Tell of Numbers Games," *Wall Street Journal,* December 12, 2002, A1, A13.

8. Stephanie Saul, "Fraud Case Filed against Ex-Officers of Bristol," *New York Times,* June 16, 2005, C1, C17.

9. Steven C. Tighe, *Bristol-Myers: Analysis Reveals Excess Inventory in the Trade,* Merrill Lynch & Co., March 25, 2002.

10. In this analysis, it is essential to carry out the full growth-rate calculations, rather than simply add the percentage increases for price and units, then subtract the reported revenue gain. To illustrate, suppose a manufacturer sells 100 units at $5.00 each for revenue of $500 in Year 1. In Year 2, unit sales grow by 12 percent, and the price increases by 8 percent. Revenue increases to 112 units @ $5.40 = $604.80. That represents a revenue increase of $604.8 ÷ $500 = 20.96 percent. In round terms, the revenue increase is 21 percent, rather than the sum of the percentage volume and price increases, that is, 12 percent + 8 percent = 20 percent.

11. Warren St. John, "With Games of Havoc, Men Will Be Boys," *New York Times,* May 12, 2002, Section 9, pp. 1, 4.

12. Gene Marcial, "Take-Two Gets a Second Chance," *BusinessWeek Online,* December 19, 2001.

13. Ibid.
14. Greg Chang, "Take-Two Drops on U.S. SEC's Accounting Investigation," *Bloomberg News,* February 15, 2002.
15. Ibid.
16. U.S. Securities and Exchange Commission Release No. 19260, June 9, 2005.
17. The controversy surrounding M/A-Com's adoption of the sell-in method is discussed in Vito J. Racanelli, "M/A-Com's Accounting Issue," *barrons.com,* June 15, 2015.
18. Chip Cummins, "Wal-Mart's Net Income Increases 28%, but Accounting Change Worries Investors," *Wall Street Journal,* August 10, 2000, A6.
19. Heather Landy, "Wal-Mart 2nd-Quarter Net to Miss Forecasts," *Bloomberg,* August 9, 2000.
20. Linda Sandler, "Bally Total Fitness's Accounting Procedures Are Getting Some Skeptical Investors Exercised," *Wall Street Journal,* August 26, 1998, C2.
21. Eric Matejevich, "Bally Total Fitness: Flexing Its Muscles; Buy Reiterated," *Merrill Lynch HYLights,* September 2, 1999, 18–24.
22. Sandler, "Bally," C2.
23. "BJ's Wholesale Club, Inc. Says Membership Income Accounting Complies with All Applicable Standards," *Business Wire,* September 3, 1998.
24. Elizabeth MacDonald, Laura Johannes, and Emily Nelson, "Discount-Club Retailers Shift Accounting," *Wall Street Journal,* October 28, 1998, B4.
25. "MemberWorks Reports Record Fiscal 2000 Fourth Quarter Financial Results," *Business Wire,* July 28, 2000.
26. Elizabeth MacDonald, "Are Those Revenues for Real?" *Forbes,* May 29, 2000, 108–110. The author credits Bear Stearns & Co. with identifying 120 companies that announced they had changed or would change their revenue recognition policies in recent months.
27. "Sequoia, Ex-Officials Settle SEC Charges of Inflating Results," *Wall Street Journal,* February 17, 1996, B6.
28. *SEC v. Scott A. Livengood, John W. Tate, and Randy S. Casstevens*, SEC Complaint against Scott A. Livengood, John W. Tate, and Randy S. Casstevens, May 4, 2009.
29. Mark Maremont and Rick Brooks, "Krispy Kreme Franchise Buybacks May Spur New Concerns," *Wall Street Journal,* May 25, 2004, C4–C5.
30. Gretchen Morgenson, "Did Someone Say Doughnuts? Yes. The S.E.C." *New York Times,* July 30, 2004, C1, C6.
31. Mark Maremont and Rick Brooks, "Krispy Kreme Operating Chief to Join Restoration Hardware," *Wall Street Journal,* August 17, 2004, B3.
32. Lauren R. Rublin, "Full of Holes," *Barron's,* September 13, 2004, 16.
33. Melanie Warner, "Report Details Some Failures That Hurt Krispy Kreme," *New York Times,* August 11, 2005, C7.
34. Alex Berenson and Lowell Bergman, "Under Cheney, Halliburton Altered Policy on Accounting," *New York Times,* May 22, 2002, C1–C2.
35. Ibid., C2.
36. *SEC Charges Halliburton and Two Former Officers for Failure to Disclose a 1998 Change in Accounting Practice*, Securities and Exchange Commission Press Release, August 3, 2004.

37. Melody Peterson, "S.E.C. Charges Grace and 6 Former Executives with Fraud," *New York Times,* December 23, 1998, C1, C6.
38. Ann Davis, "SEC Claims Profit 'Management' by Grace," *Wall Street Journal,* April 7, 1999, C1, C20.
39. Ibid., C20.
40. Ibid.
41. Peter Ramjug, "W. R. Grace Settles SEC Income Manipulation Case," *Reuters,* June 30, 1999.
42. Michael C. Jensen, "Why Pay People to Lie?" *Wall Street Journal,* January 8, 2001, A32.
43. Elizabeth MacDonald and Daniel Kruger, "Aiding and Abetting," *Forbes,* April 2, 2001, 82–84.
44. Ibid., 84.
45. Davis, "SEC Claims," C1.
46. "Cincinnati Milacron Overstated Earnings by $300,000 for Half," *Wall Street Journal,* August 4, 1993, C9.
47. "Net of First Financial Management Corp. Restated for 3 Periods," *Wall Street Journal,* December 30, 1991, B7.
48. Shawn Young and Dennis K. Berman, "SEC Staff Recommends Penalty against Lucent of $25 Million," *Wall Street Journal,* March 18, 2004, B5.
49. Carol J. Loomis, "The Whistleblower and the CEO," Fortune, July 7, 2003, 88–96.

CHAPTER 7   Expense Recognition

1. John Jannarone, "Hidden Flaw in P&G's Diamond Deal," *Wall Street Journal,* September 27, 2011.
2. Bill Alpert, "Getting to the Nut of the Problem," *Barron's Online,* November 5, 2011.
3. *Bloomberg News,* "Nortel to Restate Results of Past Years," October 23, 2003.
4. Ian Austen, "Nortel Faces Credibility Questions in New Audit," *New York Times,* March 22, 2004, C1–C6.
5. Ibid., C6.
6. Ibid.
7. Ibid.
8. Mark Heinzl, "Nortel's Books Face SEC Investigation," *Wall Street Journal,* April 6, 2004, A3, A6.
9. *Financial Times,* "Wrong Number, Approximately," August 30, 2004, 10.
10. Mark Heinzl, "Nortel Again Delays Financial Report," *Wall Street Journal,* November 12, 2004, A3, A8.
11. Ken Brown and Mark Heinzl, "Nortel Board Finds Accounting Tricks behind '03 Profits," *Wall Street Journal,* July 2, 2004, A1, A8.
12. This account draws on Floyd Norris, "Now G.M. Has Woes on Audits," *New York Times,* March 18, 2006, C1, C4.
13. Joseph B. White and Lee Hawkins Jr., "GM Will Restate Results for 2001 in Latest Stumble," *Wall Street Journal,* November 10, 2005, A1, A13.
14. Ibid., A13.

15. Floyd Norris, "The World Is Volatile, So Why Should Earnings Show Smooth Gains?" *New York Times,* November 28, 2003, C1.
16. Alex Berenson, "Report Says Freddie Mac Misled Investors," *New York Times,* July 24, 2003, C1–C2.

CHAPTER 8   The Applications and Limitations of EBITDA

1. Failures by leveraged buyouts largely accounted for the escalation in the default rate on speculative grade bond issuers, as reported by Moody's Investors Service, from 3.5 percent in 1988 to a peak of 10.5 percent in 1991.
2. William H. Beaver, "Financial Ratios as Predictors of Failure," *Journal of Accounting Research* (Supplement 1966), 71–111.
3. The development of this tradition is more fully explored in Martin S. Fridson, "EBITDA Is Not King," *Journal of Financial Statement Analysis* (Spring 1998), 59–62.
4. Edward I. Altman, "Financial Ratios, Discriminant Analysis, and the Prediction of Corporate Bankruptcy," *Journal of Finance* (September 1968), 589–609.
5. Richard Bernstein, "An Analysis of Low EV/EBITDA," Merrill Lynch & Co., September 4, 2001.

CHAPTER 9   The Reliability of Disclosure and Audits

1. Patricia Kowsmann, Paul J. Davies, and Juliet Chung, "Wirecard's Fall Puts Spotlight on Its Auditor," *Wall Street Journal,* June 29, 2020, B5.
2. Brooke Masters, "Auditors Keep Falling into the Same Trap," *Financial Times,* July 1, 2020, p. 15.
3. Anna Maria Andriotis, Paul J. Davies, and Juliet Chung, "Wirecard Was Fined by Visa, Mastercard," *Wall Street Journal,* July 28, 2020, B1, B10.
4. Robbie Whelan, Craig Karmin, and Jean Eaglesham, "Cover-Up Jolts Real-Estate Empire," *Wall Street Journal,* October 30, 2014, C10–C11.
5. Richard T. McGuire, "Marcato Sends Letter to American Realty Capital Properties," PRNewswire, June 3, 2014.
6. Mark Maurer, "SEC Probes Firms' EPS Manipulation," *Wall Street Journal,* October 11, 2021, B6.
7. Malenko, Nadya and Grundfest, Joseph A., and Shen, Yao, "Quadrophobia: Strategic Rounding of EPS Data," (August 9, 2020). Rock Center for Corporate Governance at Stanford University Working Paper No. 65.
8. Cassell Bryan-Low, "Accounting Firms Earn More from Consulting," *Wall Street Journal,* April 16, 2003, C9.
9. Ibid.
10. This discussion draws extensively on Jonathan Weil, "Behind Wave of Corporate Fraud: A Change in How Auditors Work," *Wall Street Journal,* March 25, 2004, A1, A14.
11. Ibid., A14.

12. This discussion draws extensively on Mark Maremont and Deborah Solomon, "Behind SEC's Failings: Caution, Tight Budget, '90s Exuberance," *Wall Street Journal*, December 24, 2003, A1, A5.

13. Ibid., A5.

14. Jeanne Patterson and Nell Minow, "Blame Directors for Accounting Practices, Managing Earnings," *Pensions & Investments*, May 28, 2001, 12.

CHAPTER 10   Mergers-and-Acquisitions Accounting

1. Abraham J. Briloff, "Pooling and Fooling," *Barron's*, October 23, 2000, 26.

2. Elizabeth MacDonald, "Merger-Accounting Method Under Fire," *Wall Street Journal*, April 15, 1997, A4.

3. John Dizard, "When Accountants Go Goodwill Hunting," *Financial Times*, May 30, 2003, 25.

4. Ciara Linnane, Francine McKenna, and Katie Marriner, "SEC May Be Set to Crack Down on Companies that Adjust Revenue." *MarketWatch*, November 26, 2019.

5. For a good discussion of this point, see Jonathan Ford, "Goodwill Witchcraft Led to GE's monster $17 billion write-down," *Financial Times*, October 8, 2018. Note that the $17 billion figure refers to the portion of the GE write-down announced on October 1, 2018, that was specifically related to goodwill created in the acquisition of Alstom's energy businesses.

6. Ed Crooks, "GE's $23bn Hit Reveals Goodwill Turned Bad," *Financial Times*, October 5, 2018, 16.

7. Ben Worthen, Paul Sonne, and Justin Scheck, "Long Before H-P Deal, Autonomy's Red Flags," *Wall Street Journal*, November 27, 2012, A1, A14.

8. "Delivering Alpha," CNBC.com, November 21, 2012.

9. John Carney, "How Jim Chanos Spotted the HP Scandal," CNBC.com, November 20, 2012.

10. Stanley Marrical, Plaintiff. *Complaint filed in United States District Court, Northern District of California, San Jose Division, December 19, 2012*, 34.

11. Ben Worthen, "H-P Says It Was Duped, Takes $8.8 Billion Charge," *Wall Street Journal*, November 21, 2012, A1, A14.

12. "Delivering Alpha." Autonomy founder Mike Lynch disputed Ellison's statement that the company had been shopped prior to its acquisition by Hewlett-Packard. "If some bank happened to come with us on a list, that is nothing to do with us." Ellison retorted that Lynch had accompanied investment banker Frank Quattrone on the "sales pitch" and that Oracle still had the PowerPoint slides from the presentation.

13. Stanley Marrical, 30–31.

14. Quentin Hardy and Michael J. de la Merced, "Hewlett's Loss: A Folly Unfolds, by the Numbers," *New York Times*, November 21, 2012, A1, B6.

15. James B. Stewart, "From H.P., a Blunder that Seems to Beat All," *New York Times*, December 1, 2012. Stewart argued that Hewlett-Packard's acquisition of Autonomy deserved consideration for the title of worst corporate deal of all time.

CHAPTER 11   Is Fraud Detectable?

1. David J. Lynch, "SEC Returns to Policing Accounting Fraud," *Financial Times*, June 14, 2016, 16.
2. Messod D. Beneish, "The Detection of Earnings Manipulation," *Financial Analysts Journal*, September–October 1999, 24–36.
3. David F. Larcker and Anastasia A. Zakolyukina. *Detecting Deceptive Discussions in Conference Calls*, Working Paper Series No. 63 (Stanford, CA: Rock Center for Corporate Governance, 2010).
4. Dain C. Donelson, Matthew S. Ege, and John M. McInnis, "Internal Control Weaknesses and Financial Reporting Fraud," *Auditing: A Journal of Practice & Theory*: August 2017, 45–69.
5. Gretchen Morgenson, "Sarbanes-Oxley, Bemoaned as a Burden, Is an Investor's Ally," *New York Times*, September 10, 2017, BU1.
6. Paul Calluzzo, Wei Wang, and Serena Wu (2016) "Catch Me If You Can: Financial Misconduct around Corporate Headquarters Relocations." Presented to Eleventh Annual Conference of the Financial Intermediation Research Society (FIRS), Lisbon, Portugal, June 3, 2016.
7. Jo Craven McGinty, "To Find Fraud, Just Do the Math," *Wall Street Journal*, December 6–7, 2014, A2.
8. FN Dan Amiram, Zahn Bozanic, and Ethan Rouen, "Financial Statement Errors: Evidence from the Distributional Properties of Financial Statement Numbers," *Review of Accounting Studies*, December 2015, 1540–1593.
9. FN Jean Eaglesham and Michael Rapoport, "SEC Gets Busy with Accounting Inquiries," *Wall Street Journal*, January 21, 2015, C1–C2.
10. Nicholas Stein, "The World's Most Admired Companies," *Fortune*, October 2000.
11. Jeremy Gerard, "Did Goldman Sachs on TV Kill 'Enron' on Broadway?" *Bloomberg News*, May 11, 2010.
12. John R. Emshwiller, and Rebecca Smith, "Behind Enron's Fall, a Culture of Operating outside Public's View," *Wall Street Journal*, December 5, 2001, A1, A10.
13. Richard A. Oppel Jr. and Andrew Ross Sorkin, "Enron Admits to Overstating Profits by About $600 Million," *New York Times*, November 9, 2001, C1, C5.
14. Dan Ackman, "Enron the Incredible," *Forbes.com*, January 15, 2002.
15. "Jeff Skilling's Spectacular Career," www.chron.com/disp/story.mpl/jenny/2404018.html.
16. Jonathan Weil, "Energy Traders Cite Gains, but Some Math Is Missing," *Wall Street Journal*, September 20, 2000, Texas Journal section, 1.
17. Ibid.
18. Joe Nocera, "Tipping over a Defense of Enron," *New York Times*, January 6, 2007, C1, C8.
19. Anne Kates Smith, "Enron's Biggest Assets Are on Paper," *U.S. News & World Report*, June 18, 2001, 30.
20. Milt Freudenheim, "Hospital Chain Is Accused of Accounting Fraud," *New York Times*, March 20, 2003, C1, C4.
21. Simon Romero, "The Rise and Fall of Richard Scrushy, Entrepreneur," *New York Times*, March 21, 2003, C4.

22. Judy Mathewson, Keith Snider, William McQuillen, and James Rowley, "HealthSouth, Scrushy Accused of $1.4 Billion Fraud," *Bloomberg News,* March 19, 2003.
23. Freudenheim, "Hospital Chain," C4.
24. Ann Carrns, Carrick Mollenkamp, Deborah Solomon, and John R. Wilke, "HealthSouth Case Unveils a Shock Strategy," *Wall Street Journal,* April 4, 2003, C1, C9.
25. Jonathan Weill, "Accounting Scheme Was Straightforward but Hard to Detect," *Wall Street Journal,* March 20, 2003, C1, C13.
26. Reed Abelson, "HealthSouth Fires Chief Executive and Audit Firm," *New York Times,* April 1, 2003, C1, C13.
27. Kurt Eichenwald, "Key Executive at HealthSouth Admits to Fraud," *New York Times,* March 27, 2003, C1–C2.
28. David Voreacos, with reporting by Bob Van Voris, "HealthSouth Officers Plead Guilty to $2.5 Billion Fraud," *Bloomberg News,* April 3, 2003.
29. Greg Farrell, "Scrushy Sticks to His Defense: They're All Lying," *USA Today,* November 5, 2003, 1B–2B.
30. Carrick Mollenkamp and Ann Carrns, "As Trial Looms, HealthSouth's Ex-CEO Starts a TV Show," *Wall Street Journal,* March 3, 2004, B1, B5.
31. Simon Romero, "Will the Real Richard Scrushy Please Step Forward," *New York Times,* February 17, 2005, C1, C6.
32. Brian Grow, "All Scrushy, All the Time," *BusinessWeek,* April 12, 2004, 86–87.
33. Reed Abelson and Jonathan Glater, "A Style That Connected with Hometown Jurors," *New York Times,* June 29, 2005, C1, C4.
34. Adrian Michaels and Lisa Fingeret Roth, "HealthSouth Auditors Facing Federal Probe," *Financial Times,* March 28, 2003, 17.
35. Jonathan Weil and Cassell Bryan-Low, "Audit Committee Met Only Once during 2001," *Wall Street Journal,* March 21, 2003, A2, A10.
36. Joann S. Lublin and Ann Carrns, "Directors Had Lucrative Links at HealthSouth," *Wall Street Journal,* April 11, 2003, B1, B3.
37. Gail Edmondson, with David Fairlamb and Nanette Byrnes, "The Milk Just Keeps on Spilling," *BusinessWeek,* June 24, 2004, 54–58.
38. Ibid., 55–58.
39. Oliver Holtaway, "Tragedy or Farce?" *US Credit* (February 2004), 22–26.
40. The *spread* is the risk premium on the issue, measured in the yield differential between Parmalat debt and default-risk-free government debt. Parmalat's bonds yielded around 8 percent, a high rate compared with bonds of other companies with the same (Triple-B) credit rating.
41. Holtaway, "Tragedy," 26.
42. Joanna Speed and Nic Sochovsky, *Parmalat: The Straws That Break the Camel's Back*, Merrill Lynch & Co., December 5, 2002.
43. Edmondson, "The Milk," 55.
44. Daniel J. Wakin, "There Were Earlier Signs of Trouble at Parmalat," *New York Times,* January 14, 2004, C1, C6.
45. Jing Yang, "Behind the Fall of China's Luckin Coffee: A Network of Fake Buyers and a Fictitious Employee," *Wall Street Journal,* May 28, 2020.

CHAPTER 12   Forecasting Financial Statements

1. A less restrictive type of covenant merely prohibits incurrence of new debt or payment of dividends that would cause financial measures to deteriorate below a targeted level. No violation occurs if, for example, net worth declines as a result of operating losses.
2. Charley Grant, "Heard on the Street: CVS Deal Debate Isn't Over," *Wall Street Journal,* February 12, 2020.
3. Stan Manoukian, "Hertz Corporation Research Update," Independent Credit Research LLC, April 27, 2020.

CHAPTER 13   Credit Analysis

1. In practice, the U.S. Bankruptcy Code encourages companies to reorganize, rather than simply liquidate, if they become insolvent. Typically, a reorganization results in settlement of creditors' claims via distribution of securities of a firm that has been rehabilitated through forgiveness of a portion of its debt. Determination of the value of securities awarded to each class of creditor is related to asset protection, however, so the analysis that follows applies equally to reorganization and liquidation.
2. The comments on preferred stock in this paragraph also apply generally to preference stock, which is similar to preferred stock in form but junior to it in the capital structure.
3. In this and subsequent definitions of total capital, minority interest is included. This item should be viewed as equity in leverage calculations because it involves no contractual payment and ranks junior to debt.
4. Nick Fielding, Richard Thomson, and Larry Black, "Undisclosed Debt Worries Hang over O&Y," *The Independent,* May 10, 1992, Business on Sunday Section, 1.
5. Technically speaking, the effective tax rate is somewhat manageable, even though the statutory rate is not. It is nevertheless useful to calculate the operating margin separately from the pretax margin, to measure management's operating prowess separately from its financial acumen.
6. *Noble Group, a Repeat of Enron First Report: Noble's Associates and Noble Agri.* Iceberg Research, February 15, 2015, 2
7. Abheek Bhattarchaya, "Noble Group Distracted by Bonfire of the Equity," *Wall Street Journal,* July 2, 2015.
8. See Edward I. Altman, Robert G. Haldeman, and Paul Narayanan, "Zeta Analysis: A New Model to Identify Bankruptcy Risk of Corporations," *Journal of Banking and Finance,* June 1977, 29–54.
9. See, for example, Sharon Out, Joyce Jiang, Kuan-Heng Chen, Kumar Kanthan, Atsi Sheth, Anne Van Pragh, Richard Cantor, Annual default study: Following a sharp rise in 2020, corporate defaults will drop in 2021, Moody's Investors Service, January 28, 2021. The analysts report average one-year default rates for the period 1983–2020 that increase with each step down the rating scale, from 0.00% for issuers rate Aaa to 34.52% for issuers rated Ca or C.

10. Altman, Haldeman, and Narayanan set the Zeta model's cutoff score (the level at which a loan request is rejected on grounds of excessive default risk) with an explicit goal of achieving the optimal trade-off between the costs of making loans that default and rejecting loans that do not default.
11. Christopher M. McHugh, ed., *The 2000 Bankruptcy Yearbook & Almanac* (Boston: New Generation Research, 2000), 187–190.

CHAPTER 14 Equity Analysis

1. Dividends, unlike interest payments on debt, are payable at the discretion of the board of directors, rather than in fulfillment of a contractual obligation. They are consequently subject to greater variability – through reduction, increase, or suspension – than bond coupons or scheduled principal repayments.
2. Bethany McLean, "Hocus-Pocus: How IBM Grew 27 percent a Year," *Fortune,* June 26, 2000, 165.
3. The notion that a company can increase its market capitalization by boosting its financial leverage appears to fly in the face of a fundamental tenet of modern finance. Nobel economics laureates Franco Modigliani and Merton Miller demonstrated that under certain critical assumptions, a company's stock market value was insensitive to the proportions of debt and equity in its capital structure. Modigliani and Miller followed up on this pioneering work, however, by exploring what happened when the assumptions were relaxed to reflect real-world conditions. In particular, they and subsequent researchers found that the company's stock market value could in fact rise as a result of boosting financial leverage to take fuller advantage of the tax shield provided by debt. Interest on borrowings is a tax-deductible expense, whereas dividends on stock are not.
4. To back out the 2019 year-end debt ratio, add back to the year-end 2020 long-term debt of $167 million the $14 million paid down in 2020. Reduce the year-end 2020 shareholders' equity of $502 million by the $44 million ($66 million net income minus $22 million of dividends) increase during 2020. Year-end 2019 long-term debt of $181 million thus equals 28 percent of $181 million plus $458 million, or $639 million.
5. See https://www.spglobal.com/marketintelligence/en/news-insights/latest-news -headlines/as-lbos-surged-in-q4-20-us-purchase-price-multiples-hit-new-heights -62227223
6. Note, however, the uncertainties associated with reserve valuations, discussed in Chapter 2 under the heading "The Value Problem."
7. Baruch Lev and Anup Srivastava, "Explaining the Recent Failure of Value Investing," SSRN, 2020.

accelerate To demand immediate repayment of debt in default, exercising thereby a right specified in the loan contract.

Accounting Principles Board (APB) Formerly, a rule-making body of the American Institute of Certified Public Accountants. Predecessor of the Financial Accounting Standards Board (see).

accrual accounting An accounting system in which revenue is recognized during the period in which it is earned and expenses are recognized during the period in which they are incurred, whether or not cash is received or disbursed.

adjusted funds from operations (AFFO) A measure of cash flow from operations for real estate investment trusts (REITs) considered more indicative than funds from operations (see). It is defined as funds from operations plus rent increases minus capital expenditures minus routine maintenance amounts.

APB Accounting Principles Board (see).

bona fide profit A reported profit that represents a genuine increase in wealth as opposed to one that exploits a flaw in the accounting system and reflects no economic gain.

book-to-market ratio A stock valuation measure calculated by dividing a company's total book value (total assets minus total liabilities) by its market value (share price times number of shares outstanding). Proponents of value investing (see) perceive bargains in stocks of companies with book-to-market ratios greater than one.

book value The amount at which an asset is carried on the balance sheet. Book value consists of the asset's construction or acquisition cost, less depreciation (see) and subsequent impairment of value, if applicable. An asset's book value does not rise as a function of an increase in its market value or inflation. (See also *historical cost accounting.*)

breakeven rate The production volume at which contribution (see) is equivalent to fixed costs (see), resulting in a pretax profit of zero.

Example:

$$
\begin{aligned}
\text{Price per unit} &= \$2.50 \\
\text{Variable cost per unit} &= \$1.00 \\
\text{Fixed costs} &= \$600 \\
\text{To calculate breakeven: } [(\$2.50 - \$1.00) \times B] - \$600 &= 0 \\
(\$1.50 \times B) &= \$600 \\
B &= 400 \text{ units}
\end{aligned}
$$

broadcast cash flow   A measure of financial performance used by operators of radio and television stations, defined as Operating Income + Depreciation and Amortization + Corporate Overhead − Cash Outlays for Acquisition of New Programming + Amortization of Cost of Previously Acquired Programming.

business cycle   Periodic fluctuations in economic growth, employment, and price levels. Phases of the classic cycle, in sequence, are peak, recession, trough, and recovery.

capital-intensive   Characterized by a comparatively large proportion of plant and equipment in asset base. The heavy depreciation charges that arise from capital intensity create a high level of fixed costs and volatile earnings.

capitalization (of an expenditure)   The recording of an expenditure as an asset, to be written off over future periods, on the grounds that the outlay produces benefits beyond the current accounting cycle.

carrying cost   Charges associated with warehousing of goods, such as financing, insurance, storage, security, and spoilage.

cash conversion cycle (CCC)   A measurement of the number of days required to convert working capital items (inventory, receivables, and payables) into cash. Its calculation, as formulated by Investopedia, is:

$$
CCC = DIO + DSO{-}DPO
$$

where:　DIO = Days of inventory outstanding
　　　　DSO = Days sales outstanding
　　　　DPO = Days payables outstanding

The components of CCC are calculated as follows:

$$
DIO = (\text{Average inventory}/\text{Cost of goods sold}) \times 365\,\text{days}
$$

> **where:** Average inventory = (Beginning inventory
> + Ending inventory) / 2
>
> DSO = Average accounts receivable/Revenue
> per day

> **where:** Average accounts receiveable = (Beginning accounts receivable
> + Ending accounts receivable) / 2
>
> DPO = Average accounts payable/Cost of
> goods sold per day

> **where:** Average accounts payable = (Beginning accounts payable
> + Ending accounts payable / 2

Smaller numbers are desirable for DIO and DSO, while a larger number is desirable for DPO. It is a cause for concern when a company has significantly more days in its cash conversion cycle than comparable companies in its industry.

cash-on-cash profit In real estate, the cash flow from a property divided by the cash equity invested. Unlike conventional rate-of-return measures calculated in accordance with accrual accounting (see), cash-on-cash profit is not reduced by noncash charges such as depreciation (see). This reflects a presumption that land and buildings tend to increase in value over time, rather than lose value through wear and tear, as in the case of plant and equipment.

channel stuffing Artificially inflating reported revenues by intentionally shipping distributors or retailers more inventory than ultimate customers can absorb during the period.

Chapter 11 Under the Bankruptcy Code, a method of resolving bankruptcy that provides for reorganization of the failed firm as an alternative to liquidating it.

class-action suit A type of lawsuit filed under Federal Rule of Civil Procedure 23, which allows one member of a large group of plaintiffs with similar claims to sue on behalf of the entire class, provided certain conditions are met. Damages awarded in certain class-action suits have been large enough to compromise the solvency of corporate defendants.

comparability In accounting, the objective of facilitating financial comparisons of a group of companies, achieved by requiring them to use similar reporting practices.

compound annual growth rate (CAGR) The mean annual growth rate of an investment over a chosen multi-year period. It represents the growth rate that would have increased the investment's value from the initial level to the final value if it had increased by the same percentage in each year.

Example:

Year	Value of Asset ($)
0	377
1	421
2	414
3	487
4	541
5	596

The year-to-year increase in the asset's value has been uneven, ranging from −1.7 percent in Year 2 to 17.6 percent in Year 4. If the increase had been 9.6 percent in each year, however, the value would have grown from the beginning figure of $377 to the terminal figure of $596. CAGRs can be calculated quickly using calculators that can easily be found online.

consolidation (of an industry)   A reduction in the number of competitors in an industry through business combinations.

contribution   Revenue per unit minus variable costs (see) per unit.

convertible   With reference to bonds or preferred stock, redeemable at the holder's option for common stock of the issuer, based on a specified ratio of bonds or preferred shares to common shares. (See also *exchangeable.*)

cost of capital   The rate of return that investors require for providing capital to a company. A company's cost of capital consists of the cost of capital for a risk-free borrower, a premium for business risk (the risk of becoming unable to continue to cover operating costs), and a premium for financial risk (the risk of becoming unable to continue covering financial costs, such as interest). The risk-free cost of capital is commonly equated with the prevailing interest rate on U.S. Treasury obligations.

cumulative   A characteristic of the dividends of most preferred stocks whereby any dividends in arrears must be paid before dividends may be paid to common shareholders.

days sales outstanding (DSO)   A measure of liquidity that can signal a problems in collecting on receivables or indicate channel stuffing (see). The ratio is defined as: accounts receivable ÷ (annual sales / 365 days)

default   The failure of a debt obligor to make a scheduled interest or principal payment on time. A defaulting issuer becomes subject to claims against its assets, possibly including a demand by creditors for full and immediate repayment of principal.

depreciation   A noncash expense meant to represent the amount of capital equipment consumed through wear and tear during the period.

derivative   (see *financial derivative*).

dilution   A reduction in present shareholders' proportional claim on earnings. Dilution can occur through the issuance of new shares in an acquisition if the earnings generated by the acquired assets are insufficient to maintain the level of earnings per share previously recorded by the acquiring company. Existing shareholders' interest is likewise diluted if the company issues new stock at a price below book value. In this circumstance, a dollar invested by a new shareholder purchases a larger percentage of the company than is represented by a dollar of net worth held by an old shareholder.

discount rate   The interest rate used to equate future value (see) with present value (see). Also referred to as cost of capital (see).

discounted cash flow   A technique for equating future cash flows to a present sum of money, based on an assumed interest rate. For example, $100 compounded annually at 8 percent over three years will cumulate to a sum of $125.97, ignoring the effect of taxes. This figure can be calculated via the equation

$$P \times (1 + r)^n = F$$

where: P = Principal value at beginning of period (Present value)
r = Interest rate
n = Number of periods
F = Principal value at end of period (Future value)

In this case, $100 \times (1.08)^3 = $125.97. (Note that this formula implicitly assumes reinvestment of cash interest received at the original rate of interest throughout the period.)

If $125.97 three years hence is equivalent to $100 today – given the assumed discount rate (see) of 8 percent per annum – then the ratio $100.00/$125.97, or 0.794, can be used to determine the present value (see) of any other amount discounted back from the same date and at the same rate.

By using the same general formula, it is possible to assign a value to an asset, based on a series of cash flows it is expected to generate. By way of illustration, suppose the right to distribute a particular product is expected to generate cash flow of $5,000 a year for four years, then expire, leaving no terminal value. At a discount rate of 15 percent, the distribution rights would be valued at $14,820, derived as follows:

Year	Expected Cash Flow	Discount Factor	Present Value
1	$5,000	.870	$4,350
2	$5,000	.756	$3,780
3	$5,000	.658	$3,290
4	$5,000	.572	$2,860
		Total:	$14,280

discretionary cash flow   Cash flow that remains available to a company after it has funded its basic operating requirements. There is no universally accepted, precise definition of discretionary cash flow, but conceptually it includes funds from operations less required new investment in working capital and nondiscretionary capital expenditures. The latter figure is difficult to quantify with precision, but it exceeds the required maintenance level required to keep existing plant and equipment in good working order. Ordinarily, some additional expenditures, which may be designated semidiscretionary, are necessary to keep a company competitive with respect to capacity, costs, and technology. Only a portion of the total capital budget, including expansion-oriented outlays that can be deferred in the event of slower-than-expected growth in demand, can truly be considered discretionary. In a similar vein, mandatory principal repayments of debt, by definition, cannot be regarded as discretionary. Still, a company with strong cash flow and the assurance, as a practical matter, of being able to refinance its maturing debt, has considerable freedom in the disposition even of amounts that would appear to be earmarked for debt retirement.

diversification   In portfolio management, the technique of reducing risk by dividing one's assets among a number of different securities or types of investments. Applied to corporate strategy, the term refers to participation in several unrelated businesses. The underlying premise is often countercyclicality, or the stabilization of earnings over time through the tendency of profits in certain business segments to be rising at times when they are falling in others.

double-entry bookkeeping   A system of keeping accounts in which each entry requires an offsetting entry. For example, a payment to a trade creditor causes both cash and accounts payable to decline.

Dow Jones Industrial Average   A widely followed index of the U.S. stock market composed of the common stocks of 30 major industrial corporations.

EBIT   Earnings before deduction of interest expense and income taxes.

EBITDA   Earnings before deduction of interest expense, income taxes, depreciation, and amortization.

economies of scale   Reductions in per unit cost that arise from large-volume production. The reductions result in large measure from the spreading of fixed costs (i.e., those that do not vary directly with production volume) over a larger number of units than is possible for a smaller producer.

economies of scope   Reductions in per unit cost that arise from applying knowledge or technology to related products.

external growth   Revenue growth achieved by a company through acquisition of other companies.

factor   A financial institution that provides financing to companies by buying accounts receivable at a discount.

Fair Value Accounting   An accounting system in which certain assets and liabilities are recorded at their market values. Also known as *mark-to-market accounting.*

FASB   Financial Accounting Standards Board (see).

Financial Accounting Standards Board (FASB)   A rule-making body for the accounting profession. Its members are appointed by a foundation, the members of which are selected by the directors of the American Institute of Certified Public Accountants.

financial derivative   A financial instrument with a return linked to the performance of an underlying asset, such as a bond or a currency.

financial flexibility   The ability, achieved through such means as a strong capital structure and a high degree of liquidity, to continue to invest in maintaining growth and competitiveness despite business downturns and other financial strains.

financial leverage   (See *leverage (financial).*)

fixed costs   Costs that do not vary with the volume of production. Examples include rent, interest expense, senior management salaries, and, unless calculated by the units-of-production method, depreciation (see).

fixed-rate debt   A debt obligation on which the interest rate remains at a stated level until the loan has been liquidated. (Compare *floating-rate debt.*)

floating-rate debt   A debt obligation on which the interest rate fluctuates with changes in market rates of interest, according to a specified formula. (Compare *fixed-rate debt.*)

free cash flow   Operating cash flow minus capital expenditures and dividends.

fresh start accounting   Accounting for a company that emerges from bankruptcy, in which assets and liabilities are recorded at fair value, with the result that the new reporting entity's financial statements generally are not comparable to the prebankruptcy historical statements.

fundamental analysis   A form of security analysis aimed at determining a stock or bond's intrinsic value, based on such factors as the issuer's expected earnings and financial risk. In contrast, technical analysis aims to predict a security's future value based on its past price changes.

funds from operations (FFO)   A measure of cash flow from operations for real estate investment trusts (REITs). It is defined as net income plus amortization plus depreciation minus capital gains from property sales

future value   The amount to which a known sum of money will accumulate by a specified future date, given a stated rate of interest. For example, $100 compounded annually at 8 percent over three years will cumulate to a sum of $125.97, ignoring the effect of taxes. This figure can be calculated via the formula

$$P \times (1 + r)^n$$

where: P = Principal at beginning of period
r = Interest rate
n = Number of periods

In this case, $100 \times (1.08)^3 = \$125.97$. (This formula implicitly assumes that cash interest received will be reinvested at the original rate of interest throughout the period.) (See also *discounted cash flow, net present value,* and *present value*.)

GAAP   Generally accepted accounting principles (see).

GDP   Gross domestic product (see).

generally accepted accounting principles   Rules that govern the preparation of financial statements, based on pronouncements of authoritative accounting organizations such as the Financial Accounting Standards Board, industry practice, and the accounting literature (including books and articles).

goodwill   A balance sheet item arising from accounting for a business combination, representing the excess of the purchase price over the acquired company's tangible asset value.

Gross domestic product   The value of all goods and services that residents and non-residents produce in a country (see *GDP*).

guidance   An earnings per share projection provided to investors to convey management's expectations.

historical cost accounting   An accounting system in which assets are recorded at their original value (less any applicable depreciation or other impairment of value), notwithstanding that the nominal dollar value of the assets may rise through some cause such as inflation or increased scarcity. (See also *book value*.)

hostile takeover   An acquisition of a corporation by another corporation or by a group of investors, typically through a tender for outstanding shares, in the face of initial opposition by the acquired corporation's board of directors.

initial public offering (IPO)   A first-time sale of stock to the public by a previously privately owned company. The IPO process is called going public.

internal growth   Revenue growth achieved by a company through capital investment in its existing business.

internal rate of return   The discount rate that makes the net present value (*see*) of all future cash flows equal to zero. Internal rate of return can be calculated in Excel using the IRR function.

internally generated funds   Cash obtained through operations, including net income, depreciation, deferred taxes, and reductions in working capital.

investor-relations officer   An individual designated by a corporation to handle communications with securities analysts.

involuntary inventory accumulation   An unintended increase in a company's inventory levels, resulting from a slowdown in sales that is not offset by a reduced rate of production.

LBO   Leveraged buyout (see).

leverage (financial)   The use of debt financing in hopes of increasing the rate of return on equity. In the following example, the unleveraged company, with no debt in its capital structure, generates operating income of $19.0 million, pays taxes of $4.0 million, and nets $15.0 million for a return on equity (net income divided by shareholders' equity) of 10.0 percent. The leveraged company, with an equivalent amount of operating income, relies on long-term debt (at an interest rate of 4 percent) for one-third of its capital. Interest expense causes its net income before taxes to be lower ($17.0 million) than the unleveraged company's ($19.0 million). After taxes, the leveraged company earns less ($13.2 million) than the unleveraged company ($15.0 million), but on a smaller equity base ($100 million versus $150 million) provides shareholders a higher rate of return (13.2 percent versus 10.0 percent).

	($ Million)	
	Unleveraged Company	Leveraged Company
Operating income	$ 19.0	$ 19.0
Interest expense	0.0	2.0
Net income before taxes	19.0	17.0
Taxes	4.0	3.8
Net income	$ 15.0	$ 13.2
Long-term debt	$ 0.0	$ 50.0
Shareholders' equity	150.0	100.0
Total capital	$150.0	$150.0
Net income/Shareholders' equity	10.0%	13.2%

Note, however, that leverage works in reverse as well. In the following scenario, operating income turns negative (to −$5.0 million) at both companies. With no interest expense, the unleveraged company manages to net −$3.9 million for a −2.6 percent return on equity. The leveraged company, obliged to pay out $2.0 million in interest while operating at a loss, suffers a sharper decline in return on equity (to −5.5 percent). Incurring financial leverage increases the risk to equity holders, whose returns become more subject to fluctuations. The greater the percentage of the capital structure that consists of debt, the greater the potential for such fluctuations.

	($ Million)	
	Unleveraged Company	Leveraged Company
Operating income	$ 10.0	$ 10.0
Interest expense	0.0	6.0
Net income before taxes	10.0	4.0
Taxes	3.4	1.4
Net income	$ 6.6	$ 2.6
Long-term debt	$ 0.0	$ 50.0
Shareholders' equity	150.0	100.0
Total capital	$150.0	$150.0
Net income/Shareholders' equity	4.4%	2.6%

leverage (operating)   The substitution of fixed costs (see) for variable costs (see) in hopes of increasing return on equity. In the following example, Company A's cost structure is dominated by variable expenses, of which labor represents a substantial portion. A 5 percent increase in sales volume (from 500,000 to 525,000 units) raises the rate of return on shareholders' equity from 11.0 percent to 15.0 percent. Company B, on the other hand, has installed labor-saving equipment that sharply reduces man-hours per unit of production. Its variable costs are lower than Company A's ($31.60 versus $41.60 per unit), but as a function of its greater depreciation (see) charges, its fixed costs are higher ($30 million versus $25 million per annum). The benefit of Company B's higher operating leverage is that a 5 percent increase in its unit sales raises its return on shareholders' equity from 11.0 percent to 15.7 percent, a larger boost than Company A receives from a comparable rise in volume. By the same token, Company B's return on shareholders' equity will fall more sharply than Company A's if unit volume at both companies instead recedes from 500,000 to 500,000 units.

	Company A		Company B	
Sales (units)	500,000	525,000	500,000	525,000
Price per unit	$ 100.0	$ 100.0	$ 100.0	$ 100.0
Fixed costs ($ million)	$ 25.0	$ 25.0	$ 30.0	$ 30.0
Variable cost per unit	$ 41.6	$ 41.6	$ 31.6	$ 31.6
	($ Million)			
Sales	$ 50.0	$ 52.5	$ 50.0	$ 52.5
Fixed costs	25.0	21.8	30.0	30.0
Variable costs	$ 20.8	$ 21.8	$ 15.8	$ 16.6
Income before taxes	4.2	5.7	5.0	6.7
Taxes	$ 0.9	$ 1.2	$ 0.9	$ 1.2
Net income	$ 3.3	$ 4.5	$ 3.3	$ 4.7
Shareholders' equity	$ 30.0	$ 30.0	$ 30.0	$ 30.0
Net income / Shareholders' equity	11.0%	15.0%	11.0%	15.7%

leveraged buyout (LBO)   An acquisition of a company or a division, financed primarily with borrowed funds. Equity investors typically hope to profit by repaying debt through cash generated by operations (and possibly from proceeds of asset sales), thereby increasing the net value of their stake.

liquidity   The ability of a company to meet its near-term obligations when due.

macroeconomic   Pertaining to the economy as a whole or its major subdivisions, such as the manufacturing sector, the agricultural sector, the government. (See also *microeconomic*.)

market capitalization   The aggregate market value of all of a company's outstanding equity and debt securities. Also used loosely to represent the product of a company's share price and number of shares outstanding. (See also *total enterprise value*.)

market-to-book ratio   A stock valuation measure calculated by dividing a company's market value (share price times number of shares outstanding) by its total book value (total assets minus total liabilities). Proponents of value investing (see) perceive bargains in stocks of companies with market-to-book ratios below 1.0 times.

mark-to-market accounting   The practice of valuing a holding of a financial instrument according to its fair market price on the date of the financial statement. If the instrument does not trade on a regular basis, a current market value may be inferred from the prices of comparable instruments that do.

mature   With respect to a product, firm, or industry, at a stage of development at which the rate of sales growth remains positive but no longer exceeds the general growth rate of the economy.

microeconomic   Pertaining to a small segment of the economy, such as an individual industry or a particular firm. (See also *macroeconomic*.)

multiple   With respect to a common stock, the ratio of the share price to earnings per share. Similarly, the price paid in an acquisition can be viewed as a multiple of the acquired company's earnings, cash flow, or EBITDA (see).

multivariate   In the field of quantitative modeling, having the characteristic of employing more than one explanatory factor.

net present value   The present value (see) of a stream of future cash inflows, less the present value of an associated stream of current or future cash outflows. This calculation is useful for comparing the attractiveness of alternative investments, as shown in the example. Both proposed capital projects require an expenditure of $60 million during the first year. Project A generates a higher cash flow, without trailing off in the latter years as Project B is projected to do. Residual value in year 10 is likewise superior in Project A. Even so, Project B is the more profitable investment, based on a higher net present value ($17.7 million versus $14.3 million for Project A).

Net Present Value Illustration (Presumed Discount Rate = 20%) ($000,000 omitted)

					Year							Net Present Value
	0	1	2	3	4	5	6	7	8	9	10	
Project A												
Cash flow*	(40)	(20)	16	18	21	24	24	26	26	26	20	
Discount factor	1.000	.833	.694	.579	.482	.402	.335	.279	.233	.194	.162	
Present value	(40.00)	+ (16.66)	+ 11.10	+ 10.42	+ 10.12	+ 9.65	+ 8.04	+ 7.25	+ 6.06	+ 5.04	+ 3.24	= 14.26
Project B												
Cash flow*	(10)	(50)	17	20	22	23	23	23	22	21	17	
Discount factor	1.000	.833	.694	.579	.482	.402	.335	.279	.233	.194	.162	
Present value	(10.00)	+ (41.65)	+ 11.80	+ 11.58	+ 10.60	+ 9.25	+ 7.71	+ 6.42	+ 5.13	+ 4.07	+ 2.75	= 17.66

*Figures in parentheses represent projected outflows, i.e., construction costs. Figures for years 2–9 represent projected inflows, i.e., net income plus noncash expenses. Year 10 figure represents expected residual value of equipment.

New Economy The sector composed of young, high-growth industries based on cutting-edge technology. New Economy companies are generally engaged in providing novel products and services, or new ways to provide them, rather than traditional manufacturing or commodity-driven activites.

nominal dollar A monetary sum expressed in terms of its currency face amount, unadjusted for changes in purchasing power from a designated base period. (See also *real dollar*.)

operating leverage (See *leverage (operating)*.)

organic growth Increases in revenues and earnings arising from internal operations as opposed to mergers and acquisitions.

payout ratio Dividends per share divided by earnings per share. In financial theory, a low payout ratio (other than as a result of a dividend reduction forced on the company by financial distress) is generally viewed as a sign that the company has many opportunities to reinvest in its business at attractive returns. A high payout ratio, in contrast, is appropriate for a company with limited internal reinvestment opportunities. By distributing a large percentage of earnings to shareholders, the company enables them to seek more attractive returns by investing elsewhere.

pooling-of-interests A mergers-and-acquisitions accounting method abolished in by FASB 2001. Under this method, the assets of both companies in the transaction were recorded at book value. The combined entity thereby avoided the negative earnings impact of goodwill amortization.

portfolio A group of securities. Barring the unlikely circumstance that all securities contained in a portfolio produce identical returns in all periods, it generally produces a steadier return than a single security. The comparative stability arises from the tendency of declines in the prices of certain securities to be offset by rises in the prices of others during the same period. (See *diversification*.)

present value The sum that, if compounded at a specified rate of interest, or discount rate (see), will accumulate to a particular value at a stated future date. For example: To calculate the present value of $500, five years hence at a discount rate of 7 percent, solve the equation:

$$\frac{F}{(1+r)^n}$$

where: F = Future value
r = Interest rate
n = Number of periods
p = Present value

In this case $500/(1.07)^5 = $356.49. (See also *discounted cash flow, future value*, and *net present value*.)

pro forma   Describes a financial statement constructed on the basis of specified assumptions. For example, if a company made an acquisition halfway through its fiscal year, it might present an income statement intended to show what the combined companies' full-year sales, costs, and net income would have been, assuming that the acquisition had been in effect when the year began.

purchase accounting   A method of accounting for acquisitions superseded in 2007 by FASB's introduction of **purchase acquisition accounting**. Purchase accounting in its original form was considered more conservative than **pooling-of-interests** accounting, as it resulted in annual charges to earnings for amortization of goodwill.

purchase acquisition accounting   The method of accounting for acquisitions required by FASB since 2007. It is also known as "acquisition accounting." Under this method, the acquirer records the acquired company's assets at fair market value. Any excess of the purchase price over the acquired company's net value is recorded as goodwill and is subsequently amortized.

rationalization   In reference to a business or an industry, the process of eliminating excess capacity and other inefficiencies in production.

real dollar   A monetary sum expressed in terms of its purchasing-power equivalent, relative to a designated base period. For example, at the end of the third quarter of 2001, $500 (face amount) had only 56.1 percent of the purchasing power that $500 had in the base period 1982–1984. The erosion reflected price inflation during the intervening years. The real value of $500 in September 2001 was therefore $280.50 in 1982–1984 dollars. This calculation employs a series of the purchasing power of the consumer dollar, published by the United States Bureau of Labor Statistics. See the Bureau's website, www.bls.gov. (See also *nominal dollar*.)

reorganization proceedings   A procedure under Chapter 11 of the Bankruptcy Code that permits a bankrupt company to continue in operation, instead of liquidating, while restructuring its liabilities with an aim toward ensuring its future financial viability.

reported earnings   A company's profit or loss for a specified period, as stated in its income statement. The figure may differ from the company's true economic gain or loss for the period for such reasons as delayed recognition of items affecting income, changes in accounting practices, and discrepancies between accruals and actual changes in asset values.

Disparities between reported and economic earnings can also arise from certain nuances of inventory accounting. For example, under the last-in, first-out (LIFO) method, a company's inventory account may include the historical acquisition costs of goods purchased several years earlier and unaffected (for book purposes) by inflation in the interim period. To the extent that a surge in sales causes a company to recognize the liquidation of older inventories during the current period, revenues will reflect postinflation (i.e., higher) values, but expenses will not. The mismatch will produce unusually wide reported profit margins in the current period, even though the nominal dollar (see) gains arising from inflation are in reality benefits that accumulated over several preceding periods.

run rate A financial projection derived by annualizing results achieved over a shorter period.

sale-leaseback A transaction in which a company sells an asset and immediately leases it back. The lessee thereby obtains cash while retaining use of the asset. An additional motivation for the transaction may be a difference in the marginal tax rates of the lessee and lessor. The tax shelter provided by depreciation charges on the asset are more valuable to the party paying the higher tax rate.

same-store sales A measure of revenue growth for retailing chains, consisting of the increase in revenue in a quarter or year over the preceding comparable period, for stores that were open during both periods. This measure excludes sales growth that reflects opening of additional stores.

scale economies (See *economies of scale.*)

SEC Securities and Exchange Commission (see).

Securities and Exchange Commission (SEC) An arm of the federal government that regulates the issuance and trading of securities, the activities of investment companies and investment advisers, and standards for financial reporting by securities issuers.

sensitivity analysis The testing of what-if scenarios in financial statement analysis. Typically, sensitivity analysis measures the potential impact (on earnings, cash flow, etc.) of a change of a stated amount in another variable (sales, profit margins, etc.). In connection with financial forecasting, sensitivity analysis may be used to gauge the variation in projected figures that will occur if a particular assumption proves either too optimistic or too pessimistic by a given amount.

SFAS Statement of Financial Accounting Standards. Designation for a numbered series of statements of accounting rules promulgated by the Financial Accounting Standards Board (see).

shakeout A reduction in the number of competitors (through failures or through mergers) that typically occurs as a rapidly growing industry begins to mature. Factors that may contribute to a firm's survival during a shakeout include advantages in raising new capital, economies of scale (see), and superior management.

short interest ratio The ratio between the number of a company's shares that are sold short and remain uncovered and the stock's average daily trading volume. A high ratio indicates a widespread expectation that the stock's price will decline.

slack Unutilized productive capability within a company. Although the term ordinarily connotes inefficiency, management may have a conscious strategy of maintaining a certain amount of slack. For example, a company may benefit from keeping skilled employees on the payroll during recessions, when demand can be met with a reduced workforce. The cost savings entailed in laying off the workers may be offset by the costs of replacing them with equally skilled employees during the next boom. Another example is a backup trading floor maintained by a company engaged in trading securities or commodities. The associated cost may be justified by the potentially devastating loss of business that could result in a shutdown of the primary trading floor because of a natural disaster or civil disturbance.

standard error of estimate A measure of the scatter of the observations in a regression analysis. In statistical terms, the standard error of the estimate is equivalent to the standard deviation of the vertical deviations from the least-squares line.

statutory tax rate The percentage of pretax income that would be recorded as income tax if all of a company's reported income were subject to the corporate tax rate specified by federal law. Disparities between the statutory rate and the effective rate (that which is actually recorded) arise from such reasons as tax credits and differences between U.S. and foreign tax rates.

straight-line method A depreciation method that charges off an equivalent portion of the asset in each period. During inflationary periods, straight-line depreciation may understate the true economic impact of capital consumption. That is, as the replacement cost of the asset rises in nominal terms, the dollar amount required to offset wear and tear during a period grows to exceed a pro rata write-off based on the original acquisition cost. In these circumstances, accelerated methods of depreciation, which result in larger amounts being written off in earlier than in later years, represent more conservative reporting of expenses.

subordinated debt Borrowings that have a lesser preference in liquidation vis-à-vis senior debt. In the event of a bankruptcy, subordinated lenders' claims cannot be provided for until senior claims have been satisfied.

synergy An increase in profitability arising from a merger or acquisition, relative to the stand-alone profitability of the companies involved. Synergy may result from economies of scale (see) or economies of scope (see).

technical default A default on debt that does not involve failure to make a scheduled payment of principal or interest but instead results from the violation of a covenant requirement, such as maintaining a minimum ratio of earnings to interest expense.

Tobin's Q Market Value of Equity/Replacement Cost of Assets, applied to either a company or the equity market as a whole. Popularized by economist James Tobin. Also known as the Q Ratio.

total enterprise value The value that a business would fetch if put up for sale, commonly estimated as a multiple of its sales, earnings, or EBITDA (see). (See also *market capitalization.*)

value investing An investment strategy consisting of selecting stocks perceived to be trading below their intrinsic value. Underlying this approach is a belief that the stock market frequently overreacts to both good and bad news, causing long-term not to be reflected in companies' share prices.

variable costs Costs that increase as the volume of production rises. Examples include materials, fuel, power, and wages.

working capital   Current assets minus current liabilities. Working capital is commonly employed as an indicator of liquidity, but care must be taken in interpreting the number. The balance sheets of some corporations that are strong credits by all other methods ordinarily have little (or even negative) working capital. These companies manage inventories closely and extract generous terms from creditors, including long payment periods, which result in chronically high trade payable balances. In such cases, no threat of illiquidity is implied by the fact that more liabilities than assets will be liquidated during the current operating cycle.

Further Reading

Fabozzi, Frank J., with the assistance of Francesco A. Fabozzi and Steven A. Mann (eds.), *The Handbook of Fixed Income Securities*, 9th ed. New York: McGraw Hill, 2021.

Gitman, Lawrence J. and Chad Z. Zutter, *Principles of Managerial Finance*, 14th ed. London: Pearson Higher Ed, 2019.

Holland, David A. and Bryant A. Matthews, *Beyond Earnings: Applying the HOLT CFROI® and Economic Profit Framework*. Hoboken, NJ: John Wiley & Sons, 2018.

Kricheff, Robert S. *A Pragmatist's Guide to Leveraged Finance: Credit Analysis for Below-Investment-Grade Bonds and Loans*, 2nd ed. Petersfield, Hampshire: Harriman House, 2021.

Lev, Baruch and Feng Gu. *The End of Accounting and the Path Forward for Investors and Managers* 1st ed. Hoboken, NJ: John Wiley & Sons, 2016.

McConnell, Campbell R. *Economics: Principles, Problems and Policies*, 10th ed. New York: McGraw-Hill, 1987.

Moyer, Stephen. *Distressed Debt Analysis: Strategies for Speculative Investors*. Ft. Lauderdale, FL: J. Ross Publishing, 2004.

O'Hara, Neil. *The Fundamentals of Municipal Bonds*, 6th ed. Hoboken, NJ: John Wiley & Sons, Inc., 2012.

Reilly, Frank K., Keith C. Brown, and Sanford J. Leeds. *Investment Analysis and Portfolio Management*, 11th ed. Boston: Cengage, 2018.

Roe, Mark J. *Bankruptcy and Corporate Reorganization: Legal and Financial Materials*, 4th ed. St. Paul, Minnesota: The Foundation Press, 2021.

Shim, Jae K., Joel G. Siegel, and Anique Quereshi. *Dictionary of Accounting Terms*, 6th ed. New York: Barron's, 2014.

Stewart III, G. Bennett. *Best-Practice EVA: The Definitive Guide to Measuring and Maximizing Shareholder Value*. Hoboken, NJ: John Wiley & Sons, 2013.

Ziegel, Arnold. *Fundamentals of Credit and Credit Analysis: Corporate Credit Analysis*. Stowe, Vermont: Mountain Mentors Associates, 2014.

Martin Fridson is Chief Investment Officer at Lehmann Livian Fridson Advisors LLC and publisher of the *Income Securities Investor* newsletter. Over a 25-year span with brokerage firms including Salomon Brothers, Morgan Stanley, and Merrill Lynch, he became known for his innovative work in credit analysis and investment strategy. For the last nine years of that span, participants in the Institutional Investor All-America research survey ranked Fridson number one in high-yield bond strategy. Fridson has served as president of the Fixed Income Analysts Society, governor of the Association for Investment Management and Research (now CFA Institute), and director of the New York Society of Security Analysts (now CFA Society New York). Since 1989 he has served as book review editor for the CFA Institute, initially at *Financial Analysts Journal* and now at *Enterprising Investor*.

The *New York Times* described Fridson as "one of Wall Street's most thoughtful and perceptive analysts." *Investment Dealers Digest* called him "perhaps the most well-known figure in the high-yield world." In 2000, Fridson became the youngest person inducted into the Fixed Income Analysts Hall of Fame. The Financial Management Association named him Financial Executive of the Year in 2002. In 2017 he received the Ben Graham Award from the CFA Society New York.

Fridson is the author of six books on investments and political economy. The *Boston Globe* said *Unwarranted Intrusions: The Case Against Government Intervention in the Marketplace* (2006), should be short-listed for best business book of the decade. A study based on 16 core journals ranked Fridson among the ten most widely published authors in finance in the period 1990–2001. His writings have appeared in *Barron's*, the *Financial Times*, and *WSJ.com*. He is a regular contributor to Forbes.com's *Intelligent Investing* as well as a frequent guest on CNBC, Bloomberg, and *Consuelo Mack WealthTrack* on PBS. Fridson received a Bachelor of Arts cum laude from Harvard College and a Masters of Business Administration from Harvard Business School.

Fernando Alvarez (PhD New York University) is currently Adjunct Associate Professor of Finance and Economics at the Columbia University

Graduate Business School, where he teaches Entrepreneurship Finance. From 2003 until 2008, he was Associate Professor in the Finance and Economics Department and Director of Entrepreneurship Programs at Rutgers Business School, Newark and New Brunswick. He has taught at New York University's Stern School of Business, where he was Clinical Associate Professor on Innovation and Entrepreneurship from 1998 to 2003, and Babson College in Wellesley, MA, where he was Assistant Professor of Finance from 1992 to 1996. He was visiting Associate Professor of Finance at Rutgers from 1996 to 1998.

He has taught Financial Management, Long-Term Finance with an emphasis in Shareholder Value/Economic Value Added, Short-Term Finance and Cash Flow Management, Fixed Income Analysis, Investments, Financial Statement Analysis, and Portfolio Analysis and Management. He was affiliated with the Shulman Chartered Financial Analyst Review Program in Boston. He has also taught a seminar in financial engineering at ITESM Graduate School of Management in Mexico City. Prof. Alvarez has a B.S. in Civil Engineering from the University of Nebraska at Lincoln.

Professor Alvarez's primary research areas include the growth of entrepreneurial firms, financing for start-up and growth, and the interaction of strategy, financial statement analysis, and valuation models in business decisions. His writings include the management of cash flows resulting from changes in working capital requirements, the structure of cash flows after the IPO, and the uses and sources of capital for the entrepreneurial firm. His research has been funded by the MacArthur Foundation, the Kaufman Foundation, U.S. Trust Bank of Boston, and Wells Fargo Bank.

He is co-author, with Martin Fridson, of the fourth edition of *Financial Statement Analysis: A Practitioner's Guide* (John Wiley & Sons, 2011). He contributed a chapter on business planning for the *Next Generation Business Handbook* (John Wiley & Sons, 2004), where he was recognized as one of the 50 thought leaders of tomorrow. From 1999 to 2003, he was on the Advisory Board of McGraw-Hill's Annual Editions in Entrepreneurship. Professor Alvarez has written or supervised over 50 cases and technical notes developed for the purposes of class discussion in entrepreneurship courses and cash flow analysis.